UNDERSTANDING
THE BOOK OF
REVELATION

UNDERSTANDING THE BOOK OF REVELATION

JAY A. PARRY • DONALD W. PARRY

DESERET BOOK COMPANY
SALT LAKE CITY, UTAH

Library of Congress Cataloging-in-Publication Data

Parry, Jay A.
   Understanding the book of Revelation / Jay A. Parry and Donald W.
Parry.
     p.   cm.
   Includes bibliographical references and index.
   ISBN 1-57345-438-9
   1. Bible. N.T. Revelation—Commentaries. 2. Church of Jesus
Christ of Latter-day Saints—Doctrines. I. Parry, Donald W.
II. Title.
BS2825.3.P37   1998
228'.07—dc21

                                98-30965
                                    CIP

Printed in the United States of America   72082-6424

10 9 8 7 6 5 4 3 2 1

To our parents,
Atwell and Elaine Parry,
who taught us truths they never doubted

CONTENTS

ACKNOWLEDGMENTS

We are grateful to many individuals who have contributed to this study of the book of Revelation. We thank Richard D. Draper, professor of ancient scripture at Brigham Young University and an outstanding student of the book of Revelation, for reading the entire manuscript and making many helpful suggestions. We appreciate the reviews of our manuscript by Brigham Young University professors Susan Easton Black, Truman Madsen, and Joseph Fielding McConkie. We thank Vicki Parry and Allison Clinger who read the manuscript and gave invaluable feedback.

The staff at Deseret Book has done much to turn this work from manuscript into a finished book. We're grateful for the leadership of Sheri Dew and Kent Ware and the ever-excellent editing of Suzanne Brady. We thank Ruth Howard and Celeste Howard, who proofread the galleys, and Leslie Stitt, who wrote the index. Others who made significant contributions to the task of creating the book are Ronald O. Stucki, art director, and Patricia J. Parkinson, typographer.

Though this work has required the assistance of these and other people, the authors alone are responsible for its content.

LIST OF ABBREVIATIONS

GNB	Good News Bible
JB	Jerusalem Bible
JST	Joseph Smith Translation of the Bible
KJV	Holy Bible, Authorized King James Version
LB	Living Bible
NEB	New English Bible
NIV	New International Version of the Holy Bible
RSV	Holy Bible, Revised Standard Version

—◦◦◦—

INTRODUCTION

The book of Revelation was written by John the beloved apostle. He identifies himself in five places in the book: four times by name (1:1, 4, 9; 22:8) and once as simply "a servant of God" (JST 1:1). John, called a "[son] of thunder" by Jesus Christ (Mark 3:17), was a son of Zebedee and brother of James. He was a fisherman during an early period of his life (Mark 1:19–20). He wrote the Gospel of John and at least three epistles (1, 2, and 3 Jn.), was called and ordained to serve as one of the twelve apostles, and served as a member of the First Presidency during his day.[1] Eventually John was translated and became "as flaming fire and a ministering angel" to "minister for those who shall be heirs of salvation who dwell on the earth" (D&C 7:6; 3 Ne. 28:6–7). Our latter-day scriptures give additional insight into John and his sacred mission; we have, for example, the words of Nephi, who beheld a heavenly vision similar to John's (1 Ne. 14), as well as the words of Jesus (3 Ne. 28:6), Moroni (Ether 4:16), and Joseph Smith (D&C 7; 27:12).

It tells us much about John to know that he was blessed with the Second Comforter. Joseph Smith explained that this gift "is no more nor less than the Lord Jesus Christ Himself. . . . When any man obtains this last Comforter, he will have the personage of Jesus Christ to attend him, or appear unto him from time to time, and even He will manifest the Father unto him, and they will take up their abode with him, and the visions of the

---

[1] Many authors have taught that Peter, James, and John composed the First Presidency of their day (see, for example, Taylor, *Gospel Kingdom,* 138). Joseph Fielding Smith, in *Doctrines of Salvation,* 3:152, wrote that "Peter, James, and John, acted as the First Presidency of the Church in their day."

heavens will be opened unto him, and the Lord will teach him face to face, and he may have a perfect knowledge of the mysteries of the Kingdom of God; and this is the state and place the ancient Saints arrived at when they had such glorious visions—Isaiah, Ezekiel, *John upon the Isle of Patmos,* St. Paul in the three heavens, and all the Saints who held communion with the general assembly and Church of the Firstborn."[2]

We are greatly blessed to be able to read, study, and ponder John's "glorious vision," received while on the Isle of Patmos, as set forth in the book of Revelation.

WHAT IS THE BOOK OF REVELATION?

The book of Revelation records John's "glorious vision" received "on the Lord's day" while he was banished to the Isle of Patmos for preaching the gospel and for bearing testimony of Jesus Christ. (Patmos is one of a group of islands in the Aegean Sea.) The opening lines of the book inform us that John received his vision from Jesus Christ, who sent it by a heavenly messenger (1:1).

The chief purpose of the book seems to be to prepare us for the last days and Christ's second coming, or "things which must shortly come to pass" (1:1), because "the time of the coming of the Lord draweth nigh" (JST 1:3). Major themes include the following:

Jesus Christ. The most important aspect of the book of Revelation is that it reveals Jesus Christ to us. The first chapter presents a view of the glorious resurrected Lord, and every subsequent chapter throughout the book sets forth doctrines pertaining to his atoning sacrifice, his love and mercy for us, his divine judgments upon the wicked, and his rewards for the righteous. The book of Revelation is a Christ-centered text, as indicated by its variety and number of names and titles of the Lord. There are forty-six names and titles of Deity in the book (including both the Father and the Son), used a total of 199 times (see Appendix 1).

The broad range of the names that John received in his revelation is instructive. The names or titles *Christ* (four times), *First Begotten of the Dead, Jesus* (five times), *Jesus Christ* (six times), *Living God, Lord Jesus, Lord Jesus Christ,* and especially *Lamb* (twenty-eight times) point to the atonement of Jesus. The name or titles *Alpha and Omega* (four times),

---

[2] *Teachings of the Prophet Joseph Smith,* 150–51; emphasis added.

Beginning and the Ending (three times), *First and the Last* (four times), and *Him Which Is, and Which Was, and Which Is to Come* (four times) indicate the eternal nature of the mission of Jesus, which spans the beginning of eternity through his atoning sacrifice to the judgment and end of the world. The names or titles *Almighty, Almighty God, God* (eighty-three times), *God Almighty, God of Heaven, God of the Earth, King of Kings* (two times), *King of Saints, Lion of the Tribe of Judah, Lord* (nine times), *Lord God* (three times), *Lord God Almighty* (five times), *Lord God Omnipotent, Morning Star,* and *Prince of the Kings of the Earth* refer to Jesus as the God of eternal power, authority, dominion, might, eminence, and glory.

The last days. Revelation is a guidebook for understanding the last days, or "things which must shortly come to pass" (1:1; 4:1; 22:6). Joseph Smith taught: "John saw that only which was lying in futurity and which was shortly to come to pass. See Rev. i:1–3, which is a key to the whole subject."[3] Nephi prophesied that John would "write concerning the end of the world" (1 Ne. 14:22). One scholar noted, "By far the largest portion of the book describes the events that immediately precede the second coming of the Savior."[4]

Several chapters of Revelation are devoted to the judgments of God. In addition, John presents many details pertaining to two prophets who will prophesy and minister in Jerusalem, the blessings designed for the righteous, and the judgments awaiting those who belong to Babylon.

The Second Coming. Almost all aspects of the book of Revelation seem to pertain in some way to the last days and the Lord's glorious second coming. John provides many glimpses into these future events, preparing us for the days ahead. Revelation 19, for instance, uses a multitude of images and symbols to describe the magnificent coming of Christ to the earth to "judge and make war" (v. 11). His names are *Faithful and True* (v. 11), *The Word of God* (v. 13), and *King of Kings and Lord and of Lords* (v. 16). This last name is written "on his thigh" (v. 16); he is dressed in red apparel that has been "dipped in blood" (v. 13); he is riding on a white horse; he wears many crowns upon his head; and "out of his mouth" proceeds the word of God (v. 15). Dressed in white linen and mounted on white horses, the armies of heaven follow him.

---

[3] *Teachings of the Prophet Joseph Smith,* 289.
[4] Lund, "Seeing the Book of Revelation," 52.

Good versus evil. Revelation is a book of contrasts between God and Satan, heaven and earth (and hell), Saints and sinners, righteousness and worldliness. The term *heaven,* for instance, is used fifty-six times by John; the word *earth,* often representing worldliness, is used seventy-nine times. These contrasts reflect Satan's attempt to counterfeit the things of God; they also apply to the continual spiritual battle between God and his Saints and Satan and his followers. Thus heaven stands opposite to earth, exalted Saints oppose damned souls, hymns of praise to God oppose the cries of anguish from the wicked, the number seven opposes the number 666, Michael and his angels oppose Satan and his angels, and Christ enthroned in the highest heaven opposes Satan dwelling in the abyss below (see Appendix 2).

God's judgments against the wicked. The book of Revelation lists God's judgments against sinners and the rebellious. In an orderly manner, and often one by one, God will send his judgments against the earth as a testimony and a warning to earth's inhabitants, with the desire that they repent of their manifold transgressions. The judgments, which accompany the opening of the sixth and seventh seals, the blowing of the seven trumpets, and the pouring out of the bowls, include earthquakes, signs in the heavens, the darkening of the sun, lightnings, thunderings, plagues, pestilences, and wars.

Safety for the righteous. Again and again the Lord indicates that the righteous will receive spiritual protection when God sends his judgments to the earth. Revelation 1:3 tells us very clearly that if we read and understand the things of the book, we will be "blessed." In the seven letters to the seven churches, we are told that those who overcome the world are given seven promises that pertain to the temple and to eternal life: The righteous will partake of the tree of life (2:7); they will not be hurt by the second death (2:11); they will receive hidden manna, a white stone, and a new name (2:17); they will have power over kingdoms (2:26); they will be clothed in white raiment (3:4–5); they will dwell in the heavenly temple (3:12); and they will sit upon the throne of Jesus (3:21).

The temple in heaven. John speaks of the "temple which is in heaven" (14:17) or the "temple of heaven" (16:17), which is John's name for the celestial kingdom. His description and detail of the temple in heaven is unsurpassed among all of revealed scripture. In fact, the temple in heaven serves as a backdrop for much of his vision: in Revelation 4:1, John looks and sees "a door . . . opened in heaven," and a voice instructs him to "come up hither" and enter the heavenly temple. He does so while "in the Spirit" (1:10) and sees many things that may have reminded him of the earthly temple of Jerusalem, such as the seven-branched lamp stand, trumpets, the altars of sacrifice and incense, sacred vestments, the altar's four horns, ark of the covenant, golden censer, incense and incense bowls, mercy seat (throne), priestly/angelic officiants, cherubim-like creatures, and the Lamb. We see other elements of the temple as we progress through the vision.

ISN'T THE BOOK OF REVELATION DIFFICULT TO UNDERSTAND?

Revelation contains scores of symbols and images that may make the book difficult to read and understand. John writes in veiled, symbolic language, using such images as beasts, stars, lamps of fire, a serpent, a dragon, a woman, a morning star, a white stone, ten horns, seven trumpets, a sea of glass, feet like fine brass, a thief, a rainbow, a lion, an eagle, a blood-red moon, a burning mountain, locusts, scorpions, a pit, lions' heads, a leopard, a lamb, waters, frogs, a millstone, a bride and her husband, precious stones, sand, gold, and crystal (for these and other symbols used in Revelation, see Appendix 3).

Although these symbols may at first intimidate us as we read, they are meant to be understood, especially with the spirit of prophecy and revelation and after much study. It may surprise us to learn that Joseph Smith taught that "the book of Revelation is one of the plainest books God ever caused to be written."[5] An angel explained to Nephi that "the things which [John] shall write are just and true; and . . . at the time the book proceeded out of the mouth of the Jew, the things which were written were *plain and pure, and most precious and easy to the understanding* of all men" (1 Ne. 14:23; emphasis added).

On one occasion Elder Bruce R. McConkie asked, "Are we expected to understand the book of Revelation?" and then responded, "Certainly. Why else did the Lord reveal it? The common notion that it deals with beasts and plagues and mysterious symbolisms that cannot be understood is just not true. It is so far overstated that it gives an entirely erroneous feeling about this portion of revealed truth. . . . If we apply ourselves with full

---

[5] *Teachings of the Prophet Joseph Smith,* 290.

purpose of heart, we can catch the vision of what the ancient Revelator recorded."[6]

Many resources are available to assist us in understanding the book of Revelation. Joseph Smith provided us with a number of insights found in his teachings, now published in a variety of formats: the Joseph Smith Translation of the Bible, the Book of Mormon, and Doctrine and Covenants 77, 88, and 130. Many of the symbols used in the New Testament book of Revelation are also found in other books of scripture, including the Old Testament books of Isaiah, Ezekiel, Jeremiah, and Daniel. And many of the symbols and expressions of Revelation are explained in the book itself (see Appendix 3).

WHY SHOULD WE STUDY THE BOOK OF REVELATION?

Of all the books of the Bible, except perhaps Isaiah, Revelation may be the most valuable in helping us to understand the great events of the latter days. Revelation gives us a marvelous panoramic view of eternity—from the premortal existence to mortality to life in the celestial kingdom. Revelation is a Christ-centered text; it teaches us many important truths about his divine mission, mortal ministry, atoning sacrifice, resurrection, kingship, and glory. Revelation contains numerous truths pertaining to the last days that are not found elsewhere in the scriptures. Revelation, with its symbols, images, commandments, and detailed prophecies, helps us to prepare for the Second Coming.

THE FOCUS OF THIS BOOK

Perhaps more volumes have been written on the book of Revelation than on any other single book in the Bible. It has captured the imagination of people for centuries, and it holds particular interest for us today because much of it deals with events that may well transpire during our lifetimes. The book is so complex that entire volumes have been written on the few verses dealing directly with the seven seals, or on the even fewer verses that tell us of the number of the beast. Other volumes have treated issues of apocalyptic literature or John's first-century world view.

---

[6] McConkie, "Understanding the Book of Revelation," 87.

Of necessity, then, we have had to be selective in the kinds of issues we have discussed in this volume, and we made a conscious decision to omit certain areas of focus. We have not treated in these pages the various schools of thought on how to interpret Revelation. We have given only a limited amount of space to interpretations that seem to miss the mark, even though some such interpretations have become widespread. We have not discussed the nature of apocalyptic literature in general nor the place of Revelation in that genre in specific. As a rule, we have not dealt with the civil, religious, political, and cultural dynamics of the late first century. Each of these is important in its place, but space in this particular work seemed better used on John's specific message for our day.

It was our purpose from the outset to try to create a commentary that would be helpful to lay readers and scholars alike. But we are not seeking to create a comprehensive scholarly treatment of the book of Revelation. Our desire was to find meaning in John's vision for our day, to seek to understand what people in the twentieth and twenty-first centuries might need or want to know about what John saw and heard while "in the Spirit on the Lord's day" (1:10). At the same time, it was our desire to bear testimony of Jesus Christ, his power, his plan, and his love and to share the reassurances we found in Revelation that even though the last days will be days of tribulation, they will also be days of triumph: though we will have great occasion of sorrow in the Lord's judgments, we will have even greater occasion of rejoicing in his gracious deliverance.

Although we have spent considerable time, effort, and prayer in preparing this book, we would, frankly, be uncomfortable being viewed as the last word on any part of the commentary. We hope that readers will combine any insights they gain from these pages with others they acquire elsewhere, including from the Spirit and their own scriptural study, to come to an even more complete and deeper understanding of these important words of John the Seer.

Tools for Understanding the Book of Revelation

This volume contains tools that will help in understanding John's marvelous vision. First and most important, it uses the scriptures revealed through the Prophet Joseph Smith—the Joseph Smith Translation, the Book of Mormon, the Doctrine and Covenants, and the Pearl of Great

Price—and the teachings and sermons in which Joseph Smith interpreted different parts of Revelation.

The chapters of Revelation are divided here into individual units of thought, thereby helping us understand each part more fully. A phrase-by-phrase (sometimes word-by-word) commentary covers all twenty-two chapters of the book of Revelation. The resource most frequently used in creating this commentary was the words of the prophets, both ancient and modern. Helpful background to the words, images, and symbols used by John is also provided.

The text of the book of Revelation presented in *Understanding the Book of Revelation* includes alternate readings from the Joseph Smith Translation. It also includes clarifications of archaic words. Brackets in the text indicate a word or phrase that has been added or altered from the King James Version of the Bible. Ellipses indicate a word or words that are not present in the Joseph Smith Translation. Brackets and ellipses are accompanied by explanatory footnotes. Scripture citations with only chapter and verse numbers are from Revelation unless otherwise indicated. Citations such as 2:3a and 2:3b refer, respectively, to the first and second half of the verse cited. Phrases in quotation marks but without a source citation are from the passage of Revelation under discussion. Full references for the sources in the footnotes are found in the Bibliography.

Individuals who study the book of Revelation will better understand God's designs for the future of the world and its inhabitants and prepare themselves better for the days ahead. In doing so, such individuals will find peace and calmness in their lives, because the Lord has promised us, "If ye are prepared ye shall not fear" (D&C 38:30).

REVELATION
1

THINGS WHICH MUST SHORTLY COME TO PASS (1:1–3)

Revelation begins by introducing the main characters and the chief purpose of the book. The main characters are Jesus Christ; John the Revelator; an angel who revealed things to John; and John's audience, those who read and understand his words. From our perspective, the purpose of the book is twofold. First, John bore solemn testimony of Christ (he "[bore] record of the word of God, and of the testimony of Jesus Christ") throughout the book, focusing on the Savior's divine mission, infinite atonement, and second coming. Second, the book prepares us, the readers in the latter days ("they who hear and understand," JST 1:3), for the last days ("things which must shortly come to pass") and for the second coming of Jesus Christ ("coming of the Lord," JST 1:3).

Revelation 1:1–3

> 1 The Revelation of [John, a servant of God, which was given]¹ unto him [of Jesus Christ, to show]² unto his servants things which must shortly come to pass; [that]³ he sent and signified . . . ⁴ by his angel unto his servant John.
> 2 Who [bore]⁵ record of the word of God, and of the testimony of Jesus Christ, and of all things that he saw.

---

¹ JST 1:1 indicates that the Revelation was given to the apostle John.
² JST 1:1 replaces the archaic English word *shew* with *show.*
³ JST 1:1 adds the relative pronoun *that.*
⁴ JST 1:1 omits the pronoun *it,* which is unnecessary here.
⁵ JST 1:2 replaces *bare* with *bore.*

3 Blessed [are they who read],[6] and they [who hear and understand][7] the
words of this prophecy, and keep those things which are written therein: for
the time [of the coming of the Lord draweth nigh].[8]

NOTES AND COMMENTARY

1:1 *Revelation.* The entire book is a revelation, or prophecy (1:3; 22:7,
10, 18–19).

John. An apostle of the Lord, son of Zebedee, and brother of James.

servant of God. The scriptures describe a servant of God as an individual who is "free from sin" through the atonement of Christ (Rom. 6:17–23)
and who does "the will of God from the heart" (Eph. 6:6). Moses (1 Chr.
6:49; 2 Chr. 24:9), Paul (Titus 1:1), Timotheus (Philip. 1:1), James (James
1:1), Alma (Alma 8:19), and other prophets and apostles (11:18; D&C
1:14; Amos 3:7) are "servants of God." Many of our day are also called servants, meaning "servants of God" (D&C 36:5; 52:3, 28–29; see also Rev.
7:3–4).

which must shortly come to pass. Joseph Smith taught: "The things
which John saw had no allusion to the scenes of the days of Adam, Enoch,
Abraham or Jesus, only so far as is plainly represented by John, and clearly
set forth by him. John saw that only which was lying in futurity and which
was shortly to come to pass. See Rev. i:1–3, which is a key to the whole
subject. . . . Also Rev. iv:1."[9]

The Prophet further proclaimed, "Now, I make this declaration, that
those things which John saw in heaven had no allusion to anything that had
been on the earth previous to that time, because they were the representation of 'things which must shortly come to pass,' and not of what has
already transpired."[10]

Nephi prophesied that John would "write concerning the end of the
world" (1 Ne. 14:22). One scholar notes: "The entire vision from beginning
to end takes 317 verses, and yet John spends only eleven verses (or about
3.5 percent) on the first five thousand years of history, which is about 71

---

[6] JST 1:3 replaces the phrase *is he that readeth* with *are they who read.*
[7] JST 1:3 replaces the relative pronoun *that* with the relative pronoun *who.* The JST also adds the
word *understand,* which clarifies the meaning of the text.
[8] JST 1:3 replaces the expression *the time is at hand* with the phrase *the time of the coming of the
Lord draweth nigh* to clarify the meaning of the text.
[9] *Teachings of the Prophet Joseph Smith,* 289.
[10] *Teachings of the Prophet Joseph Smith,* 290.

percent of the earth's total seven thousand years of recorded history. Without a doubt, the vast majority of the vision focuses on things 'which must be hereafter' (Rev. 4:1). Furthermore, on closer examination, we see that the focus is even more limited than that. . . . The Millennium itself is treated in only seven verses. (See Rev. 20:1–7.) By far the largest portion of the book describes the events that immediately precede the second coming of the Savior."[11] (See also 22:6.)

sent and signified by his angel. Angels, or God's heavenly messengers, play a significant role in Revelation. An angel assisted in the delivery of the revelation to John (1:1; 22:6, 8, 16). Angels are God's heavenly witnesses (3:5) and stand near to worship God in heaven (5:11; 7:11; 14:10). Four angels stand at the four corners of the earth ready to carry out judgments upon the earth (7:1), but a fifth angel ascends from the east (7:2), instructing the four to withhold their judgments for the time being; later the four angels are set loose (9:15). Seven angels who stand before God are each given a trumpet (8:2) and are prepared to sound them (8:6); then one by one they blow their trumpets (8:7–8, 10, 12; 9:1, 13–14; 11:15), announcing judgments upon the earth.

Further, an angel uses a golden censer (a small utensil used for incense) to bring judgments to the earth (8:3–5); another flies through heaven saying, "Woe, woe, woe" (8:13); still "another mighty angel come down from heaven" stands upon the sea and the earth and gives a little book to John (10:1, 5, 8–10); a different angel instructs John to "measure the temple of God, and the altar, and them that worship therein" (11:1); and Michael and his angels war against the dragon and his angels (12:7), while the dragon and his angels are cast to the earth (12:9). John sees another angel fly through heaven "having the everlasting gospel" (14:6), and this angel is followed by others (14:8–9, 15, 17, 18, 19), who work acts of God. John sees seven angels with seven plagues exit the heavenly temple (15:1, 6–8) and pour out judgments upon the earth (16:1, 3–5, 8, 10, 12, 17). John sees other great angels participating in God's plan of salvation (18:1, 21; 19:17; 20:1) and twelve angels standing at the twelve gates of heaven (21:12).

1:2 *Who [bore] record of the word of God.* John, as a special witness of Christ, bears testimony of him who is called the "Word of God" (19:13;

---

[11] Lund, "Seeing the Book of Revelation," 51–52.

see also 1 Jn. 1:1; D&C 93:8). "Word of God" also refers to scriptural records. In this case, the phrase may mean either or both.

1:3 *Blessed.* A similar statement is repeated at the end of the vision: "Blessed is he that keepeth the sayings of the prophecy of this book" (22:7). "Blessed" is used here and six other times in Revelation (14:13; 16:15; 19:9; 20:6; 22:7, 14), to introduce seven statements similar to the Beatitudes (see Appendix 4).

[they who read/hear/understand]. This passage speaks of spiritual understanding, or understanding by the Spirit. Jesus said, "Who hath ears to hear, let him hear" (Matt. 13:9; 13:43), and King Benjamin told his people, "Open your ears that ye may hear, and your hearts that ye may understand" (Mosiah 2:9; see also D&C 136:32). Unfortunately, there are those who will not attune themselves to understand spiritual things; such have "stopped their ears, that they should not hear" (Zech. 7:11) and are "a rebellious house, which have eyes to see, and see not; they have ears to hear, and hear not" (Ezek. 12:2; Jer. 5:21).

this prophecy. A reference to the entire book of Revelation (22:7, 10, 18–19).

Blessed . . . keep those things which are written. Those who treasure the words of John will be blessed.

time [of the coming of the Lord draweth nigh]. At the end of John's prophecy the Lord promises, "I come quickly" (22:12) and "Surely I come quickly" (22:20). See commentary on 2:5.

IDENTIFICATION OF JESUS CHRIST TO THE CHURCH (1:4–8)

The book of Revelation contains several truths about the Lord and his divine mission. He is called *Jesus Christ, First Begotten of the Dead, Prince of the Kings, Alpha and Omega, the Beginning and the Ending, Lord,* and *Almighty.* Regarding his premortal life, he is referred to as "Alpha" and "beginning" and is twice identified as one "who was." Concerning his mortal mission, Jesus is the being who was "pierced" and became the "first begotten of the dead," demonstrated love, and cleansed us from our sins with his blood. Regarding the time subsequent to his mortal ministry, Jesus is the one "who is to come," the "Omega," and the "ending." At his second coming Jesus Christ will come in clouds, accompanied with Saints; all shall see him and all kindreds will "wail because of him." Jesus is the "Prince of the kings," and as such he rules heavenly ministrants ("angels") and servants; possesses a throne, glory, and dominion; has the power to make individuals kings and priests; is clothed with glory; bestows "grace" and "peace" upon worthy individuals; and has a divine Father.

Revelation 1:4–8

4 [Now this is the testimony of John to the seven servants who are over the seven churches in Asia. Grace unto you, and peace from him who is, and who was, and who is to come; who hath sent forth his angel from before his throne, to testify unto those who are the seven servants over the seven churches.][12]
5 [Therefore, I, John, the faithful witness, bear record of the things which were delivered me of the angel, and from Jesus Christ][13] the first begotten of the dead, and the Prince of the kings of the earth.
6 [And unto him who loved us, be glory; who washed us from our sins in his own blood],[14] and hath made us kings and priests unto God, . . . [15] his Father. To him be glory and dominion, for ever and ever. Amen.
7 [For behold, he cometh in the clouds with ten thousands of his saints in the kingdom, clothed with the glory of his Father.][16] And every eye shall see him; and they who pierced him, and all kindreds of the earth shall wail because of him. Even so, Amen.
8 [For he saith,][17] I am Alpha and Omega, the beginning and the ending, . . . [18] the Lord, [who is, and who was, and who][19] is to come, the Almighty.

NOTES AND COMMENTARY

1:4 *testimony of John.* The book of Revelation is a testimony of Jesus Christ and his divine mission, characteristics, judgments, and especially his atoning sacrifice. It contains the testimony of John (1:2, 5, 9), whose testimony is shared by others (19:10). It mentions the testimony of martyrs who were slain because of their testimonies of Christ (6:9; 20:4) and two latter-day prophets who bear witness of Jesus (11:3, 7). Premortal Saints overcame Satan and his angels by the "blood of the Lamb" and by the "word of

---

[12] JST 1:4 adds, omits, and alters many words of this verse.
[13] JST 1:5 adds a long note of clarification and identifies John as the faithful witness of Jesus Christ.
[14] JST 1:6 adds these important words.
[15] JST 1:6 omits the conjunction *and.*
[16] JST 1:7 adds the preposition *For* and clarifies that Jesus will come "in the clouds with ten thousands of his saints in the kingdom, clothed with the glory of his Father."
[17] JST 1:8 adds this phrase.
[18] JST 1:8 omits the word *saith.*
[19] JST 1:8 changes the relative pronoun *which* to *who.*

their testimony" (12:11), and Saints of the latter days will also war with
Satan because of their testimonies of Jesus (12:17).

seven servants. Seven specific ecclesiastical leaders over the seven
churches of Asia Minor.

seven churches. Seven branches of the Church were listed by John:
Ephesus, Smyrna, Pergamos, Thyatira, Sardis, Philadelphia, and Laodicea.
These were cities, roughly thirty to forty-five miles apart, located in Asia
Minor, or what is now present-day Turkey. Other branches of the Church
known to exist in Asia during this time include Hierapolis (Col. 4:13),
Colossae (Col. 1:2), Troas (2 Cor. 2:12), Magnesia, and Tralles.[20]

Seven is a symbolic number, denoting wholeness and completeness.
The seven churches may, therefore, represent the entire Church of Jesus
Christ.

Grace unto you, and peace. Greetings of grace and peace are elements
common to ancient epistles. Here they indicate that John sends his message
to the seven churches in style like an epistle.

him who is/was/is to come. Used twice in Revelation (1:4, 8; 4:8; see
also 11:17; 16:5), this expression is a commentary on the Hebrew name
Yahweh (*Jehovah* is the usual anglicized form),[21] which denotes existence
or being. Verse 18 explains further: "I am he that liveth, and was dead; and,
behold, I am alive for evermore." Similar expressions in Revelation include
"Alpha and Omega," "the beginning and the ending" (1:8), "the first and
the last" (1:11). And other scriptures read: "listen to the voice of the Lord
your God, even Alpha and Omega, the beginning and the end, whose
course is one eternal round, the same today as yesterday, and forever"
(D&C 35:1); and "the Lord Omnipotent who reigneth, who was, and is
from all eternity to all eternity" (Mosiah 3:5). Each expression encompasses all states of existence for God: past, present, and future. Hence Jehovah is Endless ("Endless is my name," Moses 1:3), Eternal (Hel. 13:38),
and Everlasting (Isa. 9:6).

his throne. Christ's throne, located in the "temple in heaven" (14:17;
16:17), which is John's name for the celestial kingdom,[22] is a symbol of his
divine kingship (see commentary on 4:2).

---

[20] On the other churches of the period, see Charles, *Critical and Exegetical Commentary,* 1:8.

[21] Ford, *Revelation,* 376.

[22] For a discussion of the temple in heaven, see Parry and Parry, "Temple in Heaven," in *Temples
of the Ancient World,* ed. Parry, 515–32. See also the commentary on 21:22.

1:5 *faithful witness.* John, as a member of the Quorum of the Twelve Apostles, stands as a special witness of Jesus' infinite atonement and divine Sonship. John was banished to Patmos, evidently for being a faithful witness (1:9).

first begotten of the dead. As it was Jesus' birthright, as the firstborn of the Father in the spirit, to be chosen as the Redeemer,[23] it was also his privilege to become the firstborn from the dead (see also Col. 1:18). In other words, he was the first of all beings on this earth to be resurrected.

Prince of the kings. This title anticipates Christ's title of *King of kings* in Revelation 17:14 and 19:16. Jesus is of royal blood, a prince to his Father, the King. Jesus is also the "King of Zion" (Moses 7:53), "King of glory" (Ps. 24:7), and "King of the Jews" (Matt. 2:2). He, with his Father, is exalted above all kings who will rule in the kingdom of God.

1:6 *him who loved us.* Jesus loves us so much that he gave his life for us (Gal. 2:20; Eph. 5:2, 25).

washed us from our sins in his own blood. Faithful temple worshippers approach the most holy places after they have been washed, both ritually and symbolically, with water (Ex. 29:4; Heb. 9:9–10). Those who prove faithful will metaphorically receive another washing, not with water but with the blood of the Lamb (1 Jn. 1:7). The expression "washed us . . . in his own blood" refers to individuals who become pure "because of their faith, and the repentance of all their sins" (3 Ne. 27:19) through the blood that Christ shed. They then are made "kings and priests" (1:6). The pronoun *us* refers to John as well as to the righteous Saints of his day and of all ages.

kings and priests. John and others were made kings and priests by God (5:10; 20:6): "Those holding the fullness of the Melchizedek Priesthood are kings and priests of the Most High God, holding the keys of power and blessings."[24]

unto God, his Father. Heavenly Father is both Jesus' Father and God as well as our Father and God (John 20:17). Joseph Smith expounded on this expression from the King James Version of the Bible, "unto God, and his Father," in his sermon dated 16 June 1844, in which he explained the plurality of Gods. He first read Revelation 1:6 and then stated, "It is altogether

---

[23] Taylor, *Mediation and Atonement,* 136–37.
[24] *History of the Church,* 5:555.

correct in the translation." He continued, "I will preach on the plurality of Gods. . . .

"I have always declared God to be a distinct personage, Jesus Christ a separate and distinct personage from God the Father, and that the Holy Ghost was a distinct personage and a Spirit: and these three constitute three distinct personages and three Gods. . . .

" . . . Hence the doctrine of a plurality of Gods is as prominent in the Bible as any other doctrine."[25]

glory and dominion. These are two aspects of full salvation, or exaltation. Christ is "the prototype or standard of salvation; . . . salvation consists in the *glory,* authority, majesty, power and *dominion* which Jehovah possesses and in nothing else."[26] (See also Dan. 7:14.) Glory seems to suggest Christ's light and resplendence; dominion indicates his sovereignty over us and all his creations.[27]

1:7 *he cometh.* John testifies that Jesus Christ will come.

in the clouds. At the time of his second coming, Jesus will descend in clouds of glory (Dan. 7:13; Matt. 24:30; Acts 1:9–11; D&C 34:7; 45:16). With him, righteous Saints "shall be caught up together . . . in the clouds" (1 Thes. 4:17). Clouds represent the glory of the Lord (D&C 84:5; Ezek. 10:3–4), act as the chariot of God upon which he travels through the heavens (Ps. 104:3; Isa. 19:1), and symbolize a veil that ofttimes conceals his presence from mortals (Ex. 19:9, 16; 24:15–18; 3 Ne. 18:38).

with ten thousands of his saints. In the past the Lord traveled with "ten thousands of saints" (Deut. 33:2), and Enoch prophesied that the Lord would come "with ten thousands of his saints" at the Second Coming (Jude 1:14). These people will come in clouds of glory; they may be Saints who have been blessed with exaltation. "Ten thousands" is an ancient way of saying "great numbers."

clothed with the glory of his Father. Christ will wear red garments at his coming (Isa. 63:1–2; D&C 133:48) and will be clothed in brilliant light and glory.

every eye shall see him. All peoples of the earth and every individual shall see Christ when he comes in glory at his second coming. "Then shall

---

[25] *Teachings of the Prophet Joseph Smith,* 369, 370; see the entire text of this sermon, 369–76.
[26] *Lectures on Faith,* 7:9; emphasis added.
[27] *Webster's New Collegiate Dictionary,* s.v. "dominion," "glory."

all the tribes of the earth mourn, and they shall see the Son of man coming in the clouds of heaven with power and great glory" (Matt. 24:30).

they who pierced him. This passage refers to those who participated in the crucifixion of Jesus, piercing his hands and his feet with nails. Zechariah prophesied, "They shall look upon me whom they have pierced" (Zech. 12:10). This passage may also speak of those who reject Jesus Christ after having known him and his goodness (see also Heb. 6:6).

all kindreds . . . shall wail because of him. This scene, which pertains to the wicked, will fulfill Zechariah's prophecy that "they shall look unto me whom they have pierced, and they shall mourn for him" (Zech. 12:10). Matthew also prophesied: "And then shall all the tribes of the earth mourn, and they shall see the Son of man coming in the clouds of heaven with power and great glory" (Matt. 24:30; see also Rev. 6:15–17).

Even so, Amen. This phrase is "the double affirmation . . . [which] is the Spirit's seal to this striking prophetic testimony. The 'Even so' is Greek, the 'Amen' is Hebrew. To both Gentiles and Jews his Word is unchangeable."[28]

1:8 *Alpha and Omega.* Alpha and omega are the first and last letters of the Greek alphabet, here signifying Christ as the First and the Last, the Beginning and the End (1:17; 21:6; 22:13; Isa. 41:4; 48:12).

Almighty. The descriptive title *Almighty* occurs eight times in Revelation (1:8; 4:8; 11:17; 15:3; 16:7, 14; 19:15; 21:22), revealing Jesus as a God of great power and might—he is mightier than all.

JOHN WAS IN THE SPIRIT ON THE LORD'S DAY (1:9–10A)

John experienced tribulations and was banished to the Isle of Patmos for preaching the gospel. As a preface to his vision of the Lord (1:10b–16), John explains, he "was in the Spirit on the Lord's day."

Revelation 1:9–10a

9 I John, who also am your brother, and companion in tribulation, and in the kingdom and patience of Jesus Christ, was in the isle that is called Patmos, for the word of God, and for the testimony of Jesus Christ.
10a I was in the Spirit on the Lord's day,

---

[28] Scott, *Exposition of the Revelation of Jesus Christ,* 30.

NOTES AND COMMENTARY

1:9 *your brother, and companion in tribulation.* John was a brother in the gospel (19:10; 22:9) and he, like other Church members (6:11; 12:10), suffered the trials and tribulations of mortality and of membership in the Lord's kingdom.

patience of Jesus Christ. The word *patience* is found seven times in Revelation (1:9; 2:2–3, 19; 3:10; 13:10; 14:12), each time speaking of the Saints' endurance of trials and tribulation. The New English Bible gives a helpful alternative reading: "I, John, your brother, who share with you in the suffering and the sovereignty and the endurance which is ours in Jesus . . . "

isle that is called Patmos. The Isle of Patmos was an island among the Sporades, which are islands in the Aegean Sea. It was used as a place of banishment. John suggests two reasons why he was banished to Patmos: for preaching "the word of God" and for bearing "testimony of Jesus Christ."

1:10a *I was in the Spirit.* Lehi was similarly "overcome with the Spirit, [and] was carried away in a vision" (1 Ne. 1:8), and Ezekiel testified, "The spirit lifted me up, and took me away" (Ezek. 3:14). Being "in the Spirit" seems to be both a prerequisite and a vehicle for receiving a vision from God. Today we might describe this state as "being filled with the Spirit," although the instances spoken of in scripture probably involve being filled with the Spirit to a greater degree than we commonly experience or contemplate. See commentary on 17:3.

on the Lord's day. This phrase most likely refers to the Sabbath.

JOHN'S VISION OF CHRIST IN THE TEMPLE IN HEAVEN (1:10B-16)

John beholds and describes the glorious, resurrected Jesus Christ. He first sees seven golden candlesticks, representing the seven churches (1:20). That is followed by a vision of Jesus himself, who is described with images that recall a burning candlestick or lampstand: Jesus' eyes ("as a flame of fire") and his feet ("as if they burned in a furnace") recall the fire of the lampstand; his feet ("like unto fine brass") recall the metal of the lampstand; the "white," mentioned twice, and Jesus' countenance, which is "as the sun shining in his strength," are comparable to the brightness of the burning lampstand, which may have the appearance of a bright, white, burning light. That Jesus is in the "midst of the seven candlesticks," or the seven churches, provides comfort to his Saints, who know that the Lord visits his church and spends time among his people.

John's vision of Christ appears to take place in the celestial kingdom, or, more specifically, "the temple which is in heaven" (14:17). The most definitive single source on the heavenly temple is recorded in the Revelation of John, where the backdrop for much of John's apocalyptic vision was the temple in heaven. John's experience with the heavenly temple began with an ablutionary rite of approach (1:5–6), in which the apostle was washed in the blood of Jesus and made a king and a priest. Then, while John was "in the Spirit on the Lord's day" (1:10), he found himself standing before the seven golden lampstands (1:12), suggesting the candlestick with "seven lamps" (Ex. 26:37) that in the days of the Mosaic tabernacle was located in the "holy place" of the tabernacle (Ex. 26:33–35). John's observation of the seven lampstands shifted into a divine vision of the glorified Jesus (1:13–18), and the symbol of the Lord (the lampstand) actually became that which was symbolized (the Lord). In Revelation 4:1, John beholds an open door in heaven that led from the Holy Place to the celestial Holy of Holies, or the throne room of God.[29]

The prophets Daniel, in the book of Daniel, and Joseph Smith, in the Doctrine and Covenants, also received visions of the Savior and used language similar to that of John's in Revelation to describe those visions (see Table 1).

Table 1

Source	John (Rev. 1:13–16)	Daniel (Dan. 10:5–6)	Joseph Smith (D&C 110:2–4)
Identity	one like unto the Son of man	a certain man	the Lord
Vesture	clothed with a garment down to the foot	clothed in linen	no comment

---

[29] For additional aspects of John's vision of the temple in heaven, see Parry and Parry, "Temple in Heaven," *Temples of the Ancient World,* ed. Parry, 515–32.

Table 1—Continued

Source	John (Rev. 1:13–16)	Daniel (Dan. 10:5–6)	Joseph Smith (D&C 110:2–4)
Girdle	and girt about the paps with a golden girdle	whose loins were girded with fine gold of Uphaz	no comment
Head	his head and his hairs were white like wool, as white as snow	his face as the appearance of lightning	the hair of his head was white like the pure snow
Counte-nance	his countenance was as the sun [shining] in his strength	no comment	his countenance shone above the brightness of the sun
Eyes	and his eyes were as a flame of fire	his eyes as lamps of fire	his eyes were as a flame of fire
Feet	And his feet like unto fine brass, as if they burned in a furnace	his arms and his feet like in colour to polished brass	under his feet was a paved work of pure gold, in color like amber
Voice	his voice as the sound of many waters	the voice of his words like the voice of a multitude	his voice was as the sound of the rushing of great waters

Revelation 1:10b–16

10b and heard behind me a great voice, as of a trumpet,
11 Saying, I am Alpha and Omega, the first and the last: and, What thou seest, write in a book, and send it unto the seven churches which are in Asia; unto Ephesus, and unto Smyrna, and unto Pergamos, and unto Thyatira, and unto Sardis, and unto Philadelphia, and unto Laodicea.
12 And I turned to see [from whence] the voice [came][30] that spake with me. And being turned, I saw seven golden candlesticks;
13 And in the midst of the seven candlesticks one like unto the Son of man, clothed with a garment down to the foot, and girt about the paps with a golden girdle.

---

[30] JST 1:12 replaces *seeing the voice* with *from whence . . . came.*

14 His head and his hairs were white like wool, as white as snow; and his eyes were as a flame of fire;
15 And his feet like unto fine brass, as if they burned in a furnace; and his voice as the sound of many waters.
16 And he had in his right hand seven stars: and out of his mouth went a sharp two-edged sword: and his countenance was as the sun [shining][31] in his strength.

NOTES AND COMMENTARY

1:10b *great voice*. The great, or distinctive, voice belongs to Jesus.

as of a trumpet. The word *as* occurs some fifty-six times in Revelation, usually to introduce a symbol. Here the symbol is "a trumpet." The voice of the Lord is as distinctive as the sound of a trumpet, an instrument that is used to awaken, herald, proclaim, and call to arms. In a corresponding manner, Alma the Younger wished that he could "speak with the trump of God, with a voice to shake the earth" (Alma 29:1).

1:11 *I am Alpha and Omega/first and . . . last*. Jesus identifies himself to John. For a description of these titles, see commentary on 1:8.

write in a book. The present-day text of Revelation consists of twenty-two chapters. The text of Revelation, possibly written upon a papyrus scroll, may have extended some twelve feet. John is commanded eight times in Revelation to "write," or record what he is given.

seven churches. See commentary on 1:4.

1:12 *I turned to see*. John, while "in the Spirit," seems to have been transported to the heavenly temple's counterpart of the earthly temple's "holy place" (Ex. 26:33), where the sacred lampstand was found. Expecting to see the one who spoke to him, John turns; first he sees seven golden candlesticks, and then he beholds Jesus Christ "in the midst of the seven candlesticks."

the voice . . . that spake with me. The voice belongs to Jesus, identified in the preceding verse.

seven golden candlesticks. The candlesticks represent the "seven churches" (see commentary on 1:20).

1:13 *in the midst of the seven candlesticks*. John sees Christ in "the midst of the seven candlesticks," meaning the "seven churches" (1:20). This symbolism suggests that Christ visits his church and spends time with the righteous. Christ taught, "Where two or three are gathered together in

---

[31] JST 1:16 changes *shineth* to *shining*.

my name, there am I in the midst of them" (Matt. 18:20) and "Lo, I am with you alway" (Matt. 28:20; see also 2 Cor. 6:16).

one like unto the Son of man. John sees Jesus, the "Son of man." Similar phraseology is found elsewhere: Daniel saw "one like the Son of man" (Dan. 7:13; see also Dan. 3:25); John beheld a "white cloud, and upon the cloud one sat like unto the Son of man" (14:14); and Abraham recorded that in the premortal council "the Lord said: Whom shall I send? And one answered like unto the Son of Man: Here am I, send me" (Abr. 3:27). Many versions of the Bible indicate that John saw "one like a son of man" (NEB, NIV, RSV), meaning "a being who looked like a man" (GNB).

The book of Moses enlightens us regarding Jesus' sacred title, "Son of Man." Moses 6:57 states that in the "language of Adam," God the Father is named "Man of Holiness" and "the name of his Only Begotten is the Son of Man, even Jesus Christ." Thus "Son of Man" is a shortened form of "Son of Man of Holiness."

clothed with a garment down to the foot, and girt about the paps with a golden girdle. In this vision the resurrected Lord appears in the vestments that symbolically suggest both a priest and a king, wearing a robe and a golden girdle (Ex. 28:4; 39:29).[32] The word *paps* is an archaic word meaning "breasts." The word *girdle* could be translated "sash." The New International Version renders this passage as "dressed in a robe reaching down to his feet and with a golden sash around his chest."

1:14 *His head and his hairs were white like wool, as white as snow.* White is a symbol of light, purity, and triumph; therefore, John sees the Lord in brilliant glory. The word *wool* recalls Jesus as the Lamb of God, who was sacrificed for our sins.

eyes . . . as a flame of fire. (See also 2:18; 19:12.) Eyes can represent knowledge (D&C 77:4) and here may specifically refer to God's omniscience and ability to penetrate all things. "Flame of fire" describes his brilliant glory. Joseph Smith described Jesus similarly: "His eyes were as a flame of fire" (D&C 110:3).

1:15 *feet like unto fine brass.* "Fine brass" suggests beauty and permanence (see also Ezek. 1:7; Dan. 10:6). John beholds the Lord's great glory and beauty, from the head to the feet.

---

[32] Mounce, *Book of Revelation,* 58.

voice as the sound of many waters. The voice of the Lord is as "many waters" (see also Ezek. 43:2), "as the sound of the rushing of great waters" (D&C 110:3), "like the noise of great waters" (Ezek. 1:24), "as the voice of many waters, and as the voice of a great thunder" (D&C 133:22), and "like the voice of a multitude" (Dan. 10:6). These expressions seem to describe the power, authority, uniqueness, and intensity that exists in the Lord's voice.

Of course, sometimes the Lord's voice comes much more quietly, though still with great power. To the Nephite Saints gathered at the temple of Bountiful, the voice of God "was not a harsh voice, neither was it a loud voice; nevertheless, and notwithstanding it being a small voice it did pierce them that did hear to the center, insomuch that there was no part of their frame that it did not cause to quake; yea, it did pierce them to the very soul, and did cause their hearts to burn" (3 Ne. 11:3).

1:16 *right hand.* "The right hand of God is associated with righteousness (Ps. 48:10; Isa. 41:10), power (Ex. 15:6; Ps. 89:13), and covenant making (Isa. 62:8). With his right hand, the Lord executes justice (3 Ne. 29:4, 9), dispenses the law (Deut. 33:2), and saves his people (Ps. 17:7; 20:6); [and] created the heavens and the earth (Isa. 48:13). After the divine judgment, the righteous will dwell eternally at the right hand of God (Mosiah 26:23–24; D&C 29:27)."[33]

seven stars. These stars are the "seven servants [or leaders] of the seven churches" (1:20). The "seven stars," or servants in his right hand, indicate that they are in God's special protection and are under his direction. The stars in Jesus' right hand may also show that he has perfect, or complete ("seven"), power and dominion over the cosmos and all his creations.

out of his mouth went a sharp two-edged sword. The "two-edged sword" is the word of God (D&C 6:2; Rev. 2:12, 16; 19:15). According to Paul, "The word of God is quick, and powerful, and sharper than a two-edged sword, piercing even to the dividing asunder of soul and spirit, and of the joints and marrow, and is a discerner of the thoughts and intents of the heart" (Heb. 4:12). Why is the word of God like a sword with two cutting edges (two-edged), rather than single edged? Because God's word is extremely powerful, able to pierce the very soul.

---

[33] McConkie and Parry, *Guide to Scriptural Symbols,* 93.

his countenance was as the sun [shining] in his strength. Christ's glory is greater than the noonday sun (Mal. 4:2; Matt. 17:2). His servants are compared to the stars (1:20), which pale in comparison.

JOHN FEARS, AND JESUS COMFORTS HIM (1:17–19)

Upon seeing the Lord, John falls at his feet with fear (1:17). Jesus lays his right hand on him and identifies himself as the resurrected Lord: "I am he that liveth, and was dead; and, behold, I am alive for evermore" (1:18). Jesus then commands John to write about the vision (1:19; 1:11).

Revelation 1:17–19

> 17 And when I saw him, I fell at his feet as dead. And he laid his right hand upon me, saying unto me, Fear not; I am the first and the last:
> 18 I am he that liveth, and was dead; and, behold, I am alive for evermore, Amen; and have the keys of hell and of death.
> 19 Write the things which thou hast seen, and the things which are, and the things which shall be hereafter.

NOTES AND COMMENTARY

1:17 *I saw him.* John bears witness that he saw the Lord in the heavenly temple. Similarly, Joseph Smith and Sidney Rigdon testified, "For we saw him" (D&C 76:23). Many other prophets have so testified—and the righteous may see him in his earthly temple (D&C 97:16; 110:8).

I fell. Perhaps John falls because he feels great reverence for the Lord, or maybe he falls because he feels great awe and fear at being in the presence of such a great and glorious heavenly being. Other prophets have felt compelled to fall on their faces, including Abraham (Gen. 17:3), Joshua (Josh. 5:14), Peter, James, and John (Matt. 17:6), the brother of Jared (Ether 3:6), and the Nephite multitude (3 Ne. 11:12).

he laid his right hand upon me. Like the comforting hand of a loving parent upon a troubled child, the divine hand, accompanied with the words "Fear not," still John's fear. A similar event is recorded in Matthew's account of the three apostles on the Mount of Transfiguration, in which it is recorded that Peter, James, and John "fell on their face, and were sore afraid"; but Jesus touched them and said, "Arise, and be not afraid" (Matt. 17:6–7).

right hand. See commentary on 1:16.

I am the first and the last. See commentary on 1:8.

1:18 *I am he that liveth, and was dead; . . . I am alive for evermore.* These three statements speak of Christ's postmortal power, the life that he has in himself, and his exaltation.

keys of hell and of death. To possess keys is to have power, authority, and the right of presidency (3:7; 9:1; Matt. 16:19). Jesus has presiding authority over death and hell, meaning over the grave and the spirit world. Hence, he has complete power over all who inhabit the spirit world, including the hosts of evil beings. He has power to bring forth the Resurrection and to redeem us from hell (2 Ne. 9:10–13).[34]

1:19 *Write.* John is commanded to write about the things that he sees in the vision (see commentary on 1:11). Six centuries earlier Nephi learned that "the Lord God hath ordained [John] the apostle of the Lamb of God" to write his vision (see 1 Ne. 14:24–27).

things which thou hast seen. This phrase may refer to John's vision of the resurrected Christ (1:12–18).

things which are. This phrase may refer to John's vision of the seven churches, which were historically contemporary (see commentary on 1:4).

things which shall be hereafter. This phrase may refer to Revelation 4 through 22, a great prophecy that pertains to things that would exist in the future (note the pivotal "after this" [4:1] which separates Revelation 1 through 3 from the remaining chapters). Joseph Smith declared, "John had the curtains of heaven withdrawn, and by vision looked through the dark vista of future ages, and contemplated events that should transpire throughout every subsequent period of time, until the final winding up scene."[35]

THE MYSTERY OF THE SEVEN STARS AND SEVEN CANDLE-STICKS (1:20)

Many of the symbols of the book of Revelation are explained within the book of Revelation itself. Here we are enlightened concerning the meaning of the seven stars and the seven candlesticks.

---

[34] On Jesus' possession of keys, see *Teachings of the Prophet Joseph Smith,* 323; *Discourses of Brigham Young,* 378; *Discourses of Wilford Woodruff,* 26–27; Smith, *Doctrines of Salvation,* 2:267.

[35] *Teachings of the Prophet Joseph Smith,* 247.

Revelation 1:20

> 20 [This is]³⁶ the mystery of the seven stars which thou sawest in my right hand, and the seven golden candlesticks. The seven stars are the [servants]³⁷ of the seven churches: and the seven candlesticks which thou sawest are the seven churches.

NOTES AND COMMENTARY

1:20 *mystery of the seven stars.* "The seven stars are the servants," or leaders, "of the seven churches."

right hand. See commentary on 1:16.

seven golden candlesticks. The candlesticks represent the seven churches (see commentary on 1:4). They are not the light that shines, for Jesus is the light. Rather, the churches are the branches, or supports, that hold up the light to the world. As Jesus explained to the righteous Nephites: "Therefore, hold up your light that it may shine unto the world. Behold I am the light which ye shall hold up, that which ye have seen me do" (3 Ne. 18:24).

---

³⁶ JST 1:20 adds these two words.
³⁷ JST 1:20 changes *angels* to *servants*.

REVELATION
2

To the Church in Ephesus:
The Righteous Partake of the Tree of Life (2:1–7)

The letters to the seven churches have a threefold application. First, the letters were likely sent to the seven churches of Asia, which may have been under the jurisdiction of the apostle John himself; hence, each letter contains information that fits a local and historical context.

Second, the number seven symbolically indicates completion or wholeness and thus has meaning for the entire church of Christ. Thus the contents of all seven letters apply to all Saints of all ages subsequent to the time of John's book of Revelation. Certainly the problems and challenges set forth in the letters are experienced by God's people in all ages, and the promises and rewards in the letters are directed to all Church members.

Third, the seven letters are personalized and directed to each member of the Church, regardless of geographical locale or dispensation. Note the many second-person personal pronouns—"thou," "thee," and "thy"—in the seven letters and the individual expressions "he that hath an ear" or "to him that overcometh." (A chart outlining the letters to the seven churches and their contents is contained in Appendix 4.)

The Lord, through John, is the author of the letter to the servant of the Church of Ephesus. Presumably the servant, a presiding authority, received the letter and read it to members of his congregation. The Lord commends the community of Saints for their faithful labor, patience during persecution and tribulation, and for hating the evil works of the Nicolaitans. He is also aware that the Saints cannot tolerate evil and that they successfully tested and then revealed false apostles who were among them. But the Church members need to repent for leaving their "first love."

Jesus Christ promises those who are spiritually alert ("he that hath an ear, let him hear what the Spirit saith") and who overcome the world that they will be permitted to partake of the fruit of the tree of life and become exalted souls.

Revelation 2:1–7

1 Unto the [servant][1] of the church of Ephesus write; These things saith he that holdeth the seven stars in his right hand, who walketh in the midst of the seven golden candlesticks;
2 I know thy works, and thy labour, and thy patience, and how thou canst not bear them which are evil: and thou hast tried them which say they are apostles, and are not, and hast found them liars:
3 And hast borne, and hast patience, and for my name's sake hast laboured, and hast not fainted.
4 Nevertheless I have somewhat against thee, because thou hast left thy first love.
5 Remember therefore from whence thou art fallen, and repent, and do the first works; or else I will come unto thee quickly, and will remove thy candlestick out of his place, except thou repent.
6 But this thou hast, that thou hatest the deeds of the Nicolaitans, which I also hate.
7 He that hath an ear, let him hear what the Spirit saith unto the churches; To him that overcometh will I give to eat of the tree of life, which is in the midst of the paradise of God.

NOTES AND COMMENTARY

2:1 *[servant] of the church of Ephesus.* The servant is the ecclesiastical leader of the Saints in Ephesus, which was a major city of Asia Minor, now called Turkey. The city of approximately 250,000 residents had a theater, library, paved streets (the main road was lined with impressive columns), and baths. Ephesus was the center for the imperial cult, and one of its three temples, the temple of Diana (Artemis to the Greeks), was one of the seven wonders of the world. That temple, which contained an image of the goddess Diana, "whom all Asia and the world worshippeth" (Acts 19:27), was an impressive architectural structure, with intricate ornamentation, the finest Greek art, and one hundred marble columns (fifty-five feet high). The temple stood on a huge platform that covered approximately one hundred thousand square feet, which is the size of two American football fields.

---

[1] JST 2:1 replaces *angel* with *servant.*

Paul visited Ephesus during his third missionary journey and remained there for two years, preaching the gospel to both Jews and Greeks (Acts 19:8, 10). He later returned to Ephesus and preached repentance, prophesied, and stated, "I ceased not to warn every one night and day with tears" (Acts 20:31). One of Paul's epistles (Ephesians) is addressed to the Saints of Ephesus.

he that holdeth the seven stars in his right hand. This person is Jesus, as we see in John's description of the resurrected Christ: "And he had in his right hand seven stars" (1:16).

who walketh in the midst of the . . . candlesticks. The language of this passage recalls 1:13: "And in the midst of the seven candlesticks one like unto the Son of man."

2:2 *I know thy works.* This phrase, given to all seven churches (2:9, 13, 19; 3:1, 8, 15), speaks concerning the Lord's omniscience. The scriptures bear witness that God "knoweth all things, and there is not anything save he knows it" (2 Ne. 9:20). Doctrine and Covenants 38:1–2 similarly states: "Thus saith the Lord your God, even Jesus Christ, the Great I AM, Alpha and Omega . . . The same which knoweth all things, for all things are present before mine eyes."

The Lord has full knowledge of the deeds—good and evil—of all who belong to the seven churches. He knows their labor and patience and how they tried the false apostles. He is fully aware of their tribulation and poverty (2:9); he comprehends "where Satan's seat is" and knows Antipas who was martyred for the faith (2:13); he understands the charity, service, and faith of the Saints (2:19); and he recognizes that some of the Saints are lukewarm rather than cold or hot (3:15).

thou canst not bear them which are evil. The Lord commends the Saints for avoiding the wicked.

thou hast tried them which say they are apostles, and are not. The false apostles mentioned here may be the apostates from within ("of your own selves") of which Paul had warned the elders of Ephesus: "After my departing shall grievous wolves enter in among you, not sparing the flock. Also of your own selves shall men arise, speaking perverse things, to draw away disciples after them" (Acts 20:29–30). Paul encountered false apostles on other occasions (2 Cor. 11:13–14, 22–28).

The Lord established means for his ancient church to judge and prove those who claimed to be apostles. In our dispensation, he revealed: "For it shall come to pass that the inhabitants of Zion shall judge all things pertaining to Zion. And liars and hypocrites shall be proved by them, and they who are not apostles and prophets shall be known" (D&C 64:38–39).

2:3 *hast borne, and hast patience.* The Ephesian Saints bore many tribulations and much persecution and yet remained patient, looking forward to victory over evil and eternal life.

for my name's sake hast laboured, and hast not fainted. The Saints never tire of serving and ministering to their sisters and brothers in Christ's name. Nephi was a great example of this characteristic, for he "with unwearyingness declared the word" of God to his people (Hel. 10:4).

2:4–5 *I have somewhat against thee . . . hast left thy first love.* The Lord condemns the Church members here because they have abandoned their original love for him and for their sisters and brothers in the gospel. Biblical scholar Krodel writes, "Without love toward God, toward brothers and sisters, a church ceases to be a church in spite of its commendable orthodoxy and brave endurance of hardships."[2] Because those in the Church have left their first love, they are "fallen" and commanded to "repent, and do the first works" by regaining their lost love of Christ.

2:5 *I will come unto thee quickly.* This expression, repeated several times in Revelation (2:16; 3:11; 22:7, 12, 20) and in the Doctrine and Covenants (D&C 33:18; 34:12; 35:27; 39:24; 49:28; 68:35; 88:126), warns us to be prepared always for the coming of the Lord, which will occur speedily.

The expression often accompanies statements of comfort and information, such as these: "I come quickly: blessed is he that keepeth the sayings of . . . this book" (22:7); "I come quickly; and my reward is with me" (22:12); "the kingdom is yours until I come. Behold, I come quickly" (D&C 35:27); and "I will be your ruler when I come; and behold, I come quickly" (D&C 41:4). Also it frequently is found with admonitions such as these: "Be patient in tribulation until I come; and, behold, I come quickly" (D&C 54:10); "Pray always, that ye may not faint, until I come. Behold, and lo, I will come quickly" (D&C 88:126); and "Be faithful until I come, for I come quickly" (D&C 112:34).

I . . . will remove thy candlestick. This candlestick represents the church at Ephesus (1:20). If the Saints do not repent for leaving their first love (1:4), the Lord will remove them from their place. Elder Bruce R.

---

[2] Krodel, *Revelation,* 108.

McConkie taught, "Any congregation of saints which is not true and faithful shall lose its place in the true Church."[3]

2:6 *hatest the deeds of the Nicolaitans.* God commends the Church for hating the evil deeds of the Nicolaitans, because he hates their deeds, as well. The Nicolaitans "appear to have been characterized by sensuality, seducing Christians to participate in the idolatrous feasts of pagans, and to unchastity. . . . The Nicolaitans taught that, in order to master sensuality, one must know the whole range of it by experience; and that he should therefore abandon himself without reserve to the lusts of the body, since they concerned only the body and did not touch the spirit."[4]

Elder Bruce R. McConkie explained that the Nicolaitans were "members of the Church who were trying to maintain their church standing while continuing to live after the manner of the world. They must have had some specific doctrinal teachings which they used to justify their course. . . . Whatever their particular deeds and doctrines were, the designation [Nicolaitans] has come to be used to identify those who want their names on the records of the Church, but do not want to devote themselves to the gospel cause with full purpose of heart. Thus, on July 8, 1838, the Lord said: 'Let my servant Newel K. Whitney be ashamed of the Nicolaitane band and of all their secret abominations' (D&C 117:11)."[5]

2:7 *He that hath an ear, let him hear what the Spirit saith.* Those who have the spiritual ears to understand God's messages declared by the Holy Spirit will do so. The subject is singular, for the injunction is directed to each individual with spiritual ears. This injunction is repeated seven times in the letters to the seven churches (2:11, 17, 29; 3:6, 13, 22; 13:9).

To him that overcometh. This phrase also is directed to each individual who overcomes the world. It is found seven times in the letters to the seven churches (2:11, 17, 29; 3:6, 13, 22; 13:9).

Individuals overcome Satan and the wicked world by being faithful (D&C 61:9; 63:20), believing that "Jesus is the Son of God" (1 Jn. 5:5), obeying the commandments (D&C 50:35), and being "born of God" (1 Jn. 5:4). Those who overcome will "eat of the tree of life" (2:7), "not be hurt of the second death" (2:11), "eat of the hidden manna" and receive "a white stone and . . . a new name" (2:17), receive "power over [many kingdoms]"

---

[3] McConkie, *Doctrinal New Testament Commentary,* 3:446.
[4] Vincent, *Word Studies in the New Testament,* 439.
[5] McConkie, *Doctrinal New Testament Commentary,* 3:446.

(2:26), "be clothed in white raiment" (3:5), become "a pillar" in the celestial temple, and receive God's name (3:12). In short, individuals who overcome evil will inherit eternal life.

eat of the tree of life. Because of their transgression, Adam and Eve became mortal and were forbidden access to the tree of life (Gen. 3:22). Through the atonement of Jesus Christ, all who overcome death receive the promise and blessing to "eat of the tree of life," meaning the consequences of the fall of Adam have been overturned. Humanity will receive immortality, and the righteous will gain eternal life and "enter in through the gates" of the celestial kingdom (22:14).

TO THE CHURCH IN SMYRNA: THE RIGHTEOUS ARE NOT HURT OF THE SECOND DEATH (2:8–11)

The Lord, described as "the first and the last, which was dead, and is alive," is the author of the letter to the servant of the Church in Smyrna. The letter features many contrasting elements: "the first" and "the last," "dead" and "alive," "poverty" and "rich," they which "say they are Jews" but "are not," and "death" and "crown of life." These contrasts emphasize that Church members will suffer and receive tribulations during mortality but will ultimately, if they are faithful, be crowned with eternal life.

This is the shortest of the seven letters and, like the letter to the Saints in Philadelphia, it contains no condemnation of the Saints.

Revelation 2:8–11

> 8 And unto the [servant][6] of the church in Smyrna write; These things saith the first and the last, which was dead, and is alive;
> 9 I know thy works, and tribulation, and poverty, (but thou art rich) and I know the blasphemy of them which say they are Jews, and are not, but are the synagogue of Satan.
> 10 Fear none of those things which thou shalt suffer: behold, the devil shall cast some of you into prison, that ye may be tried; and ye shall have tribulation ten days: be thou faithful unto death, and I will give thee a crown of life.
> 11 He that hath an ear, let him hear what the Spirit saith unto the churches; He that overcometh shall not be hurt of the second death.

---

[6] JST 2:8 replaces *angel* with *servant*.

NOTES AND COMMENTARY

2:8 *[servant] of the church in Smyrna.* The servant is the ecclesiastical leader of the Saints in Smyrna, which was a prosperous commercial center thirty-five miles north of Ephesus. It had at least two temples, one dedicated to the goddess Roma and the other built in honor of the Emperor Tiberius. Smyrna is now called Izmir and is a large city in present-day Turkey.

the first and the last. See commentary on 1:4, 8.

which was dead, and is alive. See commentary on 1:4, 18.

2:9 *I know thy works.* See commentary on 2:2.

I know the blasphemy of them which say they are Jews, and are not. The word translated "blasphemy" may also be translated as "slanderous accusations" (JB). One commentator explains: "The Jews of Smyrna may have called themselves the synagogue of God. John denounced them with bitter irony as a synagogue of Satan, because Satan, the devil, in the form of Roman authorities, uses Jewish slander to throw some Christians of Smyrna into prison."[7] (See also Rom. 9:6; 2 Ne. 30:1–2.)

2:10 *Fear none of those things which thou shalt suffer.* In verses 9 and 10, the terms "tribulation," "poverty," "suffer," "tried," "tribulation," and "death" represent our mortal suffering and experience. The letter to the church in Smyrna contrasts these terms with the promise of life ("crown of life") and power over the second death in verses 10 and 11.

devil shall cast some of you into prison, that ye may be tried. Public authorities, while hearkening to the voice of the devil, will cast some of the Saints of Smyrna into prison.

ye shall have tribulation ten days. The period "ten days" denotes a time of testing or of probation (Dan. 1:12, 14), such as mortality. This number contrasts with such scriptural terms as "eternity," "everlasting," and "forever." The Saints will be tested for a short period (ten days) compared to the length of eternity.

thou faithful unto death. This expression is synonymous with the well-known phrase "endure to the end" (1 Ne. 13:37; D&C 14:7).

I will give thee a crown of life. The crown of life is the crown of "honor, immortality, and eternal life" (D&C 124:55), which is reserved for each one who "endureth temptation" and loves the Lord (James 1:12), who

---

[7] Krodel, *Revelation,* 112.

has faith and "work[s] righteousness" (D&C 20:14), and who is "faithful unto the end" (D&C 81:6; see also D&C 66:12).

2:11 He that hath an ear. See commentary on 2:7.

He that overcometh. See commentary on 2:7.

not be hurt of the second death. John tells us who will receive the second death, and then he defines it: "The fearful, and unbelieving, and the abominable, and murderers, and whoremongers, and sorcerers, and idolaters, and all liars, shall have their part in the lake which burneth with fire and brimstone: which is the second death" (21:8; see also Jacob 3:11; D&C 63:17). The Book of Mormon calls the second death a "spiritual death," meaning to "die as to things pertaining unto righteousness" (Alma 12:16; Hel. 14:18). Spiritual death is also defined as separation from God (D&C 29:41). Here, the Lord promises us that if we overcome the world and evil, we will not be hurt by the second death.

TO THE CHURCH IN PERGAMOS: THE RIGHTEOUS RECEIVE HIDDEN MANNA, A WHITE STONE, AND A NEW NAME (2:12–17)

Church members in Pergamos were persecuted by those who were not Christians, especially members of the pagan community, who accused the Christians of "hatred against the human race," "atheism," and advocating a "mischievous superstition." It was the custom of the persecutors to cry out to the Christians, "Away with the atheists."[8] Further, the Saints were evidently persecuted for refusing to worship pagan idols and were ostracized from social and political functions.

Jesus, the author of this letter, commends the Saints for holding fast to his name and refusing to deny the faith, but he criticizes a few for holding to the doctrines of Balaam and the Nicolaitans, which doctrines teach idolatry and sexual sin. He commands such to repent.

To those who overcome the world, Jesus promises "hidden manna," a "white stone," and a "new name."

Revelation 2:12–17

12 And to the [servant][9] of the church in Pergamos write; These things saith he which hath the sharp sword with two edges;

---

[8] Krodel, *Revelation,* 114.
[9] JST 2:12 replaces *angel* with *servant.*

13 I know thy works, and where thou dwellest, even where Satan's seat is: and thou holdest fast my name, and hast not denied my faith, even in those days wherein Antipas was my faithful martyr, who was slain among you, where Satan dwelleth.

14 But I have a few things against thee, because thou hast there them that hold the doctrine of Balaam, who taught Balac to cast a stumblingblock before the children of Israel, to eat things sacrificed unto idols, and to commit fornication.

15 So hast thou also them that hold the doctrine of the Nicolaitans, which thing I hate.

16 Repent; or else I will come unto thee quickly, and will fight against them with the sword of my mouth.

17 He that hath an ear, let him hear what the Spirit saith unto the churches; To him that overcometh will I give to eat of the hidden manna, and will give him a white stone, and in the stone a new name written, which no man knoweth saving he that receiveth it.

NOTES AND COMMENTARY

2:12 *[servant] of the church in Pergamos.* The servant is the ecclesiastical leader of the Saints in Pergamos (or Pergamum), which was in Asia Minor, or present-day Turkey. This city housed a world-famous library and several temples built in honor of Augustus, Rome, and other deities. One temple was dedicated to Asclepius, the god of healing, and sick people were presented at this temple with the hope of being healed. Another temple, built in honor of Zeus, stood on a hill overlooking the city, and its altar looked like a huge throne sitting upon a hill. Animal sacrifices were offered there day and night as a reminder to onlookers that the temple was extremely significant to the community.

he which hath the sharp sword with two edges. It is Christ who has the sharp sword (see commentary on 1:16).

2:13 *I know thy works.* See commentary on 2:2.

I know . . . where thou dwellest. Jesus is omniscient (see commentary on 2:2). It must have given the Saints at Pergamos peace of mind and courage in the midst of the persecution to know that God had full knowledge of their lives, their works, and even their place of residence.

where Satan's seat is . . . where Satan dwelleth. This passage may refer specifically to the enormous altar dedicated to the god Zeus, which had the appearance of a throne and stood on a hill overlooking Pergamos. It may also refer generally to the pagan cults of Athena, Asclepius, Dionysus, and Zeus, in which the power of Satan was manifest through false religious systems that promoted the worship of the emperor as a god. Satan's throne stands in stark contrast to the exalted and eternal thrones of Christ and God (4:2–4; D&C 76:107–8).

thou holdest fast my name. Apparently Christians who were sentenced to prison or death could save themselves by cursing Christ and worshipping at the emperor's altar.[10] The Lord commends the Saints of Pergamos for confessing his name "before men" (Matt. 10:32–33).

Antipas was my faithful martyr. We know little about Antipas, other than that he was a martyr from Pergamos who died for the sake of Jesus and his gospel. See commentary on 6:9.

2:14 *I have a few things against thee.* Although Jesus commends the Saints of Pergamos for "hold[ing] fast" to his name (2:13), he calls them to repentance for believing the doctrines of Balaam and the Nicolaitans.

doctrine of Balaam. The doctrine of Balaam was to eat things sacrificed unto idols, to commit fornication (Num. 25:1–3), and to engage in priestcrafts. Balaam, the son of Beor, convinced many from Israel to commit fornication with Moabite women and to worship false gods (Num. 31:16); he was also involved in divining for hire with Balak, the king of Moab (Num. 22–24; Deut. 23:4; 2 Pet. 2:15–16; Jude 1:11). After meeting in council in Jerusalem, the early apostles had specifically enjoined the saints to "abstain from meats offered to idols" (Acts 15:6, 29).

Balac. This king of Moab (whose name is also spelled Balak) used money to encourage Balaam to curse the children of Israel (Num. 22–24; Josh. 24:9; Judg. 11:25).

eat things sacrificed unto idols. For religious and social reasons the Saints at Pergamos were encouraged by their fellow citizens to eat the meat sacrificed to the idols of the temples of Zeus, Augustus, and Rome. To do so, however, was to practice Balaam's doctrine (Num. 31:16).

commit fornication. This phrase refers to physical fornication, or sexual sin (9:21), as well as to spiritual fornication, or idolatry (14:8; 17:2, 4; 18:3, 9; 19:2).

2:15 *doctrine of the Nicolaitans.* See commentary on 2:6.

2:16 *I will come unto thee quickly.* See commentary on 2:5.

will fight against them with the sword of my mouth. The sword of God's mouth is the word of God (see commentary on 1:16). One way that God fights against the wicked "with the sword of [his] mouth" is through

---

[10] Krodel, *Revelation,* 116.

his judgments, which are decreed and sent by his word (see Lev. 26:25; Judg. 7:20; Isa. 34:5; Ezek. 14:21; D&C 101:10).

2:17 *He that hath an ear.* See commentary on 2:7.

To him that overcometh. See commentary on 2:7.

will I give to eat of the hidden manna. Manna is the food that Israel received from heaven for forty years while they wandered in the wilderness (Ex. 16:15, 35). The hidden manna refers to Jesus, who is the "true bread from heaven" (John 6:32). Jesus said: "I am [the] bread of life. Your fathers did eat manna in the wilderness, and are dead. This is the bread which cometh down from heaven, that a man may eat thereof, and not die. I am the living bread which came down from heaven: if any man eat of this bread, he shall live for ever" (John 6:48–51). Jesus is "hidden," or unseen and unknown by the wicked, but is revealed to him or her who overcomes.

The phrase "hidden manna" may also refer to eternal truths from and about Christ that are revealed only in the temple, "mysteries" given only to those who seek diligently for them (see Matt. 13:11–12; 1 Tim. 3:16; 1 Ne. 2:16; 10:19; Alma 12:9; D&C 76:5–7).

give him a white stone. The white stone is a urim and thummim for each individual who enters the celestial kingdom; written upon this white stone will be a new name. Doctrine and Covenants 130:8–11 explains: "The place where God resides is a great Urim and Thummim. This earth, in its sanctified and immortal state, will be made like unto crystal and will be a Urim and Thummim to the inhabitants who dwell thereon, whereby all things pertaining to an inferior kingdom, or all kingdoms of a lower order, will be manifest to those who dwell on it; and this earth will be Christ's. Then the white stone mentioned in Revelation 2:17, will become a Urim and Thummim to each individual who receives one, whereby things pertaining to a higher order of kingdoms, will be made known; and a white stone is given to each of those who come into the celestial kingdom, whereon is a new name written, which no man knoweth save he that receiveth it. The new name is the key word."

new name. In a different context, Abraham (Gen. 17:5), Sarah (Gen. 17:15), and Jacob (Gen. 32:28) were given new names by the Lord. Isaiah prophesied that Israel would "be called by a new name, which the mouth of the Lord shall name" (Isa. 62:2; 65:15). God revealed to John that "him that overcometh will I make a pillar in the temple of my God . . . : and I will write upon him the name of my God . . . : and I will write upon him my new name" (3:12).

The new name is written on the white stone that is "given to each of those who come into the celestial kingdom. . . . The new name is the key word." The new name, similar to the white robe of Revelation 3:5, 6:11, and 7:9, symbolizes a new existence, or a new life.

TO THE CHURCH IN THYATIRA: THE RIGHTEOUS WILL HAVE POWER OVER KINGDOMS (2:18–29)

Jesus Christ addresses the Church members in Thyatira, declaring that he knows their works (the word *works* is repeated three times), charity, service, faith, and patience. Notwithstanding their positive behavior, Jesus condemns some of the members for permitting the evil Jezebel to teach fornication and idolatry among them. Jezebel and her followers, if they fail to repent, will die a spiritual death and will be cast into hell. Church members who refuse to follow Jezebel's teachings are commanded to endure to the end. If such overcome the world, they are promised they will be given "power over many kingdoms," which they will rule with justice and equity. They are also promised the "morning star."

Revelation 2:18–29

> 18 And unto the [servant][11] of the church in Thyatira write; These things saith the Son of God, who hath his eyes like unto a flame of fire, and his feet are like fine brass;
> 19 I know thy works, and charity, and service, and faith, and thy patience, and thy works; and the last to be more than the first.
> 20 Notwithstanding I have a few things against thee, because thou sufferest that woman Jezebel, which calleth herself a prophetess, to teach and to seduce my servants to commit fornication, and to eat things sacrificed unto idols.
> 21 And I gave her space to repent of her fornication[s];[12] and she repented not.
> 22 Behold, I will cast her into [hell],[13] and them that commit adultery with her into great tribulation, except they repent of their deeds.
> 23 And I will kill her children with death; and all the churches shall know that I am he which searcheth the reins and hearts: and I will give unto every one of you according to your works.
> 24 But unto you I say, and unto the rest in Thyatira, as many as have not this doctrine, and which have not known the depths of Satan, as they speak; I will put upon you none other burden.

[11] JST 2:18 replaces *angel* with *servant*.
[12] JST 2:21 makes the word *fornication* plural.
[13] JST 2:22 replaces *bed* with *hell*.

25 But that which ye have already hold fast till I come.
26 And [to him who][14] overcometh, and keepeth my [commandments][15] unto the end, . . . [16] will I give power over [many kingdoms];[17]
27 And he shall rule them with [the word of God];[18] [and they shall be in his hands][19] as the vessels [of clay in the hands][20] of a potter; [and he shall govern them by faith, with equity and justice],[21] even as I received of my Father.
28 And I will give him the morning star.
29 He that hath an ear, let him hear what the Spirit saith unto the churches.

NOTES AND COMMENTARY

2:18 *[servant] of the church in Thyatira.* The servant is the ecclesiastical leader of the Saints in Thyatira, the fourth of seven churches identified in Revelation 2 and 3. Thyatira, a city located in Asia Minor, or modern-day Turkey, was a commercial town of traders and craftsmen who included tanners, potters, bakers, leatherworkers, metal workers, dyers, and wool workers. A temple named after Tyrimnos, or Apollo, the son of Zeus, was an important religious symbol for this community.

These things saith the Son of God. Jesus Christ is the author of the revelation.

who hath . . . eyes like unto a flame/feet like . . . brass. The language recalls John's description of the resurrected Jesus recorded in Revelation 1:14–15. There the Lord is described as having "eyes . . . as a flame of fire, and his feet like unto fine brass." This passage anticipates another description of Christ's appearance in 19:12, which states that "his eyes were as a flame of fire." Doctrine and Covenants 110:3 uses the same expression: "His eyes were as a flame of fire."

2:19 *I know thy works.* See commentary on 2:2.

I know thy . . . charity/service/faith/patience. Jesus commends the members of the Church in Thytira for their good works.

---

[14] JST 2:26 changes the phrase *he that* to *to him who.*
[15] JST 2:26 replaces *works* with *commandments.*
[16] JST 2:26 omits *to him.*
[17] JST 2:26 replaces the phrase *the nations* with *many kingdoms.*
[18] JST 2:27 omits *a rod of iron* and adds *the word of God.*
[19] JST 2:27 adds the phrase *and they shall be in his hands.*
[20] JST 2:27 adds the phrase *of clay in the hands.*
[21] JST 2:27 omits the phrase *shall they be broken to shivers* and adds the phrase *and he shall govern them by faith, with equity and justice.*

the last to be more than the first. The Jerusalem Bible reads, "I know how you are still making progress." The Saints' spiritual lives are improving and they are becoming better people, unlike the Saints of Ephesus, who have fallen (2:5).

2:20 *I have a few things against thee.* Even though the Lord commends the Saints for their fine works (2:19), he condemns them for permitting a woman called Jezebel to teach false doctrines.

Jezebel, which calleth herself a prophetess. This woman was not Jezebel, the wife of king Ahab, who helped lead Israel to idolatry (2 Kgs. 9:22; 1 Kgs. 16:31–33), although there are points in common between these two individuals. The Jezebel of the church at Thyatira was a false prophetess, who taught false doctrines, seduced some of the Church members to commit fornication, and encouraged them to eat food that was sacrificed to idols. Inasmuch as Jezebel refused to repent of her wickedness, God "cast her into hell" (JST 2:22).

to commit fornication. This passage may refer both to the sexual sin and to the spiritual sin of idolatry, which is spiritual fornication. Individuals and organizations in all ages act as Jezebel, leading those who will follow "into forbidden paths" where they are "lost" (1 Ne. 8:28; see also Rev. 2:14).

to eat things sacrificed unto idols. Thyatira was a city of craftsmen and merchants who belonged to guilds. These guilds periodically held religious banquets at which animals were sacrificed to their gods and then eaten. Jezebel may have taught that it was acceptable for Church members to participate in such occasions connected to idol worship and to partake of things sacrificed to idols. See commentary on 2:14.

2:21 *I gave her space to repent of her fornication[s].* The Lord's true prophets, possibly the apostle Paul or John himself, preached the true gospel and repentance to Jezebel. She had adequate warning to repent of her evil deeds.

2:22 *I will cast her into [hell].* Nephi uses similar language, declaring that "all those who preach false doctrines, and all those who commit whoredoms . . . shall be thrust down to hell" (2 Ne. 28:15); he calls hell "that awful hell, which . . . was prepared for the wicked" (1 Ne. 15:29).

them that commit adultery with her. All souls who commit adultery (or idolatry, which is spiritual adultery) will be cast down to hell, unless "they repent of their deeds."

2:23 *I will kill her children.* Jezebel and Ahab's children suffered horrible deaths (2 Kgs. 10:1, 7), and in a similar manner the children of Jezebel of Thyatira will be destroyed. Another interpretation is that those who follow Jezebel in her sins, the children of her iniquities, will suffer spiritual death.

I am he which searcheth the reins and hearts. This expression recalls a passage in Psalm 7:9: "for the righteous God trieth the hearts and reins." God knows every thought and intent of all humans and is therefore able to judge accordingly and to "give unto every one of you according to your works." The New International Version renders the very literal expression "reins and hearts" as the more understandable "hearts and minds."

2:24 *as many as have not this doctrine.* Church members of Thyatira who do not accept Jezebel's false doctrines and seductions will not have the burdens of sin and guilt placed upon them. Fornication and idolatry, two extremely grievous sins, may be described as the "depths of Satan."

2:25 *hold fast till I come.* "Hold fast" means to endure to the end and recalls for us the iron rod. Lehi saw individuals "pressing forward; and they came and caught hold of the end of the rod of iron; and they did press their way forward, continually holding fast to the rod of iron, until they came forth and fell down and partook of the fruit of the tree" (1 Ne. 8:30). Church members who hold fast, or endure to the end, will eventually reach the tree of life and partake of its fruit (2 Ne. 31:20; Rev. 22:2, 14). The iron rod is the word of God, and we are promised that "whoso would hearken unto the word of God, and would hold fast unto it, they would never perish" (1 Ne. 15:24; 1 Thes. 5:21).

2:26–27 *[to him who] overcometh.* See commentary on 2:7.

keepeth my [commandments] unto the end. This language corresponds with the common Book of Mormon expression "to endure to the end" (see, for example, 1 Ne. 13:37; 22:31; 2 Ne. 9:24).

will I give power over [many kingdoms]. Those who overcome receive a promise similar to that given to Jesus, as recorded in Psalm 2:6–9, a section that deals with the temple, kingship, and the doctrine of divine sonship. The expression "will I give power over many kingdoms" in Revelation recalls "I shall give thee the heathen for thine inheritance, and the uttermost parts of the earth for thy possession" (Ps. 2:8); the phrase "he shall rule them with the word of God" parallels "Thou shalt break them with a rod of iron" (Ps. 2:9); and the expression "they shall be in his hands as the vessels of clay in the hands" corresponds with "thou shalt dash them in pieces like a potter's vessel" (Ps. 2:9). Other parallels may also be noted. The implication is that we will receive as Jesus receives, being joint-heirs with him of the gifts and power and dominion of the Father (Rom. 8:17).

"Many kingdoms" refers to eternal kingdoms, not to temporal kingdoms. The Saints are invited to "come up unto the crown prepared for you, and be made rulers over many kingdoms" (D&C 78:15).

2:27 *he shall rule them with [the word of God].* Exalted Saints will rule "many kingdoms" with God's word. Perhaps this expression means that the Saints will rule by the truth and correct principles that come from God (see commentary on 12:3).

[they shall be in his hands] as the vessels [of clay in the hands]. He who rules over many kingdoms is likened to a potter; the kingdoms are similar to clay vessels. The potter has control and power over his creation made of clay.

[he shall govern them by faith, with equity and justice]. The one who overcomes will rule and govern with faith (which is God's power) and with righteousness, having perfect "equity and justice."

even as I received of my Father. He who overcomes will receive eternal rewards (such as having "power over many kingdoms," 2:26), just as Christ received rewards from his Father. Such will be "heirs of God, and joint-heirs with Christ" (Rom. 8:17).

2:28 *I will give him the morning star.* This expression may have at least two meanings. First, Jesus Christ is "the bright and morning star" (22:16). The promise of "the morning star" may be the promise of the Second Comforter, which is that "when any man obtains this [Second] Comforter, he will have the personage of Jesus Christ to attend him, or appear unto him from time to time, and even He will manifest the Father unto him, and they will take up their abode with him, and the visions of the heavens will be opened unto him, and the Lord will teach him face to face."[22] Second, God gives eternal life to those who overcome; they will become like Christ, who is the "bright and morning star."

2:29 *He that hath an ear.* See commentary on 2:7.

---

[22] *Teachings of the Prophet Joseph Smith,* 151.

REVELATION
3

TO THE CHURCH IN SARDIS: THE RIGHTEOUS WILL BE CLOTHED IN WHITE RAIMENT (3:1–6)

In Revelation 3:2–3, Jesus Christ directs five imperatives to the Saints in Sardis: "be watchful," "strengthen," "remember," "hold fast," and "repent." These five imperatives indicate the needs of the Church members in Sardis and were to assist them in their quest for righteousness. This passage also likens Jesus to a thief who will quickly come in judgment upon the wicked, who were not looking for his coming.

The next three verses contain marvelous promises directed to those who overcome the world, for such will be "clothed in white raiment," symbolizing eternal life because of personal purity and Christ's atoning sacrifice. Those who overcome will also have their names written in the book of life, meaning they will possess eternal life and will inhabit God's heavenly kingdom.

Revelation 3:1–6

> 1 And unto the [servant][1] of the church in Sardis write; These things saith he [who][2] hath the seven [stars, which are the seven servants of God];[3] I know thy works, that thou hast a name that thou livest, and art [not][4] dead.

---

[1] JST 3:1 replaces *angel* with *servant.*
[2] JST 3:1 changes the relative pronoun *that* to the relative pronoun *who.*
[3] JST 3:1 replaces *Spirits of God and the seven stars* with *the seven stars, which are the seven servants of God.*
[4] JST 3:1 adds *not.*

2 Be watchful [therefore],[5] and strengthen [those who][6] remain, [who][7] are
ready to die: for I have not found thy works perfect before God.
3 Remember therefore how thou hast received and heard, and hold fast,
and repent. If therefore thou shalt not watch, I will come on thee as a thief,
and thou shalt not know what hour I will come upon thee.
4 Thou hast a few names even in Sardis which have not defiled their garments; and they shall walk with me in white: for they are worthy.
5 He that overcometh, the same shall be clothed in white raiment; and I
will not blot out his name out of the book of life, but I will confess his
name before my Father, and before his angels.
6 He that hath an ear, let him hear what the Spirit saith unto the churches.

NOTES AND COMMENTARY

3:1 *[servant] of the church in Sardis.* The servant is the ecclesiastical
leader of the Saints in Sardis. Once the capital of the ancient kingdom of
Lydia, Sardis was a city thirty miles south of Thyatira, in Asia Minor, or
present-day Turkey. This commercial city was known for its wealth, which
it obtained in part through its trade in clothing.

he [who] hath the seven [stars]. This expression speaks of Christ, as
we see in 1:16: "He had in his right hand seven stars." The seven stars represent the seven servants of the seven churches (1:20).

I know thy works. See commentary on 2:2.

thou hast a name that thou livest, and art [not] dead. The Saints of
Sardis were not dead as to the things of the Spirit, although they still had
need of repentance (3:2–3).

3:2 *strengthen [those who] remain, [who] are ready to die.* The Saints
are instructed to strengthen those who are weak in the faith and close to
spiritual death.

I have not found thy works perfect before God. God stated in the previous verse, "I know thy works." Here he adds that these works are less than
perfect, suggesting they lack integrity, or wholeness.

3:3 *Remember . . . thou hast received and heard.* This phrase may indicate that the Saints were to remember that they have received the gospel
with all of its blessings; they have heard the word of God.

hold fast. See commentary on 2:25.

---

[5] JST 3:2 adds *therefore.*

[6] JST 3:2 replaces the phrase *the things which* with *those who.*

[7] JST 3:2 changes the relative pronoun *that* to the relative pronoun *who.*

repent. The Church members' works are not "perfect before God" (3:2), and therefore they are commanded to repent.

If therefore thou shalt not watch. The concluding verse of the parable of the ten virgins contains the command, "Watch therefore, for ye know neither the day nor the hour wherein the Son of man cometh" (Matt. 25:13).

I will come on thee as a thief. This expression is recorded twice in Revelation, here, and again in 16:15. Most scriptural texts state that it is not the Lord but "the day of the Lord" (1 Thes. 5:2, 4; 2 Pet. 3:10), "desolation" (D&C 45:19), or "the coming of the Lord" (D&C 106:4) that comes as a thief. The Lord himself will come in glory for all to see (19:11–16). A thief secures his goods by stealth, always quickly, unexpectedly, and usually under the cover of night; the second coming of Christ is likened unto such. Modern revelation makes it clear that Christ comes not as a thief to the "children of light" but to the "world" (D&C 106:4–5).

3:4 *Thou hast a few names . . . which have not defiled their garments.* The garments represent the individual who wears them. White garments signify a holy and undefiled person; defiled garments symbolize one who is evil and bears the stains of sin. In Sardis there were a "few names," or individuals, who were pure and undefiled, who had not spotted their garments with sin. *Garments* in this verse also has application to temples and temple covenants. See commentary on 6:11.

they shall walk with me in white. A few of the Saints will walk in white garments with Christ because "they are worthy"—they have been obedient to all the Lord required of them and have received of the blessings of the Atonement.

3:5 *He that overcometh.* See commentary on 2:7.

the same shall be clothed in white raiment. See commentary on 6:11. These are they who are transformed into new persons by Jesus' atoning sacrifice and who have no filthy spots created by the blood and sins of the world. Exalted persons are they who "have washed their robes, and made them white in the blood of the Lamb" (7:14); they who "have *put on* Christ" (Gal. 3:27; emphasis added). The white clothing, with the new name, signifies a new state of existence.

I will not blot out his name out of the book of life. The book that figures so prominently in the book of Revelation (13:8; 17:8; 20:12, 15; 21:27; 22:19) contains the names of those who will receive eternal life. It is the "record which is kept in heaven" (D&C 128:7), which contains the names of the righteous (Alma 5:58). The book belongs to the Lamb (21:27), who blots out the names of sinners from it (Ex. 32:32–33) but does not remove the names of those who overcome the world and are clothed in white raiment.

I will confess his name before my Father. Jesus taught, "Whosoever . . . shall confess me before men, him will I confess also before my Father which is in heaven" (Matt. 10:32).

before his angels. The angels are heavenly witnesses; they will witness Jesus' acknowledgment of the names of the righteous before the Father (Luke 12:8–9; 1 Tim. 5:21).

3:6 *He that hath an ear.* See commentary on 2:7.

unto the churches. The message to Sardis (and to all seven churches) is for the Saints of every era.

TO THE CHURCH IN PHILADELPHIA: THE RIGHTEOUS WILL DWELL IN THE HEAVENLY TEMPLE (3:7–13)

Jesus identifies himself to Church members in Philadelphia as the one who is holy, true, and possesses "the key of David" (3:7). He commends the Saints there for keeping his commandments and for refusing to deny his name; he offers them no criticism. Because the Saints have kept Christ's words, he will keep them "from the hour of temptation," and he promises to "come quickly," a promise that was also made to the Church members in Ephesus and Pergamos. He also commands them to "hold . . . fast," a commandment also made to Church members in Thyatira and Sardis. Verses 11 through 12 contain terms that recall the ancient temple, including "crown," "pillar in the temple," "and "new name"; these same terms pertain to the righteous, who will wear the crown of victory, become permanently connected to the heavenly temple, and receive a new name.

Most of these words of admonishment, commendation, and promise apply to us, who live in the closing years of the dispensation of the fulness of times.

Revelation 3:7–13

⋅7 And to the [servant]⁸ of the church in Philadelphia write; These things

---

⁸ JST 3:7 replaces *angel* with *servant.*

saith he that is holy, he that is true, he that hath the key of David, he that openeth, and no man shutteth; and shutteth, and no man openeth;

8 I know thy works: behold, I have set before thee an open door, and no man can shut it: for thou hast a little strength, and hast kept my word, and hast not denied my name.

9 Behold, I will make them of the synagogue of Satan, which say they are Jews, and are not, but do lie; behold, I will make them to come and worship before thy feet, and to know that I have loved thee.

10 Because thou hast kept the word of my patience, I also will keep thee from the hour of temptation, which shall come upon all the world, to try them that dwell upon the earth.

11 Behold, I come quickly; hold that fast which thou hast, that no man take thy crown.

12 Him that overcometh will I make a pillar in the temple of my God, and he shall go no more out: and I will write upon him the name of my God, and the name of the city of my God, which is new Jerusalem, which cometh down out of heaven from my God: and I will write upon him my new name.

13 He that hath an ear, let him hear what the Spirit saith unto the churches.

NOTES AND COMMENTARY

3:7 *[servant] of the church in Philadelphia.* The servant is the ecclesiastical leader of the Saints in Philadelphia, a city in Asia Minor thirty-five miles southeast of Sardis. Philadelphia was likely founded and named after Attalus II Philadelphos, a king of Pergamum. The city was well-known for its religious festivals and temples.

he that is holy, he that is true. These descriptive titles identify Jesus Christ as the speaker. He is both *holy,* meaning sanctified and godly, and *true,* meaning steadfast and just. Elsewhere Jesus is called "Holy One of God" (Mark 1:24), "Holy One of Israel," (2 Ne. 9:41), "Faithful and True" (19:11), "true God" (1 Jn. 5:20), and "true Messiah" (1 Ne. 10:14).

he that hath the key of David. Jesus Christ possesses the "key of David." Because David was the great king of Israel, to hold the key of David suggests holding the power of government. Christ, who "hath the key of David," is the rightful, eternal king of Israel (Isa. 44:6; Jer. 23:5; 1 Tim. 6: 14–15; 2 Ne. 10:14) and governor of the entire world (see Ps. 47:7; Alma 5:50; D&C 45:49). Elder Bruce R. McConkie explained: "In ancient Israel, David was a man of blood and battle whose word was law and whose very name was also a symbol of power and authority. Accordingly, when Isaiah sought to convey a realization of the supreme, directive control and power resident in our Lord, the Son of David, he spoke these words in the Lord's name: 'And the key of the house of David will I lay upon his shoulder; so he shall open, and none shall shut; and he shall shut, and none shall open.' (Isa. 22:22.) . . . Thus, the key of David is the absolute power resident in Christ whereby his will is expressed in all things both temporal and spiritual."[9]

he that openeth, and no man shutteth; and shutteth, and no man openeth. Similar language is also found in Isaiah 22:22 and is the same as the sealing power mentioned in Matthew 16:16–19 and Helaman 10:4–10. Jesus Christ, "the keeper of the gate" (2 Ne. 9:41), holds the keys to permit the righteous to enter the gates to the celestial kingdom as well as the keys to lock the wicked into an eternal prison (D&C 29:27–29; 76:44). Compare also John 10:7, 9, in which Christ is called the "door of the sheep."

3:8 *I know thy works.* See commentary on 2:2.

I have set before thee an open door. In the context of the previous verse, "open door" here refers to the opportunity to enter God's kingdom. For the early Christians, an open door represented having the opportunity to share the gospel (1 Cor. 16:9; 2 Cor. 2:12; Col. 4:3).

thou hast a little strength. The Lord commends the Saints for having spiritual strength, for being obedient ("hast kept my word"), and for refusing to deny his name. Yet they are not as strong as they might be, having but "a little strength."

3:9 *synagogue of Satan.* New Testament scholar Metzger comments: "Since John himself had been born a Jew, we must not take the expression 'those of the synagogue of Satan' (3:9) in an anti-Jewish or anti-Semitic sense. The synagogue at Philadelphia was criticized, not for being Jewish, but for being hostile to Christians."[10]

I will make them to come and worship before thy feet. Those who belong to the synagogue of Satan and who were hostile to faithful Christians will someday acknowledge the truth and know that God loves his Saints.

3:10 *thou hast kept the word of my patience, I also will keep thee.* The Jerusalem Bible clarifies this challenging wording with this reading: "Because you have kept my commandment to endure trials, I will keep you safe in the time of trial which is going to come for the whole world."

[9] McConkie, *Doctrinal New Testament Commentary,* 3:457–58.
[10] Metzger, *Breaking the Code,* 41.

3:11 *I come quickly.* See commentary on 2:5.

hold that fast which thou hast. See commentary on 2:25.

that no man take thy crown. Joseph Smith said of this verse: "If the Saints are not to reign, for what purpose are they crowned? In an exhortation of the Lord to a certain church in Asia, which was built up in the days of the Apostles, unto whom He communicated His word on that occasion by His servant John, He says [quotes Rev. 3:11]."[11]

3:12 *Him that overcometh.* See commentary on 2:7.

will I make a pillar in the temple of my God. Exalted Saints are compared to the pillars of a temple, which are stable, strong, and permanent fixtures of the temple precinct. In a similar manner the Saints will stand forever in the heavenly temple, never to be removed by evil forces. John explains that such individuals will "go no more out" of the temple. Compare Galatians 2:9, in which Peter, James, and John were "pillars" in the church.

I will write upon him the name of my God. The first of three names that Christ will give the righteous is the name of his God (14:1; D&C 133:18), meaning the Saints will become like and will belong to their Father in Heaven; thus, those who have God's name upon them are gods (D&C 132:20).[12]

name of the city of my God, which is new Jerusalem. The second of three names that Christ will give the righteous is "New Jerusalem," meaning they will become eternal citizens of God's celestial city.

I will write upon him my new name. The third of three names that Christ will give the righteous is his own new name. Because an individual's "new name" is kept private—"no man knoweth saving he that receiveth it" (2:17)—this suggests that those who receive Christ's new name will have become one with him. John explains that "his name shall be in their foreheads" (22:4; see commentary there).

3:13 *He that hath an ear.* See commentary on 2:7.

---

[11] *History of the Church,* 2:20.
[12] See also Orson Pratt, *Journal of Discourses,* 14:242–43.

TO THE CHURCH IN LAODICEA: THE RIGHTEOUS WILL SIT UPON THE THRONE OF JESUS (3:14–22)

In this letter to Church members in Laodicea, Jesus identifies himself with three expressions: "the Amen," "the faithful and true witness," and "the beginning of the creation of God" (3:14). He repeats what he has told the other six churches, saying, "I know thy works" (3:15) and then follows that with the well-known phrase "Thou art lukewarm, . . . I will spue thee out of my mouth" (3:16). Jesus describes the lukewarm Saints with five terms: "wretched, and miserable, and poor, and blind, and naked" (3:17), terms that apply to their spiritual state rather than their physical condition.

Christ counsels the Saints; he commands them to "be zealous" and to "repent" and invites them to open the door and receive great spiritual blessings, including the presence of the Lord. Those who overcome the world will receive a throne in Heavenly Father's kingdom.

Revelation 3:14–22

> 14 And unto the [servant][13] of the church of the Laodiceans write; These things saith the Amen, the faithful and true witness, the beginning of the creation of God;
> 15 I know thy works, that thou art neither cold nor hot: I would thou wert cold or hot.
> 16 So then because thou art lukewarm, and neither cold nor hot, I will spue thee out of my mouth.
> 17 Because thou sayest, I am rich, and increased with goods, and have need of nothing; and knowest not that thou art wretched, and miserable, and poor, and blind, and naked:
> 18 I counsel thee to buy of me gold tried in the fire, that thou mayest be rich; and white raiment, that thou mayest be clothed, and that the shame of thy nakedness do not appear; and anoint thine eyes with eye salve, that thou mayest see.
> 19 As many as I love, I rebuke and chasten: be zealous therefore, and repent.
> 20 Behold, I stand at the door, and knock: if any man hear my voice, and open the door, I will come in to him, and will sup with him, and he with me.
> 21 To him that overcometh will I grant to sit with me in my throne, even as I also overcame, and am set down with my Father in his throne.
> 22 He that hath an ear, let him hear what the Spirit saith unto the churches.

---

[13] JST 3:14 replaces *angel* with *servant.*

NOTES AND COMMENTARY

3:14 *[servant] of the church of the Laodiceans.* The servant is the ecclesiastical leader of the Saints in Laodicea, a city in Asia Minor, or present-day Turkey. Laodicea was founded by the Syrian king Antiochus II and named after his wife Laodice. It was settled at the junction of important trade highways and subsequently became an important center for commerce, banking, medicine, and industry. Its medical school produced a special ointment, or eye salve, that was exported throughout the land. Its industrial center produced linen and wool garments.

Amen, the faithful and true witness. These three titles of Christ attest to his divine character, for he is reliable, faithful, and true. "The word *amen* connotes the idea of that which has been unalterably confirmed (Num. 5:22), or that which is sure, trustworthy, and faithful."[14]

beginning of the creation of God. Christ is the "firstborn of every creature" (Col. 1:15). In his own words he testified, "I was in the beginning with the Father, and am the Firstborn" (D&C 93:21).

3:15 *I know thy works.* See commentary on 2:2.

thou art neither cold nor hot: I would thou wert cold or hot. With all of its importance as a city of commerce and trade, Laodicea lacked sufficient fresh water for its inhabitants and visitors, so water was piped to this community from springs located several miles away. By the time the water arrived in Laodicea, it was likely lukewarm, unpleasant to drink, and good only to be "spewed out of the mouth." Hence, the water at Laodicea lacked the cold freshness for weary travelers and the healing elements for the physically ill and afflicted found in hot water.

Lukewarm water is a metaphor for some members of the Church in Laodicea (and in any era) who lack gospel zeal (see the command in 3:19 to "be zealous") and complete faithfulness. These may be the same of whom it is written, "These are they who are not valiant in the testimony of Jesus; wherefore, they obtain not the crown over the kingdom of our God" (D&C 76:79).

3:16 *thou art lukewarm . . . I will spue thee out of my mouth.* This metaphor speaks of Church members who are not valiant in their faith; such will God reject, as if ejecting them out of his mouth like bad water. See commentary on 3:15.

---

[14] McConkie and Parry, *Guide to Scriptural Symbols,* 115.

3:17 *I am rich, and increased with goods.* This phrase may refer to the wealthy conditions of the Church members of Laodicea, a prosperous city known for its banking center and clothing factories. The people say, "I am rich," referring to their silver and gold, but the Lord, referring to their spiritual condition, corrects them, saying, "Thou art wretched, and miserable, and poor, and blind, and naked." The people are "naked," without sacred garments (3:4–5), blind to gospel truths, and poor as to spiritual things.

3:18 *I counsel thee.* The "Wonderful Counsellor" (Isa. 9:6) advises his Saints to seek eternal riches, such as "gold tried in the fire" and "white raiment."

to buy of me gold tried in the fire. Here the Saints are counseled to "buy of me gold," perhaps meaning they are to pay the price for eternal riches and exaltation through obedience and sacrifice. "Gold tried in the fire" symbolizes Saints who are precious and pure and who, after the resurrection, become incorruptible. The Saints become like gold when they pass through the "furnace of affliction" (Isa. 48:10; 1 Pet. 1:7). Zechariah wrote, "And I will bring the third part through the fire, and will refine them as silver is refined, and will try them as gold is tried: they shall call on my name, and I will hear them: I will say, It is my people: and they shall say, The Lord is my God" (Zech. 13:9).

that thou mayest be rich. He who is spiritually rich is he who "hath eternal life" (D&C 6:7).

white raiment. See commentary on 3:5; 6:11.

shame of thy nakedness. Shame and *nakedness* are often used synonymously in the scriptures (Isa. 47:3; 2 Ne. 9:14). Those who are not clothed in the white garment will be filled with shame.

anoint thine eyes with eye salve. The medical profession of Laodicea used Phrygian-powdered stone to create an eye salve that was used far and wide for healing. In this verse the Lord does not refer to the manmade eye salve, of course, but to a spiritual eye salve that permits individuals to see with their spiritual eyes (Matt. 6:22). Recall what the Lord said to Enoch: "Anoint thine eyes with clay, and wash them, and thou shalt see. And he did so"; and Enoch then saw things that "were not visible to the natural eye" (Moses 6:35–36; John 9:6).

3:19 *As many as I love, I rebuke and chasten.* God's actions have always been motivated out of his love for us, "for whom the Lord loveth he correcteth" (Prov. 3:12), and "for whom the Lord loveth he chasteneth, and

REVELATION 3:14-22 • [53]

scourgeth every son whom he receiveth" (Heb. 12:6). He chastens us in order to turn us to him (1 Cor. 11:32; Hel. 12:3; D&C 95:1; 105:6).

be zealous therefore, and repent. Zealous means to be fervently devoted to a purpose. This command is directed to Church members who are lukewarm in their faith and who lack zeal in the gospel (see commentary on 3:15–16).

3:20 *I stand at the door, and knock.* God makes the initial contact with us by coming to our door and knocking. What is the door? Perhaps the door is our heart, which is the key to who we are and what we desire. It is our hearts that Christ wants to change; it is our hearts that must be broken. How does Christ knock? He sends the Spirit, prophets, teachers, and provides us with the scriptures. If we hearken to the voice of the Spirit, he will bring us more fully to Christ—so much so that eventually he will bring us to the Second Comforter, and we will enjoy an intimacy as expressed in the words, "I will sup with him and he with me." In short, we must open the door and invite Christ into our hearts and our lives (D&C 88:63).

I will come in to him, and will sup with him, and he with me. This very personal and sacred promise refers to Christ, the Second Comforter, who promises to "attend" the righteous and pure individual and "appear unto him from time to time, and even He will manifest the Father unto him, and they will take up their abode with him."[15] The idea of supping with Christ suggests that not only will he visit them and quickly deliver a message but he will also spend time with them, sitting and breaking bread with them.

3:21 *To him that overcometh.* See commentary on 2:7.

will I grant to sit with me in my throne. God empowers those who overcome trial and temptation to become like him; the righteous become exalted beings, sitting as kings upon heavenly thrones. Enoch said to God, "Thou hast made me, and given unto me a right to thy throne, and not of myself, but through thine own grace" (Moses 7:59). Similarly, Jesus promised the Twelve Apostles "twelve thrones" (Matt. 19:28). Joseph Smith defined the expressions "heirs of God" and "joint heirs with Jesus Christ," saying the righteous are to "inherit the same power, the same glory and the same exaltation, until you arrive at the station of a God, and ascend the throne of eternal power, the same as those who have gone before."[16]

---

[15] *Teachings of the Prophet Joseph Smith,* 151.
[16] *Teachings of the Prophet Joseph Smith,* 347.

even as I also overcame. How do we overcome the world as Christ overcame it? Christ's instructions to his apostles have relevance to us: "Ye are they which have continued with me in my temptations. And I appoint unto you a kingdom, as my Father hath appointed unto me" (Luke 22:28–29). How did Jesus reach his exalted station? "Why; I do the things I saw my Father do when worlds came rolling into existence. My Father worked out his kingdom with fear and trembling, and I must do the same; and when I get my kingdom, I shall present it to my Father, so that he may obtain kingdom upon kingdom."[17]

and am set down with my Father in his throne. When Jesus "shall deliver up the kingdom, and present it unto the Father, spotless, saying: I have overcome and have trodden the wine-press alone, even the wine-press of the fierceness of the wrath of Almighty God," he shall "be crowned with the crown of his glory, to sit on the throne of his power to reign forever and ever" (D&C 76:107–8).

3:22 *He that hath an ear.* See commentary on 2:7.

---

[17] *Teachings of the Prophet Joseph Smith,* 347.

REVELATION
4

THE THRONE ROOM IN THE TEMPLE IN HEAVEN (4:1–11)

While receiving his vision of Jesus Christ, John envisions (1:10) the holy place of the temple in heaven (1:12). It is in the holy place that he receives the revelation of the seven churches. Afterward John sees a door that "was opened into heaven," and a heavenly voice invites him to "come up hither" to receive "things which must be hereafter." John ascends to the holy of holies, or the throne room of the temple, which is one and the same as the celestial kingdom. Again, John is "in the spirit," meaning that though his body is likely still on the Isle of Patmos, he is viewing things as they appear in heaven and then describing his vision by using symbolic terms.

While in the throne room, John is permitted to behold the eternal glory of the Father, who is sitting upon the throne. Twenty-four elders, seven servants of God, and four beasts are all glorifying God. John uses symbolic language to describe the scene. God the Father is the center of activity as he sits upon his throne, surrounded by living creatures and exalted Saints. The vision does not describe God himself but provides a glorious description of the things around him, such as brilliant colors and glorious lights. God, like his heavenly messengers, is "glorious beyond description" (JS–H 1:32). Jesus Christ, who was introduced to John in Revelation 1:10–16 (see commentary there) stands in the Father's presence in the throne room of the temple of heaven (5:1).

John uses symbolism to describe the four beasts and their activities. The four beasts occupy a hierarchically significant position in the throne room, for they are located very near the throne. They rest neither day nor night but continually worship God by saying, "Holy, holy, holy, Lord God Almighty, which was, and is, and is to come." Each of the four beasts possesses eyes before, behind, and within, signifying light and knowledge. Each possesses six wings, "a representation of power, to move, to act" (D&C 77:4). The beasts worship God, and, as sentinels, protect God's holiness from the unauthorized trespass of unworthy, or unclean, things and individuals.

John also sees twenty-four elders worshipping the Father, submitting themselves before him by casting their crowns before the throne while exclaiming, "Thou art worthy, O Lord, to receive glory and honour and power: for thou hast created all things, and for thy pleasure they are and were created" (4:11).

There are several brief songs or hymnlike passages in Revelation, two of which are in this section (4:8, 11).

Revelation 4:1–11

1 After this I looked, and, behold, a door was opened [into][1] heaven: and the first voice which I heard was as it were of a trumpet talking with me; which said, Come up hither, and I will [show][2] thee things which must be hereafter.
2 And immediately I was in the spirit: and, behold, a throne was set in heaven, and one sat on the throne.
3 And he that sat was to look upon like a jasper and a sardine stone: and there was a rainbow round about the throne, in sight like unto an emerald.
4 And [in the midst of][3] the throne were four and twenty seats: and upon the seats I saw four and twenty elders sitting, clothed in white raiment; and they had on their heads crowns of gold.
5 And out of the throne proceeded lightnings and thunderings and voices: and there were seven lamps of fire burning before the throne, which are the seven [servants][4] of God.
6 And before the throne there was a sea of glass like unto crystal: and in the midst of the throne [were the four and twenty elders];[5] and round about the throne, were four beasts full of eyes before and behind.
7 And the first beast was like a lion, and the second beast like a calf, and the third beast had a face as a man, and the fourth beast was like a flying eagle.
8 And the four beasts had each of them six wings about him; and they were full of eyes within: and they rest not day and night, saying, Holy, holy, holy, Lord God Almighty, which was, and is, and is to come.
9 And when those beasts give glory and honour and thanks to him that [sits][6] on the throne, who liveth for ever and ever,

---

[1] JST 4:1 replaces *in* with *into.*
[2] JST 4:1 replaces the archaic *shew* with *show.*
[3] JST 4:4 replaces the phrase *round about* with *in the midst of."*
[4] JST 4:5 replaces *Spirits* with *servants.*
[5] JST 4:6 add the phrase *were the four and twenty elders.*
[6] JST 4:9 changes past tense *sat* to present tense *sits.*

10 The four and twenty elders fall down before him that [sits]⁷ on the throne, and worship him that liveth for ever and ever, and cast their crowns before the throne, saying,

11 Thou art worthy, O Lord, to receive glory and honour and power: for thou hast created all things, and for thy pleasure they are and were created.

NOTES AND COMMENTARY

4:1 *After this I looked.* This formula indicates that a new vision has begun (7:1, 9; 15:5; 18:1; 19:1; Dan. 7:6–7).

door was opened [into] heaven. The door opens to the throne room of heaven, which may be parallel to the holy of holies in the earthly temple. John, while "in the spirit" (4:2), is about to view the most holy place, the place where God sits and rules (Ezek. 1:1).

first voice. The voice is that of Jesus Christ, first identified in 1:10–11.

trumpet. The voice of the Lord is as distinctive and clear as a trumpet (1:10). Trumpets are associated with the temple elsewhere in scripture; in Exodus (19:16, 19; 20:18), for example, the trumpet is associated with Mount Sinai, which served as a temple to Moses and the Israelites.⁸

Come up hither. John is commanded to "come up" to the throne room, suggesting an ascension from the holy place to the most holy, as in the structure of the earthly temple. Similarly, Moses was commanded to "come up unto the Lord" (Ex. 19:24) to the mountain sanctuary.

I will [show] thee things which must be hereafter. Jesus himself shows John several scenes of heaven (4:2–5:14) and then events that would yet occur upon the earth.⁹

4:2 *I was in the spirit.* See commentary on 1:10.

throne was set in heaven. The Jerusalem Bible renders this passage: "a throne was standing in heaven." Heavenly Father possesses and sits upon the throne (3:21; 4:2–3, 9–10; 5:7, 13; 6:16; 7:10; 12:5; 19:4; 22:1, 3), which is at the center of activity in the temple in heaven. Twenty-four exalted elders and their thrones (4:4); many angels (5:11; 7:11, 15); four living creatures (4:6); a "great multitude, which no man could number" (7:9); seven lamps of fire, signifying the seven servants (4:5); and the 144,000 high priests, in whose "mouth was found no guile" and who sing a

---

⁷ JST 4:10 replaces *sat* with *sits.*

⁸ On Mount Sinai as a temple, see Parry, "Sinai as Sanctuary and Mountain of God," in *By Study and Also by Faith,* ed. Lundquist and Ricks, 1:482–500.

⁹ *Teachings of the Prophet Joseph Smith,* 289.

new song (14:1–3, 5), are all "in the midst of," "round about," or "before" the throne of God. Jesus Christ is also "in the midst of the throne" (5:6; 7:17), which he shares with his Father (3:21; 22:1, 3). The golden altar (8:3) and the sea of glass (4:6) are before the throne as well. The throne is the source of lightnings, thunderings, and voices (4:5).

one sat on the throne. John refers to God the Father approximately twelve times as the "one seated on the throne," which represents God's kingship and dominion. In Abraham, Facsimile 2:3, God is pictured sitting upon his throne, "clothed with power and authority."

4:3 *he that sat was to look upon like a jasper and a sardine stone.* God the Father cannot adequately be described with mere words from the human language, so John portrays him "as the brilliance of light reflected from precious stones."[10] Ezekiel describes the Lord in a similar manner (Ezek. 1:26–28; see also Ps. 104:2; 1 Tim. 6:16). Jasper and sardine stone are the last and the first of the twelve stones of the high priest's breastplate of judgment (Ex. 28:15–20), perhaps indicative of Christ as the "first and the last." They are also among the stones of the Garden of Eden (Ezek. 28:13) and the foundation stones of the heavenly city (21:19–20)—the first and last Zion communities on the earth.

there was a rainbow round about the throne, in sight like unto an emerald. John uses symbols, the rainbow and the emerald, to denote the great brilliance, glory, brightness, and light that surround God and his throne. Ezekiel used similar language (Ezek. 1:26–28). The emerald is the fourth of the twelve precious stones of the high priest's breastplate (Ex. 28:17–21), representing the tribe of Judah, or Christ, who was of Judah. The emerald is also one of the foundation stones of the heavenly city (21:19–20). It seems significant that emerald, a brilliant color of green, would be used to symbolize the very wellspring of life.

4:4 *[in the midst of] the throne were four and twenty seats.* The twenty-four seats, or thrones, are for the twenty-four elders.

four and twenty elders. Doctrine and Covenants 77:5 reads: "Q. What are we to understand by the four and twenty elders, spoken of by John? A. We are to understand that these elders whom John saw, were elders who had been faithful in the work of the ministry and were dead; who belonged to the seven churches, and were then in the paradise of God."

---

[10] Mounce, *Book of Revelation,* 120.

Each of the elders is "clothed in white raiment," and each possesses his own crown, throne, harp, and golden bowl of incense (4:4; 5:8). The harp and incense are used during their worship of God. The incense represents "the prayers of saints" (5:8), and the harps are perhaps played by the elders themselves as they sing the new song (5:9–10). The elders praise the Lord: "Thou art worthy, O Lord, to receive glory and honour and power" (4:11), "We give thee thanks, O Lord God Almighty, which art, and wast, and art to come" (11:17), and "Amen; Alleluia" (19:4). The new song they sing to the Lamb includes the words "thou wast slain, and hast redeemed us to God by thy blood" (5:9). Four times John witnesses the elders "fall down" to worship God, who "sat on the throne" (4:10; 5:14; 11:16; 19:4), and once he observes them as they "fell down before the Lamb" (5:8). Each of the elders is a king and priest, who will "reign on the earth" (5:10; see 1:6). One of the elders speaks to John two times, helping him to understand his vision (5:5; 7:13).

The number twenty-four may represent the 24,000 Levite priests who were assigned to temple work (1 Chr. 23:3–4; 24:1–19); or the number may represent the twelve patriarchs of the house of Israel and the Twelve Apostles, both of which are identified in Revelation (5:6; 21:12, 14). Although these elders were actual men who lived upon the earth during mortality, here they represent all of the redeemed who will receive thrones and crowns in heaven.

clothed in white raiment. The white raiment represents the light, glory, and purity of the exalted soul who wears it. Also, among the Greeks and Romans, white symbolized victory—those "clothed in white raiment" are those who have overcome the world (3:5).

on their heads crowns of gold. The crowns symbolize kingship, dominion, authority, and power. The twenty-four elders are God's kings and priests, who will "reign on the earth" (5:10) after the judgment and resurrection.

4:5 *out of the throne proceeded lightnings and thunderings and voices.* The lightnings and thunderings portray the power and brilliance associated with God's presence (Ex. 19:16–18; Ps. 77:18) and demonstrate that he has supreme control over the elements of heaven and earth. The voices "out of the throne" may be those of God and the Lamb (see Ps. 18:12–15; Job 37:2–5). The terms *lightnings, thunderings,* and *voices* are found four times in Revelation and are often accompanied with descriptions of earthquakes and hail (4:5; 8:5; 11:19; 16:18). Some translations of this verse omit *voices* and instead associate the sounds with the thunder (NEB, JB, NIV).

seven lamps of fire burning before the throne. The seven lamps are the seven servants of God, previously identified in Revelation ("which are before his throne," 1:4). The burning fires speak of their exalted nature; like God, they dwell in "everlasting burnings in immortal glory."[11]

4:6 *before the throne there was a sea of glass like unto crystal.* The throne overlooks a sea of glass, which "is the earth, in its sanctified, immortal, and eternal state" (D&C 77:1). Joseph Smith explained that "when the earth was sanctified and became like a sea of glass, it would be one great urim and thummim, and the Saints could look in it and see as they are seen."[12] Doctrine and Covenants 130:6–9 adds further insight: "The angels do not reside on a planet like this earth; but they reside in the presence of God, on a globe like a sea of glass and fire, where all things for their glory are manifest, past, present, and future, and are continually before the Lord. The place where God resides is a great Urim and Thummim. This earth, in its sanctified and immortal state, will be made like unto crystal and will be a Urim and Thummim to the inhabitants who dwell thereon, whereby all things pertaining to an inferior kingdom, or all kingdoms of a lower order, will be manifest to those who dwell on it." Regarding this great Urim and Thummim, Brigham Young explained, "When you wish to know anything, you can look in this earth, and see all the eternities of God."[13]

The sea of glass is also described as "a sea of glass mingled with fire" (15:2), where exalted beings stand with their harps and sing unto God: "Great and marvellous are thy works, Lord God Almighty; just and true are thy ways, thou King of saints. Who shall not fear thee, O Lord, and glorify thy name? for thou only art holy: for all nations shall come and worship before thee; for thy judgments are made manifest" (15:3–4).

round about the throne, were four beasts. Some biblical commentators place one of the four beasts at each of the four sides of the throne, where they serve as guardians of the throne. This role is similar to that played by the biblical cherubim (see, for example, Gen. 3:24; Ex. 25:18–22).[14]

---

[11] *Teachings of the Prophet Joseph Smith,* 347.
[12] *History of the Church,* 5:279.
[13] Brigham Young, *Journal of Discourses,* 8:200.
[14] Davis, *Heavenly Court, 4–5,* 126–31.

In this verse and elsewhere, John speaks of two types of beasts in Revelation: he envisions actual living creatures (Greek *zoon*) that exist in heaven (4:6–9; 5:6–14; 6:1–7; 7:11; 14:3; 15:7; 19:4), and he speaks of other beasts (Greek *therion*), referring both to earthly beasts as well as to symbolic or fantastic beasts (6:8; 11:7; 13:1–18; 14:9, 11; 15:2; 16:2, 10, 13; 17:1–18; 19:19–20; 20:4, 10). The word *beast* used in this passage could more accurately be translated "living creature." In fact, the choice of the King James Version translators to use the word *beast* is particularly unfortunate, since these creatures are living, dynamic beings filled with intelligence and glory.

Joseph Smith suggested that the four beasts "lived on another planet than ours."[15] The four beasts in this passage in Revelation are actual beasts that exist in heaven. "John saw the actual beast in heaven, showing to John that beasts did actually exist there. . . .

"John saw curious looking beasts in heaven; he saw every creature that was in heaven,—all the beasts, fowls and fish in heaven,—actually there, giving glory to God. . . .

"I suppose John saw beings there of a thousand forms, that had been saved from ten thousand times ten thousand earths like this,—strange beasts of which we have no conception: all might be seen in heaven. The grand secret was to show John what there was in heaven. John learned that God glorified Himself by saving all that His hands had made, whether beasts, fowls, fishes or men; and He will glorify Himself with them.

"Says one, 'I cannot believe in the salvation of beasts.' Any man who would tell you that this could not be, would tell you that the revelations are not true. John heard the words of the beasts giving glory to God, and understood them. God who made the beasts could understand every language spoken by them. The four beasts were four of the most noble animals that had filled the measure of their creation, and had been saved from other worlds, because they were perfect: they were like angels in their sphere. We are not told where they came from, and I do not know; but they were seen and heard by John praising and glorifying God."[16]

John informs us that the four beasts are capable of worshipping God (4:8; 5:8–10): they invite John to "come and see" the events pertaining to

---

[15] Ehat and Cook, *Words of Joseph Smith,* 171.
[16] *History of the Church,* 5:343–44.

the first four seals (6:1–7), and one of the beasts delivers the "seven golden vials full of the wrath of God" to the seven angels (15:7). The four beasts may be akin to those spoken of in Isaiah 6:2–3 and Ezekiel 1:5–14.

A modern revelation adds additional light concerning the four beasts: "They are figurative expressions, used by the Revelator, John, in describing heaven, the paradise of God, the happiness of man, and of beasts, and of creeping things, and of the fowls of the air; that which is spiritual being in the likeness of that which is temporal; and that which is temporal in the likeness of that which is spiritual; the spirit of man in the likeness of his person, as also the spirit of the beast, and every other creature which God has created" (D&C 77:2).

Doctrine and Covenants 77:3 reads: "Q. Are the four beasts limited to individual beasts, or do they represent classes or orders? A. They are limited to four individual beasts, which were shown to John, to represent the glory of the classes of beings in their destined order or sphere of creation, in the enjoyment of their eternal felicity."

full of eyes before and behind. The eyes of the beasts "are a representation of light and knowledge, that is, they are full of knowledge" (D&C 77:4).

4:7 *like a lion/calf/man/flying eagle.* Ezekiel describes a similar vision (Ezek. 1:10). One commentator suggests: "The living creatures are symbolic of creation and the divine immanence. They are what is noblest (lion), strongest (ox), wisest (man), and swiftest (eagle)."[17] Another suggests that the four faces of the beasts correspond to the banners of the "four chief tribes of Israel," as does still another: "The description of the camp of Israel in Numbers locates the four chief tribes in the following positions: Judah on the east (2:3), Reuben on the south (2:10), Ephraim on the west (2:18), and Dan on the north (2:25). The insignias for these tribes were: Judah, lion; Reuben, man; Ephraim, ox; and Dan, eagle."[18]

4:8 *four beasts had each of them six wings.* The beasts' wings "are a representation of power, to move, to act, etc." (D&C 77:4).

they were full of eyes within. The beasts' eyes "are a representation of light and knowledge, that is, they are full of knowledge" (D&C 77:4). In the previous verse, John explained that the beasts had eyes both "before

---

[17] Ford, *Revelation,* 75.
[18] Davis, *Heavenly Court,* 133.

and behind." Now we learn that they have eyes inside as well. Other translations make this clear: "eyes all over, inside and out" (NEB), and "eyes all
the way around as well as inside" (JB). The symbolism of "light and
knowledge" is reinforced by the presence of eyes inside as well as outside,
back as well as front.

they rest not day and night. It is the unceasing disposition of the four
living creatures to worship God at all times.

Holy, holy, holy, Lord God Almighty. Similarly, when Isaiah envisions
the heavenly temple, he witnesses the seraphim honoring God with the
threefold repetition "Holy, holy, holy, is the Lord of hosts" (Isa. 6:3). The
threefold repetition emphasizes the superlative degree: God is the holiest of
all creatures in the universe. *Holy* speaks concerning the wonderful sepa-
rateness of God, his distinctiveness in perfection and power.

which was, and is, and is to come. See commentary on 1:4.

4:9 *beasts give glory and honour and thanks.* The living creatures worship alongside the twenty-four elders by rendering "both vocal (4:8–9; 5:9–
10) and instrumental adoration (5:8)" of God.[19]

to him that [sits] on the throne. See commentary on 4:2.

who liveth for ever and ever. Elsewhere in scripture, it is written,
"Behold, I am the Lord God Almighty, and Endless is my name, for I am
without beginning of days or end of years; and is not this endless?" (Moses
1:3; 7:35).

4:10 *four and twenty elders fall down before him that [sits] on the
throne.* The elders prostrate themselves before God in an act of worship
and as a posture of exceptional reverence.

cast their crowns before the throne. The crowns are gifts from God to
the twenty-four elders (2:10; 4:4). By casting their crowns before the
throne, perhaps as a gesture or symbol of humility, the elders submit themselves to God and give homage and honor to him who is the King of kings.

4:11 *Thou art worthy, O Lord, to receive glory and honour and power.*
The elders' worship is different from that of the creatures, for the elders
address God directly and speak of his creative work rather than his
attributes. *Worthy* here means fully qualified.

thou hast created all things. Both God and his son Jesus Christ are
called Creator. Joseph Smith wrote: "Everlasting covenant was made

---

[19] Davis, *Heavenly Court,* 130.

between three personages before the organization of this earth, and relates to their dispensation of things to men on the earth; these personages, according to Abraham's record, are called God the first, the Creator; God the second, the Redeemer; and God the third, the witness or Testator."[20]

The Lord explained to Moses: "And by the word of my power, have I created them, which is mine Only Begotten Son, who is full of grace and truth. And worlds without number have I created; and I also created them for mine own purpose; and by the Son I created them, which is mine Only Begotten" (Moses 1:32–33).

for thy pleasure they are and were created. Many versions read "by thy will" in place of "for thy pleasure"; the Jerusalem Bible, for example, reads, "It was only by your will that everything was made and exists." A revelation in the Doctrine and Covenants explains why the earth was created: "For after it hath filled the measure of its creation, it shall be crowned with glory, even with the presence of God the Father; that bodies who are of the celestial kingdom may possess it forever and ever; for, for this intent was it made and created, and for this intent are they sanctified" (D&C 88:19–20).

---

[20] *Teachings of the Prophet Joseph Smith,* 190.

REVELATION
5

The Lamb Takes the Sealed Book (5:1–14)

Revelation 5 continues the record of John's vision of the heavenly temple, in which he sees God the Father sitting upon his throne surrounded by living creatures and twenty-four elders, all of whom are worshipping him. In chapter 5 John sees God the Father sitting on his throne with a sealed book in his right hand. John sees and hears an angel ask, "Who is worthy to open the book?" When no one can be found who is able or worthy to open the book or even "to look thereon," John weeps "much." One of the twenty-four elders, introduced in the previous chapter, comforts John and commands him to "weep not," because there is one worthy to open the book, and he is called "the Lion of the tribe of Juda." John looks, perhaps expecting to see this worthy Lion, but instead he sees a Lamb with the marks of a slaughtered creature but who now stands victorious over death. The Lamb steps forward and takes the book from the right hand of the Father.

This chapter presents a "new song" that is sung to honor and glorify God and Christ. The first stanza is sung by the twenty-four elders, who focus upon two signal topics: first, Christ suffered death and brought redemption by his blood; and second, Christ has made worthy individuals to be kings and priests, who will eventually reign upon the earth. The second stanza is sung by the elders, the beasts, and by numerous angels with a "loud voice," perhaps because of their great number. They focus on the worthiness of the slain Lamb and his great power, strength, and glory. The third stanza, sung by creatures who belong to heaven, earth, and the sea, pertains to the exalted Lamb, who sits upon the throne, having blessing, glory, and power. At the conclusion of the new song the four beasts say "amen" and the twenty-four elders fall down and worship the Lord. The new song repeats the following terms two times, perhaps for emphasis: *God, Lamb, worthy, slain* [Lamb], *power, honor, glory, blessing,* and *ever* (that is, "for ever and ever").

Revelation 5:1–14

1 And I saw in the right hand of him that [sits]¹ on the throne a book written within and on the backside, sealed with seven seals.

2 And I saw a strong angel [and heard him]² proclaiming with a loud voice, Who is worthy to open the book, and to loose the seals thereof?

3 And no man in heaven, nor in earth, neither under the earth, was able to open the book, neither to look thereon.

4 And I wept much, because no man was found worthy to open and to read the book, neither to look thereon.

5 And one of the elders saith unto me, Weep not: behold, the Lion of the tribe of Juda, the Root of David, hath prevailed to open the book, and to loose the seven seals thereof.

6 And I beheld, and, lo, in the midst of the throne and of the four beasts, and in the midst of the elders, stood a Lamb as it had been slain, having [twelve]³ horns and [twelve]⁴ eyes, which are the [twelve servants]⁵ of God sent forth into all the earth.

7 And he came and took the book out of the right hand of him that sat upon the throne.

8 And when he had taken the book, the four beasts and four and twenty elders fell down before the Lamb, having every one of them harps, and golden vials full of odours, which are the prayers of saints.

9 And they sung a new song, saying, Thou art worthy to take the book, and to open the seals thereof: for thou wast slain, and hast redeemed us to God by thy blood out of every kindred, and tongue, and people, and nation;

10 And hast made us unto our God kings and priests: and we shall reign on the earth.

11 And I beheld, and I heard the voice of many angels round about the throne and the beasts and the elders: and the number of them was ten thousand times ten thousand, and thousands of thousands;

12 Saying with a loud voice, Worthy is the Lamb that was slain to receive power, and riches, and wisdom, and strength, and honour, and glory, and blessing.

13 And every creature which is in heaven, and on the earth, and under the earth, and such as are in the sea, and all that are in them, heard I saying, Blessing, and honour, and glory, and power, be unto him that sitteth upon the throne, and unto the Lamb for ever and ever.

14 And the four beasts said, Amen. And the four and twenty elders fell down and worshipped him that liveth for ever and ever.

---

¹ JST 5:1 replaces *sat* with *sits.*

² JST 5:2 adds *and heard him.*

³ JST 5:6 changes *seven* to *twelve.*

⁴ JST 5:6 changes *seven* to *twelve.*

⁵ JST 5:6 changes the phrase *seven spirits* to *twelve servants.*

NOTES AND COMMENTARY

5:1 *I saw in the right hand.* The book with seven seals is in Heavenly Father's right hand, which is the hand "associated with righteousness (Ps. 48:10; Isa. 41:10), power (Ex. 15:6, 12; Ps. 89:13), and covenant making (Isa. 62:8). With his right hand, the Lord executes justice (3 Ne. 29:4, 9), dispenses the law (Deut. 33:2), and saves his people (Ps. 17:7; 20:6); with his right hand he created the heavens and the earth (Isa. 48:13)."[6]

him that [sits] on the throne. God the Father. See commentary on 4:2.

book. This book "contains the revealed will, mysteries, and the works of God; the hidden things of his economy concerning this earth during the seven thousand years of its continuance, or its temporal existence" (D&C 77:6). Orson F. Whitney explained: "The book which John saw represented the real history of the world—what the eye of God has seen, what the recording angel has written; and the seven thousand years, corresponding to the seven seals of the Apocalyptic volume, are as seven great days during which Mother Earth will fulfill her mortal mission, laboring six days and resting upon the seventh, her period of sanctification. These seven days do not include the period of our planet's creation and preparation as a dwelling place for man. They are limited to Earth's 'temporal existence,' that is, to Time, considered as distinct from Eternity."[7]

written within and on the backside. The technical term for this book is an *opistographi,* which is a scroll that has writing on both sides. Ezekiel's scroll is similarly described: "I looked, . . . and [the scroll] was written within and without: and there was written therein lamentations, and mourning, and woe" (Ezek. 2:9–10). The book in God's right hand overflows with his "revealed will, mysteries, and . . . works" (D&C 77:6).

sealed with seven seals. Each of the seven seals corresponds with one of the seven millennia of the earth's temporal existence. The Lord revealed that "the first seal contains the things of the first thousand years, and the second also of the second thousand years, and so on until the seventh" (D&C 77:7).

A seal is an impression of a signet (a finger ring or similar object with an engraved design) in wax that is designed to fasten and seal a scroll or document. Gottfried Fitzer, a biblical scholar, explains the significance of

---

[6] McConkie and Parry, *Guide to Scriptural Symbols,* 93.
[7] Whitney, *Saturday Night Thoughts,* 11.

the seal and how it was used in the ancient Near East. First, kings possessed seals that were unique and not easily duplicated, lest someone attempt to counterfeit the seal and imitate the authority of the king. God's seal was unique, and no one in heaven or on earth, save Christ himself, was permitted to open the seals (5:2–3). Second, "the seal served as a legal protection and guarantee in many ways, especially in relation to property. All objects suitable for sealing could be marked as the property of the owner in this way."[8] God owned the book and the seals that sealed it. No other individual, save the Lamb of God, was empowered to open it. Third, the seal proved the identity of its owner. The seal of God, with which the book was sealed, indicated to onlookers and observers the identity of the true King. Fourth, "the holder of the seal is the holder of power and has his place in a duly constituted order. Might and right come together in the seal."[9] Christ, by virtue of his worthiness to open the seals, held great power in the cosmos. That is indicated in the statement that Christ "hath prevailed to open the book." Fifth, "the seal was also meant to protect a document against inappropriate or premature disclosure."[10] God's sealed book was closed until he revealed its contents through Christ, who opened the seals one at a time (6:1, 3, 5, 7, 9; 8:1), according to the foreordained time schedule of God. And finally, "the seal makes a document legally valid."[11] God's sealed book was opened in a legal and official manner: the King, who sat on his throne in the heavenly temple, delivered the sealed book in his right hand to his chief administrator, and hosts of beings stood as witnesses.

5:2 *I saw a strong angel . . . proclaiming with a loud voice.* The identity of the "strong angel" is not revealed. It may be Michael, Gabriel, Raphael, or any other mighty angel. John later witnesses "a mighty angel" performing sacred work (10:1; 18:1). The angel proclaims with a loud voice so that all the millions in heaven who are witnessing these events will hear him. The expression "loud voice" is used twelve times in Revelation (5:12; 6:10; 7:2, 10; 8:13; 10:3; 12:10; 14:7, 9, 15; 19:17).

Who is worthy to open the book? The strong angel asks the hosts of heaven this question. We learn in Revelation 5:3 and 5 that Jesus Christ is the only one in heaven or on earth who is worthy to open the book. Why?

----

[8] *Theological Dictionary of the New Testament,* 7:940, s.v. "seals, sealing."

[9] *Theological Dictionary of the New Testament,* 7:942, s.v. "seals, sealing."

[10] *Theological Dictionary of the New Testament,* 7:945, s.v. "seals, sealing."

[11] *Theological Dictionary of the New Testament,* 7:945, s.v. "seals, sealing."

Perhaps because Jesus Christ is the only one qualified to bring about the eternal and infinite atonement for the inhabitants of this world, the history of which is contained in the book to be opened.

5:3 *no man in heaven, nor in earth, neither under the earth.* No individual (angels, or exalted Saints) in heaven, no flesh (mortals) upon the earth, and no disembodied spirit (either righteous or evil) under the earth was permitted to "open the book" or even to "look thereon." See also Philippians 2:10.

5:4 *I wept much.* John sorrows that no one can open the book.

5:5 *one of the elders saith unto me.* One of the twenty-four elders interprets for John here and again in 7:13.

Weep not. John is told to "weep not" because there is an individual who is able to open the book.

Lion of the tribe of Juda, the Root of David, hath prevailed to open the book. In 5:6 Christ is called "Lamb," but here he is called "Lion," a creature hostile and adverse to the Lamb. Christ as the Lamb portrays one who is submissive, as a sacrificial victim who is "brought as a lamb to the slaughter" (Isa. 53:7), or one who condescended to descend below all things. Christ as the Lion depicts one who has power over all creatures and is a majestic, fearless king (as a lion is "king of the beasts") who possesses great strength. In this context the title is especially appropriate, because just as a lion prevails over other creatures, so Christ "prevailed to open the book" with seven seals (or, according to RSV, Christ "has conquered, so that he can open the scroll and its seven seals").

Jesus is a member "of the tribe of Juda," whose emblem is the lion (Gen. 49:9). Paul stated that Jesus "sprang out of Juda" (Heb. 7:14), and Christ himself declared, "I am the root and the offspring of David" (22:16). Christ as the "Root" provides spiritual water, nourishment, and life to his people (Isa. 11:1, 10; 53:2; John 15:1–7).

5:6 *in the midst of the throne . . . stood a Lamb as it had been slain.* The elder instructs John to "weep not" and to "behold the Lion," but unexpectedly John sees a Lamb that possesses the marks of one who was slain. He sees Christ who, though slain for the sins of the world, now stands in great majesty as a lion stands as the king of all creatures. Christ stands now in the inner circle of the multitudes in heaven. He is standing near his Father's throne, which is surrounded by the four beasts and the twenty-four elders.

Christ is called Lamb twenty-seven times in Revelation. Elsewhere the prophets write of the Lamb: "Behold the Lamb of God, which taketh away the sin of the world" (John 1:29); "Christ our passover is sacrificed for us" (1 Cor. 5:7); and "ye know that ye were not redeemed with corruptible things, as silver and gold . . . but with the precious blood of Christ, as of a lamb without blemish and without spot" (1 Pet. 1:18–19).

The expression "as it had been slain" indicates that the Lamb, although risen from the dead and possessing eternal life, in this vision to John carried the marks of his sacrifice in his hands, feet, and side. The Book of Mormon testifies that the Nephite Saints at the temple in Bountiful "went forth, and thrust their hands into his side, and did feel the prints of the nails in his hands and in his feet; and this they did do, going forth one by one until they had all gone forth, and did see with their eyes and did feel with their hands, and did know of a surety and did bear record, that it was he, of whom it was written by the prophets, that should come" (3 Ne. 11:15; see also John 20:25, 27).

having [twelve] horns and [twelve] eyes, which are the [twelve servants] of God. The Lamb's twelve horns and twelve eyes are figurative, representing the Twelve Apostles, who are empowered by the Lamb to administer his gospel throughout the earth. The horns represent power (1 Sam. 2:10; Jer. 48:25; Ps. 75:10); the "eyes" may refer to the powers of seership held by apostles.

sent forth into all the earth. The expression "sent forth" defines the meaning of the word *apostle,* which means "one sent forth."[12]

5:7 *he came and took the book.* God remains seated on the throne as Jesus Christ comes and takes the book from his right hand. For more about "right hand," see commentary on 5:1.

5:8 *when he had taken the book.* The moment that Christ takes the book from God, the beasts and elders, with their harps and golden bowls, fall down to worship Christ.

four beasts and four and twenty elders fell down before the Lamb. Previously the beasts and elders had fallen down to worship God the Father (4:10); now they prostrate themselves before Jesus Christ. Three more times they will fall down before the Father (5:14; 11:16; 19:4).

---

[12] The LDS Bible Dictionary states that *apostle* means "one sent forth" (612, s.v. "apostle").

having every one of them harps. Biblical scholars Bratcher and Hatton explain: "This seems to say that every one of the four living creatures and the twenty-four elders had a harp and golden bowls filled with incense, although some would restrict it to the twenty-four elders."[13] Worship in heaven evidently includes music from harps. In this verse there are twenty-eight harps; in Revelation 14:1-3 it appears that each of the 144,000 high priests has a harp; and in Revelation 15:2 all exalted Saints possess "harps of God."

golden vials full of odours. A better translation is "golden bowls full of incense."[14] These bowls of incense recall those used during the ancient Israelite temple service by priestly officiants (1 Kgs. 7:50).

John informs us that the incense represents "the prayers of the saints" (see also Ps. 141:2). As the priestly ministrants offered incense upon the altar in the earthly temple twice daily, the Saints prayed in the courtyard of the temple (Luke 1:10); the twenty-four elders present the prayers, represented by incense, to God. Later in Revelation we read: "And another angel came and stood at the altar, having a golden censer; and there was given unto him much incense, that he should offer it with the prayers of all saints upon the golden altar which was before the throne. And the smoke of the incense, which came with the prayers of the saints, ascended up before God out of the angel's hand" (8:3-4). An apocryphal source adds, "I am Raphael, one of the seven holy angels, who present the prayers of the saints, and who go in and out before the glory of the Holy One" (Tobit 12:15; see also 3 Baruch 11).

5:9 *they sung a new song.* The words of this "new song," sung by the twenty-four elders and the four beasts, are addressed to Jesus (note the second-person pronouns *thou* and *thy*). The song emphasizes Christ's atoning sacrifice ("thou wast slain," "by thy blood") and the resultant benefits for humankind ("hast redeemed us," "hast made us . . . kings and priests"). Compare also Doctrine and Covenants 88:98-102, which contains the words to another "new song."

Thou art worthy to take the book. The verse explains why Jesus is worthy to take the book from God's right hand: he wrought the eternal and

---

[13] Bratcher and Hatton, *Handbook on the Revelation of John,* 102.
[14] See, for example, NIV.

infinite atonement, a fact expressed as "thou wast slain, and hast redeemed us to God by thy blood."

for thou wast slain, and hast redeemed us to God by thy blood. These words are the foundation of the song, because Christ's sacrifice made him worthy to take the book and will allow the Saints to become kings and priests and reign on the earth. Mormon taught that the redeemed will "dwell in the presence of God in his kingdom, to sing ceaseless praises with the choirs above, unto the Father, and unto the Son, and unto the Holy Ghost" (Morm. 7:7).

every kindred, and tongue, and people, and nation. John uses this phraseology in Revelation seven times to represent a great host of people from all lands and nations as well as every language and extended family. Five times the phrase refers to peoples upon the earth (10:11; 11:9; 13:7; 14:6; 17:15), and twice it refers to redeemed Saints who dwell in heaven (5:9; 7:9). It is clear that the exalted souls will include individuals from all lands, peoples, and languages. Truly, as Nephi taught, "there is one God and one Shepherd over all the earth" (1 Ne. 13:41).

5:10 *made us unto our God kings and priests.* Through his atonement Jesus Christ "made us . . . kings and priests"; individuals cannot become kings and priests on their own (see commentary on 1:6) but become such in God's temples. That God's kings and priests are from "every kindred, and tongue, and people, and nation" suggests that the gospel will be preached to all peoples throughout the world and those who accept the gospel will worship in the temples of the Lord that are now being established throughout the earth.

we shall reign on the earth. Our earth will become a celestial kingdom, and exalted Saints who have become kings and queens unto God will reign there. A modern revelation states: "The poor and the meek of the earth shall inherit it. Therefore, it must needs be sanctified from all unrighteousness, that it may be prepared for the celestial glory; for after it hath filled the measure of its creation, it shall be crowned with glory, even with the presence of God the Father" (D&C 88:17–19).

5:11 *I beheld, and I heard.* John sees and hears the angels, beasts, and elders praise the Lamb.

ten thousand times ten thousand, and thousands of thousands. One hundred million (ten thousand times ten thousand equals one hundred million), and "thousands of thousands" of angels near God's throne revere the

Lamb. The number may be taken literally, or it may signify a great, indefinite number. In any case, John witnesses a great number of angels praising the Lamb.

5:12 *Saying with a loud voice.* The unified sound of more than one hundred million beings produces a "loud voice."

Worthy is the Lamb that was slain. The phrase recalls 5:9, which explains why the Lamb was worthy to open the book.

to receive power/riches/wisdom/strength/honour/glory/blessing. "The angels repeat three of the elders' terms of praise: glory, honor, and power, and add wealth, wisdom, might, and blessing (5:13). The seven terms symbolize the fullness of the praise."[15]

5:13 *every creature which is in heaven/on the earth/under the earth/in the sea.* After witnessing the sacred adulation of more than one hundred million angels, John listens to all creatures of the earth and sea praise the Lamb. They repeat four of the seven terms of praise voiced by the angels: *blessing, honor, glory,* and *power.* The section anticipates this modern revelation, which has similar themes.

"Let the mountains shout for joy, and all ye valleys cry aloud; and all ye seas and dry lands tell the wonders of your Eternal King! And ye rivers, and brooks, and rills, flow down with gladness. Let the woods and all the trees of the field praise the Lord; and ye solid rocks weep for joy! And let the sun, moon, and the morning stars sing together, and let all the sons of God shout for joy! And let the eternal creations declare his name forever and ever!" (D&C 128:23).

Joseph Smith said: "Revelation 5:13 proves that John saw beasts in heaven and heard them speak praise to God. [I] do not know what language they speak."[16]

unto him that sitteth upon the throne, and unto the Lamb. The sacred praise of every creature is directed to God the Father, who sits upon his throne, and to Jesus Christ.

5:14 *four beasts said, Amen.* After the elders sing a new song (5:9–10), the angels praise the Lamb (5:12), and every creature glorifies God and the Lamb. The four beasts then close these threefold praises by saying "Amen" (see commentary on 3:14).

---

[15] Metzger, *Breaking the Code,* 54.
[16] Ehat and Cook, *Words of Joseph Smith,* 190.

four and twenty elders fell down and worshipped him that liveth for ever and ever. This is the third of five occasions in which the elders fall down and worship Deity (4:10; 5:8; 11:16; 19:4).

REVELATION
6

THE OPENING OF FOUR SEALS: TYPES OF THINGS TO COME (6:1–8)

John describes the Lamb's opening of the first four seals, which contain brief information about the first four thousand years of the earth's "temporal existence" (D&C 77:6). Comparatively little attention is given in Revelation to these and the fifth seal, for only eleven verses are dedicated to them. One commentator points out that John's entire revelation "from beginning to end takes 317 verses, and yet John spends only eleven verses (or about 3.5 percent) on the first five thousand years of history."[1]

At the opening of each seal, one of the four beasts invites John to "come and see." John responds with "and I saw," "and I beheld," "and I looked," followed by a brief description of what he sees: four horses and their riders. Each horse is a different color (white, red, black, and pale), and each is interpreted symbolically. Three of the four horsemen possess objects: the first has a bow and a crown, the second a sword, and the third a pair of balances. The fourth horseman does not possess an object, but he is named "Death" (the first three horsemen are not named). Each of the four horses, horsemen, and the objects or name attached to them tells us something about the thousand years that each represents.

Beyond what is mentioned in Revelation 6:1–8, we know very little about the four horsemen, who travel in silence, and their horses. We do not know their origin or their direction of travel. Do they come from heaven or

---

[1] Lund, "Seeing the Book of Revelation," 51.

hell?[2] Are they destroying angels from God executing his divine plan to destroy the wicked, or are they evil men from hell who are asserting their agency to kill and cause wars and famines upon the earth? Are the four horsemen related to the four destroying angels described in Revelation 7? Do they correspond in some manner with the four horses of Zechariah 1:8–11; 6:2–3? Do the four horsemen and their horses pertain only to the first four thousand years, or are they also types of things to come?

Joseph Smith taught, "John saw beasts that had to do with things on the earth, but not in past ages. The beasts which John saw had to devour the inhabitants of the earth in days to come [quotes Revelation 6:1–4]."[3] This statement suggests that the activities of the four horses and horsemen, representing the first four thousand years, also typify wars, famines, and tribulations yet to come upon the earth.

The number four has symbolic importance in Revelation, where we read about the four living creatures (4:6, 8; 5:6, 8, 14), the four horses, and the four horsemen who correspond with the first four seals (announced by the four beasts; 6:1–8), the "four angels standing on the four corners of the earth, holding the four winds of the earth" (7:1), and the "four quarters of the earth" (20:8).

The first seals are linked together into a unified group of four (four seals, four horses, four horsemen, four statements from four beasts), while the final three seals belong to a second group. This pattern of one group of four and one group of three parallels that pattern set forth for the seven trumpets (Rev. 8–9) and the seven vials (Rev. 16).

According to one scholar, the number four "has its origin in the orientation to four sides which, as before, behind and to right and left, are suggested by man's physical constitution. The four corners of heaven or the world embrace the whole of man's horizon."[4] The following table sets forth the structure of Revelation 6:1–8.

<hr/>

[2] The phrase *and there went out* (4:1) is used often of angels who go out of the temple in heaven, suggesting that the four horsemen also went out from heaven (14:15, 17). In 15:6, the "seven angels came out of the temple, having the seven plagues."
[3] *Teachings of the Prophet Joseph Smith,* 290.
[4] *Theological Dictionary of the New Testament,* 8:128, s.v. "four"; see also Bullinger, *Number in Scripture,* 123–34.

Table 2

Four Horses	White (6:1–2)	Red (6:3–4)	Black (6:5–6)	Pale (6:7–8)
Lamb opens four seals	Lamb opened one of the seals . . .	when he had opened the second seal,	when he had opened the third seal,	when he had opened the fourth seal,
Four beasts speak	noise of thunder, saying,	I heard the second beast say,	I heard the third beast say,	I heard the voice of the fourth beast say,
Words of the four beasts	Come and see.	Come and see. . . .	Come and see.	Come and see.
John beholds	And I saw,		And I beheld,	And I looked,
Objects or description of the four horsemen	he that sat on him had a bow; and a crown was given unto him: . . .	there was given unto him a great sword.	he that sat on him had a pair of balances in his hand. . . .	his name that sat on him was Death,. . . . .
Significance of the four horsemen	he went forth conquering, and to conquer.	. . . power was given to him that sat thereon to take peace from the earth, and that they should kill one another: . . .	A measure of wheat for a penny, and three measures of barley for a penny; and see thou hurt not the oil and the wine.	Hell followed with him. And power was given unto them over the fourth part of the earth, to kill with sword, and with hunger, and with death, and with the beasts of the earth.

Revelation 6:1–8

1 And I saw when the Lamb opened one of the seals, [one of the four

beasts],[5] and I heard, as it were, the noise of thunder, saying, Come and see.

2 And I saw, and behold a white horse: and he that sat on him had a bow; and a crown was given unto him: and he went forth conquering, and to conquer.

3 And when he had opened the second seal, I heard the second beast say, Come and see.

4 And there went out another horse that was red: and power was given to him that sat thereon to take peace from the earth, and that they should kill one another: and there was given unto him a great sword.

5 And when he had opened the third seal, I heard the third beast say, Come and see. And I beheld, and lo a black horse; and he that sat on him had a pair of balances in his hand.

6 And I heard a voice in the midst of the four beasts say, A measure of wheat for a penny, and three measures of barley for a penny; and see thou hurt not the oil and the wine.

7 And when he had opened the fourth seal, I heard the voice of the fourth beast say, Come and see.

8 And I looked, and behold a pale horse: and his name that sat on him was Death, and Hell followed with him. And power was given unto them over the fourth part of the earth, to kill with sword, and with hunger, and with death, and with the beasts of the earth.

NOTES AND COMMENTARY

6:1 *I saw . . . and I heard.* As John witnesses the opening of the first seal, he hears something resembling the noise of thunder.

Lamb opened one of the seals. The Lamb, who now has the sealed book in his own hand, opens the first seal, which "contains the revealed will, mysteries, and the works of God" (D&C 77:6) for the first one thousand years of the earth's temporal existence. The time frame here, according to one estimate, is approximately 4000 to 3000 B.C. Elder Orson F. Whitney wrote, "According to received chronology—admittedly imperfect, yet approximately correct—four thousand years, or four of the seven great days given to this planet as the period of its 'temporal existence,' had passed before Christ was crucified; while nearly two thousand years have gone by since."[6]

By virtue of his supreme, divine, and infinite sacrifice, Jesus Christ is worthy to open the seals (see commentary on 5:9). Only he can open the view of the earth's temporal existence that is the history of humankind upon the earth.

---

[5] JST 6:1 moves the phrase *one of the four beasts* from one place in the verse to another.
[6] Whitney, *Saturday Night Thoughts,* 12; see also McConkie, *Doctrinal New Testament Commentary,* 3:476; "Book of Revelation Overview," 50–53.

noise of thunder. This sound probably denotes the powerful voice of the beast. Heavenly voices, including that of the Father (John 12:29), are often likened to thunder (10:3; 14:2; 19:6).

[one of the four beasts] . . . saying, Come and see. The beast guides John; this may be the first beast, which "was like a lion" (4:7). For "beast," see commentary on 4:6.

6:2 *white horse . . . he that sat on him had a bow.* Elder Bruce R. McConkie identifies the rider of the "white horse" as Enoch, who was "a general over the armies of the saints."[7] Moses 7:13–16 supports this idea, explaining that Enoch "led the people of God, and their enemies came to battle against them; . . . and all nations feared greatly, so powerful was the word of Enoch, and so great was the power of the language which God had given him. There also came up a land out of the depth of the sea, and so great was the fear of the enemies of the people of God, that they fled and stood afar off and went upon the land which came up out of the depth of the sea. And the giants of the land, also, stood afar off; and there went forth a curse upon all people that fought against God; and from that time forth there were wars and bloodshed among them; but the Lord came and dwelt with his people, and they dwelt in righteousness."

went forth conquering, and to conquer. The white horse and crown speak symbolically of victory, and the bow represents war. Conceivably the white horse and its rider can symbolize any of the righteous men of this time period who fought and prevailed against evil, including Adam or his descendants.

6:3 *when he had opened the second seal.* John sees Christ open the second seal, which "contains the revealed will, mysteries, and the works of God" (D&C 77:6), for the second thousand years of the earth's temporal existence. The time frame here, according to one estimate, is approximately 3000 to 2000 B.C.[8]

I heard the second beast say, Come and see. The beast, which may be the second beast identified earlier that was "like a calf" (4:7), guides the Revelator. For "beast," see commentary on 4:6.

6:4 *there went out another horse that was red.* The time represented by the second seal was an era of war and bloodshed. The color red signifies

---

[7] McConkie, *Doctrinal New Testament Commentary,* 3:477.
[8] Whitney, *Saturday Night Thoughts,* 12; McConkie, *Doctrinal New Testament Commentary,* 3:478.

bloodshed; the horse, according to prophetic symbolism, represents a means of transport in war (Job 39:19–24). The rider of the horse carries a large, or "great sword," a symbol of war (3 Ne. 2:19; D&C 45:33) and a weapon designed expressly to take human lives. In addition, the rider is empowered to "take peace from the earth, and that they should kill one another" (6:4). John does not identify the rider; it is possible that the rider symbolizes all wicked and bloodthirsty men who murder and make war.

Moses identifies this era as a time when "the wickedness of man was great in the earth, and that every imagination of the thoughts of his heart was only evil continually. . . . The earth also was corrupt before God, and the earth was filled with violence. And God looked upon the earth, and, behold, it was corrupt; for all flesh had corrupted his way upon the earth. And God said unto Noah, The end of all flesh is come before me; for the earth is filled with violence through them; and, behold, I will destroy them with the earth. Make thee an ark" (Gen. 6:5, 11–14). So great was the violence and wickedness during the period of this seal that God destroyed all flesh, except the eight souls who were aboard the ark.

to take peace from the earth. A similar phrase is used in a modern revelation: "The day speedily cometh; the hour is not yet, but is nigh at hand, when *peace shall be taken from the earth,* and the devil shall have power over his own dominion" (D&C 1:35; emphasis added).

6:5 *when he had opened the third seal.* John witnesses Christ open the third seal, which "contains the revealed will, mysteries, and the works of God" (D&C 77:6), for the third thousand years of the earth's temporal existence. The time frame here, according to one estimate, is approximately 2000 to 1000 B.C.[9]

I heard the third beast say, Come and see. The beast, which may be the third beast identified earlier who "had a face as a man" (4:7), guides John. For "beast," see commentary on 4:6.

black horse. The time represented by the third seal was an era of great famine. John sees a black horse, black being the color of extreme hunger and famine (Lam. 4:8–9). In the hand of the rider he sees a pair of balances, which are used to measure the food during the famine, a practice known from earlier times (Lev. 26:26). For instance, on one occasion the Lord

[9] Whitney, *Saturday Night Thoughts,* 12; McConkie, *Doctrinal New Testament Commentary,* 3:479.

prophesied through Ezekiel that he would cause a famine by "break[ing] the staff of bread in Jerusalem"; the Jerusalemites, he explained, would "eat bread by weight, and with care; and they shall drink water by measure" (Ezek. 4:16).

During this thousand-year time span, Abraham records, "a famine prevailed throughout all the land of Chaldea, and my father was sorely tormented because of the famine. . . . Now the Lord God caused the famine to wax sore in the land of Ur, insomuch that Haran, my brother, died" (Abr. 1:30; 2:1). As Abraham and Sarai traveled through the land, he stopped and "built an altar in the land of Jershon, and made an offering unto the Lord, and prayed that the famine might be turned away from my father's house, that they might not perish. . . . And I, Abraham, concluded to go down into Egypt, to sojourn there, for the famine became very grievous" (Abr. 2:17, 21).

We recall that Joseph, the great-grandson of Abraham, interpreted Pharaoh's dream of a famine that would last seven years and would "consume the land" (Gen. 41:30). The famine existed in Egypt as well as other lands. Genesis 41 relates: "And the famine was over all the face of the earth . . . and the famine waxed sore in the land of Egypt. And all countries came into Egypt to Joseph for to buy corn; because that the famine was so sore in all lands" (Gen. 41:56–57). Jacob, Joseph's father, also experienced the famine while dwelling in Canaan, and he sent ten of his sons to Egypt to buy corn (Gen. 42:1–5).

6:6 *I heard a voice in the midst of the four beasts.* Again, one of the "beasts" interprets for John.

measure of wheat for a penny/three measures of barley for a penny. A measure (approximately one quart) represents the daily food ration of one adult, and a penny (Matt. 20:2) was one day's pay. Barley, the food of the destitute, cost a third as much as wheat. The measurement of small quantities of food speaks of a time of famine.

hurt not the oil and the wine. "The warning against hurting the oil and wine sets limits to the destruction about to be carried out by the horseman. Since the roots of the olive and vine go deeper [than the roots of barley and wheat], they would not be affected by a limited drought that would all but destroy the grain."[10]

---

[10] Mounce, *Book of Revelation,* 144.

6:7 *when he had opened the fourth seal.* John sees Christ open the fourth seal, which "contains the revealed will, mysteries, and the works of God" (D&C 77:6) for the fourth thousand years of the earth's temporal existence. The time frame here, according to one estimate, is approximately 1000 B.C. to A.D 1.[11]

I heard the voice of the fourth beast say, Come and see. The beast, perhaps the fourth beast identified earlier that "was like a flying eagle" (4:7), guides John. For "beast," see commentary on 4:6.

6:8 *pale horse.* The color described here reminds us of a corpse and of death. The rider's name is Death, and one named Hell follows after him to receive the dead. We are not told how Hell travels, whether by horse or on foot. John informs us that Death will kill one-fourth of earth's inhabitants by sword, famine, plague, and wild beasts. Ezekiel calls these four ways to die (sword, famine, plague, and wild beasts) the "four sore judgments" (Ezek. 14:21) that God sends upon the wicked.

Certainly the millennium of the fourth seal was an era of numerous wars. In the biblical world alone we are aware of wars between the Northern Kingdom of Israel and the Southern Kingdom of Judah; there were also wars among other Near Eastern groups, including the Assyrians, Persians, Babylonians, Syrians, and Egyptians.

Hell followed with him. The horseman named Death and his companion Hell (signifying spirit prison) are given power over a quarter of the people of earth. The verse in Revelation recalls a prophecy of Isaiah: "Hell hath enlarged herself, and opened her mouth without measure: and their glory, and their multitude, and their pomp, and he that rejoiceth, shall descend into it" (Isa. 5:14).

power was given unto them over the fourth part of the earth. During the time period of the fourth seal Death (followed by Hell) destroys one quarter of the earth's inhabitants.

to kill with sword/hunger/death/beasts. See "pale horse," above.

---

[11] Whitney, *Saturday Night Thoughts,* 12; McConkie, *Doctrinal New Testament Commentary,* 3:481.

THE OPENING OF THE FIFTH SEAL:
THE MARTYRS' CRIES (6:9–11)

At the opening of the fifth seal, John sees individuals who were slain because of their testimonies of Christ. After listening to their prayers offered unto God "with a loud voice," he then witnesses that each of the martyrs is given the white robes of salvation.

Revelation 6:9–11

9 And when he had opened the fifth seal, I saw under the altar the souls of them that were slain for the word of God, and for the testimony which they held:
10 And they cried with a loud voice, saying, How long, O Lord, holy and true, dost thou not judge and avenge our blood on them that dwell on the earth?
11 And white robes were given unto every one of them; and it was said unto them, that they should rest yet for a little season, until their fellowservants also and their brethren, that should be killed as they were, should be fulfilled.

NOTES AND COMMENTARY

6:9 *when he had opened the fifth seal.* The Lamb opens the fifth seal, which "contains the revealed will, mysteries, and the works of God" (D&C 77:6), for the fifth thousand years of the earth's temporal existence. The time frame here, according to one estimate, is approximately A.D. 1 to 1000.[12]

under the altar the souls of them that were slain for the word of God, and for the testimony. The Revelator sees those who have suffered or would suffer martyrdom for the sake of Christ and his gospel, such as Antipas of Pergamos (2:13). Such martyrs and their spilled blood are likened to sacrificial animals, whose blood was poured out at the foot of the altar by the priests (Lev. 4:7). John may have seen the martyrs Joseph Smith and Hyrum Smith under the altar. John Taylor wrote that the "innocent blood" of Joseph and Hyrum, "with the innocent blood of all the martyrs under the altar that John saw, will cry unto the Lord of Hosts till he avenges that blood on the earth" (D&C 135:7).

---

[12] Whitney, *Saturday Night Thoughts,* 12; McConkie, *Doctrinal New Testament Commentary,* 3:482.

The martyrs were slain for two reasons: for preaching the word of God and for their testimonies of Christ. John was exiled to the Isle of Patmos for identical reasons (1:9).

6:10 *they cried with a loud voice.* The prayer of the martyrs is loud because of their great number and their anguish (5:12).

how long . . . dost thou not judge and avenge our blood. From the martyrdom of Abel, whose "blood crieth unto [God] from the ground" (Gen. 4:10; Luke 11:50–51), to the deaths of Joseph and Hyrum Smith, whose "innocent blood" spilled "on the floor of Carthage jail" (D&C 135:7), martyrs for Jesus Christ cry out to God, "How long, O Lord, holy and true, dost thou not judge and avenge our blood on them that dwell on the earth?" Similarly, the psalmist prayed, "Lord, how long shall the wicked, how long shall the wicked triumph?" (Ps. 94:3), and Habakkuk cried, "O Lord, how long shall I cry, and thou wilt not hear!" (Hab. 1:2). But Jesus assures us, "Shall not God avenge his own elect, which cry day and night unto him, though he bear long with men?" (JST Luke 18:7). The martyrs will not stop petitioning the Lord "till he avenges that blood on the earth" (D&C 135:7).

When will God "judge and avenge" the innocent blood of the martyrs? That judgment and avenging may begin when he sends the judgments of the seven trumpets and seven bowls, as set forth in Revelation.

6:11 *white robes were given unto every one of them.* A white robe is the dress of the glorified Christ (3 Ne. 11:8; see also "robe of righteousness," 2 Ne. 4:33), heavenly messengers (1 Ne. 8:5; 14:19; JS-H 1:32), and exalted Saints (3:4–5; 7:9; 2 Ne. 9:14; D&C 109:76). Here the martyrs are given white robes, signifying that they have made the Atonement effective in their lives and have "washed their robes, and made them white in the blood of the Lamb" (7:14). Jesus taught how one should wash his robes: "And no unclean thing can enter into his kingdom; therefore nothing entereth into his rest save it be those who have washed their garments in my blood, because of their faith, and the repentance of all their sins, and their faithfulness unto the end" (3 Ne. 27:19; 1 Ne. 12:10).

Garments and robes are images often used to symbolize the inner state of the persons wearing them (Morm. 9:35; Ether 13:10). For example, the wearing of white robes represents an individual becoming an immortal, celestial person with a celestial body. Hence, the white robes identified in this passage refer to the celestial bodies of glory and light possessed by the martyrs.

rest yet for a little season. The martyrs are instructed to wait until after the martyrdom of other Saints. The Prophet Joseph Smith, his brother Hyrum, and the two prophets of Revelation 11 may be included in this group of individuals who would "be killed as they were." The martyrs were to rest until the allotted number of those who were to join them in martyrdom was complete (see RSV, NEB, JB, NIV, and GNB).

THE OPENING OF THE SIXTH SEAL: WARNING VOICES (6:12–17)

This section sets forth seven signs of the times that will occur after the opening of the sixth seal but before the second coming of the Lord. The seven signs are the earthquake, the darkened sun, the blood-red moon, falling stars, the heavens opening as a scroll, the movement of mountains and islands, and fear coming upon humanity. Many passages of scripture parallel this section.

These signs of the times warn the earth's inhabitants that the end of the earth is near. They are designed, in part, to encourage the wicked to repent of their sins. In fact, many will misinterpret these signs, believing that the time of the Second Coming has actually arrived. They will say, "The great day of his wrath is come, and who shall be able to stand?" (6:17). But the scriptures inform us that Jesus will not make his great appearance until sometime after the opening of the seventh seal (D&C 77:12–13).

These signs are imminent. On 27 December 1832, the Lord revealed, "Not many days hence and the earth shall tremble and reel to and fro as a drunken man; and the sun shall hide his face, and shall refuse to give light; and the moon shall be bathed in blood; and the stars shall become exceedingly angry, and shall cast themselves down as a fig that falleth from off a fig-tree" (D&C 88:87).

Revelation 6:12–17

> 12 And I beheld when he had opened the sixth seal, and, lo, there was a great earthquake; and the sun became black as sackcloth of hair, and the moon became as blood;
> 13 And the stars of heaven fell unto the earth, even as a fig tree casteth her untimely figs, when she is shaken of a mighty wind.

14 And the heaven[s opened][13] as a scroll [is opened][14] when it is rolled
together; and every mountain and island [was][15] moved out of [its place].[16]
15 And the kings of the earth, and the great men, and the rich men, and the
chief captains, and the mighty men, and every bondman, and every free
man, hid themselves in the dens and in the rocks of the mountains;
16 And said to the mountains and rocks, Fall on us, and hide us from the
face of him that sitteth on the throne, and from the wrath of the Lamb.
17 For the great day of his wrath is come; and who shall be able to stand?

NOTES AND COMMENTARY

6:12 *he . . . opened the sixth seal.* Christ opens the sixth seal, which
"contains the revealed will, mysteries, and the works of God" (D&C 77:6),
for the sixth thousand years of the earth's temporal existence. The time
frame here, according to one estimate, is approximately A.D. 1000 to
2000.[17]

there was a great earthquake. Earthquakes, along with other catastrophic events, signify "great and terrible judgments of the Lord" (1 Ne.
12:4–5; Isa. 29:6; Ezek. 38:19–20). Before the Second Coming, God sends
earthquakes to those who do not believe in Jesus Christ, for "they that
believe not in him [the Messiah] shall be destroyed, both by fire, and by
tempest, and by earthquakes, and by bloodsheds, and by pestilence, and by
famine" (2 Ne. 6:15).

Earthquakes also serve as warning voices to earth's wicked inhabitants: "The Lord shall utter his voice out of heaven, saying: Hearken, O ye
nations of the earth. . . . How oft have I called upon you by the mouth of my
servants, and by the ministering of angels, and by mine own voice, and by
the voice of thunderings, and by the voice of lightnings, and by the voice of
tempests, and by the voice of earthquakes, and great hailstorms, and by the
voice of famines and pestilences of every kind, and by the great sound of a
trump, and by the voice of judgment" (D&C 43:23–25).

Doctrine and Covenants 87 teaches: "With famine, and plague, and
earthquake, and the thunder of heaven, and the fierce and vivid lightning also, shall the inhabitants of the earth be made to feel the wrath, and

---

[13] JST 6:14 changes the phrase *heaven departed* to *heavens opened.*
[14] JST 6:14 adds the phrase *is opened.*
[15] JST 6:14 replaces *were* with *was.*
[16] JST 6:14 replaces the phrase *their places* with *its place.*
[17] Whitney, *Saturday Night Thoughts,* 12; McConkie, *Doctrinal New Testament Commentary,*
3:485–86.

indignation, and chastening hand of an Almighty God, until the consumption decreed hath made a full end of all nations" (v. 6).

And again, the Lord has revealed that "after your [the Lord's servants] testimony cometh wrath and indignation upon the people. For after your testimony cometh the testimony of earthquakes, that shall cause groanings in the midst of her, and men shall fall upon the ground and shall not be able to stand. And also cometh the testimony of the voice of thunderings, and the voice of lightnings, and the voice of tempests" (D&C 88:88–90).

The great earthquake identified in Revelation 6:12 will serve as a testimony and a warning voice to earth's people that the Lord is God. It may cause the sun to become black and the moon to look like blood. Other earthquakes are identified in 11:13; 16:17–20.

sun became black as sackcloth. The sun will look as if it is covered with black sackcloth, which is made from the hair of black goats. Sackcloth symbolizes mourning and its connection with darkening the sun implies that all God's creations are in mourning over the wickedness of the world. As seen by the inhabitants of the earth, the sun may appear to be darkened on account of volcanic ash, dust, smoke, or other such things. This darkening may be a result of the "great earthquake," or some other cause. We must remember that "the events of that day shall be so unprecedented and so beyond human experience, that the prophets are and have been at an almost total loss for words to describe those realities pressed in upon them by the spirit of revelation."[18]

Many prophecies have testified of this great event: "the sun shall be turned into darkness" (Joel 2:31); "shall the sun be darkened" (Matt. 24:29; JS–M 1:33); "the sun shall be darkened" (D&C 29:14; 34:9; 45:41); "the sun shall hide his face, and shall refuse to give light" (D&C 88:87).

moon became as blood. The moon does not become actual blood but becomes "as blood," probably meaning that it will look red to the inhabitants of the earth. This change in the appearance of the moon may be the result of the earthquake spoken of in this same verse, which would send a great amount of dust and debris into the atmosphere, which could make the moon appear red "as blood." Many prophets have foretold this event, using such phrases as "the moon into blood" (Joel 2:31; Acts 2:20), "the moon shall be turned into blood" (D&C 29:14), "and the moon be turned into

---

[18] McConkie, *Doctrinal New Testament Commentary,* 3:486.

blood" (D&C 34:9; 45:42), and "the moon shall be bathed in blood" (D&C 88:87).

6:13 *stars of heaven fell unto the earth.* Many of the stars that we see in the sky are much larger than our sun, and their size alone, not to mention their extreme heat, would pulverize and melt the earth. Elder Bruce R. McConkie explained: "Such an earthquake has never before been known (16:17–21), and it shall appear to man on earth as though the stars in the sidereal heavens are falling. And in addition, as here recorded, some heavenly meteors or other objects, appearing as stars, will fall 'unto the earth.'"[19]

Other prophets besides John have foreseen this event. They write: "the stars shall fall from heaven" (Matt. 24:29; JS–M 1:33; D&C 29:14); and "the stars shall refuse their shining, and some shall fall" (D&C 34:9); "the stars fall from heaven" (D&C 45:42); "and the stars shall become exceedingly angry, and shall cast themselves down as a fig that falleth from off a fig-tree" (D&C 88:87).

as a fig tree casteth her untimely figs. "Untimely figs" should read "unripe figs," referring to winter figs that frequently fall off the tree during a great storm or a great gust of wind. Isaiah's words are similar: "And the heavens shall be rolled together as a scroll: and all their host shall fall down, as the leaf falleth off from the vine, and as a falling fig from the fig tree" (Isa. 34:4).

6:14 *heaven[s opened] as a scroll.* This difficult expression parallels a similar one in Isaiah 34:4; there, however, the heavens are "rolled together as a scroll," whereas here they are "opened as a scroll."

The expression "heavens opened as a scroll" may correspond with an experience described by Wilford Woodruff. "When the five men entered the camp there was not a cloud to be seen in the whole heavens, but as the men left the camp there was a small cloud like a black spot appeared in the north west, and it began to unroll itself like a scroll, and in a few minutes the whole heavens were covered with a pall as black as ink. This indicated a sudden storm which soon broke upon us."[20]

every mountain and island [was] moved out of [its place]. This movement may be the result of the "great earthquake" spoken of in 6:12. In the

[19] McConkie, *Doctrinal New Testament Commentary,* 3:486.
[20] *History of the Church,* 2:104.

following verse we learn that fearful individuals also hide in the "rocks of the mountains."

6:15 *kings of the earth . . . and every free man, hid themselves.* John lists seven categories of individuals here, the number seven denoting completeness.[21] The list includes individuals belonging to the upper social class (kings; great, rich, and mighty men; and chief captains), middle class (free men), and lower class (bondmen)—all of whom will be affected by these cataclysmic events. Children are not included in this list, perhaps because of their innocence before God.

Why will people attempt to hide themselves from God? Three times Isaiah states that they will do so because of their "fear of the Lord" (Isa. 2:10, 19, 21), which fear is due to their wickedness and its consequences. Similarly, after their transgression, Adam and Eve also "hid themselves" from God (Gen. 3:8–10).

According to Doctrine and Covenants 29:15, these signs of the times will cause "weeping and wailing among the hosts of men." Meanwhile the righteous, or those who worship the Lord in his sacred temples, will receive deliverance. The prophet Joel stated, "Whosoever shall call on the name of the Lord shall be delivered: for in mount Zion and in Jerusalem shall be deliverance" (Joel 2:32). A modern revelation, speaking of the same events, commands us to "be not troubled" (D&C 45:35).

6:16 *said to the mountains and rocks, Fall on us, and hide us.* Jesus Christ prophesied of these events to "a great company of people" who followed him as he walked to Calvary: "Then shall they begin to say to the mountains, Fall on us; and to the hills, Cover us" (Luke 23:27–30; Hosea 10:8).

face of him that sitteth on the throne. This expression is a reference to God the Father (see commentary on 4:2).

wrath of the Lamb. This phrase speaks of Jesus' righteous indignation.

6:17 *great day of his wrath is come.* It is the wicked who, as they hide themselves in the rocks, make this statement because of their fear. Because of the extraordinary events described in verses 12 through 14, the wicked will believe it is the end of the world. Though these events are certainly signs of the times, they do not occur at the Second Coming, for the

---

[21] These verses also depict seven consequences of man's wickedness: the earthquake, the darkened sun, the moon turned red, the falling stars, the opening of the heavens, the mountains and islands moving from their places, and the fear of all mankind.

revelations state explicitly that Christ will not come until after the opening of the seventh seal (see, for example, D&C 77:12–13). In John's book of Revelation, Christ does not make his great appearance until Revelation 19.

Further, the same prophetic writers who prophesied of the darkening of the sun, the moon becoming as blood, and stars falling from heaven (see commentary on 6:12–14) record that those events would occur before the Second Coming, not at the Second Coming: "The sun shall be turned into darkness, and the moon into blood, *before* the great and terrible day of the Lord come" (Joel 2:31; emphasis added; see also Acts 2:20); "but, behold, I say unto you that *before* this great day shall come the sun shall be darkened" (D&C 29:14; emphasis added); "but *before* that great day shall come, the sun shall be darkened (D&C 34:9; emphasis added); "and *before* the day of the Lord shall come, the sun shall be darkened" (D&C 45:42; emphasis added). Doctrine and Covenants 88:87 notes that these events will occur "not many days hence."

who shall be able to stand? The psalmist asked, "Thou, even thou, art to be feared: and who may stand in thy sight when once thou art angry?" (Ps. 76:7).

REVELATION
7

SEALING OF THE 144,000 DURING THE SIXTH SEAL (7:1–8)

The question posed at the end of Revelation 6: "Who shall be able to stand?" when the Lord sends his great judgments upon the earth is answered in Revelation 7: Those who possess the seal of the living God. This sealing secures and protects the righteous from the great destructions that will be poured out upon the earth's inhabitants, including the desolations that accompany the blowing of the seven trumpets and the pouring out of the seven vials (bowls) in Revelation 8, 9, and 16. Joseph Smith taught that the sealing mentioned here "signifies sealing the blessing upon their heads, meaning the everlasting covenant, thereby making their calling and election sure."[1] The number of those sealed are 144,000; they are all high priests.

The events portrayed in this section will occur during our dispensation; they continue the events surrounding the opening of the sixth seal, which is discussed in Revelation 6:12 and in Doctrine and Covenants 77: "Q. What time are the things spoken of in this chapter [Revelation 7] to be accomplished? A. They are to be accomplished in the sixth thousand years, or the opening of the sixth seal" (v. 10).

Revelation 7:1–8

> 1 And after these things I saw four angels standing on the four corners of the earth, holding the four winds of the earth, that the wind should not blow on the earth, nor on the sea, nor on any tree.

---

[1] *Teachings of the Prophet Joseph Smith,* 321.

2 And I saw another angel ascending from the east, having the seal of the living God: and [I heard him cry]² with a loud voice to the four angels, to whom it was given to hurt the earth and the sea,
3 Saying, Hurt not the earth, neither the sea, nor the trees, till we have sealed the servants of our God in their foreheads.
4 And . . . ³ the number of them [who] were sealed: . . . an hundred and forty and four thousand of all the tribes of the children of Israel.
5 Of the tribe of Juda were sealed twelve thousand. Of the tribe of Reuben were sealed twelve thousand. Of the tribe of Gad were sealed twelve thousand.
6 Of the tribe of Aser were sealed twelve thousand. Of the tribe of Nepthalim were sealed twelve thousand. Of the tribe of Manasses were sealed twelve thousand.
7 Of the tribe of Simeon were sealed twelve thousand. Of the tribe of Levi were sealed twelve thousand. Of the tribe of Issachar were sealed twelve thousand.
8 Of the tribe of Zabulon were sealed twelve thousand. Of the tribe of Joseph were sealed twelve thousand. Of the tribe of Benjamin were sealed twelve thousand.

NOTES AND COMMENTARY

7:1 *after these things.* After the events recorded in Revelation 6.

I saw four angels. In his vision, John sees "four destroying angels holding power over the four quarters of the earth,"⁴ who are "sent forth from God, to whom is given power over the four parts of the earth, to save life and to destroy; these are they who have the everlasting gospel to commit to every nation, kindred, tongue, and people; having power to shut up the heavens, to seal up unto life, or to cast down to the regions of darkness" (D&C 77:8).

These angels are those who in 1831 were "waiting the great command to reap down the earth, to gather the tares that they may be burned" (D&C 38:12). Joseph Fielding Smith wrote that these four angels "seem to fit the description of the angels spoken of in the parable of the wheat and the tares (Matt. 13:24–43; and D&C 86:1–7) who plead with the Lord that they might go forth to reap down the field. They were told to let the wheat and the tares grow together to the time of the end of the harvest, which is the end of the world (Matt. 13:38–39). . . . These are now at work in the earth on their sacred mission."⁵

---

² JST 7:2 replaces *he cried* with *I heard him cry.*
³ JST 7:4 omits *I heard* and *and there . . . sealed* and changes the pronoun *which* to *who.*
⁴ *Teachings of the Prophet Joseph Smith,* 321.
⁵ Smith, *Church History and Modern Revelation,* 2:70.

Wilford Woodruff confirmed that the four angels are now at work: "Those angels have left the portals of heaven, and they stand over this people and this nation now, and are hovering over the earth waiting to pour out the judgments. And from this very day they shall be poured out."[6]

standing on the four corners of the earth. This phrase seems to indicate that the four angels have power and authority ("standing" shows ascendancy or control; 10:2, 5) over the entire earth ("four corners of the earth" means the whole earth).

holding the four winds of the earth. The four winds originate from God, who uses them to scatter and destroy people and nations (Jer. 49:35–36; Zech. 2:6; Dan. 7:2; 11:4). The four winds are also sometimes connected with gathering peoples from all parts of the world (Matt. 24:31; D&C 133:7; JS–M 1:37). Here and in the following two verses the four winds are equated with damaging the earth, sea, and trees. God empowers the four angels to hold back the four winds, which appear to be metaphors of destruction, until his mortal servants are protected and sealed against the coming tribulations (Ezek. 9:4–6; see commentary on 7:2). Elsewhere, the book of Revelation makes it evident that angels are given control of the elements: in 14:18 and 16:5 we read of the angel "which had power over fire" and "the angel of the waters."

wind should not blow on the earth/sea/tree. It is unclear whether this expression refers to the actual destruction of land and waters (through natural disasters) or to the destruction of a portion of humankind (also through natural disasters), with the earth, sea, and trees being symbols of humanity.[7]

7:2 *another angel ascending from the east.* "The angel ascending from the east is he to whom is given the seal of the living God over the twelve tribes of Israel; wherefore, he crieth unto the four angels having the everlasting gospel, saying: Hurt not the earth, neither the sea, nor the trees, till we have sealed the servants of our God in their foreheads. And, if you will receive it, this is Elias which was to come to gather together the tribes of Israel and restore all things. . . .

"[John's little book] was a mission . . . for him to gather the tribes of Israel; behold, this is Elias, who . . . must come and restore all things" (D&C 77:9, 14).

---

[6] Woodruff, "Temple Worker's Excursion," 512.
[7] "The trees, especially vulnerable to gusts of wind, represent all the living." D'aragon, "Apocalypse," in *Jerome Biblical Commentary,* ed. Brown, 477.

Who is the angel who ascends from the east? Sidney B. Sperry reasoned that "from the teaching in verses 9 and 14 [of D&C 77] one cannot help concluding (1) that John the Revelator has a commission to gather together the tribes of Israel and (2) that he is the Elias who, as it is written, must come and restore all things. If these conclusions are correct . . . then we are driven to a third conclusion, namely, that John the Revelator is the angel ascending from the east as related in Rev. 7:2."[8]

east. This is the source of Christ's coming and light. Christ will come from the east, as will the light that will accompany his second coming.

seal of the living God. This seal pertains to the Abrahamic covenant and making one's calling and election sure, as Joseph Smith explained: "Four destroying angels holding power over the four quarters of the earth until the servants of God are sealed in their foreheads, which signifies sealing the blessing upon their heads, meaning the everlasting covenant, thereby making their calling and election sure. When a seal is put upon the father and mother, it secures their posterity, so that they cannot be lost, but will be saved by virtue of the covenant of their father and mother."[9]

"A measure of this sealing is to confirm upon their head in common with Elijah the doctrine of election or the covenant with Abraham—which when a father and mother of a family have entered into, their children who have not transgressed are secured by the seal wherewith the parents have been sealed. And this is the oath of God unto our father Abraham, and this doctrine shall stand forever."[10]

In another setting, Ezekiel envisioned the sealing, or marking, on the foreheads of the righteous and the subsequent destruction of the wicked as prefiguring the events recorded in Revelation 7:1–8: "And the Lord said unto him, Go through the midst of the city, through the midst of Jerusalem, and set a mark upon the foreheads of the men that sigh and that cry for all the abominations that be done in the midst thereof. And to the others he said in mine hearing, Go ye after him through the city, and smite: let not your eye spare, neither have ye pity: Slay utterly old and young, both maids, and little children, and women: but come not near any man upon whom is the mark" (Ezek. 9:4–6).

---

[8] Sperry, *Doctrine and Covenants Compendium,* 367.
[9] *Teachings of the Prophet Joseph Smith,* 321.
[10] Ehat and Cook, *Words of Joseph Smith,* 241.

The seal of the righteous recalls the mark of blood at Passover (Ex. 12:13). At that time those who possessed the mark of lamb's blood—that is, those who desired to make Christ's atonement effective in their lives—were spared the plague of God (Isa. 44:5; Gal. 6:17).

In short, God marks and seals the righteous with his seal, making them his and placing them under his protection. In the last days, those who possess God's seal on their foreheads will not be destroyed by the "four winds of the earth" (7:1–3). Joseph Smith explained: "Then, having this promise [of one's calling and election made sure] sealed unto them, it was an anchor to the soul, sure and steadfast. Though the thunders might roll and lightnings flash, and earthquakes bellow, and war gather thick around, yet this hope and knowledge would support the soul in every hour of trial, trouble and tribulation."[11]

As a counterfeit to the true and sacred things of God, Satan places a mark on the forehead or the right hand of his followers (13:16; 14:9). These followers, however, will not be protected from God's "four winds," and they eventually will be destroyed by God (see commentary on 13:16; see also 16:2; 19:20).

[I heard him cry] . . . to the four angels. The "angel ascending from the east," who holds authority over the four angels, gives them direction (see also 7:3).

7:3 *Hurt not the earth, neither the sea, nor the trees.* See commentary on 7:1.

sealed the servants of our God. See commentary on 7:2.

7:4 *number . . . sealed . . . an hundred and forty and four thousand.* A heavenly messenger informs John that the number of them who are sealed is 144,000. These sealed individuals "are high priests, ordained unto the holy order of God, to administer the everlasting gospel; for they are they who are ordained out of every nation, kindred, tongue, and people, by the angels to whom is given power over the nations of the earth, to bring as many as will come to the church of the Firstborn" (D&C 77:11).

On 4 February 1844, Joseph Smith commented regarding the 144,000: "I attended prayer-meeting with the quorum in the assembly room, and made some remarks respecting the hundred and forty-four thousand mentioned by John the Revelator, showing that the selection of persons to form

---

[11] *Teachings of the Prophet Joseph Smith,* 298.

that number had already commenced."[12] He explained: "There will be 144,000 saviors on Mount Zion, and with them an innumerable host that no man can number. Oh! I beseech you to go forward, go forward and make your calling and your election sure."[13]

Revelation 14:3–5 explains that the 144,000 are "redeemed from the earth," are "virgins," "follow the Lamb whithersoever he goeth," are "the firstfruits unto God," and are "without fault before . . . God" (see commentary on 14:3–5). Many commentators believe that the number 144,000 is not to be taken literally but that it signifies all the redeemed of the Lord.[14]

tribes of the children of Israel. John is told that twelve thousand individuals from each of the tribes of Judah, Reuben, Gad, Asher, Nepthalim, Manasseh, Simeon, Levi, Issachar, Zabulon, Joseph, and Benjamin will be sealed—a total of 144,000 people. Judah heads the list instead of Reuben, probably because Christ belongs to the tribe of Judah (Heb. 7:14), and because Reuben lost the birthright. The tribe of Joseph is mentioned, as is that of his son Manasseh. But Joseph's other son, Ephraim, is not mentioned, nor is Dan. John provides no clue why the names on the list differ from those of the original twelve tribes.

A GREAT MULTITUDE OF EXALTED SOULS PRAISE GOD (7:9–17)

In an interlude between the events associated with the sixth (6:12–7:8) and the seventh seals (8:1) are portrayed events reserved for the righteous that will occur in the celestial kingdom (compare Joseph Smith's vision of the celestial kingdom, D&C 137). This vision continues the heavenly scene described in Revelation 4 and 5, in which the four living creatures, twenty-four elders, and a host of angels gathered and worshipped around God's throne. Revelation 7:9–17 provides hope for all who experience the plagues and tribulations that are set forth in Revelation (see especially chapters 8–9, 16). Those who persevere and endure to the end will reap great eternal blessings: they will possess white robes of light and glory and have in their hands the palms of victory and joy; they will serve God eternally in his temple and never again experience the hunger, thirst, and heat

[12] *History of the Church,* 6:196.
[13] *Teachings of the Prophet Joseph Smith,* 366.
[14] Draper, *Opening the Seven Seals,* 83; Metzger, *Breaking the Code,* 61.

associated with mortality, for Jesus Christ himself will feed them and give them fresh and pure water from his "living fountains"; in this wonderful and glorious setting God himself will "wipe away all tears from [their] eyes."

This portion of Revelation contains two hymn-like sayings. The first, recorded in 7:10 and spoken by innumerable exalted souls who stand before God and Jesus Christ, pertains to the salvation that comes from God and Christ. The second, recorded in 7:12, is uttered by angels, the four living creatures, and the twenty-four elders, all of whom open and close the hymn with "Amen." The focus of this hymn is reverence and thanksgiving to God.

One of the elders serves as a guide to John by teaching him of the great blessings reserved for those who inherit the celestial kingdom. The teaching takes place in a question and answer format, similar to that of Nephi's great vision recorded in 1 Nephi 11.

Revelation 7:9–17

9 After this I beheld, and, lo, a great multitude, which no man could number, of all nations, and kindreds, and people, and tongues, stood before the throne, and before the Lamb, clothed with white robes, and palms in their hands;

10 And cried with a loud voice, saying, Salvation to our God which sitteth upon the throne, and unto the Lamb.

11 And all the angels stood round about the throne, and about the elders and the four beasts, and fell before the throne on their faces, and worshipped God,

12 Saying, Amen: Blessing, and glory, and wisdom, and thanksgiving, and honour, and power, and might, be unto our God for ever and ever. Amen.

13 And one of the elders answered, saying unto me, What are these which are arrayed in white robes? and whence came they?

14 And I said unto him, Sir, thou knowest. And he said to me, These are they which came out of great tribulation, and have washed their robes, and made them white in the blood of the Lamb.

15 Therefore are they before the throne of God, and serve him day and night in his temple: and he that sitteth on the throne shall dwell among them.

16 They shall hunger no more, neither thirst any more; neither shall the sun light on them, nor any heat.

17 For the Lamb which is in the midst of the throne shall feed them, and shall lead them unto living fountains of waters: and God shall wipe away all tears from their eyes.

NOTES AND COMMENTARY

7:9 *great multitude, which no man could number.* In Revelation 5:11 John saw that there were one hundred million, plus "thousands of thousands," of angels around God's throne. Here John witnesses innumerable exalted Saints from all nations, extended families, and languages standing before God and Jesus Christ in heaven.

clothed with white robes. Exalted Saints wear white robes, signifying that they have overcome Satan and made the atonement of Christ effective in their lives (7:14). See commentary on 6:11.

palms in their hands. "Palms," or palm branches, symbolize victory and joy (D&C 109:76; 1 Maccabees 13:51; 2 Maccabees 10:7). The "palms in their hands," meaning the hands of the exalted Saints, recalls Jesus' triumphal entry into Jerusalem before his sacrifice, when his disciples "took branches of palm trees, and went forth to meet him, and cried, Hosanna: Blessed is the King of Israel that cometh in the name of the Lord" (John 12:13). The symbolic "robes of righteousness," "palms in [the] hands," and "crowns of glory" are the attire of the exalted Saint in heaven (D&C 109:76).

7:10 *cried with a loud voice.* The hymn is sung by exalted souls, and they will sing again when Babylon falls (19:1). The voice is loud here because of the sheer numbers who are crying with the loud voice, "a great multitude, which no man could number" (7:9).

Salvation to our God . . . and unto the Lamb. The multitude directs their words to both the Father and the Son. Joseph Smith defined salvation as "nothing more nor less than to triumph over all our enemies and put them under our feet."[15] Certainly this definition fits nicely into this context of victory and exaltation. The term *salvation* is used on two other occasions when the multitude sings a hymn (12:10; 19:1). Other versions clarify the confusing phrase "salvation *to* our God." For instance, the Revised Standard Version says, "Salvation belongs to our God," and the Good News Bible reads, "Our salvation comes from our God."

7:11 *all the angels stood round about the throne . . . and worshipped God.* In an earlier scene (5:11–14) the angels directed their devotion to Christ, but here they bow down before God the Father.

---

[15] Dahl and Cannon, *Teachings of Joseph Smith,* 600.

7:12 *Amen: Blessing/glory/wisdom/thanksgiving/honour/power/might. . . . Amen.* The seven attributes of God uttered by the angels represent the totality of his perfections, for the number seven represents completion. The angels begin and close their statement of worship with "Amen," one of the titles of Christ (3:14). "The word *amen* connotes the idea of that which has been unalterably confirmed (Num. 5:22), that which is sure, trustworthy, and faithful."[16]

7:13–14 *arrayed in white robes.* One of the twenty-four elders, acting as a guide and an interpreter for John, asks him, "What are these which are arrayed in white robes" and "Whence came they?" John's response to his heavenly guide is simply, "Sir, thou knowest." The elder then explains that these exalted Saints are those who have experienced tribulation during mortality and have made the Atonement effective in their lives by washing their robes in Christ's blood (through repentance, obedience, and endurance). See commentary on 6:11.

great tribulation. Tribulation has always been part of the lives of those who accept and follow Christ (John 16:33; 2 Tim. 3:12; D&C 138:13), and eternal blessings and glory come after great tribulation (D&C 58:3–4). The tribulation mentioned here "is referring primarily to that final series of woes which will immediately precede the end. It is the hour of trial that is to come upon the whole world (3:10)."[17]

washed their robes, and made them white in the blood of the Lamb. This statement is a common one in the Book of Mormon. It is clear that one's robes become pure and white through that individual's faith, faithfulness, and belief in Christ and his atoning sacrifice (1 Ne. 12:10–11; Alma 5:21; Morm. 9:6). See commentary on 6:11.

7:15 *Therefore are they before the throne of God.* The adverb *therefore* has a conjunctive force between verses 14 and 15: it is because the Saints have "washed their robes" in Christ's blood that they are able to stand before God in heaven (D&C 121:45).

serve him day and night in his temple. The exalted Saints serve God "forever in his kingdom, where, in the literal sense, there is neither night nor a temple. See Rev. 21:22–23."[18]

---

[16] McConkie and Parry, *Guide to Scriptural Symbols,* 115.
[17] Mounce, *Book of Revelation,* 164.
[18] McConkie, *Doctrinal New Testament Commentary,* 3:496.

One way that we may gain the privilege of serving God day and night in the heavenly temple is to serve God regularly and often in the earthly temple. President Spencer W. Kimball interpreted this verse in this way: "I can envision not only many more temples, as the Lord directs us when and where to build them, but I foresee the day when we will make around the clock use of all these sacred, holy edifices. I repeat a statement made at the dedication of the great temple in Washington . . . : 'The day is coming and not too far ahead of us when all temples on this earth will be going day and night.'"[19]

he that sitteth on the throne shall dwell among them. A better translation for the phrase "shall dwell among them" may be found in the Jerusalem Bible, which reads "will spread his tent over them." This expression recalls the tabernacle of Moses, which was a tent. Similar to the way the earthly temple renders spiritual protection for those who worship therein, here God himself will serve as a temple and provide eternal shelter for the righteous.

7:16 *They shall hunger no more, neither thirst . . . neither shall the sun light on them, nor any heat.* The language of 7:16 recalls Isaiah 49:10: "They shall not hunger nor thirst; neither shall the heat nor sun smite them: for he that hath mercy on them shall lead them, even by the springs of water shall he guide them." It also recalls Psalm 121:6: "The sun shall not smite thee by day, nor the moon by night." This symbolic language indicates that exalted souls will not suffer the tribulations associated with mortality, such as fatigue, hunger, and thirst.

In the literal sense, it will not be necessary for the sun to shine on those who inherit the celestial kingdom because "the glory of God did lighten it, and the Lamb is the light thereof" (21:23; 22:5; Isa. 60:19).

7:17 *Lamb . . . shall feed them.* Many translations say the "Lamb . . . will be their shepherd" (RSV, NEB, JB, NIV, GNB; see also Isa. 40:11; Ezek. 34:23; John 10:11–16).

lead them unto living fountains of waters. Metaphorically, Christ is the "fountain of living waters" (Jer. 17:13) and the "fountain of all righteousness" (Ether 12:28). He says to those who are spiritually thirsty, "I will give unto him that is athirst of the fountain of the water of life freely" (21:6;

---

[19] Kimball, "Temples—Now and in the Future," 4–5.

22:17). A parallel is found in 22:1, which speaks of a "pure river of water of life, clear as crystal, proceeding out of the throne of God and of the Lamb."

God shall wipe away all tears. The language of this passage recalls Isaiah's prophecy that "the Lord God will wipe away tears from off all faces" (Isa. 25:8). Later in Revelation we read, "God shall wipe away all tears from their eyes; and there shall be no more death, neither sorrow, nor crying" (21:4). Tears come from the pain and sorrow associated with mortality: affliction, pain, death, and personal sin. When he dwells with us after his coming, Jesus Christ, who is well acquainted with grief (Isa. 53:3), will remove the pains of our mortality.

REVELATION
8

SILENCE IN HEAVEN; ANGELS PREPARE TO SOUND THEIR TRUMPETS (8:1–5)

Several events occur in the temple in heaven when Christ opens the seventh and final seal and silence reigns in heaven for "about . . . half an hour." The seven angels are each given a trumpet, and they prepare themselves to sound them. An eighth angel performs duties similar to those of a priestly functionary of the earthly temple: while standing at the altar he offers the incense offering unto God as the Saints are praying. Afterwards he takes the censer, fills it with the coals from the altar of sacrifice, and casts the coals downward from heaven unto the earth, symbolizing the judgments of God that are cast down on earth's inhabitants. All of this presumably occurs during the silence in heaven, which lasts for "about the space of half an hour" (8:1).

Revelation 8:1–5

> 1 And when he had opened the seventh seal, there was silence in heaven about the space of half an hour.
> 2 And I saw the seven angels which stood before God; and to them were given seven trumpets.
> 3 And another angel came and stood at the altar, having a golden censer; and there was given unto him much incense, that he should offer it with the prayers of all saints upon the golden altar which was before the throne.
> 4 And the smoke of the incense, which came with the prayers of the saints, ascended up before God out of the angel's hand.
> 5 And the angel took the censer, and filled it with fire of the altar, and cast it into the earth: and there were voices, and thunderings, and lightnings, and an earthquake.

REVELATION 8:1–5 • [103]

NOTES AND COMMENTARY

8:1 *when he had opened the seventh seal.* Christ opens the seventh seal, which "contains the revealed will, mysteries, and the works of God" (D&C 77:6), for the seventh thousand years of the earth's temporal existence.

The number seven signifies completion. During the seventh seal we anticipate the completion of God's work, as indicated by Doctrine and Covenants 77:12: "In the beginning of the seventh thousand years will the Lord God sanctify the earth, and *complete* the salvation of man. . . . The sounding of the trumpets of the seven angels are the preparing and *finishing* of his work, in the beginning of the seventh thousand years."

silence in heaven. (See also D&C 88:95). This silence seems to last through the activities of the angel at the altar described in 8:2–5, after which "voices and thunderings" followed by the sounding of the first trumpet break the stillness of heaven. The meaning of silence here is obscure, although it may have one or more meanings.

Several scriptural passages equate silence with God's withholding his judgments upon the wicked. When there is silence in heaven, no judgments are sent upon the earth. God breaks the silence by sending his judgments. The psalmist prophesied: "Our God shall come, and shall not keep silence: a fire shall devour before him, and it shall be very tempestuous round about him. He shall call to the heavens from above, and to the earth, that he may judge his people" (Ps. 50:3–4). Also, "Keep not thou silence, O God: hold not thy peace, and be not still, O God. For, lo, thine enemies make a tumult: and they that hate thee have lifted up the head. . . . O my God, make them like a wheel; as the stubble before the wind. As the fire burneth a wood, and as the flame setteth the mountains on fire; so persecute them with thy tempest" (Ps. 83:1–2, 13–14; 35:22–23; Hab. 2:20–3:2). After listing many evils of the people, the Lord then promises through Isaiah, "I will not keep silence, but will recompense, even recompense into their bosom" (Isa. 65:6). A latter-day revelation reveals, "For all flesh is corrupted before me; and the powers of darkness prevail upon the earth, among the children of men, in the presence of all the hosts of heaven—which causeth silence to reign, and all eternity is pained, and the angels are waiting the great command to reap down the earth, to gather the tares that they may be burned" (D&C 38:11–12). In Revelation silence is interrupted and followed with God's judgments.

Silence in heaven may take place while the Saints pray. The phrase "prayers of the saints" is mentioned in these verses twice, and the offering of incense (symbolizing the prayers, Luke 1:10) by an angel of God takes a central place in this scene. All of the creatures and exalted Saints in heaven are silent as the mortal Saints' prayers are offered to God (8:3). "Is it too fanciful to suppose, as some have suggested, that everything in heaven halts so that the prayers of the saints may be heard?"[1]

about the space of half an hour. It is uncertain if this time is to be taken literally. "The half hour, it has been speculated, may actually approach twenty-one years, based on the Lord's time being 1,000 years to the day (see Abr. 3:4; 2 Pet. 3:8). If such is correct, it will be a period when all will seem to be at rest, a return to the normal after the pounding taken during the sixth seal. The earth will cease to shake, the stars to fall, and the cosmos will return to a definite pattern. However, no matter what the duration, wickedness will not cease."[2]

8:2 *I saw the seven angels which stood before God.* Probably during the "half hour" of silence, John notices the seven angels receive seven trumpets. In 8:6 he will see them prepare to blow their trumpets, and in the next verse the first angel blows his trumpet. The chief goal of these angels is to prepare for the second coming of Christ: "The sounding of the trumpets of the seven angels are the preparing and finishing of [God's] work . . . the preparing of the way before the time of [Christ's] coming" (D&C 77:12). This will occur "in the beginning of the seventh thousand years" (D&C 77:12).

These seven angels are men who belong or have belonged to our earth (D&C 130:5). They may be the same seven angels who pour out the seven plagues upon the earth's inhabitants, as identified in Revelation 15:1, 6–8; 16:1. The seven priests who blew the seven trumpets and walked with the Lord's ark of the covenant in ancient Israel (Josh. 6:13) were shadows and types of these seven angels from heaven.

Apocryphal sources name the seven angels as Uriel, Raphael, Raguel, Michael, Saraqael, Gabriel, and Remiel (1 Enoch 20:1–8). All of these names end in the particle *el,* which means "God." One source states, "I am Raphael, one of the seven holy angels which present the prayers of the

---

[1] Metzger, *Breaking the Code,* 62.
[2] Draper, *Opening the Seven Seals,* 91.

saints, and which go in and out before the Holy One" (Tobit 12:15). Luke 1:19 records, "I am Gabriel, that stand in the presence of God," and we know of Michael, Gabriel, and Raphael from modern-day revelation (D&C 128:21).

seven trumpets. The seven trumpets will be blown after the opening of the seventh seal, or "in the beginning of the seventh thousand years"; their purpose is to prepare the way for the Second Coming (D&C 77:12). At the sounding of each trump, great destructions occur upon the earth. For instance, as the first angel sounds his trump, "there followed hail and fire mingled with blood, and they were cast upon the earth: and the third part of trees was burnt up, and all green grass was burnt up" (8:7; see commentary on 8:6–13).

Trumpets were used in war in ancient Israel, which is in keeping with the context of their use here. Trumpets also played a prominent role in the Israelite temple and may have served as types of the trumpets that sound from the temple in heaven. Nehemiah 12:41 and 1 Chronicles 15:24, for example, indicate that "there were seven trumpets in the temple orchestra."[3] Trumpets were blown during times of peace and burnt offerings (Num. 10:10; 2 Chr. 29:27–28), at certain feasts and at a new moon (Lev. 23:24; Num. 29:1), during solemn assemblies and fasting (Joel 2:15), on the Day of Atonement (Lev. 25:8–9), and at the dedication of the temple (2 Chr. 5:12–14).

The scriptures inform us that the day of the Lord will be announced by the sounding of a trumpet (Joel 2:1; Zeph. 1:14–16; Isa. 27:13; Zech. 9:14).

8:3 *another angel.* This angel is not one of the seven identified in the previous verse.

stood at the altar, having a golden censer; and there was given unto him much incense. A censer is a utensil, perhaps similar to a large spoon or very small shovel, which was used for the incense rite. It was employed by the priestly officiant for carrying a few of the burning coals. The action of the angel recalls the activities of the priests in the Israelite temple system, in which the high priest took a "censer full of burning coals of fire from off the altar" (Lev. 16:12) and poured a handful of incense into the burning coals, creating a cloud of incense that ascended into the sky (Num. 16:17–

[3] Ford, *Revelation,* 136.

19). The burning incense symbolizes the prayers of the righteous, which ascend from the earth unto the throne of God (see commentary on 5:8).

that he should offer it with the prayers of all saints. In the Mosaic temple system the priest offered up the incense inside the temple at the same time that the multitude outside offered their prayers (Luke 1:10). Similarly, in the temple in heaven the angelic minister offers incense simultaneous "with the prayers of all saints" (see commentary on 5:8). Thus, as Elder Bruce R. McConkie explained, "The saints on both sides of the veil join in worshipping the Lord."[4]

golden altar which was before the throne. The golden altar is the altar of incense, located before God's throne in the temple in heaven. Similarly, the incense alter of the earthly temple was covered with gold and was situated before the mercy seat, or Jehovah's throne (Ex. 30:1–6; 39:38). This altar may or may not be the same as that mentioned earlier in the verse; it is impossible to tell.

8:4 *smoke of the incense . . . ascended up before God.* See commentary on 8:3.

8:5 *filled it with fire . . . and cast it into the earth.* This rite copies, on a grander scale, a practice in ancient Israel in which the burning coals were cast near the sacrificial altar (Num. 16:36–40). Once they were scattered throughout the city (Ezek. 10:2–7). The same angel who offered incense upon the golden altar now fills the censer with "fire of the altar" and casts it down to the earth. This action symbolizes the pouring out of God's judgments upon earth and her inhabitants soon after the opening of the seventh seal. The burning coals recall the brimstone and fire that were cast down upon the wicked inhabitants of Sodom and Gomorrah. It is interesting to note that the first three trumpet blasts bring fire upon the earth (8:7–10).

there were voices/thunderings/lightnings/earthquake. See commentary on 4:5. The sound of the voices and thunderings shatter the silence in heaven that endured for half an hour (see 8:1).

FIRST FOUR TRUMPETS BRING JUDGMENTS (8:6–13)

The following instructs us concerning the blasts of the trumpets:

---

[4]McConkie, *Doctrinal New Testament Commentary,* 3:498.

The seven angels will blow their trumpets at the beginning of the seventh thousand-year period to prepare the earth's inhabitants for the Second Coming (D&C 77:12).

The trumpets' blasts bring calamities upon the earth, which warn its inhabitants of greater destructions that will accompany the pouring out of the seven bowls identified in Revelation 16.

The calamities that accompany the blowing of the trumpets also encourage the earth's inhabitants to repent (9:20–21; 16:9, 11).

There is a progression of the degree of destruction in the groups of the seven seals, trumpets, and bowls: the fourth horseman affected a fourth part of the earth (6:8), the first four angels' trumpets are directed to one-third of the earth ("third part" is used twelve times in this section), and "the bowls complete the wrath of God (16:17)."[5] The multiple mention of "third part" may have a historical precedent. Just as one-third of heaven's hosts were cast out for rebellion, so will one-third of the earth be smitten for the wickedness of her inhabitants.

The judgments of the first four trumpets are directed to nature and the elements (land, trees, grass, sea, fresh waters) and to heavenly bodies (sun, moon, stars), although humanity will be affected indirectly. The final three trumpets, represented by a threefold woe, are aimed directly at humanity.

The events that accompany the seven trumpets correspond to and recall the plagues of Egypt during the time of Moses: the hail, blood, and fire of the first trumpet parallel the seventh plague, in which God plagued Egypt with "hail, and fire mingled with the hail, very grievous, such as there was none like it in all the land of Egypt since it became a nation" (Ex. 9:24); the sea becoming blood at the sound of the second trumpet recalls the first plague of Egypt, in which God turned the river into blood (Ex. 7:14–25); the waters becoming bitter at the sound of the third trumpet recalls the first plague, during which the Egyptians "lothe[d] to drink of the water of the river" (Ex. 7:18); the sound of the fourth trumpet will bring darkness, which parallels the ninth plague, during which God brought three days of darkness over Egypt, "even darkness which may be felt" (Ex. 10:21); and the locusts connected with the fifth trumpet (9:1–11) recall the locusts that plagued Egypt, destroying all vegetation "through all the land of Egypt" (Ex. 10:15).

---

[5] Mounce, *Book of Revelation,* 169.

These parallels suggest that Egypt is a type of the world and wickedness, and the plagues are shadows of what will come upon our world in the
last days. Also, just as God punished those who were hostile to the prophet
Moses and his people, he will again plague those who do not hearken to his
voice. God said to Pharaoh, "For I will at this time send all my plagues
upon thine heart, and upon thy servants, and upon thy people; that thou
mayest know that there is none like me in all the earth" (Ex. 9:14).

We recall that before the sounding of the seven trumpets, an angel
filled his censer with burning coals from the altar in the temple in heaven
and then cast them to the earth (8:5). This fire became, symbolically, the
fire that accompanied the first three trumpets: "the first angel sounded, and
there followed hail and fire mingled with blood"; "the second angel
sounded, and as it were a great mountain burning with fire"; and "the third
angel sounded, and there fell a great star from heaven, burning as it were a
lamp." The seven angels identified in Revelation may be the same angels
mentioned in Doctrine and Covenants 88:94–110 who will blast their trumpets.

Table 3 outlines the judgments that will accompany the blowing of the
seven trumpets.

Table 3

Seven Angels Blow Trumpets	Judgment(s)	Things Harmed or Destroyed	Percentage/ Amount of Damage	Agent of Destruction
first angel sounds trumpet (8:7)	hail and fire mingled with blood are cast upon the earth	trees and green grass	third part of trees and all green grass	burning
second angel sounds trumpet (8:8–9)	as it were a great mountain burning with fire was cast into the sea	sea, sea creatures, ships	one-third of sea becomes blood; one-third of living creatures of the sea die; one-third of ships are destroyed	blood in the sea

Table 3—Continued

Seven Angels Blow Trumpets	Judgment(s)	Things Harmed or Destroyed	Percentage/ Amount of Damage	Agent of Destruction
third angel sounds trumpet (8:10–11)	there fell a great star from heaven, burning as it were a lamp	rivers, fountains of waters, many men	third part of rivers and waters, many men die	waters are made bitter
fourth angel sounds trumpet (8:12)	none listed	sun, moon, stars, day and night	third part of the sun, moon, and stars smitten and darkened	
fifth angel sounds trumpet (9:1–12)	star falls from heaven, is given the key of the bottomless pit, and he opens the bottomless pit	sun, air, those without the seal of God	those who do not have the seal	smoke, locusts
sixth angel sounds trumpet (9:13–21)	four angels are loosed which were prepared to slay one-third of men	men	third part of men killed	horsemen and horses
seventh angel sounds trumpet (11:15–19)	uncertain	none mentioned	none mentioned	none mentioned

Revelation 8:6–13

6 And the seven angels which had the seven trumpets prepared themselves to sound.
7 The first angel sounded, and there followed hail and fire mingled with blood, and they were cast upon the earth: and the third part of trees was burnt up, and all green grass was burnt up.
8 And the second angel sounded, and as it were a great mountain burning with fire was cast into the sea: and the third part of the sea became blood;
9 And the third part of the creatures which were in the sea, and had life, died; and the third part of the ships were destroyed.
10 And the third angel sounded, and there fell a great star from heaven, burning as it were a lamp, and it fell upon the third part of the rivers, and upon the fountains of waters;
11 And the name of the star is called Wormwood: and the third part of the waters became wormwood; and many men died of the waters, because they were made bitter.
12 And the fourth angel sounded, and the third part of the sun was smitten, and the third part of the moon, and the third part of the stars; so [that]⁶ the third part of them was darkened, and the day shone not for a third part of it, and the night likewise.
13 And I beheld, and heard an angel flying through the midst of heaven, saying with a loud voice, Woe, woe, woe, to the inhabiters of the earth by reason of the other voices of the trumpet of the three angels, which are yet to sound!

NOTES AND COMMENTARY

8:6 *seven angels . . . prepared themselves to sound [trumpets].* The seven angels lift their trumpets to their mouths, ready to sound them.

8:7 *first angel sounded.* See commentary on 8:2.

hail and fire mingled with blood. The hail and fire parallel the seventh plague of Egypt: "So there was hail, and fire mingled with the hail, very grievous, such as there was none like it in all the land of Egypt since it became a nation" (Ex. 9:24). The plague that follows the sounding of the first trumpet, however, is more severe, for the hail and fire are "mingled with blood" (see also Joel 2:30). The Lord has not revealed what will cause this plague, nor have Bible scholars been able to offer reasonable explanations of what will actually happen during this plague.

the third part. A "third" means that these judgments were partial and incomplete—that, for now, God's mercy is greater than his punishment.⁷

---

⁶ JST 8:12 replaces *as* with *that.*
⁷ Mounce, *Book of Revelation,* 178; Dummelow, *One-Volume Bible Dictionary,* 1080.

third part of trees was burnt up. The four destroying angels had commanded to "hurt not the earth, neither the sea, nor the trees, till we have sealed the servants of our God in their foreheads" (7:3). Now, at the sounding of the first trumpet, hail and fire destroy one-third of the earth's "trees," which may be actual trees, for "green grass" is mentioned in the same context. The loss of one-third of the earth's trees, which produce fruit, nuts, lumber, and oxygen, would be disastrous. It is also possible that the trees here symbolize people (Ps. 1:3)—thus, this prophecy may indicate that *people* will be burned. The ordinal number *third* is used elsewhere in Revelation (8:7–10, 12; 9:15, 18; 12:4).

all green grass was burnt up. New Testament scholar Mounce believes "green grass" may mean "vegetation" in general.[8] The fire and hail that accompanies the blast of the first trumpet destroy grass and vegetation; such a catastrophe would cause a worldwide famine and millions of deaths.

8:8 *second angel sounded.* See commentary on 8:2.

as it were a great mountain burning with fire. John seems to be speaking symbolically, for he uses the expression "as it were," although the meaning of this passage has not been revealed (Jer. 51:25). Or perhaps John is describing a great volcano.

third part of the sea became blood. If the "great mountain burning with fire" were a volcano, its lava would look like blood flowing into the sea around it.[9]

This plague parallels the first plague of Egypt, when fresh waters became blood at the word of the Lord. This plague was so severe that "there was blood throughout all the land of Egypt" (Ex. 7:21). Ancient Egypt is a type of the present-day world and its wickedness, and Egypt's first plague is a type of the destruction that will fall upon the world in the days to come (see commentary on 16:3).

8:9 *third part of the [sea] creatures . . . died.* As did the freshwater fish during the first plague of Egypt (Ex. 7:21), one-third of all sea creatures will die because of the great burning mountain, identified in 8:8.

third part of the ships were destroyed. The great burning mountain destroys the ships on earth.

8:10 *third angel sounded.* See commentary on 8:2.

---

[8] Mounce, *Book of Revelation,* 179.
[9] Mounce, *Book of Revelation,* 179.

fell a great star from heaven. Whether this expression refers to a mete-
orite, nuclear bomb, or another catastrophic event is unknown. We do know
that the purpose of this destruction—"a symbol of divine visitation"[10]—is
to encourage humanity to repent and turn to God (see commentary on
9:20–21).

fell upon the third part of the rivers/fountains. The great star will fall
upon and make bitter one-third of the earth's fresh inland waters. Such a
catastrophe will certainly alter drastically the earth's ecological system, and
many will die (8:11).

8:11 *name of the star is called Wormwood.* The star is named after a
plant that has a bitter taste. In the Old Testament God sends wormwood
upon the wicked as a judgment: to an immoral woman whose "end is bitter
as wormwood" (Prov. 5:4), to wicked people whom God will cause to eat
wormwood (Jer. 9:15; Deut. 29:17–18; Lam. 3:15). Thus the star called
Wormwood will bring great bitterness upon earth's inhabitants.

Because stars represent people in other passages of scripture (12:4; Job
38:7; D&C 128:23), the star called Wormwood may represent an angel
who is sent from God with bitter judgments upon the people.[11]

third part of the waters became wormwood. Approximately one-third
of the earth's fresh waters will become bitter, causing "many men" to die.
Elder McConkie asks, "Could this be atomic fallout which shall poison a
third of the drinking water of the earth?"[12]

8:12 *fourth angel sounded.* See commentary on 8:2.

third part of the sun/moon/stars . . . was darkened. The blast of the
trumpet of the fourth angel brings total darkness for one-third of the day
and night. John's prophecy accords with other prophets who have testified
that "the day of the Lord is darkness, and not light" (Amos 5:18; Joel 2:2).
Isaiah also speaks of the darkening of the sun, moon, and stars, placing this
darkening in the context of God's punishment of the world for their evil
(Isa. 13:10–11). The events recall the ninth plague, or three days of "thick
darkness," in Egypt as well as the darkness at Christ's crucifixion, recorded
in 3 Nephi 8:20–23.

8:13 *I beheld, and heard an angel flying through the midst of heaven.*
Many versions read *eagle* rather than *angel.* The first four trumps warn the

[10] Mounce, *Book of Revelation,* 180.
[11] Davidson, *New Bible Commentary,* 1180.
[12] McConkie, *Doctrinal New Testament Commentary,* 3:499.

earth's inhabitants to repent; now one of God's messengers warns the earth's inhabitants that greater calamities are about to fall upon them. This verse parallels Doctrine and Covenants 88:92, which reads, "And angels shall fly through the midst of heaven, crying with a loud voice, sounding the trump of God, saying: Prepare ye, prepare ye, O inhabitants of the earth; for the judgment of our God is come."

with a loud voice. All of the earth's inhabitants must hear. The voice here is probably not literal; instead, it may pertain to God's judgments that accompany the sounding of the seven trumps. All of humanity will hear of these great calamities.

Woe, woe, woe, to the inhabiters of the earth. These words clearly show God's deep displeasure in the inhabitants of the earth, specifically those who choose sin and worldliness and will not repent. God's pronouncement of a woe results in a condition of woe on the earth.

Woe denotes great trouble and anguish; three woes magnify the trouble and anguish. The first woe occurs when the fifth angel sounds his trumpet (9:1–12), and the second woe accompanies the sixth angel's trumpet blast (9:13–21) and is fulfilled in Revelation 11:14, although there is an interlude in chapter 10. John does not identify the fulfillment of the third woe, although it may be connected with the bowl of judgments in Revelation 16, for we observe that as the opening of the seventh seal encompasses both the seven trumps and the seven bowls, so might the seventh trump encompass the seven bowls.

God uses three woes to encourage the wicked to repent, for he says, "Woe shall come unto the inhabitants of the earth if they will not hearken unto my words" (D&C 5:5).

—⟨ℰℰ⟩—

REVELATION
9

FIRST WOE: THE FIFTH ANGEL BLOWS HIS TRUMPET AND BRINGS JUDGMENTS (9:1–12)

The events described in this chapter will "be accomplished after the opening of the seventh seal, before the coming of Christ" (D&C 77:13). When the fifth angel blows his trumpet, John sees the complete unleashing of hell upon the earth, as the great abyss is opened and smoke billows forth onto the earth, darkening the world with great evil. This may be the time "when peace shall be taken from the earth, and the devil shall have power over his own dominion" (D&C 1:35).

Armies, many perhaps unknowingly, will be influenced and led by the devil into battle. As locusts ravage green plants and trees, the armies will scourge the men and women of the earth, save those who are citizens of Zion and who possess the seal of the living God on their foreheads (9:4; 7:3–4). The Saints, we are told in a modern-day revelation, will dwell safely in Zion (D&C 45:66–70). The series of events that accompanies the fifth and sixth trumpets is to encourage people to repent of their sins and to acknowledge God as their Lord and King (see 9:20–21).

Revelation 9:1–12

> 1 And the fifth angel sounded, and I saw a star fall from heaven unto the earth: and to [the angel]¹ was given the key of the bottomless pit.
> 2 And he opened the bottomless pit; and there arose a smoke out of the pit, as the smoke of a great furnace; and the sun and the air were darkened by reason of the smoke of the pit.
> 3 And there came out of the smoke locusts upon the earth: and unto them was given power, as the scorpions of the earth have power.

---

¹ JST 9:1 replaces the word *him* with *the angel*.

4 And it was commanded them that they should not hurt the grass of the
earth, neither any green thing, neither any tree; but only those men which
have not the seal of God in their foreheads.
5 And to them it was given that they should not kill them, but that they
should be tormented five months: and their torment was as the torment of a
scorpion, when he striketh a man.
6 And in those days shall men seek death, and shall not find it; and shall
desire to die, and death shall flee from them.
7 And the shapes of the locusts were like unto horses prepared unto battle;
and on their heads were as it were crowns like gold, and their faces were as
the faces of men.
8 And they had hair as the hair of women, and their teeth were as the teeth
of lions.
9 And they had breastplates, as it were breastplates of iron; and the sound
of their wings was as the sound of chariots of many horses running to
battle.
10 And they had tails like unto scorpions, and there were stings in their
tails: and their power was to hurt men five months.
11 And they had a king over them, which is the angel of the bottomless pit,
whose name in the Hebrew tongue is Abaddon, but in the Greek tongue
hath his name Apollyon.
12 One woe is past; and, behold, there come two woes more hereafter.

NOTES AND COMMENTARY

9:1 *fifth angel sounded.* See commentary on 8:2.

star fall from heaven. This metaphor refers to Lucifer, who is "fallen
from heaven" (Isa. 14:12). Jesus said, "I beheld Satan as lightning fall from
heaven" (Luke 10:18; Rev. 12:9).

to [the angel]. The fifth angel is given the key to the bottomless pit.
This may be the same angel identified in Revelation 20:1, who John saw
"come down from heaven, having the key of the bottomless pit."

key of the bottomless pit. According to his divine schedule, God permits the inhabitants of hell to come forth with Satan as their king (9:11),
and unleash their torment on earth's inhabitants. Later an angel will come
out of heaven with a key and a chain which he will use to bind Satan for a
thousand years (20:1–3).

bottomless pit. The pit is the abyss, or the "place of imprisonment for
disobedient spirits."[2] This is the pit identified in Joseph Smith's translation
of Isaiah 14:15, 19. The king of the abyss is Lucifer, who is also called
Abaddon and Apollyon (9:11). God, of course, has complete control over
this prison (20:1–3).

---

[2] *Theological Dictionary of the New Testament,* 1:9, s.v. "abyss."

9:2 *he opened the bottomless pit.* The angel uses the key to open the pit so that wicked spirits will unleash, perhaps as never before, their evil forces upon humanity. A prophecy delivered through Joseph Smith may allude to the opening of the pit: "For I [God] . . . will that all men shall know that the day speedily cometh; the hour is not yet, but is nigh at hand, when peace shall be taken from the earth, and the devil shall have power over his own dominion" (D&C 1:35). Joseph Smith taught: "Some may have cried peace, but the Saints and the world will have little peace from henceforth. . . . The time is soon coming, when no man will have any peace but in Zion and her stakes."[3]

there arose a smoke out of the pit . . . the sun and the air were darkened. Hell is opened and evil arises "as the smoke of a great furnace," blackening the air and hiding the sun's light. John seems to be describing darkness that "pertains to Satan, his kingdom, his disciples, and their works. The devil is the perpetrator of dark and evil things (2 Ne. 9:9; Hel. 6:28–29)."[4] The darkening of the air with evil is the result of Satan's work, for he is called "the prince of the power of the air" (Eph. 2:2). New Testament scholar Richard Draper writes: "As the pit is opened, smoke billows forth and obscures the light of the sun. Darkness reigns. Through this powerful symbol, John reveals the nature of the first thrust against mankind: a blow against the light."[5] The smoke, like the "mists of darkness" in Lehi's dream, represents evil, darkness, and "the temptations of the devil, which blindeth the eyes, and hardeneth the hearts of the children of men, and leadeth them away into broad roads, that they perish and are lost" (1 Ne. 12:17).

9:3 *there came out of the smoke locusts upon the earth.* These are not actual insects (grasshoppers; see Prov. 30:27), for they sting like scorpions, strike out at mankind, have a king, and are commanded not to eat vegetation (9:3–5, 11). These are actually wicked men and armies with power to torment all of humanity except those who have God's seal in their foreheads (9:4). John's imagery of locusts is similar to Joel's description of the locust-like armies that will "come up upon my land, strong, and without number. . . . He hath laid my vine waste, and barked my fig tree: he hath made it clean bare, and cast it away; the branches thereof are made white" (Joel 1:4–7; 2:25). The locusts that plagued ancient Egypt and "covered the

---

[3] *History of the Church,* 3:390–91.
[4] McConkie and Parry, *Guide to Scriptural Symbols,* 36.
[5] Draper, *Opening the Seven Seals,* 101.

face of the whole earth, so that the land was darkened" (Ex. 10:15) are types of this great army of wicked people.

unto them was given power. God gives agency to humankind, and he permits the wicked to destroy one another, but he sets boundaries for them. Compare Revelation 6:4, 8, in which power is given through the red and pale horses.

as the scorpions of the earth. Here and in 9:5 the locusts are likened to scorpions, which torment humans, often without killing them (see commentary on 9:5).

9:4 *it was commanded them.* God controls the destiny of this army of locusts and commands them to harm only those who do not have God's seal on their foreheads.

not hurt the grass/green thing/tree. These are the usual objects that locusts feed on in their developmental stages (cankerworm, palmerworm, caterpillar, locust; see Joel 1:4). The creatures of Revelation 9 are not like the locusts that plagued the Egyptians and "did eat every herb of the land, and all the fruit of the trees which the hail had left: and there remained not any green thing in the trees, or in the herbs of the field, through all the land of Egypt" (Ex. 10:15). These creatures are soldiers who seek to destroy humans. See commentary on 7:1–2.

men which have not the seal of God in their foreheads. Inhabitants of Zion (many of whom will have the seal of God) will be preserved during this time. They will dwell in the New Jerusalem, which is called "a land of peace, a city of refuge, a place of safety for the saints of the Most High God. . . . There shall be gathered unto it out of every nation under heaven; and it shall be the only people that shall not be at war one with another. And it shall be said among the wicked: Let us not go up to battle against Zion, for the inhabitants of Zion are terrible; wherefore we cannot stand" (D&C 45:66, 69–70). The righteous in the stakes of Zion will also have safety (D&C 115:5–6; 124:36). See commentary on 7:1–2.

9:5 *to them it was given that they should not kill them.* The armies of locusts will not kill humans; instead they will harm and torment them. Elder Bruce R. McConkie suggests that "perhaps John is seeing such things as the effects of poisonous gas, or bacteriological warfare, or atomic fallout, which disable but do not kill."[6]

---

[6] McConkie, *Doctrinal New Testament Commentary,* 3:502.

tormented five months. Five months is the life cycle of the locust. Here five months may represent a short period and not exactly five months.

torment of a scorpion. The scorpion's sting rarely results in death, but it causes great pain and discomfort. Torment in this context pertains to more than war and warfare. Torment is also associated with "guilt and abominations, which doth cause [the wicked] to shrink from the presence of the Lord into a state of misery and endless torment" (Mosiah 3:25). Alma spoke of both the abyss and torment when he declared: "My soul hath been redeemed from the gall of bitterness and bonds of iniquity. I was in the darkest abyss. . . . My soul was racked with eternal torment" (Mosiah 27:29).

9:6 *shall men seek death.* It seems that the torment brought about by the locusts will cause such pain that people will want to die to end their pain. In another context the Lord said, "And death shall be chosen rather than life by all the residue of them that remain of this evil family" (Jer. 8:3). Also, Job spoke of the wicked: "Which long for death, but it cometh not; and dig for it more than for hid treasures" (Job 3:21).

9:7–10 *shapes of the locusts.* John seems to be describing soldiers that are trained and equipped to fight on land, sea, or in the air, with their various types of uniforms and protective gear, including helmets, body armor, and protective masks; their war vehicles, including aircraft, helicopters, tanks, and dozens of other military machines; and their weaponry and artillery of many types and kinds, each designed to harm, maim, or kill humans. He may be describing that which belongs to military units of our era, or he may be seeing that which belongs to our own future.

Joseph Fielding Smith, citing Isaiah 5:26–30, Nahum 2:2–5, and Revelation 9:6–10, opined that the ancient prophets saw "our automobiles, our railroad trains, . . . the airplanes flying in the midst of the heavens, because we can read in the prophecies of these ancient scriptures many things that indicate that these things were revealed unto those ancient prophets."[7]

John describes the things that he envisions by using objects or creatures that were known to him in the first century after Christ: locusts, horses, crowns, hair, lions, breastplates, chariots, and scorpions. These objects and creatures create a fearsome picture of symbolic images for his audience.

---

[7] Smith, *Doctrines of Salvation,* 1:146.

shapes of the locusts were like unto horses prepared unto battle. This phrase recalls Joel 2:4, which reads: "The appearance of them is as the appearance of horses; and as horsemen, so shall they run." The image of locusts depicts an army of tens of thousands of warriors, an army so great that its soldiers darken the land and cannot be numbered. The phrase "horses prepared unto battle" portrays warriors wearing body armor similar to the protective body and headgear worn by warhorses of John's day. John's description here recalls Job's description of a warhorse (Job 39:19–24).

on their heads were as it were crowns like gold. This expression may refer to the soldier's helmet, in all of its shapes and varieties; or it may be symbolic of kings' headgear ("crowns of gold"). If the passage does pertain to kings' headgear, it may mean that governments are banding together for war.

their faces were as the faces of men. This expression seems to indicate that the locusts represent men.

9:8 *they had hair as the hair of women.* We don't know what this expression means, but there is precedent in scripture for long hair on men being seen as a sign of strength (Judg. 16:17).

their teeth were as the teeth of lions. This expression describes the warriors' ability to ravage and destroy. It also recalls Joel's description of warriors: "For a nation is come up upon my land, strong, and without number, whose teeth are the teeth of a lion, and he hath the cheek teeth of a great lion" (Joel 1:6–7). Satan himself has been called a "roaring lion, [who] walketh about, seeking whom he may devour" (1 Pet. 5:8).

9:9 *they had breastplates.* Modern soldiers' armor and protective gear covers vital organs. It may also refer to the armor of war vehicles.

sound of chariots of many horses. Natural locusts in flight make a fearful noise, and the reference here may be to the mingled sound of chariot wheels and the hooves of the horses (see Joel 2:5). Anciently the chariot and its horses were used for war, and in prophetic language they may be a metaphor for modern war vehicles (Ezek. 39:20; Dan. 11:40; Joel 2:5).

9:10 *they had tails like unto scorpions.* This expression could refer to any number of weapons.

power was to hurt men five months. This particular battle, or war, will have a limited duration. It may serve as a precursor to the great war that will accompany the blasting of the sixth trumpet, when two hundred million soldiers will fight and kill one-third of humanity (9:13–19).

9:11 *they had a king over them.* Actual locusts have no king; the locusts described in Revelation 9:6–10 are warriors, and they and their leaders hearken unto Satan, who is their king.

angel of the bottomless pit. Satan.

Abaddon/Apollyon. John gives a Hebrew name followed with the Greek equivalent, as was his custom (John 1:38, 42; 4:25; 9:7; 11:16), perhaps so that his audience will understand his words. The angel is named *Abaddon,* meaning "destruction" or "ruin"; he is also called *Apollyon,* meaning "destruction" or "destroyer." Such names relate to Satan's evil mission and goals.

9:12 *one woe is past.* The first woe occurs when the fifth angel sounds his trumpet (9:1–12); the second woe will begin with the blowing of the trumpet by the sixth angel (9:13–21). See commentary on 8:13.

SECOND WOE: THE SIXTH ANGEL SOUNDS AND BRINGS JUDGMENTS (9:13–21)

The events identified in this section will "be accomplished after the opening of the seventh seal, before the coming of Christ" (D&C 77:13). The second woe begins with the blowing of the sixth angel's trump (9:13) but is not completed until Revelation 11:14, in which John writes "the second woe is past."

The second woe brings great anguish upon humankind, for two hundred million warriors battle in war and destroy, ultimately causing the death of one-third of humanity. John uses descriptive and symbolic terms in describing this great conflagration, including *fire* (three times), *brimstone* (three times), *smoke* (twice), *lions,* and *serpents.* The sixth trump announces these events, but it is Satan and his angels who set them in motion through their evil influence and guidance. The events recall numerous other historical time periods when "Satan had great dominion among men, and raged in their hearts; and from thenceforth came wars and bloodshed" (JST Gen. 6:13).

The purpose of these events that accompany the blowing of this trump is to encourage humankind to repent of their many grievous sins, which

John lists as idolatry, murders, sorceries, fornication, and thefts. Sadly, they do not repent of their wickedness.

Revelation 9:13–21

13 And the sixth angel sounded, and I heard a voice from the four horns of the golden altar which is before God,
14 Saying to the sixth angel which had the trumpet, Loose the four angels which are bound in the [bottomless pit].[8]
15 And the four angels were loosed, which were prepared for an hour, and a day, and a month, and a year, for to slay the third part of men.
16 And the number of the army of the horsemen were two hundred thousand thousand: and I [saw][9] the number of them.
17 And thus I saw the horses in the vision, and them that sat on them, having breastplates of fire, and of jacinth, and brimstone: and the heads of the horses were as the heads of lions; and out of their mouths issued fire and smoke and brimstone.
18 By these three was the third part of men killed, by the fire, and by the smoke, and by the brimstone, which issued out of their mouths.
19 For their power is in their mouth, and in their tails: for their tails were like unto serpents, and had heads, and with them they do hurt.
20 And the rest of the men which were not killed by these plagues yet repented not of the works of their hands, that they should not worship devils, and idols of gold, and silver, and brass, and stone, and of wood: which neither can see, nor hear, nor walk:
21 Neither repented they of their murders, nor of their sorceries, nor of their fornication, nor of their thefts.

NOTES AND COMMENTARY

9:13 *sixth angel sounded.* See commentary on 8:2.

voice from the four horns of the golden altar which is before God. The voice here could be that of the angel identified in Revelation 8:3–5, who was located near this altar.

9:14 *Loose the four angels which are bound in the [bottomless pit].* The "bound" angels may belong to that group of "angels that sinned" and thus who God "cast . . . down to hell, and delivered them into chains of darkness" (2 Pet. 2:4; see also Jude 1:6). They will be set loose to prompt and persuade the wicked to kill one-third of humankind during the great war described in 9:15–19.

9:15 *prepared for an hour/day/month/year.* The time mentioned here does not indicate how long the four angels will be loosed, but it does say

---

[8] JST 9:14 replaces *great river Euphrates* with *bottomless pit.*
[9] JST 9:16 replaces *heard* with *saw.*

they will be loosed at a specific, divinely appointed time. Jerusalem Bible reads, "These four angels had been put there ready for this hour of this day of this month of this year."

slay the third part of men. The army of two hundred million individuals (see commentary on 9:16), with their modern weapons of destruction, will kill one-third of the earth's inhabitants. It is unclear whether the figure "one-third" is to be taken as literal or symbolic.

9:16 *number of the army . . . were two hundred thousand.* The number of fighting men that John "saw" was two hundred million, twice the number of the angels who were worshipping God in the celestial kingdom (5:11). The numerical figure is likely symbolic, intended to represent great hosts of warriors.

9:17 *I saw the horses in the vision, and them that sat on them.* John describes this scene of horses using various images and symbols; he makes threefold repetition of "fire" and "brimstone" (JB says "fire" and "sulfur") and twofold repetition of "smoke" and "horses" in 9:17–18. Fire, smoke (see commentary on 9:2), and brimstone may describe the bombs and destructive devices associated with present-day or future warfare. Horses often represent war vehicles (see commentary on 9:9).

9:18 *by these three was the third part of men killed.* Fire, smoke, and brimstone are the weapons of this mighty army that will destroy one-third of humanity.

9:19 *power is in their mouth, and in their tails.* The fire-breathing capacity of these lion-headed horses symbolizes "the torment of hell and [underscores their] diabolical nature."[10] Like the scorpions in 9:10, there is destructive power in the horses' tails. In fact, the tails are snakes with heads, another evidence that they are sent from the devil.[11]

9:20 *rest of the men . . . repented not.* The "rest of the men" speaks of those who are not sealed (9:4) and who survive the warfare described above. The purpose for the blowing of the sixth trumpet is manifest here: to encourage the wicked to repent, for they are idolaters, devil worshippers, murderers, fornicators, thieves, and sorcerers (9:21). The great war, however, during which one-third of humankind is destroyed, does not succeed in bringing the wicked to repentance; they "repented not of the works of their hands, that they should not worship devils, and idols," writes John.

---

[10] Draper, *Opening the Seven Seals,* 108.
[11] Mounce, *Book of Revelation,* 197.

works of their hands. This expression seems to refer to idol worship (Ps. 115:4–7; Isa. 2:8; Jer. 1:16), which consists both of images and statues created by human hands and of all the evil deeds and actions of humanity that replace one's righteous desire to serve the true and living God.

that they should not worship devils. Humanity continues to worship devils, even after the great war that destroys so many. Devil worship has long been a gross evil conducted upon the earth (Deut. 32:17; Ps. 106:37; 1 Cor. 10:20–21).

idols of gold. Nephi warned, "Yea, wo unto those that worship idols, for the devil of all devils delighteth in them" (2 Ne. 9:37). In our dispensation we are told of those who "have strayed from [God's] ordinances, and have broken [God's] everlasting covenant; they seek not the Lord to establish his righteousness, but every man walketh in his own way, and after the image of his own god, whose image is in the likeness of the world, and whose substance is that of an idol, which waxeth old and shall perish in Babylon, even Babylon the great, which shall fall" (D&C 1:15–16).

9:21 *neither repented they of their murders/sorceries/fornication/ thefts.* In the previous verse John identified idolatry as a chief sin belonging to humanity in the last days; now he lists other iniquities—murder, sorcery, fornication, and thievery—that represent all of the wickedness that will prevail upon the earth during this time.

REVELATION
10

THE MIGHTY ANGEL AND JOHN'S LATTER-DAY MISSION (10:1–11)

This chapter is an interlude, or break, between the events listed in Revelation 9 and those listed in Revelation 11. After enumerating plagues and judgments in Revelation 8 and 9, John envisions an angel, who has a small, open book in his hand, "come down from heaven" (10:1–2). John describes the angel's brilliant light and glory with four symbolic expressions: cloud, rainbow, sun, and fire. His greatness is emphasized with the expressions "mighty," "loud voice," and "as when a lion roareth" (10:1, 3). Although he is not identified by name, the angel is likely Michael, the seventh angel, who is second only to Jehovah himself in authority (see commentary on 10:1).

Emphasis is placed upon a "little book" that John is instructed to consume (it is mentioned four times: 10:2, 8, 9, 10). The book pertains to John's future work upon the earth, for he would yet prophesy to many of the earth's inhabitants.

Revelation 10:1–11

> 1 And I saw another mighty angel come down from heaven, clothed with a cloud: and a rainbow was upon his head, and his face was as it were the sun, and his feet as pillars of fire:
> 2 And he had in his [right][1] hand a little book open: and he set his right foot upon the sea, and his left foot on the earth,
> 3 And cried with a loud voice, as when a lion roareth: and when he had cried, seven thunders uttered their voices.

---

[1] The Greek reads *right hand* rather than *hand.*

4 And when the seven thunders had uttered their voices, I was about to write: and I heard a voice from heaven saying unto me, [Those things are sealed up][2] which the seven thunders uttered, and write them not.
5 And the angel which I saw stand upon the sea and upon the earth lifted up his hand to heaven,
6 And sware by him that liveth for ever and ever, who created heaven, and the things that therein are, and the earth, and the things that therein are, and the sea, and the things which are therein, that there should be time no longer:
7 But in the days of the voice of the seventh angel, when he shall begin to sound, the mystery of God should be finished, as he hath declared to his servants the prophets.
8 And the voice which I heard from heaven spake unto me again, and said, Go and take the little book which is open in the hand of the angel which standeth upon the sea and upon the earth.
9 And I went unto the angel, and said unto him, Give me the little book. And he said unto me, Take it, and eat it up; and it shall make thy belly bitter, but it shall be in thy mouth sweet as honey.
10 And I took the little book out of the angel's hand, and ate it up; and it was in my mouth sweet as honey: and as soon as I had eaten it, my belly was bitter.
11 And he said unto me, Thou must prophesy again before many peoples, and nations, and tongues, and kings.

NOTES AND COMMENTARY

10:1 *another mighty angel come down from heaven.* Three times in Revelation the angels are called "mighty" or "strong" (5:2; 10:1; 18:21). The "mighty angel" identified in this verse may be Michael, who is the chief angel, or archangel, and who stands next in authority to Jesus Christ himself.[3] Doctrine and Covenants 88:110–12 (see Dan. 12:7), which identifies Michael as the seventh angel, has some notable similarities with this section of Revelation (see Table 4).

---

[2] JST 10:4 changes the order of the words.
[3] *Teachings of the Prophet Joseph Smith,* 157–58.

Table 4

Revelation 10:1–7	Doctrine and Covenants 88:110–112
1 And I saw another mighty angel come down from heaven . . .	110 And so on, until the seventh angel shall sound his trump;
2 And he had in his hand a little book open: and he set his right foot **upon the sea**, and his left foot **on the earth . . .**	and he shall stand forth **upon the land** and **upon the sea,**
6 **And sware** by him that liveth for ever and ever, who created heaven, and the things that therein are, and the earth, and the things that therein are, and the sea, and the things which are therein**, that there should be time no longer**.	**and swear** in the name of him who sitteth upon the throne, **that there shall be time no longer**; and Satan shall be bound, that old serpent, who is called the devil, and shall not be loosed for the space of a thousand years.
7 But in the days of the voice of **the seventh angel**, when he shall begin to sound, the mystery of God should be finished, as he hath declared to his servants the prophets.	112 And Michael, **the seventh angel**, even the archangel, shall gather together his armies, even the hosts of heaven.

The similarities are striking, though we must note that Doctrine and Covenants 88:110–12 has a context different from Revelation 10:1–7.

clothed with a cloud. The mighty angel is wrapped in celestial glory (see D&C 84:5); he is clothed with glory as one wears a garment. Similarly, when Christ returns at his second coming, he will be "clothed with power and great glory" (D&C 45:44; 34:7).

rainbow was upon his head. The rainbow may refer to a glorious crown of light found upon the mighty angel's head, indicating his exalted station (4:3; Ezek. 1:28). It also suggests the Lord's covenant with Noah, signified by a rainbow, that He would again bring Zion to the earth (JST Gen. 9:21–23.)

face was as it were the sun. Like the face of Christ, whose "countenance shone above the brightness of the sun" (D&C 110:3), the mighty angel's face beams with celestial glory and brilliance.

feet as pillars of fire. The mighty angel's feet, like his body, head, and face, are likened to burning light and glory (see Dan. 10:6; Rev. 2:18).

10:2 *in his [right] hand a little book open.* This "book," or scroll, is not the same as that identified in Revelation 5:1–5, which is sealed with seven seals, for this book is described as "little" and "open" (the other book was sealed), and the angel (possibly Michael) has the book in his hand (no one but Jesus was permitted to touch the other book). The little book would be eaten by John, representing "a mission, and an ordinance, for him to gather the tribes of Israel; behold, this is Elias, who, as it is written, must come and restore all things" (D&C 77:14). See commentary on 10:8–11.

he set his right foot upon the sea/left foot on the earth. John speaks three times of the angel standing on sea and land (10:2, 5, 8). A similar expression is found in Doctrine and Covenants 88:110, where the order of "land" and "sea" is reversed. "Earth" and "sea" appear to indicate the total existence of the telestial world (Ex. 20:4, 11; Ps. 69:34). That the mighty angel has established one foot on the sea and a second on the earth may demonstrate that the telestial world is under his power and authority. It is not clear why the angel sets his right foot on the sea and his left on the earth and not the other way around.

10:3 *cried with a loud voice, as when a lion roareth.* The "loud voice" may be required so that a very large audience will hear the angel, as was the case in Revelation 7:9–10 and 8:13; or it may refer to the great authority of the angel, whose voice resembles the mighty voice of God himself, which is sometimes likened to a lion's roar (Hosea 11:10; Joel 3:16; Amos 1:2; 3:8).

seven thunders uttered their voices. The thunders are voices in heaven (6:1; 14:2; Mosiah 27:18) that respond to the loud voice of the angel. Compare the sevenfold "voice of the Lord" in Psalm 29:3. Elder Bruce R. McConkie suggests that "the seven thunders which here utter their voices are the seven angels reciting in some detail that which is to be in each of the thousand year periods of the earth's temporal continuance."[4]

Elder McConkie also provides another possible interpretation of the seven thunders: "It also appears that John's vision prefigured what is to be when the events occur and that the promised proclamations shall yet be made when the hour for Millennial peace actually arrives." Doctrine and

---

[4] McConkie, *Doctrinal New Testament Commentary,* 3:505.

Covenants 88:108–10 speaks of the seven angels, who each sound their trumps and "reveal the secret acts of men, and the thoughts and intents of their hearts, and the mighty works of God" (D&C 88:109) in each of the six thousand years of the earth's temporal existence.

10:4 *I was about to write.* John, who had previously been commanded to "write" the things of his vision (1:11, 19; 14:13; 19:9; 21:5), prepares to write the words uttered by the seven thunders. A voice from heaven stops him from writing these things and instead commands him to "seal up" the seven thunders' words and to "write them not." On other occasions, too, God has directed his prophets to "shut up the words, and seal the book" (Dan. 12:4; 2 Ne. 27:22; Ether 3:22–23, 27–28).

10:5 *the angel which I saw.* See commentary on 10:2.

stand upon the sea. See commentary on 7:1.

lifted up his hand to heaven. The mighty angel lifts his right hand (many translations read "right hand") to heaven, making the standard oath-taking gesture (Gen. 14:22; Deut. 32:40; Dan. 12:7). With one foot on the sea, the other on the land, and the right arm raised to the sky, the angel "touches the three parts of the universe because he is going to swear by him who created them."[5]

10:6 *sware by him that liveth for ever.* The language and the setting recall Daniel 12:4–7, in which Daniel sealed the book "even to the time of the end" (v. 4); he saw a "man clothed in linen, which was upon the waters of the river, when he held up his right hand and his left hand unto heaven, and sware by him that liveth for ever that it shall be for a time, times, and an half" (v. 7). In John's vision, however, the individual who stands on earth and sea swears that "there should be time no longer."

"Him that liveth for ever" is a name, or title, of God the Father (see commentary on 4:9; see also 5:14). The angel swears by using God's name, for there is no greater power and more exalted name. When God himself makes oaths with his people, he swears "by himself" because "he could swear by no greater" (Heb. 6:13). To emphasize that God is the most exalted of all, John writes that "him that liveth for ever and ever" is the same being who created heaven, earth, the sea, and all things that are found within them.

---

[5] Harrington, *Revelation,* 115.

there should be time no longer. The context of this phrase is the sounding of the seventh angel's trump, as recorded in the next verse, which reads, "When he shall begin to sound, the mystery of God should be finished" (10:7; see also D&C 88:106). This passage coincides with Revelation 11:15, when the seventh angel actually sounds his trumpet, signaling the end of the earth in its present state, or the time when the earthly kingdoms "become the kingdoms of our Lord, and of his Christ; and he shall reign for ever and ever."

In this setting, "time no longer" may refer to the beginning of the Millennium, when time as we understand it with our calendar, seasons, hours, minutes, and seconds no longer exists. This seems to be the manner in which two revelations use the phrase "time no longer": "The Lord hath redeemed his people; and Satan is bound and time is no longer. The Lord hath gathered all things in one. The Lord hath brought down Zion from above. The Lord hath brought up Zion from beneath" (D&C 84:100); and, "The seventh angel shall sound his trump; and he shall stand forth upon the land and upon the sea, and swear in the name of him who sitteth upon the throne, that there shall be time no longer; and Satan shall be bound, that old serpent, who is called the devil, and shall not be loosed for the space of a thousand years" (D&C 88:110).

The phrase could also mean "there should be no more delay," meaning that there will be no more delay before the final signs of the times are fulfilled and God sends his final judgments upon the wicked. This phrase answers the martyrs' question, "How long, O Lord, holy and true, dost thou not judge and avenge our blood on them that dwell on the earth?" (6:10).

10:7 *days of the voice of the seventh angel.* Michael, the seventh angel, sounds his trump at least twice and possibly on three different occasions (11:15; D&C 88:106, 110). This constitutes the "days of the voice of the seventh angel."

mystery of God should be finished. The "mystery of God" may pertain to the book with seven seals that "contains the revealed will, mysteries, and the works of God; the hidden things of his economy concerning this earth during the seven thousand years of its continuance, or its temporal existence" (D&C 77:6). This mystery will be finished "in the days of the voice of the seventh angel." Elsewhere the seventh angel is associated with completion, for the number seven signifies completion: when he pours out his vial, a voice from heaven says, "It is done" (16:17); and when he sounds his trump, he declares, "It is finished; it is finished!" (D&C 88:106; see also Rev. 11:15; D&C 88:110).

declared to his servants the prophets. The Lord has revealed the completion of God's mystery to many of his prophets, who are called the Lord's "servants" (2 Kgs. 17:23; Jer. 25:4; Dan. 9:10).

10:8 *voice which I heard from heaven spake unto me again.* This voice is the same that commanded John not to write the "things which the seven thunders uttered" (10:4). Here the voice commands John to take the little book from the hand of the mighty angel.

take the little book. Ezekiel and Lehi also received books from heavenly messengers (Ezek. 2:9; 1 Ne. 1:11). The command to John to eat the little book identified in Revelation 10:8–11 "was a mission, and an ordinance, for him to gather the tribes of Israel; behold, this is Elias, who, as it is written, must come and restore all things" (D&C 77:14). John's work among the tribes of Israel was confirmed with Joseph Smith's statement in June 1831 that "John the Revelator was then among the Ten Tribes of Israel who had been led away by Shalmaneser, king of Assyria, to prepare them for their return from their long dispersion, to again possess the land of their fathers."[6] In addition, John is an Elias;[7] he is identified in the revelations as one who, accompanying Peter and John, restored keys and powers to the earth through the Prophet Joseph Smith (D&C 27:12–13; 128:20).

angel which standeth upon the sea and upon the earth. See commentary on 10:2.

10:9 *I went unto the angel.* John approaches the angel to obtain the book.

eat it up. The angel commands John to eat the little book. This symbolic action has historical precedents, for Jeremiah declared unto the Lord, "Thy words were found, and I did eat them; and thy word was unto me the joy and rejoicing of mine heart" (Jer. 15:16). Ezekiel also received a book from a messenger who commanded him to "eat this [scroll], and go speak

---

[6] *History of the Church,* 1:176.
[7] The prophets spoke of Elias, who "must come and restore all things" (JST Matt. 11:15; 17:10–14; D&C 27:6–7). Joseph Fielding Smith explained that "the Elias who was to restore all things is a composite Elias. In other words, the restoration was not made by one personage, but many, and in speaking of Elias coming to restore all things, the Lord was using that title in a plural meaning, having in mind all the prophets who came to restore the fulness of the gospel. This would include John the Baptist, Peter, James and John, and every ancient prophet who restored keys from the days of Adam down." *Doctrines of Salvation,* 1:174.

unto the house of Israel. So I opened my mouth, and he caused me to eat that [scroll]. . . . Then did I eat it; and it was in my mouth as honey for sweetness" (Ezek. 3:1–3).

John partakes of God's word as contained in the little book, making it part of his soul, and he now fully understands his mission to gather the tribes of Israel.

10:9–10 *mouth sweet as honey/belly bitter.* The book is sweet when John eats it because feasting upon the word of God is always sweet, and John's mission to gather the tribes of Israel would bring joy and satisfaction to his soul. But the book is bitter in his belly because the message within the book described the woes and judgments that would come against the wicked world. Similarly, though Ezekiel's book was "as honey for sweetness," in it were "written lamentations, and mourning, and woe" (Ezek. 3:3; 2:10).

10:11 *Thou must prophesy again.* The angel who gave the book to John now promises John that he will "prophesy again before many people, and nations, and tongues, and kings." During His mortal ministry the Lord prophesied to John that he would "tarry until I come in my glory, and shalt prophesy before nations, kindreds, tongues and people" (D&C 7:3; see John 21:22–23). John thus became a translated being, "as flaming fire and a ministering angel," who would "minister for those who shall be heirs of salvation who dwell on the earth" (D&C 7:6). He "is yet alive in the flesh," explained Elder Parley P. Pratt, "and is held in reserve, to 'prophesy again before many peoples, and nations, and tongues, and kings,' as it is written."[8]

before many peoples, and nations, and tongues, and kings. John's work among the tribes of Israel (D&C 77:14) and among "those who shall be heirs of salvation" (D&C 7:6) may constitute, in part, the promise that he will "prophesy again before many peoples."

---

[8] Pratt, *Key to the Science of Theology,* 32.

REVELATION
11

TWO PROPHETS PROPHESY, WORK MIRACLES, AND ARE KILLED (11:1–14)

Again the Lord provides the righteous with hope, peace of mind, and security during the trials and tribulations of the last days. In Revelation 7:1–8 we learn of the sealing of individuals to protect them from future judgments and plagues; here we read that John measures the Saints with a measuring rod, thus protecting them from some future trials. The actions preceding the sounding of the seventh trumpet (which sounds in 11:15) are similar to the actions preceding the opening of the seventh seal (7:1–8): both serve to secure the Saints.

The principal theme of Revelation 11 is the work and ministry of two prophets who will minister in the last days in Jerusalem. Elder Parley P. Pratt summarized these events: "[John] informs us that, after the city and temple are rebuilt by the Jews, the Gentiles will tread it under foot forty and two months, during which time there will be two Prophets continually prophesying and working mighty miracles. And it seems that the Gentile army shall be hindered from utterly destroying and overthrowing the city, while these two Prophets continue. But, after a struggle of three years and a half, they at length succeed in destroying these two Prophets, and then overrunning much of the city, they send gifts to each other because of the death of the two Prophets, and in the meantime will not allow their dead bodies to be put in the graves, but suffer them to lie in the streets of Jerusalem three days and a half."[1]

---

[1] Pratt, *Voice of Warning*, 41–42.

The two prophets will prophesy "at the time of the restoration" (D&C 77:15), after the Jews "are gathered and have built the city of Jerusalem" (D&C 77:15), after the opening of the seventh seal but before the Second Coming (D&C 77:12–13), and during the events of the second woe (11:3–14). They will prophesy for 1,260 days, or three and one-half years.

Their mission will have several purposes: to "prophesy to the Jews" (D&C 77:15), to serve as "witnesses" of God and his judgments, to symbolically provide oil unto those who are preparing for Christ's coming, to work many great miracles, and to bear testimony.

They will receive power from God to prophesy, and they will be clothed in sackcloth, which symbolizes the great power possessed by the Old Testament prophets. They will have power to devour "their enemies" with fire; to "shut heaven, that it rain not"; to turn waters to blood; and to smite the earth with plagues according to their will.

The two prophets will minister in Jerusalem (D&C 77:15), where they will be killed, for "Satan shall slay them, by the hands of those in his employ, even as he slew their Lord and the prophets who were before them."[2]

There will be two prophets in order to establish God's word with more than one testimony: "In the mouth of two or three witnesses shall every word be established" (2 Cor. 13:1).

Many of the events connected to the sacred work of the two prophets recall events of the mortal ministry of Jesus Christ: the duration of their three-and-one-half year ministry, their prophesying, their working great miracles, and their control over the elements. In addition, the two prophets, like Jesus, will be anointed with oil and will be slain in Jerusalem by evil men—acts which will be followed by an ascension into heaven.

Revelation 11:1–14

1 And there was given me a reed like unto a rod: and the angel stood, saying, Rise, and measure the temple of God, and the altar, and them that worship therein.
2 But the court which is without the temple leave out, and measure it not; for it is given unto the Gentiles: and the holy city shall they tread under foot forty and two months.
3 And I will give power unto my two witnesses, and they shall prophesy a thousand two hundred and threescore days, clothed in sackcloth.

---

[2] McConkie, *Doctrinal New Testament Commentary,* 3:510.

4 These are the two olive trees, and the two candlesticks standing before the God of the earth.

5 And if any man will hurt them, fire proceedeth out of their mouth, and devoureth their enemies: and if any man will hurt them, he must in this manner be killed.

6 These have power to shut heaven, that it rain not in the days of their prophecy: and have power over waters to turn them to blood, and to smite the earth with all plagues, as often as they will.

7 And when they shall have finished their testimony, the beast that ascendeth out of the bottomless pit shall make war against them, and shall overcome them, and kill them.

8 And their dead bodies shall lie in the street of the great city, which [allegorically]³ is called Sodom and Egypt, where also our Lord was crucified.

9 And they of the people and kindreds and tongues and nations shall see their dead bodies three days and an half, and shall not suffer their dead bodies to be put in graves.

10 And they that dwell upon the earth shall rejoice over them, and make merry, and shall send gifts one to another; because these two prophets tormented them that dwelt on the earth.

11 And after three days and an half the Spirit of life from God entered into them, and they stood upon their feet; and great fear fell upon them which saw them.

12 And they heard a great voice from heaven saying unto them, Come up hither.

And they ascended up to heaven in a cloud; and their enemies beheld them.

13 And the same hour was there a great earthquake, and the tenth part of the city fell, and in the earthquake were slain of men seven thousand: and the remnant were affrighted, and gave glory to the God of heaven.

14 The second woe is past; and, behold, the third woe cometh quickly.

NOTES AND COMMENTARY

11:1 *reed like unto a rod.* A heavenly being hands John a long reed, or stick, to use as a measuring tool, and tells him to measure the temple, its altar, and the worshippers. Similarly, a "golden reed" is used to measure the wall and gates of the celestial temple (21:15), and the future temple of Jerusalem is measured with a "measuring reed" (Ezek. 40:3, 5–8; 41:8; 42:16–20) that is six cubits (about ten feet) in length.

the angel stood. Some Greek texts omit this phrase.⁴

Rise, and measure. John is told to go and measure, just as a carpenter measures before constructing or repairing. The things that John measures (the temple, the altar, and the worshippers) are established by God, or

---

³According to the reading provided by Harrington, *Revelation,* 122. The Greek word is *pneumatikos.*

⁴See note *b* to 11:1 in the LDS edition of the KJV.

protected from his judgments; they are not slated for destruction; the outer court and beyond, which have not been measured, will be affected by his judgments. John is commanded to perform a symbolic action that anticipates our own day: the temple and altar and worshippers represent the faithful, or Zion; the outer court represents the unfaithful and unbelieving, or the world. "What is thus measured is under God's special protection, as in Ezekiel and in Zechariah"[5] (see also Ezek. 40–42; Zech. 2:1–2).

Perhaps the measuring of the temple, the altar, and worshippers symbolizes "taking the measure" of worthiness to partake of blessings of the Atonement. Kenneth Strand, a New Testament scholar, points out parallels between Revelation 11:1 and Leviticus 16:6, 11, 16–18 (Leviticus 16 speaks about the Day of Atonement[6]): "It is striking . . . that the three other exact entities to be atoned for in Leviticus 16 [temple, altar, and worshipers] are precisely those three elements to be 'measured' in Rev 11:1."[7]

The term *measure* also has another application in the scriptures. In contrast to the measuring of God's righteous people, the scriptures speak of the destruction of the wicked "without measure," meaning to the fullest extent. "When the wrath of God shall be poured out upon the wicked without measure" (D&C 1:9); "mine indignation is soon to be poured out without measure upon all nations; and this will I do when the cup of their iniquity is full" (D&C 101:11; see also 109:45).

temple of God. The Greek word used here for temple is *naos,* which refers to the sanctuary itself, namely the Holy Place and the Most Holy Place, not the outer courts. This temple was not Herod's temple, which had been destroyed in A.D. 70, more than twenty years before John is instructed to "measure" the temple. This temple may be the temple that will yet be built in Jerusalem in the last days, as the prophets have declared. Ezekiel, for instance, saw and described in some detail this temple in Ezekiel 40 through 46. Joseph Smith also spoke of the future temple: "Judah must return, Jerusalem must be rebuilt, and the temple, and water come out from under the temple, and the waters of the Dead Sea be healed. It will take some time to rebuild the walls of the city and the temple."[8]

---

[5] Harrington, *Revelation,* 119.
[6] See LDS Bible Dictionary, 671, s.v. "fasts."
[7] Strand, "Overlooked Old Testament Background," 322.
[8] *Teachings of the Prophet Joseph Smith,* 286.

The phrase "temple of God" also has a symbolic meaning. Paul likened the Saints to a temple when he asked, "Know ye not that ye are the temple of God?" (1 Cor. 3:16). Later Paul wrote, "Ye are the temple of the living God" (2 Cor. 6:16). On another occasion he likened Christ to the chief cornerstone and the apostles and prophets to the building's foundation. The Saints, together with the apostles and prophets, are "an holy temple in the Lord" (Eph. 2:19–21). That is to say, the community of Saints, speaking of those who attend the temple and worship within its walls, constitute a temple of God. These are "measured" by John and receive protection from the coming judgments.

altar. This altar may refer to the altar of incense or to the great altar of sacrifice. In our day this altar refers to the sacred altars of our temples and those who surround them or kneel at them for sacred ordinances. The ordinances and the keeping of covenants associated with them protect the Saints from God's judgments.

them that worship therein. John measures temple worshippers, speaking of the Saints who worship in our temples today, to ensure their protection from God's wrath and judgments.

11:2 *court . . . without the temple . . . measure it not.* The temple in John's day had many courts; the court mentioned here may have been the court of the Gentiles. In reference to our temples today, "court" probably refers to those who do not enter and worship in God's temples, for John is commanded to "measure it not," leaving this court and its inhabitants unprotected and unsanctified (JST Ezek. 44:19; 46:20).

it is given unto the Gentiles: and the holy city shall they tread under foot. The Gentiles will trample the holy city for forty-two months. Both the old Jerusalem (Neh. 11:1; Isa. 52:1; 2 Ne. 8:24; Ether 13:5) and the New Jerusalem (21:10; D&C 133:56; Moses 7:62) are called "holy city," but here the context seems to refer only to Jerusalem.

According to Luke 21:24, "Jerusalem shall be trodden down of the Gentiles, until the times of the Gentiles be fulfilled"[9] (see also Isa. 63:18; Dan. 8:13). To trample or tread upon includes showing contempt for sacred things and to persecute, even destroy, others. The phrase "it is given" suggests that God will allow this oppression but only for a set period of time.

---

[9] The "times of the Gentiles" refers to that era when the Gentiles, rather than the Jews, are the primary recipients of the gospel. See *Discourses of Wilford Woodruff,* 132; Smith, *Restoration of All Things,* 164; McConkie, *Mortal Messiah,* 1:97n.

forty and two months. The number forty-two often signifies the period when righteousness is cut short and the wicked dominate the righteous. There will be a period in the last days when evil will reign. Even the powerful prophets of God (the two witnesses in the next verse) will be destroyed. Evil will win for the moment—but only until God's full power is unleashed.

The number forty-two is manifest scripturally in several ways, each of which equals three and one-half:

Daniel 7:25 speaks of "a time and times and the dividing of time." A "time" equals one year, "times" equal two years, and a "half" equals half a year, based on the Hebrew calendar of thirty days per month.[10] The total time is three and one-half years. A wicked king will blaspheme God and persecute the Saints for this time period (see Dan. 7:25).

Daniel 9:27 speaks of the "midst [middle] of the week." Half a week, or three and a half days, may perhaps signify years (Ezek. 4:6; Num. 14:34). Daniel prophesies that temple sacrifices will cease for this period of time (see Dan. 9:27).

Daniel 12:7, which speaks of "time, times, and an half," indicates that during this period the wicked will "scatter the power of the holy people."

Revelation 11:2 records that "forty and two months," or three and one-half years, is the length of time the Gentiles will tread the holy city.

Revelation 11:3 speaks of "a thousand two hundred and threescore days," which is another way of saying three and one-half years, or forty-two months. That is the same length of time as that spoken of in 11:2; it is also the period of time that the two prophets will prophesy before they are killed. Moreover, if we use that number with years rather than days, as in the Joseph Smith Translation rendering of Revelation 12:5, "a thousand two hundred and threescore years," we have the period of the Great Apostasy (see commentary on 12:5).

Revelation 12:14 uses the expression "a time, and times, and half a time" as another way of describing the period of the Great Apostasy.

Revelation 11:11 gives "three days and an half" as the period during which the bodies of the two prophets will lie in the streets.

Revelation 13:5 records "forty and two months," or three and one-half years, as the duration of the beast's evil activity.

---

[10] Durham, "Revelation," 26.

Forty-two months, or three and one-half, or 1,260, belong to the wicked and apparently signify their work; the number three and one-half may mean that the work of righteousness is cut short. That number is one-half of seven, the number of perfection and completion, which belongs to God and his Saints. We recall that the number seven is used symbolically many times in Revelation with regard to God and his work: "seven churches" (1:4), "seven servants" (JST 1:4), "seven golden candlesticks" (1:12), "seven stars" (1:20), "seven lamps of fire" (4:5), "seven seals" (5:5), "seven angels" with their "seven trumpets" (8:6), "seven thunders" (10:3), "seven last plagues" (15:1), and "seven vials" (17:1).[11]

Further, "the root of the Hebrew word for seven (*sheva*) is identical to the Hebrew verb that means 'to take an oath,' thus connecting the word *seven* to covenants and covenant making."[12] One-half of seven, or three and one-half, represents an incomplete covenant (religious systems that appear to be spiritual and to possess power but do not) or the broken covenant (apostate conditions).

11:3 *I will give power.* The Greek text omits the word *power*,[13] but it is clear from the context of this verse that the two witnesses will have great power indeed.

my two witnesses. The two witnesses are "two prophets that are to be raised up to the Jewish nation in the last days, at the time of the restoration, and to prophesy to the Jews after they are gathered and have built the city of Jerusalem in the land of their fathers" (D&C 77:15). Why two? Ancient Israelite law required two witnesses for testimony to be valid (Deut. 17:6; 19:15). The law of witnesses remains in effect today (D&C 6:28; 42:80–81).

They are called witnesses because they will bear testimony of Jesus Christ and his latter-day work. Revelation 11:10 calls the two witnesses "two prophets," indicating that they will have the powers and authority of prophets; Joseph Smith's translation of Isaiah 51:19 refers to them as "two sons," perhaps suggesting that they are sons of Abraham, whether literally or by covenant; Zechariah 4:3 calls them "two olive trees," indicating that

[11] Satan often attempts to counterfeit the things of God. For an illustration of Satan's use of the number seven in this way, see 12:3.
[12] McConkie and Parry, *Guide to Scriptural Symbols,* 99.
[13] Note *a* to 11:3 in the LDS edition of the KJV.

they possess oil and light (see commentary on 11:4); and Zechariah 4:14 calls them "two anointed ones."

prophesy a thousand two hundred and threescore days. The two prophets will prophesy for three and one-half years, the same length of time that the Gentiles will tread under foot the holy city. Perhaps these two events—the prophesying of the two prophets and the treading of the Gentiles—will occur at the same time. The Jerusalem Bible says that the Gentiles "will trample on the holy city for forty-two months. But I shall send my two witnesses to prophesy for those twelve hundred and sixty days" (11:2–3). It must be noted, however, that since this is a symbolic number, the time frame may not be exact.

clothed in sackcloth. The two prophets will likely not actually wear sackcloth, but sackcloth signifies that they will possess the same prophetic powers and authority to teach, warn, prophesy, and perform mighty miracles as did such ancient prophets as Moses, Elijah, and Isaiah (1 Kgs. 17; Isa. 20:2–4).

11:4 *two olive trees, and . . . two candlesticks.* The imagery of olive trees recalls the book of Zechariah, in which he asks an angel, "What are these two olive trees upon the right side of the candlestick and upon the left side thereof?" The angel's response indicates that the two prophets have been anointed with holy oil in the Lord's temple: "These are the two anointed ones, that stand by the Lord of the whole earth" (Zech. 4:11, 14).

Zechariah's images of a bowl, golden pipes, oil, olive branches, and seven lamps (Zech. 4:2–14) seem to say that the two prophets, as olive trees, will help "provide oil for the lamps of those who go forth to meet the Bridegroom."[14]

The two prophets will be like candlesticks holding up the light of Christ to shine in the darkness. Some will see the light, recognize their "good works," and "glorify [their] Father which is in heaven" (Matt. 5:16). Some will recognize Jesus through the prophets' testimony: "Therefore, hold up your light that it may shine unto the world. Behold I am the light which ye shall hold up—that which ye have seen me do" (3 Ne. 18:24).

standing before the God of the earth. This phrase recalls Zechariah 4:14: "two anointed ones, that stand by the Lord of the whole earth." The expression "standing before God" seems to place the two witnesses in a

---

[14] McConkie, *Doctrinal New Testament Commentary,* 3:510.

temple setting, as does Zechariah 4. Menahem Haran wrote: "In general, any [religious] activity to which the biblical text applies the formula 'before the Lord' can be considered an indication of the existence of a temple . . . this expression . . . actually belongs to the temple's technical terminology."[15]

11:5 *if any man will hurt them, fire proceedeth out of their mouth.* The two prophets will possess great power, similar to that of Moses (Num. 16:23–35) and Elijah (2 Kgs 1:10–14), to call upon heaven and cause fire to consume those who attempt to hurt them or to hinder their work. The two will call upon God with their mouth, and God will respond by sending the consuming fire. Although there are two witnesses, the singular "mouth" is used ("their mouth"), perhaps indicating that their message will be united.[16]

11:6 *power to shut heaven, that it rain not.* The two prophets will possess the sealing power whereby they perform great miracles among the people, including closing of the skies so that it does not rain and thus causing famine in the land. When such occurs, the land does not "yield . . . her fruit," and the people begin to "perish quickly from off the good land" (Deut. 11:17). The prophet Elijah from Gilead also "prayed earnestly" (James 5:17) and shut heaven, causing a great famine in the land. He promised King Ahab, "As the Lord God of Israel liveth, before whom I stand, there shall not be dew nor rain these years, but according to my word" (1 Kgs 17:1). Elijah's prophecy was fulfilled, and "heaven was shut up three years and six months, when great famine was throughout all the land" (Luke 4:25).

Many during mortality have held power over earth's waters, including Enoch (Moses 7:13; JST Gen. 14:30), Moses (Moses 1:25; Hel. 8:11), Jesus Christ (Mark 4:39), and others (D&C 61:27). God, of course, is the power behind these miracles (Ether 4:9).

to smite the earth with all plagues. Doctrine and Covenants 84:97 promises, "And plagues shall go forth, and they shall not be taken from the earth until I have completed my work, which shall be cut short in righteousness" (see also D&C 43:25). The plagues that will occur at the command of the two prophets are similar to those spoken of in Exodus when

---

[15] Haran, *Temples and Temple Service,* 26.
[16] So suggests Ford, *Revelation,* 171.

Moses, through the power of God, smote the land of Egypt with numerous plagues (Ex. 7–10). The two prophets' plagues may be the same as the seven plagues of the seven angels (Rev. 15:1, 6, 8); at least, the prophets' plagues anticipate and perhaps foreshadow the great plagues that will be poured out of the bowls (vials) identified in Revelation 16.

as often as they will. This phrase suggests that the prophets will conduct miracles as necessity demands, which may be frequently during their three-and-one-half-year ministry.

11:7 *finished their testimony.* God will protect the two prophets until they complete their mission; then he will permit them to be killed. Their testimony will focus on Jesus Christ (19:10).[17]

beast that ascendeth out of the bottomless pit. The bottomless pit was discussed in Revelation 9:1–2. The beast identified here may be the same as the beast identified in Revelation 13:1–8.

shall make war against them . . . and kill them. Satan and his followers have always made war with the righteous (see, for example, 12:17). The beast will war against the two prophets (possibly with the aid of "kings of the earth, and their armies," 19:19) and succeed in killing them. That the beast is making war against only two individuals underscores the tremendous power the two will hold—power greater than that of the armies of the earth. The beast and his followers will also "make war" against others (13:7), including Jesus Christ, but Jesus will "overcome them: for he is Lord of lords, and King of kings" (17:14; see also 19:11, 19).

11:8 *their dead bodies shall lie in the street.* The two prophets' bodies will lie in the street for three and one half days while the people of the earth rejoice and send gifts to one another (11:9–10). Allowing the dead to lie in view of their enemies was considered extremely disrespectful in ancient times (see Ps. 79:3–4; 2 Macc. 5:10). Joseph Smith taught, "It has always been considered a great calamity not to obtain an honorable burial: and one of the greatest curses the ancient prophets could put on any man, was that he should go without a burial."[18]

great city, which [allegorically] is called Sodom and Egypt. Jerusalem is called the "great city" (see D&C 77:15), "where also our Lord was crucified." Jerusalem is allegorically called "Sodom" (Isa. 1:10; 3:9) and

---

[17] *History of the Church,* 5:215–16; 3:389.
[18] *History of the Church,* 5:361.

"Egypt" because of the wickedness of her inhabitants. Sodom, we recall, was destroyed for her abominations and gross wickedness (Ezek. 16:49– 50; Jude 1:7), and Egypt, called "the basest of the kingdoms" (Ezek. 29:15), symbolizes worldliness and oppression of the Lord's people.

Babylon is also called the "great city" (14:8; 18:21), implying that "great city" symbolizes all of earth's cities that contain iniquitous and god- less people who war against the Lamb and his witnesses. One commentator writes that the "great city" is "every city that embodies self-sufficiency in place of dependence on the creator, achievement in place of repentance, oppression in place of faith, the beast in place of the Lamb, and murder in place of witness to God."[19]

11:9 *they of the people and kindreds and tongues and nations.* This expression signifies totality of people and indicates that the worldwide community will be involved, at least emotionally, in the slaying of the two prophets. See commentary on 5:9.

see their dead bodies three days and an half. The two prophets' bodies will lie in a highly visible place for all to see. The time of three and one- half days corresponds to the time that Jesus' body rested in the tomb ("after three days rise again," Mark 8:31; 9:31; 10:34). Perhaps more importantly, this period also parallels the number that belongs to the wicked, the cutting short of righteousness. See commentary on 11:2.

not suffer their dead bodies to be put in graves. See commentary on 11:8.

11:10 *they that dwell upon the earth.* This expression denotes was the "people and kindreds and tongues and nations" spoken of in 11:9.

shall rejoice over them, and make merry, and shall send gifts one to another. Earth's inhabitants celebrate and gloat over the death of the two prophets, who had "tormented them" by bringing forth famine and plagues and who had testified of Jesus Christ (see 11:5–7). This celebration indi- cates the gross darkness that belongs to the wicked during this period; not satisfied with the spilling of the blood of God's witnesses and leaving their bodies in the streets for all to see, they will also party, revel over their deaths, and exchange gifts. The wicked will feel they have won the victory.

11:11 *after three days and an half.* See commentary on 11:9.

---

[19] Krodel, *Revelation,* 226.

Spirit of life from God entered into them, and they stood upon their feet. These phrases recall the promise of the resurrection to the house of Israel in Ezekiel 37:10: "And the breath came into them, and they lived, and stood up upon their feet."

great fear fell upon them which saw them. Zophar taught that "the triumphing of the wicked is short" (Job 20:5), and indeed, the revelers have only three-and-one-half days to celebrate the prophets' death before they experience great terror as they witness them come back to life (Matt. 28:4).

11:12 *they heard a great voice from heaven.* The voice of a heavenly being instructs the two witnesses to "come up hither." This is the dramatic moment when God bares his arm before the nation and begins to bring an end to the rule of evil. Death is the ultimate tool of evil—what happens when even that power is removed? All others will be destroyed as well, leaving the wicked completely powerless.

they ascended up to heaven in a cloud. The prophets' ascension into heaven in a cloud parallels the ascension into heaven of both Elijah and the Lord (2 Kgs 2:11; Acts 1:9).

11:13 *same hour was there a great earthquake.* A "great earthquake" coincides with the opening of the sixth seal (6:12), and another "great earthquake" occurs after the seventh angel pours out his bowl (16:17–18). The earthquake identified here accompanies the prophets' ascension into heaven and serves as another testimony, subsequent to the testimony of the two prophets, that God lives (see D&C 88:87–89; see also commentary on 6:12).

tenth part of the city fell. The earthquake causes great destruction to the city's buildings, roads, and other structures.

were slain of men seven thousand. The earthquake destroys a great number of individuals, represented here as "seven thousand."

the remnant . . . gave glory to the God of heaven. To give glory to God, at the very least, is to acknowledge his hand in the resurrection and ascension of the two witnesses and in the earthquake (16:9; 3 Ne. 20:9; D&C 88:104; 133:38).

11:14 *second woe is past.* See commentary on 8:13.

THE SEVENTH TRUMPET SOUNDS AND
TWENTY-FOUR ELDERS WORSHIP GOD (11:15–19)

Three major events occur when Michael, the archangel, blows the seventh trumpet: heavenly voices declare the eternal kingship and reign of God and Jesus, the twenty-four elders fall on their faces and worship God, and the heavenly temple is opened for all of God's Saints to enter.

As the seventh seal includes the events connected to the seven trumpets, so the seventh trumpet seems to include the events connected with the seven vials (bowls, or seven last plagues). "The seventh trumpet . . . embraces the whole of the seven vials, or last seven plagues, which make up the 'third woe.'"[20]

Revelation 11:15–19

15 And the seventh angel sounded; and there were great voices in heaven, saying, The kingdoms of this world are become the [kingdom][21] of our Lord, and of his Christ; and he shall reign for ever and ever.
16 And the four and twenty elders, which sat before God on their seats, fell upon their faces, and worshipped God,
17 Saying, We give thee thanks, O Lord God Almighty, which art, and wast, and art to come; because thou hast taken to thee thy great power, and hast reigned.
18 And the nations were angry, and thy wrath is come, and the time of the dead, that they should be judged, and that thou shouldest give reward unto thy servants the prophets, and to the saints, and them that fear thy name, small and great; and shouldest destroy them which destroy the earth.
19 And the temple of God was opened in heaven, and there was seen in his temple the ark of his testament: and there were lightnings, and voices, and thunderings, and an earthquake, and great hail.

NOTES AND COMMENTARY

11:15 *seventh angel sounded.* "Michael, the seventh angel, even the archangel" (D&C 88:112), blows his trump.

there were great voices in heaven. The voices are not identified, but they may belong to the twenty-four elders, the four living creatures, or the great multitude of exalted souls in heaven. See commentary on 4:5.

kingdoms of this world. The world's kingdoms are like wild beasts, who have no owner or master and are untamed, uncivilized, and often

---

[20] Bullinger, *Commentary,* 369.
[21] JST 11:15 changes the plural *kingdoms* to the singular *kingdom.*

bloodthirsty. Joseph Smith explained: "You there see that the beasts [in Daniel 7:16] are spoken of to represent the kingdoms of the world, the inhabitants whereof were beastly and abominable characters; they were murderers, corrupt, carnivorous, and brutal in their dispositions. The lion, the bear, the leopard, and the ten-horned beast represented the kingdoms of the world, says Daniel."[22]

When Christ, the Lamb of God, comes in great power and glory, he will destroy these beasts, or earthly kingdoms, and establish his perfect kingdom, for he has promised, "I will be your ruler when I come" (D&C 41:4). At that time "the Lord shall be king over all the earth: in that day shall there be one Lord, and his name one" (Zech. 14:9), and he will make "a full end of all nations" (D&C 87:6).

Daniel envisioned these things: "I beheld till the thrones were cast down . . . and there was given [the Son of Man] dominion, and glory, and a kingdom, that all people, nations, and languages, should serve him: his dominion is an everlasting dominion, which shall not pass away, and his kingdom that which shall not be destroyed" (Dan. 7:9, 14).

he shall reign for ever. The tenth Article of Faith states that "Christ will reign personally upon the earth." Also, "the Lord, even the Savior, shall stand in the midst of his people, and shall reign over all flesh" (D&C 133:25).

11:16 *four and twenty elders . . . fell upon their faces, and worshipped God.* Four times John sees the elders "fall down" to worship God, who "sat on the throne" (4:10; 5:14; 11:16; 19:4), and once he observes them as they "fell down before the Lamb" (5:8).

11:17 *We give thee thanks.* In Revelation 4:9 the four living creatures who are located near God's throne give thanks to God; in Revelation 7:12 the angels who stand before God say "thanksgiving" to God; and here the twenty-four elders state, "We give thee thanks, O Lord God Almighty."

Lord God Almighty. This title of God, also used by Jacob (2 Ne. 9:46), describes God's supreme power to reign upon the earth, "because thou hast taken to thee thy great power, and hast reigned." That power was made manifest by God's triumph in raising the two prophets from the dead. Evil had appeared to triumph, but God turned seeming defeat into glorious

---

[22] *Teachings of the Prophet Joseph Smith,* 289.

victory. Do what they will, the powers of evil cannot frustrate the purposes of God— he alone is almighty.

which art, and wast, and art to come. See commentary on 1:4.

11:18 *the nations were angry, and thy wrath is come.* Psalm 2 helps us understand this section of Revelation. The psalmist wrote: "Why do the heathen rage? The kings of the earth set themselves, and the rulers take counsel together, against the Lord, and against his anointed" (Ps. 2:1–2; 46:6). That is to say, the nations are angry and they and their leaders continually war against God and Jesus Christ. The psalmist prophesies that the Lord will become the earth's king and ruler and receive as a possession "the uttermost parts of the earth" (Ps. 2:8).

The Lord's wrath ("thy wrath is come") is also mentioned in Psalm 2, where the psalmist writes that the Lord shall "speak unto them [the heathen] in his wrath, and vex them in his sore displeasure" (Ps. 2:5). Modern revelations also speak of the Lord's wrath: "Hearken, O ye people who profess my name, saith the Lord your God; for behold, mine anger is kindled against the rebellious, and they shall know mine arm and mine indignation, in the day of visitation and of wrath upon the nations" (D&C 56:1); and "with the sword and by bloodshed the inhabitants of the earth shall mourn; and with famine, and plague, and earthquake, and the thunder of heaven, and the fierce and vivid lightning also, shall the inhabitants of the earth be made to feel the wrath, and indignation, and chastening hand of an Almighty God, until the consumption decreed hath made a full end of all nations" (D&C 87:6).

time of the dead, that they should be judged. The first resurrection pertains to the prophets and Saints of God (20:4–5): "For the day cometh that the Lord shall utter his voice out of heaven; the heavens shall shake and the earth shall tremble, and the trump of God shall sound both long and loud, and shall say to the sleeping nations: Ye saints arise and live; ye sinners stay and sleep until I shall call again" (D&C 43:18; 29:12–13). Later, John will witness the "dead, small and great, stand before God; and the books were opened . . . and the dead were judged out of those things which were written in the books, according to their works" (20:12–13).

give reward unto thy servants the prophets, and to the saints. God's reward to his prophets and Saints is thus described: "And thus we saw the glory of the celestial, which excels in all things—where God, even the Father, reigns upon his throne forever and ever; before whose throne all things bow in humble reverence, and give him glory forever and ever. They who dwell in his presence are the church of the Firstborn; and they see as they are seen, and know as they are known, having received of his fulness and of his grace; and he makes them equal in power, and in might, and in dominion" (D&C 76:92–95).

small and great. Individuals from all walks of life, both prophets and Saints, who "fear," or reverence, God's name will receive an eternal reward (D&C 138:14–15).

destroy them which destroy the earth. Those who belong to Babylon, whose citizens worship the beast and have received his mark in their foreheads or hands (20:4), have sought to destroy the earth's inhabitants. Jesus Christ will destroy these destroyers and "every corruptible thing, both of man, or of the beasts of the field, or of the fowls of the heavens, or of the fish of the sea" (D&C 101:24). Note that Jesus comes to save the earth from those who would destroy it. Even the Second Coming is an act of salvation.

11:19 *temple of God was opened in heaven.* The celestial kingdom, called the "temple of heaven" (16:17; 14:17), is opened to receive the Saints who are resurrected, judged (11:18), and found worthy to enter. See commentary on 21:22.

ark of his testament. This expression refers to the ark of the testimony (also called ark of the covenant), which rested in the Israelite temple's holy of holies, into which only the high priest was permitted to enter "once every year" (Heb. 9:7). The ark was a box that held three sacred items symbolically connected to Jesus Christ's power and atonement—Aaron's rod, the pot of manna, and the tablets of the law (Heb. 9:4).[23] The lid, or covering, of the ark served as Jehovah's "seat of atonement,"[24] or "mercy seat"; it was situated between two large, gold cherubim. John's statement that "there was seen in his temple the ark of his testimony" indicates that all exalted Saints, not just the high priest of the earthly temple, will be privileged to gain access to Jesus Christ and his sacred, heavenly dwelling.

lightnings, and voices, and thunderings, and an earthquake, and great hail. See commentary on 4:5.

---

[23] For details on these items, and their connection with Christ and his atonement, see McConkie and Parry, *Guide to Scriptural Symbols,* 76–77, 81, 94.
[24] McConkie and Parry, *Guide to Scriptural Symbols,* 82–83.

REVELATION
12

THE WOMAN AND THE DRAGON (12:1–17)

The kingdom of God (the child) is born through the instrumentality of the Church (the woman). Once the kingdom is born, Satan (the dragon) and his followers make war against it, seeking to destroy it. To protect them from the attacks of Satan, the Lord removes both the Church and the kingdom of God from the earth.

This great battle was begun in premortality and was continued in the Garden of Eden: There the woman faced the serpent, learned that she would bring forth in anguish, and was told that her child would be attacked by Satan (Gen. 3:1, 15–16). The battle was renewed in the time of Christ and his apostles, when Satan attacked the Church with great vigor (1 Ne. 11:32–35). The battle continues to this day as our adversary, in his wrath, makes war with all those who "keep the commandments of God, and have the testimony of Jesus Christ" (12:17).

Revelation 12 may be divided into three parts. First, verses 1 through 5 appear to depict the establishment of the Church in the meridian of time and the beginning of the Great Apostasy. Second, verses 6 through 11 show us the war in heaven between Satan and his followers and the Lord and his followers. This war gives heightened understanding of the war between Satan and the righteous on the earth—and the outcome of the heavenly war gives us confidence that the Saints will prevail. Third, verses 12 through 17 return to the theme of the persecution of the meridian Church and the Great Apostasy that followed.

In Revelation 12 through 14, the Lord seems to be setting the stage for the great tribulations and final triumph described in the final chapters of the book. He introduces the primary players in those last events—the Church and kingdom of God, Satan, the wicked earthly kingdoms, the powerful followers of Satan, and the Lord and his angels. And he introduces the theme that will be portrayed: Satan, having been cast down from heaven to earth, will rule in terror; Satan's kingdom will eventually fail; and the Lord and his kingdom will triumph.

One commentator has written perceptively that Revelation 12 reveals "to the believing community the ultimate cause for the increased opposition and hostility they will meet in the last days. Beyond that the visions in chapter 12 form the theological heart of the entire book. In Christ, God engaged Satan in the ultimate battle of the Holy War. The redemptive triumph of Christ in his death and resurrection was the crucial defeat of Satan and the forces of evil. Yet for a time the dragon vigorously pursues the people of God. Hence there is great suffering in the final days (which extend from Pentecost to the return of Christ)."[1]

Revelation 12:1–17

1 And there appeared a great [sign in heaven, in the likeness of things on the earth];[2] a woman clothed with the sun, and the moon under her feet, and upon her head a crown of twelve stars.
2 And [the woman][3] being with child,[4] cried, travailing in birth, and pained to be delivered.
3 And she brought forth a man child, who was to rule all nations with a rod of iron; and her child was caught up unto God and . . .[5] his throne.[6]
4 And there appeared another [sign][7] in heaven; and behold, a great red dragon, having seven heads and ten horns, and seven crowns upon his heads. And his tail drew the third part of the stars of heaven, and did cast them to the earth. And the dragon stood before the woman which was . . . delivered, [ready] to devour her child [after] it was born.[8]
5 And the woman fled into the wilderness, where she [had] a place prepared of God, that they should feed her there a thousand two hundred and threescore [years].[9]

---

[1] Mounce, *Book of Revelation,* 230.
[2] JST 12:1 changes this from the KJV *wonder in heaven.*
[3] JST 12:2 changes this from the KJV *she.*
[4] This chapter of the JST makes a number of punctuation changes that have not been noted in brackets.
[5] KJV says *and to;* the change is from JST 12:3.
[6] The JST puts this verse here; the KJV puts it as verse 5.
[7] JST 12:4 changes this from the KJV *wonder.*
[8] This change is from the JST. Verse 4 in the KJV reads, " . . . the woman which was ready to be delivered, for to devour her child as soon as it was born."
[9] Changes in this verse are from JST 12:5.

6 And there was war in heaven; Michael and his angels fought against the dragon; and the dragon . . . and his angels [fought against Michael;][10]
7 And [the dragon] prevailed not [against Michael, neither the child, nor the woman which was the church of God, who had been delivered of her pains, and brought forth the kingdom of our God and his Christ.][11]
8 [Neither was there place found . . . in heaven for the great dragon, who] was cast out, that old serpent called the Devil, and [also called][12] Satan, which deceiveth the whole world: he was cast out into the earth; and his angels were cast out with him.
9 And I heard a loud voice saying in heaven, Now is come salvation, and strength, and the kingdom of our God, and the power of his Christ;
10 For the accuser of our brethren is cast down, which accused them before our God day and night.
11 [For they have overcome][13] him by the blood of the Lamb, and by the word of their testimony; [for][14] they loved not their [own lives, but kept the testimony even unto death.][15] Therefore, rejoice, [O][16] heavens, and ye that dwell in them.
12 [And after these things I heard another voice saying,] Woe to the inhabiters of the earth, [yea,] and [they who dwell upon the islands] of the sea! for the devil is come down unto you, having great wrath, because he knoweth that he hath but a short time.[17]
13 [For][18] when the dragon saw that he was cast unto the earth, he persecuted the woman which brought forth the man child.
14 [Therefore,][19] to the woman were given two wings of a great eagle, that she might [flee][20] into the wilderness, into her place, where she is nourished for a time, and times, and half a time, from the face of the serpent.
15 And the serpent [casteth][21] out of his mouth water as a flood after the woman, that he might cause her to be carried away of the flood.
16 And the earth [helpeth] the woman, and the earth [openeth] her mouth, and [swalloweth] up the flood which the dragon [casteth] out of his mouth.[22]

---

[10] The KJV reads, " . . . and the dragon fought and his angels." The change is from JST 12:6.
[11] The KJV reads, "And prevailed not; neither was their place found any more in heaven." The change is from JST 12:7.
[12] This change is from JST 12:7. The KJV reads, "And the great dragon was cast out, that old serpent, called the Devil, and Satan, which deceiveth the whole world."
[13] This change is from JST 12:11. KJV reads, "And they overcame."
[14] This change is from JST 12:11. KJV uses *and.*
[15] This change is from JST 12:11. KJV reads "and they loved not their lives unto the death."
[16] This change is from JST 12:11. KJV has *ye.*
[17] Additions are from JST 12:12.
[18] This change is from JST 12:13. The KJV uses *and.*
[19] This change is from JST 12:14. KJV uses *and.*
[20] This change is from JST 12:14. KJV uses *fly.*
[21] This change is from JST 12:15. KJV uses *cast.*
[22] These changes are from JST 12:16. KJV has *helped, opened, swallowed,* and *cast.*

17 [Therefore,][23] the dragon was wroth with the woman, and went to make war with the remnant of her seed, which keep the commandments of God, and have the testimony of Jesus Christ.

NOTES AND COMMENTARY

12:1 *there appeared a great [sign in heaven, in the likeness of things on the earth].* The sign here is a portent, or omen, of a coming event (12:3; 15:1). It appears in heaven because that is where John sees his vision—in the temple in heaven. The sign is "in the likeness of things on the earth" in that it portrays a pregnant woman who is experiencing labor, something commonly seen on the earth.

a woman clothed with the sun. Joseph Smith's translation of 12:7 makes clear that the woman represents the true Church of God, which is not just an organization but many righteous individuals joined together by covenant. In being clothed with the sun, the woman represents the destiny of those who join themselves to her and follow the Lord with pure hearts: they will be privileged to enter the celestial kingdom, "whose glory is [like] that of the sun" (D&C 76:70). In being clothed with the sun, the true Church becomes like unto God himself, who is clothed "with light as with a garment" (Ps. 104:2).

the moon under her feet. The moon represents a lesser glory than that of the sun (1 Cor. 15:40–41). The glory of the moon, which is terrestrial, is lesser than, or inferior to, the glory enjoyed by the Church and its faithful adherents. This expression could also mean that the woman has power or dominance over the moon; in other words, it may suggest that those of the Church who attain a celestial glory will have stewardship and ascendancy over those who attain a lesser glory.

a crown of twelve stars. The head of the Church is the Twelve Apostles of the Lord, who direct the Church in righteousness, under Christ (1 Ne. 1:10). This system of Church government continues to our day—the presiding officer of the Church is the senior apostle. The crown signifies the preeminent position of the apostles; stars often symbolize individual human beings (Gen. 37:9; Job 38:7; see commentary on 1:16, 20). The crown of twelve stars may also represent the twelve tribes of Israel, through whom we are able to partake of the Abrahamic covenant.

---

[23] This change is from JST 12:17. KJV uses *and.*

12:2 *[the woman] being with child.* The woman, representing the true Church, bears within her the seed of the kingdom of God (JST 12:7). The Church is the ecclesiastical arm of the Lord's work; the kingdom of God on earth, which will come to full fruition in the Millennium, will also have political power (see commentary on 12:3).

travailing in birth, and pained to be delivered. According to this symbolism, it was not an easy thing for the Church to bring forth the kingdom of God but required both sacrifice and pain. Similarly, Old Testament prophets depicted ancient Israel as a travailing woman seeking to give birth to Zion (Isa. 66:7–8; Jer. 4:31; Micah 4:10). It is uncertain what the travail and pain represent in actual history—perhaps they are related to persecution from without and apathy and apostasy from within the Church.

12:3 *she brought forth a man child.* After her travail and pain, the Church did indeed bring forth the kingdom of God. The birth occurred in the time of the original Twelve Apostles, but because of Satan's oppressions, that kingdom (which stems from the establishment of Zion) was driven from the earth before it could grow.

Elder Joseph Fielding Smith explained the difference between the Church and the kingdom of God: "After Christ comes, all the peoples of the earth will be subject to him, but there will be multitudes of people on the face of the earth who will not be members of the Church; yet all will have to be obedient to the laws of the kingdom of God, for it will have dominion upon the whole face of the earth. These people will be subject to the political government, even though they are not members of the ecclesiastical kingdom which is the Church.

"This government which embraces all the peoples of the earth, both in and out of the Church, is also sometimes spoken of as the kingdom of God, because the people are subject to the kingdom of God which Christ will set up."[24]

rule all nations with a rod of iron. It was the destiny of the kingdom of God to rule all nations, but, as John saw, because of Satan's opposition, the kingdom was not able to assume that role at the time of its birth. The rod of iron is "the word of God," as seen by Lehi and Nephi (1 Ne. 11:25). To rule by the word of God is to rule by the principles of divine truth, under the direction of the Spirit. Such rule implies priesthood direction; it is part of

---

[24] Smith, *Doctrines of Salvation,* 1:229.

the oath and covenant of the priesthood to "live by every word that procee-deth forth from the mouth of God" (D&C 84:44). Those who so live shall also so rule (Ps. 2:9; Rev. 2:27; 19:15).

her child was caught up unto God. Because of Satan's threat, the infant political kingdom of God was not allowed to remain on the earth. When all who held the keys and authorities of the kingdom were killed, those keys were returned to God by being lost to those on the earth.

his throne. The Eternal Father rules from a throne in the heavens (3:21; 4:2–6).

12:4 *another [sign] in heaven.* This sign is a portent of things to come in the vision.

a great red dragon. The dragon represents the devil, or Satan (12:8). The red here is the color of fire, symbolizing the indiscriminate destruction of the dragon—like fire, the dragon destroys all in its path. Red is also the color of sin, murder, and bloodshed (6:4; Isa. 1:18).

seven heads and ten horns/seven crowns upon his heads. Satan is found in many places, and he rules over many nations, represented by the seven crowns on seven heads (see also Dan. 7:7). Horns are a symbol of power.[25] The number ten suggests that Satan has great power, but it is nei-ther perfect nor complete; such complete power, represented by twelve horns, resides in the Lamb (JST Rev. 5:6). Yet the seven crowns indicate that Satan has perfect and complete power on earth, at least for a time. This description of the dragon is repeated in relation to one of his followers, a beast from the sea (see commentary on 13:1).

Some scholars believe that these symbols represent the earthly powers that opposed the meridian Church—which may coincide with the view of the Church members in that era. As J. R. Dummelow explained, "[Satan's] seven heads and ten horns . . . represent the Roman emperors through whom he exercised his power. The seven crowned heads perhaps signify the seven emperors, from Augustus to Titus, who had really reigned. The ten horns may stand for the same emperors with the addition of Galba, Otho, and Vitellius."[26] (These last three were pretenders to the Roman throne in A.D. 68 and 69. Some historians, however, include them in the count of the Roman emperors.) This argument is basically flawed,

---

[25] McConkie and Parry, *Guide to Scriptural Symbols,* 66.
[26] Dummelow, *Commentary on the Holy Bible,* 1082.

however: The dragon's power began long before the Roman empire and has continued long since.

his tail drew the third part of the stars of heaven, and did cast them to the earth. This passage refers to the third of the hosts of heaven who were cast out with Satan after the war in heaven. Job also refers to the premortal spirit children of God as "stars" (Job 38:4–7). This idea is repeated in 12:8 (Dan. 8:10; 2 Pet. 2:4; Jude 1:6).

the dragon stood before the woman . . . [ready] to devour her child. This passage reminds us of the serpent's presenting himself, face to face, to the first woman of our earth, Eve, in the Garden of Eden (Gen. 3:1–6). Satan traditionally places himself in the best position to do us harm (1 Pet. 5:8). Here, he stands before the Church, ready to prevent her from bearing the fruit that is the kingdom of God. Should that kingdom be born, Satan's plan will be defeated as the Lord's influence on earth spreads.

12:5 *the woman fled into the wilderness.* The Lord's people, when persecuted, have often fled into the wilderness (Ex. 2:15; 1 Kgs. 17:2–3; 19:3–4; 1 Ne. 2:2), meaning the uninhabited desert. While the child (kingdom of God) was returned to the presence of God (12:3); the woman (the Church) is also taken away from the inhabited earth. During the time of the Great Apostasy, which followed the death of Christ and his apostles, the Church was removed from the earth. See commentary on 12:14.

she [had] a place prepared of God. The Lord had foreseen that Satan would persecute the Church and was prepared to withdraw the keys and authority from the earth, to keep them with himself until the Restoration.

they should feed her there. In place of *feed,* other versions use *taken care of* (GNB, NIV, LB), *nourished* (RSV), or *sustained* (NEB). The sense of the passage is that the Lord will not allow the Church to die but will keep it in his care until it is time to restore the gospel to the earth.

a thousand two hundred and threescore [years]. The clarification of *years* in the Joseph Smith Translation rather than the King James Version *days* is an important one, for the number suggests the length of time the Church will be gone from the earth during the Great Apostasy—1,260 years. If we consider that the Apostasy ended in 1820 (when the silence of the heavens was broken during Joseph Smith's First Vision) or in 1830 (when the Church was formally organized), then the 1,260 year period began in A.D. 570 or 560. But we know that the world had plunged deep into apostasy centuries before that time.

Perhaps John saw the Renaissance and the later Reformation as part of the restoration of the gospel; latter-day prophets have taught that events of these periods did indeed pave the way for the Restoration.[27] The Renaissance began to bring light to the Dark Ages in the fourteenth and fifteenth centuries. A key date in the Renaissance was Gutenberg's invention of the printing press in about 1451. Less than a century later, in 1517, Martin Luther nailed his ninety-five theses to the door of the Castle Church in Wittenberg, Germany, sparking the beginning of the Reformation.

If we count 1,260 years before Luther's protest, we get a date of A.D. 257. If we count backwards from Gutenberg, the resulting date is A.D. 191. We could likely find other dates from which to measure the end of John's 1,260 years, but all such efforts are no more than speculative. The important point is that John saw an extended period of widespread apostasy, followed by the immeasurable blessing of the restoration of the gospel (14:6). That is probably the basic and most important understanding we can come to here: the Apostasy would last a very long time.

In 12:14, the 1,260 years is given differently, as "a time, and times, and half a time"—which may mean "one year [time], plus two years [times], plus half a year [half a time]," which equals three and one-half years, or, again, 1,260 days. Perhaps in "prophet's time" (D&C 130:4), a prophetic day sometimes equals a mortal year. Compare the similar time period—"forty and two months" (11:2), or "a thousand two hundred and threescore days" (11:3), or three and one-half years—during which Jerusalem would be besieged and the two prophets would testify in power. In the latter instances those time periods seem to be literal, rather than symbolic, months and days.

The ancient prophet Daniel dealt with similar time periods. After seeing a vision of the last days, Daniel asked, "How long shall it be to the end of these wonders?" And the answer: "It shall be for a time, times, and an half." Daniel did not understand, asked again, and was told, "From the time that the daily sacrifice shall be taken away, and the abomination that maketh desolate set up, there shall be a thousand two hundred and ninety days. Blessed is he that waiteth, and cometh to the thousand three hundred

---

[27] See, for example, Smith, *Gospel Doctrine*, 31; Smith, *Doctrines of Salvation*, 1:176–77; McConkie, *Millennial Messiah*, 90, 92–93.

and five and thirty days" (Dan. 12:6–12). Daniel's time periods are slightly different, but the application may be similar.

The specific meaning of these time periods has not been revealed, though some may come to a private understanding through personal revelation. As an angel told Daniel, "None of the wicked shall understand; but the wise shall understand" (Dan. 12:10). For further discussion of the symbolism of the numbers involved here, see commentary on 11:2.

12:6 *war in heaven.* "What kind of war? The same kind that prevails on earth; the only kind Satan and spirit beings can wage—a war of words, a tumult of opinions, a conflict of ideologies; a war between truth and error, between light and darkness, between the gospel of Jesus Christ, with all its saving power, and the false religions of the world, which have a form of godliness but are devoid of saving grace. And the battle lines are still drawn. It is now on earth as it was then in heaven; every man must choose which general he will follow."[28]

Latter-day Saints traditionally speak of the war in heaven that occurred before Satan was cast out (see 12:8), but in verses 6 and 7, John may be seeing a renewal of that war in the days of the meridian church—and beyond. Two clues support this idea: first, the Church and kingdom of God are both present during the war (12:7), and second, some of the righteous who fight in the war are killed (12:11), which cannot happen with premortal spirits.

Michael and his angels fought against the dragon. Michael, leading the hosts of the Lord, fought Satan and his followers (Dan. 10:13, 21; 12:1; Jude 1:9). The battle begun in premortality continued when Michael came to earth as Adam, the first man, and it continues to this day among Adam's descendants. The great battle between Michael and Satan, with their angels, will be fought anew at the end of the world (D&C 88:112–15).

12:7 *[the dragon] prevailed not [against Michael, neither the child, nor the woman].* Powerful as he is, Satan is not as powerful as God. Though he may gain temporary victories, ultimately Satan fails in his evil plans against Michael and his righteous descendants, against the child (the kingdom of God), and against the woman (the true Church of God).

[brought forth the kingdom of our God and his Christ]. Through her pains, the Church brought forth the kingdom, which is ruled over by both

---

[28] McConkie, *Doctrinal New Testament Commentary,* 3:518.

God the Father and his Son, Jesus Christ. This phrase is an important addition to the King James Version found in the Joseph Smith Translation.

12:8 *[Neither was there place found . . . in heaven for the great dragon, who] was cast out.* This passage seems to flash back to the time in premortality when Satan was cast out of heaven. "I beheld Satan as lightning fall from heaven," the mortal Jesus said (Luke 10:18).

Devil/Satan. Not used in the Old Testament, *devil* is a word found in the New Testament, which was translated from Greek rather than Hebrew. The word means "false accuser" or "slanderer," which is one of Satan's primary tactics against God the Father, the Lord Jesus Christ, and the followers of Christ. We learn from modern revelation that Satan was "a liar from the beginning" (D&C 93:25). The word *satan* means "adversary"—he stands in opposition to God, to good, and to all who embrace the Lord and his goodness.

deceiveth the whole world. The adversary's work of deception on earth is well documented in the scriptures (John 8:44; JST 2 Thess. 2:7–9; Rev. 16:14; 20:7–8; Mosiah 16:3; Moro. 7:17; D&C 84:49).

cast out into the earth. As a result of the war in heaven, the devil was cast from the presence of God down to the earth. As Isaiah exclaimed, "How art thou fallen from heaven, O Lucifer, son of the morning!" (Isa. 14:12).

his angels were cast out with him. Through his deceptions, Satan drew a full third of the Lord's premortal children after him—and they suffered the same consequences he did: they were cast from heaven to earth (D&C 29:37).

12:9 *I heard a loud voice saying in heaven.* John here seems to be differentiating between the voice in the vision and the normal voice of the Spirit. The voice in the vision is not a still small voice but a loud voice proclaiming to all the goodness of God. The loud voice may be the voice of an angel (8:13; 14:6–7; 19:17; D&C 88:92).

Now is come salvation/strength. With Satan cast from heaven, the Lord's plan can now begin to be effected among his children. Satan opposed the salvation that God would send through his Only Begotten Son. Now Satan is banished from heaven, and the plan can move forward, bringing redemption and spiritual blessing to all who will receive them. Other versions clarify the meaning of *strength* here. The New English Bible says,

"This is the hour of victory for our God, the hour of his sovereignty and power" (Ex. 15:2; Ps. 27:1; 37:39; 118:14; Isa. 12:2; 1 Ne. 15:15).

the kingdom of our God/the power of his Christ. With the great opponent of God's kingdom cast down, that kingdom is now ready to be established. Christ will now go forth with power to perform the Atonement and bless all mankind (Omni 1:26; Moro. 7:41).

12:10 *the accuser of our brethren.* Satan calls good evil and evil good (2 Ne. 15:20). He accuses those who are righteous ("our brethren") of being evil. Often his accusations will be made through the mouths of his followers on earth (Dan. 6:24; Matt. 27:12; D&C 122:6). Interestingly, the Hebrew word for Satan means "to accuse."

accused them before our God day and night. Satan never ceases from his evil work. He seeks constantly, both day and night, to undermine the righteous. And, as in the story of Job, he makes false accusation directly to the face of God (Job 1:6–12; 2:1–5).

12:11 *[they have overcome] him by the blood of the Lamb.* Ultimately, we conquer Satan not by our own righteousness nor by the valiant efforts of Michael, who leads the heavenly armies. We overcome as we partake of the blessings of the atonement of Christ, which atonement was wrought by the shedding of his blood (7:14; 1 Pet. 1:18–19; 1 Ne. 12:10–11; 2 Ne. 9:6–26; Alma 34:36).

by the word of their testimony. We also conquer Satan in our own lives by standing firm in our testimonies and being willing to proclaim them even in the face of opposition.

they loved not their [own lives, but kept the testimony even unto death]. Those who overcome the enticements and powers of Satan include the martyrs for truth, who love the Lord and their testimony of his word more than they love their own lives (6:9; 20:4–6).

Therefore, rejoice, [O] heavens. Those in heaven have cause to rejoice (Ps. 96:11; Isa. 49:13): Satan has been cast out; the plan can go forward; salvation has come. The rejoicing in heaven contrasts with the state of those on earth, who must deal with Satan and his deceptions. "Woe to the inhabiters of the earth" (12:12).

12:12 *[after these things].* This phrase is an addition found in the Joseph Smith Translation. Its inclusion does more than suggest a sequence in the vision, which is implied anyway. The words seem to create a separation between rejoicing in heaven in 12:11 and the woe on earth in 12:12.

I heard another voice. Apparently the voice that proclaims rejoicing in heaven is different from the voice that proclaims the woe on earth. This is another addition found in the Joseph Smith Translation.

Woe to the inhabiters of the earth. The book of Revelation has other woes pronounced on the inhabitants of the earth—plagues and judgments that will cause much loss of life and destruction. But this woe is the greatest—that Satan will dwell unseen among the Father's children on earth and will use his lies and deceptions to bring spiritual death to many (3 Ne. 9:2; Moses 7:25–26). This judgment will result in the fulfillment of Isaiah's prophecy: "The earth also is defiled under the inhabitants thereof; because they have transgressed the laws, changed the ordinance, broken the everlasting covenant. Therefore hath the curse devoured the earth, and they that dwell therein are desolate: therefore the inhabitants of the earth are burned, and few men left" (Isa. 24:5–6; D&C 5:5). The woe seems to have begun when Satan first entered the Garden of Eden and tempted Eve; it will not end until Satan has been bound with chains and cast into the bottomless pit (20:1–3).

[they who dwell upon the islands] of the sea. Even those in the farflung areas of the earth will be subject to the evil work of the devil (Ezek. 26:17).

the devil is come down unto you. Satan dwells on the same planet on which we dwell.[29]

having great wrath. The devil is angry by nature, and he is further incensed by the fate he suffered in being cast out of heaven. In his wrath he seeks to bring us to a misery like unto his own (2 Ne. 2:27; see also Rev. 14:8).

he knoweth that he hath but a short time. Satan is fully aware that he will be able to tempt us for only a brief moment of the eternities, and then he will be cast out forever (Matt. 8:29).

12:13 *he persecuted the woman.* Persecution of the Church (the woman), meaning the righteous members as well as the organization itself, has always been Satan's first order of business. He seeks to deceive the whole world, but he seems to save his persecutions for those who resist his deceptions. Jesus taught us that we should expect persecutions—and yet remain steadfast to the end (Matt. 5:11–12; John 15:21).

---

[29] Wilford Woodruff, *Journal of Discourses,* 13:163.

12:14 *to the woman were given two wings of a great eagle.* The eagle's wings symbolize deliverance from on high, which deliverance comes with swiftness and power. The Church after the days of Christ will be delivered by the same divine power that delivered the children of Israel from Egypt; as we read in Exodus, "Ye have seen what I did unto the Egyptians, and how I bare you on eagles' wings, and brought you unto myself" (Ex. 19:4; see also Deut. 32:11–12; Isa. 40:31).

[flee] into the wilderness, into her place, where she is nourished. As the children of Israel found deliverance from Egypt, symbolizing the wicked world, by fleeing into the wilderness, so will the Lord's true Church be protected "in the wilderness" when Satan attacks in the meridian of time.[30] In this case, the wilderness is a place of safety prepared for it and isolated from mortals, namely, a place in the care of God (12:5). During the period that the Church is gone from the earth, she will be "nourished" by God, which probably means he will make certain that all is in readiness when the time comes for the restoration, which began in the days of Joseph Smith.

a time, and times, and half a time. See commentary on 12:5; 13:5.

from the face of the serpent. The woman (meaning the Church) will be taken to a place where the serpent (meaning the devil) will no longer be able to harm her—that is, the protective presence of God.

12:15 *the serpent [casteth] out of his mouth water as a flood after the woman.* Before the woman (or the Church) actually departed into the wilderness (meaning the safety of heaven), the serpent (the devil) tried to destroy her with a flood. The flood from Satan's mouth could have been a torrent of lies against the Church; the flow of evil that he sent forth, seeking to overwhelm the Church; ceaseless persecution and tribulation; or the attacks of a wicked nation (Rome)—or each of these in turn. (For scriptural examples of such applications of flood waters, see Ps. 18:4, 14–15; Isa. 17:12–14; 43:2; Jer. 46:7–8; 51:55.) The real point, of course, is that Satan made great efforts to destroy the Church, and that the true power and authority of the Church survived in God's care.

12:16 *the earth [helpeth] the woman/[swalloweth] up the flood.* John's meaning here seems unclear, but nature often seems to cooperate with the God of nature to protect the Church long enough for God's purposes to be

---

[30] McConkie, *Doctrinal New Testament Commentary,* 3:519.

fulfilled (compare Num. 16:30; 26:10; Deut. 11:6). As Mormon testified, even the dust of the earth is obedient to the command of God (Hel. 12:7–19). And as we learn from Enoch, the earth itself has a spirit that loves righteousness and is pained by wickedness (Moses 7:48). Satan's river of destruction (12:15) stands in contrast to the river of life that flows from God (22:1).

12:17 *the dragon was wroth with the woman.* Satan's anger against the Church as an institution, as well as the righteous members of the Church, continues.

make war with the remnant of her seed. Satan particularly attacks those who "keep the commandments of God, and have the testimony of Jesus Christ." And his efforts are neither feeble nor sporadic. The war in heaven continues as Satan constantly brings the battle to the righteous on the earth. This verse applies not only to the gradually dwindling numbers of the righteous in Christ's Church in the meridian of time but also to the increasing numbers of righteous in the restored Church of Jesus Christ in our day.

REVELATION
13

A BEAST RISES FROM THE SEA (13:1–10)

As part of his effort to make war against the Saints, Satan summons from the sea a beast, which symbolizes certain of the "kingdoms of the earth" (JST 13:1). This beast, depicted as various wild animals, has many heads and many crowns (suggesting many different rulers or kingdoms) and many horns (suggesting much power). He is known for his blasphemy against God (13:1, 6). The world is so taken by the beast and his power that they worship him and fear him, and they worship the dragon (or devil) as well (13:4). The beast's power continues for forty-two months, during which time he fights and overcomes the Saints of God (13:5, 7).

Most commentators identify the beast as the wicked Roman emperor Nero (and, by extension, the Roman Empire itself).[1] Nero had great power and allied himself with Satan to persecute the Saints. He took his own life in A.D. 68, and in the year that followed, civil war threatened to destroy the very life of the empire. Vespasian rose to power in A.D. 69 and restored order, but during his reign he proved to be as vicious against the Christians as Nero had been.

All this seems to fit with the description of the beast and its mortal wound as found in 13:3, and this may have been the interpretation the early Christians understood. But the vision seems to lead us to another, broader level of meaning as well. The beast appears to have power that reaches worldwide—"over all kindreds, and tongues, and nations," even "all that dwell upon the earth" (13:7–8). Further, that power was appointed to

---

[1] See discussions in Harrington, *Revelation,* 138–41; Mounce, *Book of Revelation,* 246–48; Glasson, *Revelation of John,* 79–81.

continue only "forty and two months" (13:5). The second beast, which is a supporter and ally of the first, has no such time limit placed on his reign.

If we take these descriptions literally, the beast must be more than simply an emperor of Rome, however powerful he might have been in his corner of the world. Some might argue that Nero did have power over all the known world, suggesting that "all . . . nations" refers to all nations that John was familiar with. But in the very next chapter John notes that the gospel was to go to "every nation" (14:6), which certainly was not limited to the Mediterranean world.

Who, then, is the beast from the sea? Following are some clues to its identity:

1. The beast has political power—from it stem many kings (13:1; 17:12).

2. It stands in blatant opposition to God, representing blasphemy with no shame (13:1).

3. It receives its power and authority from Satan himself (13:2).

4. One of its heads receives a deadly wound by a sword and is healed (13:3, 14).

5. The whole world knows about the healing and is amazed (13:3).

6. The people of the world worship the beast (13:4, 8).

7. The world marvels at the power of the beast (13:4).

8. The beast is able to speak great things, including blasphemies (13:5, 6).

9. It has power for forty-two months (13:5).

10. It has power to make war with and overcome the Saints (13:7).

11. It has power over all nations (13:7).

12. A second beast has power to give life to an image of the first beast, enabling it even to speak (13:15).

13. The second beast causes all who do not worship the first beast to be put to death (13:15).

14. The first beast will make war against the two witnesses in Jerusalem and will kill them (11:7).

15. The first beast supports Babylon, the mother of harlots (17:7).

16. It comes from the bottomless pit and is destined to go to perdition (17:8).

17. The beast "was, and is not, and yet is" (17:8).

18. The seven heads of the beast are seven mountains (17:9).

19. The beast is eighth in a line of kings, five of which have come and gone by the time of John's vision (17:10–11).

20. It is yet to come in John's future—but it existed in some form before John's vision (17:11, 8).

21. Many kings will lend their power and strength to the beast (17:13).

22. The beast is not limited in time to the period of the Great Apostasy but will still be in power when the Lord returns in power (19:19).

23. The beast and the false prophet, who is the second beast, will both be captured at the time of the Second Coming and will be thrown into the lake of fire (19:20).

We will talk about the specific meaning of these elements, as far as they are known, in commentaries to follow. But the combination of elements gives us these essential understandings:

1. The beast is a servant of Satan and receives power from him.

2. The beast has power politically, a power that reaches to all nations.

3. It speaks blasphemies, fights and overcomes the Saints, and supports Babylon. The wicked throughout the world worship it.

4. It seems to have existed in some form before the time of Christ, and it will continue to exist as a force in the world until the Lord returns in glory.

What power in the world fits such a description? It seems to be the power of unrighteous government, or an ideology or philosophy or culture that binds many governments. Governments in any age that resist the spirit of truth, that exercise power over men and women inappropriately, that set themselves up as the source (rather than simply the protector) of people's security—all these partake of the spirit of the beast.[2]

Note that the commentary to this chapter is written primarily in the present tense. Yet much of that which is depicted in this portion of John's vision may be in the past, and much may also be in the future.

Revelation 13:1–10

1 And I [saw another sign, in the likeness of the kingdoms of the earth;] a beast rise up out of the sea, [and he stood upon the sand of the sea,] having seven heads and ten horns; and upon his horns ten crowns; and upon his heads the name of blasphemy.[3]

---

[2] For an interesting discussion of the power of wicked governments, see Andersen, *Great and Abominable Church.*
[3] Changes are from JST 13:1.

2 And the beast which I saw was like unto a leopard, and his feet were as the feet of a bear, and his mouth as the mouth of a lion; and the dragon gave him his power, and his seat, and great authority.
3 And I saw one of his heads as it were wounded to death; and his deadly wound was healed; and all the world wondered after the beast.
4 And they worshipped the dragon which gave power unto the beast; and they worshipped the beast, saying, Who is like unto the beast? who is able to make war with him?
5 And there was given unto him a mouth speaking great things and blasphemies; and power was given unto him to continue forty and two months.
6 And he opened his mouth in blasphemy against God, to blaspheme his name, and his tabernacle, and them that dwell in heaven.
7 And it was given unto him to make war with the saints, and to overcome them; and power was given him over all kindreds, and tongues, and nations.
8 And all that dwell upon the earth shall worship him, whose names are not written in the book of life of the Lamb slain from the foundation of the world.
9 If any man have an ear, let him hear.
10 He that leadeth into captivity shall go into captivity; he that killeth with the sword must be killed with the sword. Here is the patience and the faith of the saints.

NOTES AND COMMENTARY

13:1 *[another sign, in the likeness of the kingdoms of the earth].* John earlier saw a sign "in the likeness of things on the earth" (12:1). Here we see a sign, or omen, that is like unto the *kingdoms* of the earth.

a beast. The beast is a symbol of an unnamed kingdom on the earth, most likely a political kingdom. Joseph Smith taught, "When God made use of the figure of a beast in visions to the prophets He did it to represent those kingdoms which had degenerated and become corrupt, savage and beast-like in their dispositions, even the degenerate kingdoms of the wicked world. . . . The beast that rose up out of the sea should be translated the image of a beast"—meaning that it was symbolic rather than literal.[4]

The beast also represents a particular ruler over a kingdom: "There are seven kings . . . and the beast . . . is the eighth" (17:10–11). Though the beast seems to be a particular king or kingdom, his horns represent other kingdoms as well. Some have tried to identify the beast with a particular king or kingdom, such as Rome or one of its caesars, but it is more important to identify its chief characteristics.

---

[4] *History of the Church,* 5:341, 345.

rise up out of the sea. In the ancient world the sea was often associated with evil, with chaos, with the enemies of God.[5] The four beasts Daniel saw also came up from the sea (Dan. 7:3). That may suggest that the king who is the beast will literally come from the sea when he attacks the people of God. *Sea* here may symbolize the nations of the world, as *waters* does in 17:15. Thus, the beast rises to prominence from among the nations of the world.

If *sea* is to be read literally, a statement in the Doctrine and Covenants may provide an interesting connection. Said the Lord: "Behold, I, the Lord, in the beginning blessed the waters; but in the last days, by the mouth of my servant John, I cursed the waters. . . . I, the Lord, have decreed, and the destroyer rideth upon the face thereof, and I revoke not the decree" (D&C 61:14, 19).

seven heads and ten horns/upon his horns ten crowns. The beast has heads, horns, and crowns like its master, Satan—with one difference: Satan has but seven crowns (JST 12:4), whereas the beast has ten. In numerology, seven is a perfect number, but ten is not, which suggests that Satan has more complete power and sovereignty than his beast, even though the beast has a greater number of heads, horns, and crowns. This beast reappears in Revelation 17, in which we are given an interpretation of some of the symbolism. We learn that the woman who is called "Babylon the great, the mother of harlots" is carried by the beast (17:5, 7). The seven heads represent seven mountains, "on which the woman sitteth" (17:9). The heads may also represent seven kings (17:10). The ten horns represent ten kings who are yet to come (17:12; Daniel too saw ten horns on a beast, also representing kings; Dan. 7:7). These kings receive their power from the beast (17:12).

This beast is commonly understood to represent Rome or one of the evil rulers of Rome. But if Rome does fit the description in some respects, it is only as a prototype or symbol of the true beast of the last days. For even though the beast may represent a particular king or kingdom, its horns represent other kings and kingdoms, and its heads seem to represent that which supports the great Babylon of the earth, which is the embodiment of all wickedness.

---

[5] Mounce, *Book of Revelation,* 244.

upon his heads the name of blasphemy. It is in the nature of the beast to oppose and mock God, to seek to injure His good name and reputation— and to ascribe to itself the character and attributes of God.

13:2 *the beast . . . like unto a leopard/bear/lion.* The beast has power among nations and peoples in the same way vicious animals have power in their kingdoms, ruling others by fear and force. These three animals are the same as those seen by Daniel, which also rise up from the sea (Dan. 7:3–6). Daniel saw a fourth beast as well; it is not described as a particular animal but is called "dreadful and terrible, and strong exceedingly." This beast has ten horns and "a mouth speaking great things" (Dan. 7:7–8; compare Rev. 13:5). Daniel learns that "these great beasts . . . are four kings" (Dan. 7:17). He sees further that one of the horns on the last beast "made war with the saints, and prevailed against them" (Dan. 7:21; compare Rev. 13:7). The last beast "shall devour the whole earth, . . . and he shall speak great words against the most High, and shall wear out the saints of the most High" (Dan. 7:23, 25; compare Rev. 13:7). Daniel appears to have seen the same thing John saw but in a slightly different form.

the dragon gave him his power, and his seat, and great authority. The beast looks to the devil for power to rule; in turn, the devil is the master, or ruler, of the beast.

13:3 *one of his heads as it were wounded to death/deadly wound was healed.* If the heads represent kings (JST 13:1), apparently one of the kings is wounded to the point of death but will then be healed. If the heads represent kingdoms, perhaps one of the kingdoms will seem to be destroyed but will then come forth unto power once again.

This wound to a beast that is an enemy of Christ contrasts with the mortal wound the Lamb will receive on the cross (5:6, 12); and as the beast, which is anti-Christ, is healed, so also will the true Christ be healed in the resurrection. There, however, the similarity ends: Jesus Christ the Lamb will live victorious forever, while his enemy the beast will be thrown into the "lake of fire" (19:20).

all the world wondered after the beast. The people of the world see the healing of one of the heads of the beast and are amazed. Of course, the people do not view the beast as a beast—that is only the metaphor John uses to convey his message. Instead, the people are amazed at the power and resilience of the king, kingdom, or philosophy that the beast symbolizes. As an analogy, suppose that communism were to be revitalized and return to worldwide power after being repudiated in the late 1980s. That would be a source of wonderment to all the world. That is only an analogy, not an interpretation of prophetic or future events, but the analogy may be instructive in helping us to see what John seems to be describing in this verse.

13:4 *they worshipped the dragon.* In John's vision, the people of the world worship the devil. This does not mean, necessarily, that they bow down before him or that they offer prayers or oblations to him. Rather, they may follow him, subscribe to his way of thinking, and choose to do his will—some knowingly, some unknowingly.

they worshipped the beast. The people of the world worship this king, kingdom, or philosophy in the same way that they worship the devil—by following it and making it the ruling principle in their lives. The word *anti-Christ* does not appear in Revelation; in the New Testament it is found only in the epistles of John (1 Jn. 2:18, 22; 4:3; 2 Jn. 1:7). But this beast is unquestionably an anti-Christ, standing in opposition to Christ, seeking his power and authority.

Who is like unto the beast? The people of the world offer to the beast praise and admiration that should be reserved for God. In Exodus, for example, the people exclaim, "Who is like unto thee, O Lord, among the gods? who is like unto thee . . . ?" (Ex. 15:11; Ps. 89:8; Isa. 44:7; Micah 7:18). Of course, because the Lord really is preeminent, the beast, whom the people worship, will be destroyed.

13:5 *given unto him a mouth speaking great things and blasphemies.* These blasphemies might claim that the beast ought to be worshipped rather than God. In speaking of the days before the second coming of Christ, Paul spoke of "that man of sin . . . who opposeth and exalteth himself above all that is called God, or that is worshipped; so that he as God sitteth in the temple of God, shewing himself that he is God" (2 Thes. 2:3–4). The power to speak these blasphemies is given to the beast by Satan.

continue forty and two months. The beast is allowed to exercise its power for forty-two months. This number often represents the period when the wickedness of the world will hold sway (see commentary on 11:2–3). The number forty-two may not indicate an actual number of months or other specific period of time but may instead symbolize a general, prolonged, but ultimately limited, time of wickedness.

When the forty-two months are broken down into days (1,260) and then translated into years, we have the period of time that the woman finds refuge in the wilderness (12:6). Whether or not this connection applies, however, we know that the beast will have power for a finite amount of time and that in the end the Lord and his people will emerge victorious.

13:6 *blasphemy against God/his name/his tabernacle/them that dwell in heaven.* The beast speaks his blasphemy against God himself, against God's name, against God's dwelling place (the tabernacle, or temple), and against the angels and gods in heaven. The beast is opposed to all that is good (Dan. 7:8, 20, 25; 11:36) and tries to garner to himself the honor and respect that should be given only to God.

13:7 *given unto him to make war with the saints, and to overcome them.* It appears that the Lord is the one who is allowing the beast to make war with the Saints, even knowing that they will be conquered for a time. It is part of the Lord's eternal plan to allow the exercise of agency to both wicked and righteous on the earth—even if the wicked martyr the righteous in the process. The Lord takes the long, eternal view, knowing that in the end he will be able to exact full justice both from those who deserve punishment and for those who deserve comfort and reward.

We read in 12:11 that the righteous did not love their lives more than they loved the Lord, and thus they were willing to suffer martyrdom. Here that resolve is put to the test for many Saints, who pass the test by succumbing to death at the hands of the beast. Yet that death is the very means of their own victory (15:2; see also Dan. 7:21).

Joseph Smith seems to place this event "in the last days."[6] Supporting that is John's statement that the beast will still be in power when Christ comes again (19:19). If that is the case, it must be emphasized that the beast's war against the Saints will bring only a partial and temporary victory. The Great Apostasy will be followed by the restoration of the gospel. And the Lord has promised that his kingdom of the last days, once it is put in place, will never again be lost from the earth.[7] Perhaps the beast will oppose the Saints beginning in John's day—when he will overcome them so thoroughly that the Church will be lost from the earth—and continue his efforts (with varying degrees of success) until the end. Even though John

[6] *History of the Church,* 5:344.
[7] McConkie, *New Witness for the Articles of Faith,* 557–58.

sees in his vision the final triumph of Christ and his forces for good, he does not sugarcoat the events that precede the victory. Many of the righteous will suffer at the hands of Satan and his followers, but the righteous will indeed be victorious.

The beast will not restrict himself to persecution in his efforts to overcome (or *conquer;* RSV, NIV) the Saints. He will likely use all the tricks of his master, Satan, including the three great enemies of the Saints in all eras: apathy, apostasy, and sin.

power was given him over all kindreds, and tongues, and nations. The power and influence of the beast extend across the entire earth. Yet greater still is the eternal power of Christ, who "redeemed us to God by [his] blood out of every kindred, and tongue, and people, and nation" (5:9).

13:8 *all that dwell upon the earth shall worship him.* Those who worship the beast include all the people of the earth "whose names are not written in the book of life." To worship the beast is to honor and obey him. Again we see that the beast's influence is worldwide.

book of life of the Lamb. See commentary on 3:5; see also 20:12, 15.

Lamb slain from the foundation of the world. The promise of the atonement of Christ was made at the beginning, even before the creation of the world—and, through the grace of God, the power of that atonement took effect even from the time of that promise (1 Pet. 1:18–20).

13:9 *If any man have an ear, let him hear.* This is an invitation to understand and heed the words of the vision (2:7, 11, 17).

13:10 *He that leadeth into captivity shall go into captivity/killeth . . . be killed.* The Lord warns those who would follow the beast into sin that those who harm others will receive punishment to match their offenses. This statement also gives comfort to the Saints: even though the beast will lead many of the Saints into captivity, and even though he will kill many of them, in God's perfect justice he will receive in the end the same judgment he metes out (see also Jer. 15:2; 43:11; Matt. 26:52).

Here is the patience and the faith of the saints. Other translations (NIV, JB, RSV, NEB) clarify this phrase to indicate that the trials and persecution the Saints face will require much patience and faith if they hope to endure. Still another reading is the Saints know that even though some of them will suffer persecutions from those who worship the beast, in the end the Lord will execute his righteous judgments against the wicked.

A BEAST RISES FROM THE EARTH (13:11–18)

John sees a second beast, which has the same power as the beast that preceded it. The second beast appears to be like Christ (the lamb), but he really is like Satan, his master (the dragon). This beast also is a symbol of one or more kings or kingdoms of the earth.[8] The second beast causes the people of the world to worship (meaning, perhaps, to follow or to give allegiance to) the first beast. He performs great miracles to deceive people, he gives life to the image of the first beast, and he kills many who will not worship that image. This beast (or kingdom) also controls the economy of the earth (buying and selling) and requires people to associate themselves with the beast if they wish to have part in that economy.

This beast truly is an anti-Christ: he pretends to be a lamb, he performs great miracles (including fire from heaven, which all men see), he brings an image of the first beast to life, he requires the people of the world to worship that image instead of God, he takes away the exercise of agency of the people of the world. This second beast is referred to as a "false prophet" later in Revelation (16:13; 19:20; 20:10). Perhaps this beast, as a "prophet," represents religious philosophy and power, rather than the more political power of the first beast. Or perhaps he represents Satan's sophisticated propaganda machine, designed to flood the world with lies and false political and religious doctrines. Like his counterpart, he will remain in power until the Lord comes (19:19–20). His exact identity—whether as a kingdom or a false prophet—has not been revealed.

Revelation 13:11–18

> 11 And I beheld another beast coming up out of the earth; and he had two horns like a lamb, and he spake as a dragon.
> 12 And he exerciseth all the power of the first beast before him, and causeth the earth and them which dwell therein to worship the first beast, whose deadly wound was healed.
> 13 And he doeth great wonders, so that he maketh fire come down from heaven on the earth in the sight of men,
> 14 And deceiveth them that dwell on the earth by the means of those miracles which he had power to do in the sight of the beast; saying to them that dwell on the earth, that they should make an image to the beast, which had the wound by a sword, and did live.

---

[8] See *History of the Church,* 5:341.

15 And he had power to give life unto the image of the beast, that the image of the beast should both speak, and cause that as many as would not worship the image of the beast should be killed.

16 And he causeth all, both small and great, rich and poor, free and bond, to receive a mark in their right hand, or in their foreheads:

17 And that no man might buy or sell, save he that had the mark, or the name of the beast, or the number of his name.

18 Here is wisdom. Let him that hath understanding count the number of the beast: for it is the number of a man; and his number is Six hundred threescore and six.

NOTES AND COMMENTARY

13:11 *another beast coming up out of the earth.* Whereas the first beast came from the sea, the second beast comes from the land, though it is uncertain why this might be significant. The precise identity of this beast is less important than what he symbolizes: earthly kingdoms that follow Satan and lead the world away from Christ, or political, economic, and religious ideologies that seduce institutions and kingdoms into following the way of the beast and the dragon.

he had two horns like a lamb, and he spake as a dragon. This beast has the appearance of a lamb, like Jesus; outwardly he appears innocent and harmless. But when the beast speaks, his true nature is revealed—he speaks like his master, the devil. This false prophet is precisely like those the Lord warned against: "Beware of false prophets, which come to you in sheep's clothing, but inwardly they are ravening wolves" (Matt. 7:15).

13:12 *he exerciseth all the power of the first beast.* The first beast had "power . . . and great authority" given it by the devil (13:2). The first beast was so powerful that everyone feared war with it (13:4). The first beast had power "over all kindreds, and tongues, and nations" (13:7). The second beast exercised similar power in all these instances.

causeth the earth and them which dwell therein to worship the first beast. True prophets of God seek diligently to bring people to believe in Christ and worship him. The second beast, a false prophet, likewise seeks diligently to bring people to worship the first beast. His methods include wonders and miracles, threats of death (which are indeed carried out), and economic coercion. These methods are so effective that the beast succeeds in his efforts: the people of the world do indeed worship the beast. This is a continuation of the worship that started earlier (13:8).

One commentator writes, "[The] dragon, sea beast, and land beast are a satanic trinity that infiltrates the political world in order to deflect our worship from the God whom we cannot see to the authorities that we can see, and to deceive us into buying into a religion or belief-system that has visible results in self-gratification."[9]

13:13 *he doeth great wonders.* This beast performs great miracles, just as the Lord's true prophets performed miracles in earlier days (see, for example, Ex. 7–10) and as the two prophets will perform in Jerusalem (11:5–6). The beast will even have power to make fire come down from heaven "in the sight of men"—a sign and wonder like that performed by Elijah (1 Kgs. 18:38). "There shall arise false Christs, and false prophets," the Lord said, "and shall shew great signs and wonders; insomuch that, if it were possible, they shall deceive the very elect" (Matt. 24:24). And Paul warned against him "whose coming is after the working of Satan with all power and signs and lying wonders" (2 Thes. 2:9).

13:14 *deceiveth them that dwell on the earth.* Through the miracles the beast performs, he deceives the people of the world. The deception is that the beast should be worshipped, rather than Christ, and that the power behind the beast is the power of God when in reality it is Satan's power.

"The Great Imitator is able to blind the eyes and deceive the hearts of men and to put his own seal of verity, that of false miracles, on his damning philosophies. Thus those who place themselves wholly at his disposal have power to imitate the deeds of the prophets, as the magicians of Egypt imitated the miracles of Moses and as Simon the sorcerer sought to duplicate the works of Peter."[10]

The deception of the people of the world is a commentary on their spiritual state. Satan cannot deceive a person against that person's will— belief in the lies of Satan is always accompanied by choosing sin or choosing doubt in the work and message of the Lord.

miracles which he had power to do in the sight of the beast. Some versions of the Bible say that the second beast was performing his miracles "in the presence" of the first beast (LB, RSV, GNB, NEB). Others say that the second beast was acting "in behalf of" the first beast (NIV, JB). The Greek

[9] As quoted in Mounce, *The Book of Revelation,* 256.
[10] McConkie, *Doctrinal New Testament Commentary,* 3:524.

(*enopion*) clarifies further, suggesting that the second beast was acting "through the authority" of the first.

they should make an image to the beast. The second beast causes the people of the world to set up some kind of image of the first beast. We are not able to say what this means literally.

13:15 *he had power to give life unto the image of the beast.* In an amazing miracle, the second beast is able to cause the image of the beast to seem to come alive and speak. Many translations suggest that the second beast gives the "breath" of life to the image (LB, RSV, GNB, NIV, JB, NEB), another way in which the second beast acts as a counterfeit to God and his Spirit. We are not able to say what this prophecy means in literal terms.

as many as would not worship the image of the beast should be killed. This phrase indicates a true division between the people of the world. There will be two categories: those who will worship (follow, give allegiance to) the beast, and those who will resist even when threatened with death. Those who resist are those who have overcome "by the blood of the Lamb" and "loved not their lives unto the death" (12:11).

Some have suggested that this prophecy was fulfilled in the meridian of time. After the crucifixion of Christ, all members of the early Christian Church eventually died, were killed, or apostatized (the one exception, of course, is John the Revelator himself, who was translated). Certainly the demise of the meridian Church and the martyrdom of many members seem to fit at least parts of this prophecy. But many questions remain unanswered. For instance, what were the wonders and miracles performed by the Roman Empire, which persecuted the meridian Church? In what way did the Roman Empire have worldwide influence, as implied in 12:16–17? Both of these clues seem to point elsewhere to the identity of the second beast.

If this passage also has a latter-day application, it is safe to say that not all the righteous Saints will be killed—many will remain to establish Zion and to greet Christ when he returns. In this dispensation, the Church has been put on the earth to stay—it will not be removed from its place, though all powers of earth and hell be arrayed against it. But according to this prophecy, at some point many of the righteous will apparently live under the threat of a martyr's death: those who will not worship the image of the beast essentially have a death warrant on their heads. Thankfully, as Nephi saw, the saints will be "armed with righteousness and with the power of God in great glory" (1 Ne. 14:14), and they will emerge victorious.

13:16 *he causeth all . . . to receive a mark.* Earlier we saw that the righteous will receive the seal of the Lamb on their foreheads. This seal consists of the name of the Father and appears to protect the righteous from the judgments of God (7:2–3; 14:1). In contrast, the wicked—all who worship the beast—receive the mark of the beast (his name; 13:17; 14:11; 16:2; 19:20) on their foreheads or right hands. This mark appears to distinguish the wicked and enables them to buy and sell (13:17). Many have speculated on what the mark might be. Entire volumes have been written on the subject. But the Lord has not revealed the answer.

Here is one possibility, however, that may be more sound than most speculations. The seal of God is real, but it is also figurative—it cannot be seen, but those who have it know they are God's, and they are known by him. The seal is having one's calling and election made sure, being sealed up unto eternal life. That seal requires no outward mark or tattoo. It represents a way of life and its consequences.

Perhaps the mark of the beast is a parallel (though opposing) idea. Those who follow the beast do his will with their hands (symbolized by the mark on the hand) and accept and adhere to his philosophies with their minds (symbolized by the mark on the forehead).

Thus, those who give their lives to the beast and his philosophies constantly show whose they are—by the deeds of their hands and the words of their mouths (which reveal their thoughts).

13:17 *no man might buy or sell, save he that had the mark.* Here we see the extent of the power of the second beast. In 13:15 we see that the beast kills those who will not worship the first beast. Now we see that he has another threat: he controls the world economy so much that only those with the mark can engage in the essential economic activities of buying and selling. Perhaps this means that one cannot prosper without taking part in the prevailing philosophy, which is inspired by Satan.[11] Perhaps the Saints will survive by living the law of consecration.

the name of the beast, or the number of his name. The beast's name and number are synonymous. In many ancient alphabets, each letter had a

---

[11] For an interesting discussion on the economy of Babylon, see "What Is Zion? A Distant View," in Hugh Nibley, *Approaching Zion* (Salt Lake City: Deseret Book, 1989), 25–62. Other essays in the volume are equally compelling.

numerical equivalent. A graffito uncovered in Pompeii reads, "I love her whose number is 545."[12] Jewish rabbis enjoyed looking for hidden meanings in the scriptures; they called the practice of hiding numerical meanings in words *gematria.* For instance, we read in Genesis 14:14 that Abraham took 318 "trained servants" with him when he went to rescue Lot from his captors; according to gematria, the number 318 translates as *Eliezer,* the name of Abraham's chief servant.

13:18 *Here is wisdom.* John suggests that if we have understanding, we will be able to "count" the number of the beast, which will reveal his name. But lacking revelation, we are probably best served by not aligning ourselves too closely to any one interpretation.

the number of the beast. The number of the beast, which number (or name, derived from the number) constituted the mark placed on people's foreheads or right hands, was 666. The number is given as "the number of a man," meaning, perhaps, that it was not a mystical number or name but an ordinary human number or name, or it may mean that the number was that of a particular individual. If that is so, the individual is likely only a representative symbol of the beast, which goes beyond individual identities, reaching far into the past as well as into the future.

Another possibility is that the number is symbolic. The number seven indicates perfection; three sevens would suggest perfection to an emphatic level. Three sixes suggest a marked falling short of perfection. Seven could be a symbolic number for Christ; six could indicate the anti-Christ.

Most authorities interpret the number to mean the name Nero Caesar: when Nero's name is given in Hebrew (*nrwn qsr*), the numerical equivalent is 666.[13] Other possibilities include the Roman emperors Domitian or Titus, all the Roman emperors combined, the ancient Romans as a group, or the Roman Catholic Church.[14] The numerical equivalents of the names of each of these can be made to add up to 666. Many other individuals and organizations have been suggested as possibilities.

There are two complications with this approach. The first is that many early Greek manuscripts of the book of Revelation give the number as 616[15]—which would yield totally different interpretations. The second

[12] Deissmann, *Light from the Ancient East,* 277.
[13] Harrington, *Revelation,* 144; Mounce, *Book of Revelation,* 261; Glasson, *Revelation of John,* 83.
[14] Mounce, *Book of Revelation,* 261–62; Draper, *Opening the Seven Seals,* 150–51.
[15] Draper, *Opening the Seven Seals,* 150.

complication is that the beast truly seems to transcend the normal life span of individuals and institutions. He reaches around the entire world. The second beast seems to be a symbol in which we find embodied the great forces that oppose Christ and his people in the last days. Though we may not understand the interpretation of the number, we can seek to recognize the work of Satan in all its guises and then be willing to trust and follow Christ, our Savior, whatever the cost.

Even if we cannot tell who the number may literally point to, we understand the message of this passage: Satan sends forth philosophies and servants to do his work. Many who follow Christ and his perfection will suffer greatly for their opposition to Satan's program, but eventually the wicked will fall and the righteous will prevail.

REVELATION
14

THE LAMB AND HIS 144,000 (14:1–5)

These verses are placed in obvious contrast to those that immediately precede them. They give the Saints a message of hope. In Revelation 13, we see the two beasts who serve Satan and enslave the people of the world; now, at the beginning of Revelation 14, we see the Lamb standing in triumph on his temple mount. In Revelation 13, we see the peoples of the earth, who worship the beast and receive his name in their foreheads (13:4, 15–16); in Revelation 14, we see a powerful group of righteous followers of Christ, who worship him, who remain pure, and who stand faultless before God, having his name written in their foreheads (14:1, 3–5). The spreading, pervasive power of the two beasts is so great that it appears that none can withstand it. But in the few verses of chapter 14, we see that the Lord and his true followers can and will withstand that power, and they will surely prevail in the end.

Revelation 14:1–5

> 1 And I looked, and, lo, a Lamb stood on the mount Sion, and with him an hundred forty and four thousand, having his Father's name written in their foreheads.
> 2 And I heard a voice from heaven, as the voice of many waters, and as the voice of a great thunder: and I heard the voice of harpers harping with their harps:
> 3 And they sung as it were a new song before the throne, and before the four beasts, and the elders: and no man could learn that song but the hundred and forty and four thousand, which were redeemed from the earth.
> 4 These are they which were not defiled with women; for they are virgins. These are they which follow the Lamb whithersoever he goeth. These were redeemed from among men, being the firstfruits unto God and to the Lamb.

5 And in their mouth was found no guile: for they are without fault before the throne of God.

NOTES AND COMMENTARY

14:1 *a Lamb.* The Lamb is Jesus Christ (5:5–6).

mount Sion. In the Old Testament Mount Zion (Ps. 48:1–3; 74:2; 78:68; 125:1; Isa. 8:18) is located in Jerusalem. In Hebrews 12:22, Mount Sion (*Sion* is the New Testament form of *Zion*) is associated with "the heavenly Jerusalem," which is another name for the portion of New Jerusalem that will descend from on high (21:10). Modern revelation clarifies further that Mount Zion "shall be the city of New Jerusalem" (D&C 84:2; 133:18, 56). When the Lord stands on Mount Zion in the latter days, it appears he will be standing at the Mount Zion called New Jerusalem, which will be centered in Jackson County, Missouri. Yet he also will appear at Mount Olivet in Old Jerusalem, which is near the Mount Zion there, and the 144,000 may well be with him there as well.[1]

Mount Zion also sometimes refers to the temple;[2] in this part of the vision, therefore, John has seen the Lamb standing on the temple mount or in the temple itself.

an hundred forty and four thousand. This group of 144,000 consists of those who were sealed in 7:1–8. We learn in 14:3–5 that they have been "redeemed from the earth," that they are "virgins," that they "follow the Lamb whithersoever he goeth," that they are "the firstfruits unto God," and that they are "without fault before . . . God." See the commentary on 7:1–8; 14:3–5.

having his Father's name written in their foreheads. In 13:16–17, we saw that the people of the world had the name of the beast written on their foreheads. Here, the righteous have the Father's name written on their foreheads. We are marked by the name of him to whom we give our true loyalty. The reception of the Father's name is a fulfillment of the promise made to the valiant in 3:12, which records that the righteous also have written on them the name of God's holy city, New Jerusalem, as well as the new name of Christ (see commentary on 3:12). The Father's name is written on the righteous in a symbolic rather than a literal way.

---

[1] McConkie, *Doctrinal New Testament Commentary,* 3:525–26.
[2] D&C 84:32; *Anchor Bible Dictionary,* 6:1096.

There is another way in which we may receive the name of the Father and the Son in our foreheads. A name stands for the person it belongs to. When Alma asked, "Can ye look up to God at that day [the day of judgment] . . . having the image of God engraven upon your countenances?" (Alma 5:19), he may have been referring to the same idea John is speaking of here.

14:2 *a voice from heaven, as the voice of many waters, and . . . great thunder.* This voice may be that of the Lord (1:15; D&C 110:3) or of the multitude of angels in heaven (19:6). It is more likely the latter, as the angels join in the song mentioned in 14:3. The sound is so loud it is like the roar of the ocean or of a rushing river; it is like the clapping of mighty thunder (see commentary on 1:15; see also Ezek. 1:24; 43:2).

the voice of harpers harping with their harps. John also hears the sound of harps accompanying the multitude in the song. Harps appear to be the instrument most often used by those in God's heavenly kingdom (see also 5:8; 15:2).

14:3 *they sung as it were a new song.* The harpers, and perhaps others in heaven, are singing a song before the throne of God. The song and its setting are likely those described in Doctrine and Covenants 84:96–102:

For I, the Almighty, have laid my hands upon the nations, to scourge them for their wickedness. And plagues shall go forth, and they shall not be taken from the earth until I have completed my work, which shall be cut short in righteousness—until all shall know me, who remain, even from the least unto the greatest, and shall be filled with the knowledge of the Lord, and shall see eye to eye, and shall lift up their voice, and with the voice together sing this new song, saying:

> The Lord hath brought again Zion;
> The Lord hath redeemed his people, Israel,
> According to the election of grace,
> Which was brought to pass by the faith
> And covenant of their fathers.
>
> The Lord hath redeemed his people;
> And Satan is bound and time is no longer.
> The Lord hath gathered all things in one.
> The Lord hath brought down Zion from above.
> The Lord hath brought up Zion from beneath.

The earth hath travailed and brought forth her strength;
And truth is established in her bowels;
And the heavens have smiled upon her;
And she is clothed with the glory of her God;
For he stands in the midst of his people.

Glory, and honor, and power, and might,
Be ascribed to our God; for he is full of mercy,
Justice, grace and truth, and peace,
Forever and ever, Amen.

before the throne, and before the four beasts, and the elders. John reminds us that he is seeing a vision of the heavenly temple, with God's throne (4:2) before which are four beasts and exalted elders (4:4, 6–10). The singers proclaim their song in the heavenly temple.

no man could learn that song but the hundred and forty and four thousand. The song is sung by heavenly beings before the throne of God. But there are also some on earth who can learn the song—the 144,000 who stand on Mount Zion with Christ. Why are these the only ones who can learn the song? Perhaps it can be known only by revelation. Or perhaps such knowledge requires a certain relationship with God and his Spirit.

14:4 *they are virgins.* The descriptions in 14:4–5 may apply to all who are exalted, though in this case they refer particularly to the 144,000. They are virgins in having refrained from entering into any unlawful sexual intercourse. They are also virgins in having remained true to Christ as their Bridegroom (19:7; 21:9; see also Jer. 2:1–4)—in having refrained from entering into spiritual adultery (Ezek. 16; Hosea 1–3). The Lord has often referred to his true people as a virgin (2 Kgs. 19:21; Jer. 18:13; Lam. 2:13; Amos 5:2; 2 Cor. 11:2). These "virgins" are contrasted with the wicked who worship the beast in Revelation 13 and who join in consort with the "mother of harlots" that is Babylon (17:5).

follow the Lamb. Those who are chosen of Christ are those who follow him in all circumstances. These do as the man said in Luke, "Lord, I will follow thee whithersoever thou goest" (Luke 9:57; see also Mark 8:34; Matt. 19:21).

redeemed. Christ, the Redeemer, has paid the price for their sins, and they are redeemed from the demands of justice and the bonds of the devil (Mosiah 15:9; Alma 12:32–34; 34:15–16).

the firstfruits unto God. Under the law of Moses, the firstfruits of the harvest were offered to God in sacrifice (Ex. 34:22, 26). As Jesus is the firstfruits of all the dead, being the first to be resurrected (1 Cor. 15:20), so are these 144,000 "the first fruits of the harvest of salvation"[3] (see also Jer. 2:2–3).

14:5 *in their mouth was found no guile.* The 144,000 speak no deceit, being honest and true like their Master (Isa. 53:9). This characteristic is in contrast to the wicked, who include the liars (21:8), who, as we saw in their worship of the beast in Revelation 13, "changed the truth of God into a lie" (Rom. 1:25).

without fault before the throne of God. A proper sacrifice had to be without blemish (Lev. 1:3, 10; 22:21). These 144,000 are like the Lamb, "without blemish and without spot" (1 Pet. 1:19; Heb. 9:14). This purity and perfection, of course, is made possible through the sacrifice of that Lamb (Heb. 13:20–21; Moro. 10:33).

THREE ANGELS OF JUDGMENT (**14:6–13**)

John sees three angels who proclaim or bring judgment upon the world. The first angel brings "the everlasting gospel" for "every nation"—and with it brings a warning that the hour of God's judgment "is come." The second angel proclaims that Babylon, the wicked world, has fallen. The third angel announces that all those who worship the beast will be "tormented with fire and brimstone . . . forever and ever." Despite the troubles and destruction that will come to the wicked, the righteous will be blessed, and if they die, they will rest in the Lord.

Revelation 14:6–13

> 6 And I saw another angel fly in the midst of heaven, having the everlasting gospel to preach unto them that dwell on the earth, and to every nation, and kindred, and tongue, and people,
> 7 Saying with a loud voice, Fear God, and give glory to him; for the hour of his judgment is come: and worship him that made heaven, and earth, and the sea, and the fountains of waters.
> 8 And there followed another angel, saying, Babylon is fallen, is fallen, that great city, because she made all nations drink of the wine of the wrath of her fornication.

---

[3] Harrington, *Revelation,* 147.

9 And the third angel followed them, saying with a loud voice, If any man worship the beast and his image, and receive his mark in his forehead, or in his hand,

10 The same shall drink of the wine of the wrath of God, which is poured out without mixture into the cup of his indignation; and he shall be tormented with fire and brimstone in the presence of the holy angels, and in the presence of the Lamb:

11 And the smoke of their torment ascendeth up for ever and ever: and they have no rest day nor night, who worship the beast and his image, and whosoever receiveth the mark of his name.

12 Here is the patience of the saints: here are they that keep the commandments of God, and the faith of Jesus.

13 And I heard a voice from heaven saying unto me, Write, Blessed are the dead which die in the Lord from henceforth: Yea, saith the Spirit, that they may rest from their labours; and their works do follow them.

NOTES AND COMMENTARY

14:6 *another angel fly in the midst of heaven.* In latter-day revelation, the Lord clarifies that the angel John sees here has been sent to "commit" the gospel to man, suggesting that the gospel has been lost and would be restored: "And now, verily saith the Lord, . . . I have sent forth mine angel flying through the midst of heaven, having the everlasting gospel, who hath appeared unto some and hath committed it unto man, who shall appear unto many that dwell on the earth. And this gospel shall be preached unto every nation, and kindred, and tongue, and people. And the servants of God shall go forth, saying with a loud voice: Fear God and give glory to him, for the hour of his judgment is come; and worship him that made heaven, and earth, and the sea, and the fountains of waters—calling upon the name of the Lord day and night, saying: O that thou wouldst rend the heavens, that thou wouldst come down, that the mountains might flow down at thy presence" (D&C 133:36–40).

This angel is generally considered to be Moroni. We read in the Doctrine and Covenants that Moroni was the angel "whom I have sent unto you to reveal the Book of Mormon, containing the fulness of my everlasting gospel" (D&C 27:5). This angel is the angel who will sound the fifth trump at the time of the resurrection and the end of the world (D&C 88:103; see also vv. 94–110); this may or may not be the same as the angel with the fifth trump in 9:1–12.

Elsewhere Joseph Smith taught: "All the testimony is that the Lord in the last days would commit the keys of the Priesthood to a witness over all people. Has the Gospel of the kingdom commenced in the last days? . . . I have read it precisely as the words flowed from the lips of Jesus Christ. John the Revelator saw an angel flying through the midst of heaven, having the everlasting Gospel to preach unto them that dwell on the earth.

"The scripture is ready to be fulfilled when great wars, famines, pestilence, great distress, judgments, &c., are ready to be poured out on the inhabitants of the earth. John saw the angel having the holy Priesthood, who should preach the everlasting Gospel to all nations. God had an angel—a special messenger—ordained and prepared for that purpose in the last days."[4]

Joseph Smith does not clearly identify the angel here, but the context suggests that the angel would come to "commit the keys of the Priesthood"; "John saw the angel having the holy Priesthood." Moroni certainly had the priesthood, but he did not commit any priesthood keys—that was done by Peter, James, and John, Elijah, Moses, and others (D&C 110; 128:20–21).

Elder Bruce R. McConkie suggests that the angel seen by John in this verse was symbolic of many angels: "Paul makes the apt statement that the gospel consists of two parts: the word and the power. (1 Thess. 1:5.) . . . Thus the angel Moroni brought the message, that is, the word; but other angels brought the keys and priesthood, the power."[5]

Doctrine and Covenants 77:8 lends credence to the idea that many angels joined together to accomplish the restoration of the gospel. Joseph Smith speaks there by revelation of "four angels sent forth from God . . . ; these are they who have the everlasting gospel to commit to every nation, kindred, tongue, and people."

having the everlasting gospel. The gospel with its laws, principles, and powers is eternal, lasting forever. The expression "everlasting gospel" or "everlasting covenant of the gospel" appears twenty-six times in the Doctrine and Covenants (see, for example, D&C 101:22, 39).

to preach . . . to every nation. The gospel is destined to go forth to the entire world—"every nation, and kindred, and tongue, and people." This is the final divine commission the Savior gave his apostles: "Go ye therefore, and teach all nations, baptizing them in the name of the Father, and of the Son, and of the Holy Ghost" (Matt. 28:19).

---

[4] *Teachings of the Prophet Joseph Smith,* 364–65.
[5] McConkie, *Doctrinal New Testament Commentary,* 3:530.

14:7 *loud voice.* The angel's "loud voice" is intended to be heard by all. See commentary on 12:9.

Fear God, and give glory to him. The whole world has been worshipping the beast. But the angel tells them they must turn to God and reverence and honor him.

the hour of his judgment is come. Hour here is probably not literal but may represent a short period of time, as if to say, "His judgment is about to begin." *Judgment* does not refer to the Last Judgment but to the time when God will punish the world (send his judgments) for its wickedness. The judgment will be a time of terror for the wicked, but it will represent deliverance for the righteous from the rule of the wicked. This judgment and deliverance come through Christ. As he said in his final mortal days, so can Christ say again at his second coming: "Now is the judgment of this world: now shall the prince of this world be cast out" (John 12:31).

This verse, in essence, is a call to the world to repent. This call—and reminder of the hour of the Lord's judgment—was repeated early in the days of the restoration of the gospel, as seen by John. By command of the Lord, Joseph Smith placed these powerful words at the beginning of the Doctrine and Covenants:

"Hearken, O ye people of my church, saith the voice of him who dwells on high. . . .

"For verily the voice of the Lord is unto all men, and there is none to escape; and there is no eye that shall not see, neither ear that shall not hear, neither heart that shall not be penetrated. . . .

"And the rebellious shall be pierced with much sorrow; for their iniquities shall be spoken upon the housetops, and their secret acts shall be revealed. . . .

"Wherefore, fear and tremble, O ye people, for what I the Lord have decreed . . . shall be fulfilled. . . .

"Wherefore the voice of the Lord is unto the ends of the earth, that all that will hear may hear:

"Prepare ye, prepare ye for that which is to come, for the Lord is nigh;

"And the anger of the Lord is kindled, and his sword is bathed in heaven, and it shall fall upon the inhabitants of the earth. . . .

"Wherefore, I the Lord, knowing the calamity which should come upon the inhabitants of the earth, called upon my servant Joseph Smith, Jun., and spake unto him from heaven, and gave him commandments;

"And also gave commandments to others, that they should proclaim these things unto the world; and all this that it might be fulfilled, which was written by the prophets" (D&C 1:1–3, 7, 11–13, 17–18).

worship him that made heaven/earth/sea/fountains of waters. God has all power, even greater than the beast in Revelation 13. It is the true God that all mankind should worship, and none else (Ex. 20:2–6; Acts 14:15).

14:8 *there followed another angel.* John sees a second angel of judgment. This angel has yet to come, because he proclaims the fulfillment of an event yet to occur.

Babylon is fallen. Babylon, the city that was the epitome of the wicked, idolatrous, immoral world, was destroyed—and so will symbolic Babylon. This is her prophetic destiny, and it surely will occur, as many prophets have foreseen (Isa. 21:9; Jer. 51:7–8; Dan. 5:25–28). The fall of Babylon is a direct result of the judgment of God declared in 14:7; the cause of that judgment follows: she induced the people of the world to join in "fornication," which is a symbolic reference to worship of gods other than the true God. In a literal sense, the "fall of Babylon" means that the wicked world will cease to exist.

that great city. Babylon is the great city of wickedness, standing in opposition to the great city of righteousness, New Jerusalem. Anciently, Babylon was a literal city, but in prophecy she stands as a symbol of the wicked world. The New Jerusalem will be a literal city in the future; she also stands as a symbol of the union of the righteous.

she made all nations drink. Certainly Babylon did not force the people of the world to participate in sin. But through her inducements and enticements, she was able to seduce the world into accepting her godless philosophies and approaches to life. The term *drink* suggests that the wicked have truly internalized their sinfulness.

the wine of the wrath of her fornication. This expression combines two phrases that are found elsewhere in Revelation: "the wine of the wrath of God" (14:10) and "the wine of her fornication" (17:2). The Jerusalem Bible seems to fit these meanings together well in its translation: "Babylon which gave the whole world the wine of God's anger to drink." The Revised Standard Version interprets *wrath* as *passion:* "made all nations drink the wine of her impure passion." The New International Version gives the idea of madness: "made all the nations drink the maddening wine of her adulteries" (see also Jer. 51:7). *Fornication* here refers to the evil practice of leaving the true Bridegroom and going after other gods, as both the world and the Lord's people too often do (2:20). *Fornication* may also refer literally to sexual immorality, which often accompanies the grosser levels of wickedness on the earth. The underlying meaning is that Babylon (the wicked element of the world) has enticed the nations to become intoxicated with sin and that both Babylon and the nations of the world will be punished by God in his wrath. In bringing others to this fornication, Babylon is nothing less than a harlot (17:1–6).

14:9 *the third angel followed them.* In this part of the vision, John sees the angels come in a trio, the first bearing the gospel, the second proclaiming the fall of Babylon, and the third warning of the fate of those who join with the beast.

loud voice. See commentary on 12:9.

14:9–10 *If any man worship the beast/shall drink of the wine of the wrath of God.* In 13:15, we saw that all who refused to worship the beast were to be put to death. Here, in sobering contrast, we see that all who enter into such worship receive a much more terrible punishment—they receive the wrath of God into their very beings. God's punishing anger is often depicted in the Old Testament as a symbolic drink made up of his wrath, which the wicked are forced to swallow (Job 21:20; Ps. 75:8; Isa. 51:17; Jer. 25:15–28). Wine also symbolizes blood (3 Ne. 20:8; D&C 20:79); the wicked, who refuse the atoning blood of Christ, will be forced to drink of wine that typifies the blood of sinfulness (Isa. 49:26; Jacob 1:19).

14:10 *poured out without mixture into the cup of his indignation.* Speaking symbolically, God has a cup of mercy and blessing (Ps. 23:5; 116:13) and a cup of anger and vengeance (16:19; Isa. 51:17; D&C 29:17; 43:26). In the day of judgment, when "the cup of their [the world's] iniquity is full" (D&C 101:11; 103:1–3), the Lord will pour out punishment into his cup of wrath, unmixed (or undiluted) with mercy, as wine was sometimes mixed—or not mixed—with water.[6] The wicked will then be required to drink of the punishment in the Lord's cup. He cannot give mercy (meaning, grant them the blessings of the Atonement) because they did not repent.

tormented with fire and brimstone. Isaiah described the destruction of Edom (another symbol for the world, as was Babylon) in similar terms:

---

[6] Mounce, *Book of Revelation,* 273.

"The indignation of the Lord is upon all nations. . . . For it is the day of the Lord's vengeance. . . . And the streams thereof shall be turned into pitch, and the dust thereof into brimstone, and the land thereof shall become burning pitch. It shall not be quenched night nor day; the smoke thereof shall go up for ever" (Isa. 34:2, 5, 8–10). These images draw from the destruction of Sodom and Gomorrah, which is a type of the destruction of the world (Gen. 19:24–26).

The fate that has been prepared for the wicked, that of ceaseless burning and torment, was experienced to a degree by Zeezrom in the Book of Mormon: "Zeezrom lay sick . . . with a burning fever, which was caused by the great tribulations of his mind on account of his wickedness, for he supposed that Alma and Amulek were no more; and he supposed that they had been slain because of his iniquity. And this great sin, and his many other sins, did harrow up his mind until it did become exceedingly sore, having no deliverance; therefore he began to be scorched with a burning heat" (Alma 15:3; 36:12–14).

Though the fire and brimstone appear to symbolize the endless spiritual and emotional torment of the wicked, the idea of a burning hell is nevertheless scriptural and was taught by Jesus himself (Mark 9:44; Luke 16:9–31; Rev. 20:10).

in the presence of the holy angels, and in the presence of the Lamb. It increases the torment of the wicked to see the bliss and blessings of "the holy angels" and "the Lamb." This expression likely refers to the presence of Christ and his angels when they descend at the Second Coming, the time of judgment referred to in this verse (Mark 8:38).

14:11 *the smoke of their torment ascendeth up for ever and ever.* The prayers and praise of the righteous are symbolized by the smoke of incense that ascends to heaven (5:8). In contrast, the literal smoke of the burning of the city of Babylon—and the burning of the wicked—symbolizes the spiritual torment they suffer. Like the devil and his beast and false prophet, those who follow them—worshipping the beast and bearing his mark— will suffer torment "day and night for ever and ever" (20:10). Again, the eternal nature of the punishment of the wicked stands in contrast to the eternal blessing of the righteous (1:6; 11:15; Matt. 25:41, 46; Heb. 1:8). Those who suffer the greatest eternal punishment, of course, are the sons of perdition (Heb. 6:4–6; D&C 76:32–38). Those who inherit a lesser degree of glory than the celestial will also have eternal pangs of regret for that which they could have had, but chose, in sin, not to have.

no rest day nor night. The torments of the damned continue without cessation and without rest forever (Isa. 34:10; 57:20–21; Mark 9:43–49).

14:12 *Here is the patience of the saints.* In the midst of turmoil, the Saints are enjoined to continue in patient trust in God and his plan, to keep God's commandments, and to be true to their faith in Jesus Christ (see commentary on 13:10; see also 1:9; James 5:7–11; Heb. 6:12).

14:13 *a voice from heaven.* The Lord or one of his angels bears testimony to the blessing that will come to those who are faithful unto death (11:15).

Write. Here John is given exact words to include in his revelation. This commandment emphasizes the importance of what he has heard—he is specifically told to record it—and is a continuation of that which he received in 1:19.

Blessed are the dead which die in the Lord from henceforth. This statement, proclaimed by a heavenly voice, is one of seven "beatitudes" given in this revelation (1:3; 16:15; 19:9; 20:6; 22:7, 14; see also Appendix 5). The reason these faithful are to be considered blessed is then given: "They may rest from their labors; and their works do follow them" (see also Ps. 116:15). *Henceforth* means "from this time forward." Certainly, Saints in all ages are blessed when they "die in the Lord." Perhaps the use of *henceforth* underscores the truth that even though great trials lie ahead, those who continue faithful will be greatly blessed, even though they may die.

saith the Spirit. The voice of the Spirit here may be different from the "voice from heaven." But both voices proclaim eternal verities to the Lord's people, truths that bless and comfort and lift the heart in the midst of trial.

rest from their labours. For the righteous, the spirit world and the celestial world are places of peace and rest. There is no more sin or suffering, no pain or sickness or fatigue. And there is no longer need to work to earn our bread "in the sweat of [our] face" (Gen. 3:19; Job 3:17; Matt. 11:28; Philip. 1:21–23). As Alma taught, "The spirits of those who are righteous are received into a state of happiness, which is called paradise, a state of rest, a state of peace, where they shall rest from all their troubles and from all care, and sorrow" (Alma 40:12).

their works do follow them. Our good works will be known in the world to come. Also, the blessings and positive consequences of our good works go with us as we move into the spirit world and then into a state of resurrected glory (Matt. 25:31–46; Rev. 20:12). In addition, Joseph Smith reportedly taught that a better translation of this phrase is "they shall continue their work."[7] Though we may rest from earthly cares, the righteous in the spirit world and in a glorified celestial world will devote their new life and energy to the work of the kingdom.

THE ANGELS OF EARTH'S HARVEST (14:14–20)

This section gives us scenes of the two-phase harvest of the earth. First we see Christ with a sharp sickle, which he uses to select out the righteous as if they were wheat to be harvested. This harvest is that which was described by Jesus in his parable of the wheat field (see JST Matt. 13:24–30, 37–43; for a modern interpretation, see D&C 86:1–7).

Next, we see an angel gathering the wicked as if they were clusters of grapes and then casting them into a winepress that represents God's wrath. We see the blood that comes from the winepress, as juice flows from crushed grapes—blood so deep it reaches to a horse's bridle. Though this is a horrifying scene in John's vision, it is a scene not of injustice and wrong but of setting things right and fulfilling the law of justice. Whatever God in his wisdom and love decides to do is best for his children, both individually and as a group; whatever God chooses to do is both just and merciful and right (Alma 42:15).

Joel saw a similar vision: "Let the heathen be wakened, and come up to the valley of Jehoshaphat: for there will I sit to judge all the heathen round about. Put ye in the sickle, for the harvest is ripe: come, get you down; for the press is full, the fats overflow; for their wickedness is great" (Joel 3:12–13).

Revelation 14:14–20

> 14 And I looked, and behold a white cloud, and upon the cloud one sat like unto the Son of man, having on his head a golden crown, and in his hand a sharp sickle.
> 15 And another angel came out of the temple, crying with a loud voice to him that sat on the cloud, Thrust in thy sickle, and reap: for the time is come for thee to reap; for the harvest of the earth is ripe.

---

[7] Matthews, *"A Plainer Translation,"* 210.

16 And he that sat on the cloud thrust in his sickle on the earth; and the earth was reaped.
17 And another angel came out of the temple which is in heaven, he also having a sharp sickle.
18 And another angel came out from the altar, which had power over fire; and cried with a loud cry to him that had the sharp sickle, saying, Thrust in thy sharp sickle, and gather the clusters of the vine of the earth; for her grapes are fully ripe.
19 And the angel thrust in his sickle into the earth, and gathered the vine of the earth, and cast it into the great winepress of the wrath of God.
20 And the winepress was trodden without the city, and blood came out of the winepress, even unto the horses[']⁸ bridles, by the space of a thousand and six hundred furlongs.

NOTES AND COMMENTARY

14:14 *a white cloud.* This scene is reminiscent of one beheld by Daniel long before: "I saw in the night visions, and, behold, one like the Son of man came with the clouds of heaven. . . . And there was given him dominion, and glory, and a kingdom" (Dan. 7:13–14). Elsewhere we read of Christ coming "in the clouds of heaven with power and great glory" (Matt. 24:30; D&C 45:16, 44), but this appearance does not seem to be the Second Coming, when Christ returns in great power with his angels. Instead, he sits as a judge and conqueror upon the clouds in heaven. The cloud probably symbolizes Christ's glory (D&C 84:5). The whiteness of the cloud may symbolize victory, purity, and grace.

upon the cloud one sat like unto the Son of man. The Son of man here is Christ (1:12–20). After listing events of the last days, Jesus said, "And then shall they see the Son of man coming in the clouds with great power and glory. And then shall he send his angels, and shall gather together his elect from the four winds, from the uttermost part of the earth to the uttermost part of heaven" (Mark 13:26–27). See commentary on 1:13.

on his head a golden crown, and in his hand a sharp sickle. The Greek tells us that the golden crown is instead a golden wreath (*stephanos*), such as victors would wear.⁹ Christ comes victorious, with power to gather his Saints unto himself. The sharp sickle, the instrument of the gathering, may symbolize the missionaries who go forth with his true gospel, bearing the priesthood and conveying ordinances, bringing the righteous, like sheaves, into the Lord's barn (Matt. 13:30).

---

⁸ JST introduces this possessive.
⁹ Harrington, *Revelation*, 154.

14:15 *another angel came out of the temple.* This angel comes forth from the place where God is (7:15; 11:15–19), bearing the message that it is time for the final harvest of the righteous on the earth, preparatory to the burning of the wicked.

loud voice. See commentary on 12:9.

Thrust in thy sickle, and reap. The reaping in this verse refers to the gathering of the righteous out of the field that is the world (JST Matt. 13:24–30, 36–43; D&C 86:1–7). The time for that gathering has come; it is the last days, and "the harvest of the earth is ripe." *Ripe* means fully ready; the righteous have proved themselves and are ready to be gathered into the arms of their Lord.

"Behold, the field is white already to harvest," the latter-day revelation says, "therefore, whoso desireth to reap, let him thrust in his sickle with his might, and reap while the day lasts, that he may treasure up for his soul everlasting salvation in the kingdom of God" (D&C 6:3). Gathering the people of the world in harvest—for safety in the barn (or bosom) of the Lord, or for punishment and burning—has long been an image used by the Lord and his prophets (Jer. 51:33; Hosea 6:11; Matt. 9:37–38; 13:30, 40–42; Mark 4:29; Luke 10:2; John 4:35–38).

14:16 *he that sat on the cloud thrust in his sickle on the earth; and the earth was reaped.* Through his sickle (the righteous Saints), the Lord reaches down and gathers his people from every part of the world. This gathering seems to be that of those who will come unto Christ; the gathering of the wicked is depicted in 14:19–20.

Through the Prophet Joseph Smith, the Lord described the two parts of the gathering that will occur before the Millennium—the gathering of the righteous unto blessing, and the gathering of the wicked unto burning:

"But behold, in the last days, even now while the Lord is beginning to bring forth the word, and the blade is springing up and is yet tender—behold, verily I say unto you, the angels are crying unto the Lord day and night, who are ready and waiting to be sent forth to reap down the fields; but the Lord saith unto them, pluck not up the tares while the blade is yet tender (for verily your faith is weak), lest you destroy the wheat also.

"Therefore, let the wheat and the tares grow together until the harvest is fully ripe; then ye shall first gather out the wheat from among the tares, and after the gathering of the wheat, behold and lo, the tares are bound in bundles, and the field remaineth to be burned" (D&C 86:4–7).

14:17 *another angel came out of the temple which is in heaven.* That the angel comes out of the temple in heaven, where God is, suggests that he has first received his commission or assignment from God and then goes forth to accomplish it.

he also having a sharp sickle. If the sickle of the Lord (14:16) is the Saints going forth to do his work of gathering, this sickle, in the hands of an angel, may also be mortal beings doing the harvesting work of the Lord, but they are harvesting the wicked, preparing them to be crushed in the winepress of God—or, as we read elsewhere, preparing them to be burned (Matt. 13:38–40; D&C 86:7). Perhaps this is done by bearing strong testimony to all people, and those who refuse to repent are then judged worthy to be destroyed.

14:18 *another angel came out from the altar, which had power over fire.* This angel also comes from the temple but specifically from the altar. This passage may have reference to the angel in 8:3–5, who stood at the altar of incense, which was offered with the prayers of the Saints: "And the angel took the censer, and filled it with fire of the altar, and cast it into the earth" (8:5). This angel, who has authority over the fire of the altar, commands the angel with the sickle to gather the wicked to be destroyed. Ultimately, that destruction will come by fire (18:8).

a loud cry to him that had the sharp sickle. The angel from the altar commands the angel with the sickle to thrust it down to earth, to cut down and gather the wicked. The wicked are "the clusters of the vine of the earth"; they are "fully ripe" in their wickedness (contrast with the ripeness of the righteous in 14:15).

14:19 *the angel thrust in his sickle into the earth, and gathered the vine of the earth.* The wheat that represents the righteous has been gathered, separated unto itself. The ripened grapes of the vine represent the wicked, those who bring forth evil fruit (Matt. 7:16–20), who are now ready to be harvested. The angel is the destroying angel, sent forth by God to perform his work of destruction and judgment. The gathering depicted here, however, is not the end of the world, for much must still transpire. Many details of the gathering are depicted in the chapters that follow.

For now, John seems to be giving us an overview, from the war in heaven to the great and final destruction, that the righteous may know with certainty the outcome of the great conflict between good and evil, between God and the devil.

cast it into the great winepress of the wrath of God. As grapes were harvested, they were placed in a trough and trampled by foot; the juice then flowed through a duct into a lower basin. In symbolic terms, the winepress represents the great press of God's wrath (meaning the execution of his judgments), which, according to justice, exacts the full terrible payment for sin. The grapes, which represent the sinner, are trodden under foot until nothing is left but pulp and wine—the wine being a symbol of the blood of the sinner.

In performing the Atonement, Christ suffered that wrath for us, so that we might escape both the wrath and the consequent suffering if we would repent. In the time of judgment, all those who did not truly repent and come unto Christ will suffer the wrath of God themselves; it will be for them as if they themselves were cast into the winepress and trampled. "I have trodden the winepress alone," the Lord said through Isaiah, "I will tread them in mine anger, . . . and their blood shall be sprinkled upon my garments" (Isa. 63:3). Doctrine and Covenants 19:11–19 describes the suffering of Christ in performing the Atonement—and the suffering of those unrepentant souls who will be cast into the winepress themselves (see also D&C 133:46–51; Rev. 14:8–11).[10]

14:20 *the winepress was trodden without the city.* Jesus suffered for the sins of the world outside the city of Jerusalem, in the Garden of Gethsemane and later at Golgotha (Heb. 13:12; Luke 22:39–44; John 19:20). In the same way, the nations will come to their judgment outside the city of Jerusalem, with the destruction centered in the valley of Jehoshaphat (probably the Kidron valley, which runs between Jerusalem and the Mount of Olives; Joel 3:12–14; Zech. 14:1–4).[11] Because the wicked refused the blessings of the suffering of Christ—the benefits of the blood that was shed for them—they must now suffer for themselves, shedding their own blood.

blood came out of the winepress, even unto the horses'[12] bridles, . . . a thousand and six hundred furlongs. The language here is very plain: rather than using wine or red grape juice as a symbol for blood, John simply says, "blood came out of the winepress." The slaughter of the wicked in the day of their judgment creates a flood of their blood. The depth of the flow of blood reaches up to the bridle of a horse. The length of the river of blood

---

[10] Parry, Parry, and Peterson, *Understanding Isaiah,* 555.

[11] Mounce, *Book of Revelation,* 281.

[12] JST 14:20 introduces this possessive.

(sixteen hundred furlongs) is about 184 miles, or the approximate length of the land of Palestine. In this verse, the city seems to symbolize the holy places that are protected by God; the land outside the city may represent all the people of the world who are subjected to God's terrible but righteous judgments.[13]

---

[13] Mounce, *Book of Revelation,* 281.

REVELATION
15

SEVEN ANGELS WITH SEVEN PLAGUES (15:1–8)

In this scene, John sees a vision of celestial glory. He sees those who have "gotten the victory over the beast" singing a song of praise to God. Paradoxically, many who gain victory over the beast were first slain by that beast (13:7, 15); by standing firm in their testimonies, even unto death, they eventually emerge victorious. John also sees seven angels being prepared to pour out seven final judgments on the earth (15:1, 7). We do not yet see what those judgments are (that is reserved for the next chapter), but they appear to be terrible: "In them is filled up the wrath of God" (15:1).

Revelation 15:1–8

1 And I saw another sign in heaven, great and marvellous, seven angels having the seven last plagues; for in them is filled up the wrath of God.
2 And I saw as it were a sea of glass mingled with fire: and them that had gotten the victory over the beast, and over his image, and over his mark, and over the number of his name, stand on the sea of glass, having the harps of God.
3 And they sing the song of Moses the servant of God, and the song of the Lamb, saying, Great and marvellous are thy works, Lord God Almighty; just and true are thy ways, thou King of saints.
4 Who shall not fear thee, O Lord, and glorify thy name? for thou only art holy; for all nations shall come and worship before thee; for thy judgments are made manifest.
5 And after that I looked, and, behold, the temple of the tabernacle of the testimony in heaven was opened:
6 And the seven angels came out of the temple, having the seven plagues, clothed in pure and white linen, and having their breasts girded with golden girdles.

7 And one of the four beasts gave unto the seven angels seven golden [bowls][1] full of the wrath of God, who liveth for ever and ever.
8 And the temple was filled with smoke from the glory of God, and from his power; and no man was able to enter into the temple, till the seven plagues of the seven angels were fulfilled.

NOTES AND COMMENTARY

15:1 *And I saw another sign in heaven, great and marvellous.* Another sign gives us to understand that the scene in the vision has shifted. As with the other signs in John's vision, what he sees as a sign symbolizes a great truth. In this case, the truth is that God will indeed exact judgment against the wicked, a judgment that will be complete and terrible. The phrase "great and marvellous" suggests a sign that is absolutely overwhelming.

seven angels having the seven last plagues. These seven last plagues are the Lord's final attempt to cause the hearts of the wicked to be softened and to turn to him. After these plagues will come the actual fall of Babylon and the second coming of Christ. Because seven is a number signifying perfection, seven angels with seven plagues indicates perfect and complete judgment against the wicked of the earth. This prophecy is reminiscent of the curse the Lord gave against the wicked in Leviticus 26:21: "If ye walk contrary unto me, and will not hearken unto me; I will bring seven times more plagues upon you according to your sins." These plagues are poured out in Revelation 16.

in them is filled up the wrath of God. The plagues bring a full measure of God's wrath to the world but not the final consummation. That consummation comes in the chapters that follow.

15:2 *a sea of glass mingled with fire.* The sea of glass indicates a celestial sphere (D&C 130:6–7), and the presence of fire indicates the presence of God, who dwells amid everlasting burnings (Isa. 33:14–16).

them that had gotten the victory over the beast . . . stand on the sea of glass. Those who have refused to bow to the beast, either physically or spiritually, inherit a celestial glory. These may be the same Saints who were sealed in 7:1–8 and were named among the 144,000 in 14:1–5.

harps of God. The harps symbolize an attitude of worship and giving glory to God (2 Sam. 6:5; Neh. 12:27; Ps. 92:1–3; Rev. 14:2).

---

[1] The KJV *vials* may more appropriately be translated *bowls.* See, for example, RSV, GNB, NIV, and JB.

15:3 *And they sing the song of Moses . . . and the song of the Lamb.*
The song of Moses was sung by that great prophet and his followers after
they were delivered from the great "beast" called Egypt (Ex. 15:1–19). The
lyrics to the song spoken of in this verse include the words, "Great and
marvellous are thy works, Lord God Almighty; just and true are thy ways,
thou King of saints."[2] These words are not found in the song of Moses
in Exodus 15, but the common element is what is important: the Lord's
people were in bondage and trouble, and the Lord delivered them from
their enemy.

This song is also the song of the Lamb, because he is the great Deliv-
erer. The song of the Lamb will ultimately be sung by all true Saints. On
the day of resurrection, the scripture says, "The graves of the saints shall be
opened; and they shall come forth and stand on the right hand of the Lamb,
when he shall stand upon Mount Zion, and upon the holy city, the New
Jerusalem; and they shall sing the song of the Lamb, day and night forever
and ever" (D&C 133:56).

15:4 *Who shall not fear thee/all nations shall come and worship before
thee.* The Saints cry out their praise and admiration to the Lord. Shouldn't
all nations fear and honor him? Yes, the time will come when "every knee
shall bow, and every tongue confess" that the Lord is God (Rom. 14:11;
Mosiah 27:31; D&C 88:104).

The Saints in our day sing a similar song:

> How wondrous and great
> Thy works, God of praise!
> How just, King of Saints,
> And true are thy ways!
> Oh, who shall not fear thee
> And honor thy name?
> Thou only art holy,
> Thou only supreme.[3]

thy judgments are made manifest. The nations will acknowledge the
power and supremacy of God as they see them manifest through the judgments he brings on the wicked of the earth.

---

[2] This song contains phrases from many Old Testament sources, in this order: Ps. 111:2; 139:14;
Amos 4:13; Ps. 145:17; Deut. 32:4; Jer. 10:7; Ps. 86:9; Mal. 1:11.
[3] *Hymns,* 267.

15:5 *I looked.* Again the vision shifts to a new scene.

the temple of the tabernacle of the testimony in heaven was opened. The ancient tabernacle in the days of Moses was called the "tabernacle of witness" (Num. 17:7), or "tabernacle of testimony," because it contained the two stone "tables of the testimony" on which God had written (Ex. 32:15; Deut. 10:5). A clearer way of stating this is found in the New International Version: "I looked and in heaven the temple, that is, the tabernacle of testimony, was opened." The tabernacle of Moses served as a temple until Solomon's day, when a more permanent structure was built (1 Kgs. 8:18–20). When John looked into the heavens again, he saw the temple in heaven open and seven angels came out.

15:6 *the seven angels came out of the temple, having the seven plagues.* Apparently the seven angels received their charge in the temple and then emerged with the seven plagues. The number seven indicates that the judgments are perfect and complete. That the judgments come from the temple is a mark of their godly origin.

clothed in pure and white linen/their breasts girded with golden girdles. The linen dress of the angels, pure and white, indicates that they hold a sacred and holy office (Ezek. 9:2; Dan. 10:5). Linen also suggests the bride of Christ (19:7–8) and the armies of heaven (19:14). The high rank of the angels is deduced from the golden girdles (or sashes) they wear, which are like that worn by Christ himself (1:13).

15:7 *one of the four beasts.* In 4:6–9 John saw four beasts at the throne of God. In 5:8 the beasts worship the Lamb. In 6:1, 3, 5, and 7 the beasts invite John to see the events that occur when the seals on the book are opened. Now one of these same beasts, which are intelligent creatures, gives the angels the bowls that contain the judgments that are to be poured out on the earth.

seven golden [bowls] full of the wrath of God. The seven bowls contain the judgments that represent God's wrath (Rom. 1:18; Heb. 10:30–31). These judgments are poured out in the following chapter. Golden bowls, or vials, are mentioned in 5:8, symbolizing the prayers of the Saints. Perhaps the Saints' pleading for justice and deliverance is answered in the judgments in the seven golden bowls here.

who liveth for ever and ever. This interjection reaffirms the power and dominion of God (4:9; 10:6). As one who lives forever, unlike the mortals on the earth, God has full power to accomplish all his will against the wicked of the world.

15:8 *the temple was filled with smoke.* The source of the smoke is "the glory of God, and . . . his power." Smoke or a cloud is a typical sign of the presence of God. When the Lord descended on Mount Sinai "in fire," the mount "was altogether on a smoke, . . . and the smoke thereof ascended as the smoke of a furnace, and the whole mount quaked greatly" (Ex. 19:18; see also Isa. 6:4; Ezek. 10:4).

no man was able to enter into the temple. Because God is present in the heavenly temple, filling it with his glory, no one is able to go into it until the seven plagues are completed. This expression evidently indicates that God continues to actively exercise his power in judgment until the wicked are destroyed. No one can approach him, pleading mercy.

We read in the Old Testament of another circumstance in which God's power prevented man from entering His temple: "Then a cloud covered the tent of the congregation, and the glory of the Lord filled the tabernacle. And Moses was not able to enter into the tent of the congregation, because the cloud abode thereon, and the glory of the Lord filled the tabernacle" (Ex. 40:34–35; see also 1 Kgs. 8:10–11).

REVELATION
16

THE SEVEN ANGELS WITH THE BOWLS
OF GOD'S WRATH (16:1–21)

The day of God's judgment is a day of God's wrath—and that day is fast approaching. "Vengeance cometh speedily," the Lord says, "as a whirlwind it shall come upon all the face of the earth" (D&C 112:24).

The righteous will be blessed with a degree of protection: "Zion shall escape if she observe to do all things whatsoever I have commanded her" (D&C 97:25). But those among the Saints who are hypocrites have no such promise; indeed, they will be the first to be judged: "Upon my house shall it [the day of vengeance] begin, and from my house shall it go forth, saith the Lord; first among those among you, saith the Lord, who have professed to know my name and have not known me, and have blasphemed against me in the midst of my house, saith the Lord" (D&C 112:25–26).

This chapter of Revelation details the scourges and plagues that will afflict mankind in the day of the final judgments—plagues that will smite the land, the sea, the rivers, the sun, and the kingdoms of spiritual darkness. Through the power of God, the very foundations of the earth are shaken, and Babylon is prepared to be totally destroyed. These plagues may well fit the description the Lord gave us elsewhere in modern revelation: "For behold, and lo, vengeance cometh speedily upon the ungodly as the whirlwind; and who shall escape it? The Lord's scourge shall pass over by night and by day, and the report thereof shall vex all people; yea, it shall not be stayed until the Lord come; for the indignation of the Lord is kindled against their abominations and all their wicked works" (D&C 97:22–24).

And again: "Their testimony [the elders] shall also go forth unto the condemnation of this generation if they harden their hearts against them;

for a desolating scourge shall go forth among the inhabitants of the earth, and shall continue to be poured out from time to time, if they repent not, until the earth is empty, and the inhabitants thereof are consumed away and utterly destroyed by the brightness of my coming" (D&C 5:18–19).

Some commentators believe that the judgments in this chapter are a repetition of the plagues seen in Revelation 8, 9, and 11.[1] That is one possible reading; there are remarkable parallels between the two sections. But it seems more likely that Revelation 16 represents a later and more severe occurrence of plagues. In Revelation 8, for instance, a third of the sea becomes blood and a third of the creatures in the sea die (8:8–9). But in Revelation 16, all of the sea becomes blood and all creatures therein die (16:3). A comparison of the plagues in both sections shows a similar progression—as God continues to plead with and to punish the earth through his judgments, those judgments become more severe.

Revelation 16:1–21

1 And I heard a great voice out of the temple saying to the seven angels, Go your ways, and pour out the [bowls][2] of the wrath of God upon the earth.
2 And the first went, and poured out his [bowl] upon the earth; and there fell a noisome and grievous sore upon the men which had the mark of the beast, and upon them which worshipped his image.
3 And the second angel poured out his [bowl] upon the sea; and it became as the blood of a dead man: and every living soul died in the sea.
4 And the third angel poured out his [bowl] upon the rivers and fountains of waters; and they became blood.
5 And I heard the angel of the waters say, Thou art righteous, O Lord, which art, and wast, and shalt be, because thou hast judged thus.
6 For they have shed the blood of saints and prophets, and thou hast given them blood to drink; for they are [deserving].[3]
7 And I heard another [angel who came out from the altar saying],[4] Even so, Lord God Almighty, true and righteous are thy judgments.
8 And the fourth angel poured out his [bowl] upon the sun; and power was given unto him to scorch men with fire.
9 And men were scorched with great heat, and blasphemed the name of God, which hath power over these plagues: and they repented not to give him glory.
10 And the fifth angel poured out his [bowl] upon the seat of the beast; and his kingdom was full of darkness; and they gnawed their tongues for pain,

[1] See, for example, Draper, *Opening the Seven Seals,* 251.
[2] The KJV *vials* may be more appropriately translated *bowls.* See, for example, RSV, GNB, NIV, and JB.
[3] From the Greek; see note *c* to 16:6 in the LDS edition of the KJV.
[4] JST 16:7 amends this from the KJV, which reads, "And I heard another out of the altar say, . . . "

11 And blasphemed the God of heaven because of their pains and their sores, and repented not of their deeds.

12 And the sixth angel poured out his [bowl] upon the great river Euphrates; and the water thereof was dried up, that the way of the kings of the east might be prepared.

13 And I saw three unclean spirits like frogs come out of the mouth of the dragon, and out of the mouth of the beast, and out of the mouth of the false prophet.

14 For they are the spirits of devils, working miracles, which go forth unto the kings of the earth and of the whole world, to gather them to the battle of [the]⁵ great day of God Almighty.

15 Behold, I come as a thief. Blessed is he that watcheth, and keepeth his garments, lest he walk naked and they see his shame.

16 And he gathered them together into a place called in the Hebrew tongue Armageddon.

17 And the seventh angel poured out his [bowl] into the air; and there came a great voice out of the temple of heaven, from the throne, saying, It is done.

18 And there were voices, and thunders, and lightnings; and there was a great earthquake, such as was not since men were upon the earth, so mighty an earthquake, and so great.

19 And the great city was divided into three parts, and the cities of the nations fell: and great Babylon came in remembrance before God, to give unto her the cup of the wine of the fierceness of his wrath.

20 And every island fled away, and the mountains were not found.

21 And there fell upon men a great hail out of heaven, every stone about the weight of a talent: and men blasphemed God because of the plague of the hail; for the plague thereof was exceeding great.

NOTES AND COMMENTARY

16:1 *I heard a great voice out of the temple.* In 15:8 we learned that no one could enter the temple until the next seven plagues were completed. This voice might be the voice of God himself, commanding the seven angels to act.

Go your ways. The voice tells the angels to move ahead with their commission to administer plagues to the earth.

pour out the [bowls] of the wrath of God. Under the law of Moses, the priests used a sacred bowl to capture the blood of the sacrifice. As part of the ritual, the priest then sprinkled the blood around the altar (Lev. 1:5; 3:8). Perhaps in this part of the vision John is seeing a reversal of this ritual—rather than blood coming from the bowls to save the people, John sees something come from the bowls that sheds blood and punishes the

---

⁵ JST 16:14 changes the KJV *that.*

people. That which is poured from the bowls represents different manifestations of God's wrath.

16:2 *the first . . . poured out his [bowl] upon the earth; and there fell a noisome and grievous sore.* The first plague, which is directed at the wicked, is of "disgusting and virulent sores" (JB). This plague parallels the sixth plague that fell on the Egyptians in the time of Moses (Ex. 9:8–12). The contents of this bowl are poured out on the earth itself; and the affliction falls on those who dwell on the earth. The wicked have earlier worn the mark of the beast; now they will wear the mark of the wrath of God.[6]

Zechariah prophesies a plague that may be similar: "This shall be the plague wherewith the Lord will smite all the people that have fought against Jerusalem; their flesh shall consume away while they stand upon their feet, and their eyes shall consume away in their holes, and their tongue shall consume away in their mouth" (Zech. 14:12). And we read in latter-day revelation: "Their tongues shall be stayed that they shall not utter against me; and their flesh shall fall from off their bones, and their eyes from their sockets" (D&C 29:19). These descriptions sound very much like some of the effects of nuclear war.[7]

16:3 *the second angel poured out his [bowl] upon the sea; and it became as . . . blood/every living soul died in the sea.* This plague and that which follows parallel the first plague that the Lord brought on the ancient Egyptians—the waters turned to blood (Ex. 7:19–21). In 8:8–9, a third of the waters were afflicted; here, the polluted water kills every creature. This may have connection with words of the Lord given in our dispensation: "Behold, there are many dangers upon the waters, and more especially hereafter; for I, the Lord, have decreed in mine anger many destructions upon the waters" (D&C 61:4–5). We can only speculate on the cause of this destruction; it may be related to the fallout from nuclear war.

There may be another meaning to *sea* in this passage. In 17:15, the waters symbolize "peoples, and multitudes, and nations, and tongues." Perhaps here, as well, the sea represents the wicked people of the world, all of whom are eventually destroyed.

as the blood of a dead man. A person's blood gives life to the body, as water gives life to the world and the creatures thereof. But a dead man's

---

[6] Mounce, *Book of Revelation,* 293.

[7] The horrific results of atomic warfare can be read in Hersey, *Hiroshima.* For a description of the effects on the skin and eyes, see pages 59 and 67.

blood is corrupted and coagulated, no longer able to help sustain life. So shall it be with the waters of the seas as a result of this plague.

16:4 *the third angel poured out his [bowl] upon the rivers . . . they became blood.* This plague (like that of 16:3) parallels the one found in Exodus 7:19–21 (see also Ps. 78:44). In 8:10–11, a burning star turned a third of the rivers and fountains of waters bitter. Here, all the rivers and fountains are polluted, though the result is not given.

16:5 *the angel of the waters.* Anciently, the Jews believed that different angels had charge of different elements of nature. The vision of John seems to support this belief. In 7:1 we see four angels who have power over "the four winds of the earth." In 14:18 we read of an angel who has "power over fire." Here we have one or more angels who seem to have power over the fate of the waters. Or, if we read this verse more simply, we might understand that it refers only to the angel who, in 16:4, poured his bowl out upon the rivers.

Thou art righteous, O Lord, . . . because thou hast judged thus. Even though the judgments on the earth are terrible, the angel proclaims that the Lord is righteous and correct to have so judged (see Ps. 119:137). Why? The answer is given in the next verse. Not only have the people chosen lives of sin, but they have slain those who desired to follow the Lord. For such great sin, the Lord rightly punishes them with devastating judgments.

which art, and wast, and shalt be. See commentary on 1:4 (see also 1:8; 4:8; 11:17).

16:6 *For they have shed the blood of saints and prophets/given them blood to drink.* The motif of blood continues as we are reminded that the wicked have slain many of the righteous (13:7, 15; 17:6; 18:24)—and learn that, in a punishment that fits the crime, the wicked will themselves be forced to drink blood (Isa. 49:26). "To be drunk with blood . . . signifies slaughter by the sword."[8] The King James Version says the wicked are "worthy" of this punishment; a more accurate translation may be "deserving."[9]

The scriptures tell of many specific instances of martyrdom (1 Kgs. 18:13; 2 Chr. 24:20–21; Mark 6:25–28; Acts 7:57–60; 12:1–2; Rev. 2:13; 11:7; Mosiah 17:20; Alma 25:7). They also record many general statements documenting the rejection and killing of the Lord's prophets

---

[8] Davidson, *New Bible Commentary,* 1187.
[9] See note *c* to 16:6 in the LDS edition of the KJV.

(1 Thes. 2:15; Heb. 11:37; Rev. 6:9; 12:11; 16:6; Hel. 13:24; 3 Ne. 10:15). The mortal Jesus prophesied that martyrdom was precisely what many of his followers would suffer (Matt. 23:29–38; 24:9).

16:7 *I heard another [angel who came out from the altar].* Almost without exception, the altar in Revelation is connected with the judgments of God (8:3–5; 9:13–14; 14:18; the one exception is 11:1). The angel declares that God's judgments are indeed "true and righteous" (see also 15:3–5; Ps. 19:9)—as is the case with all his works.

16:8 *the fourth angel poured out his [bowl] upon the sun/scorch men with fire.* The righteous are promised in 7:16 that "neither shall the sun light on them, nor any heat," meaning that they will not suffer from the heat of the sun. But here the wicked suffer from intense heat, perhaps from the sun. This may result from a breakdown of the ozone layer of the atmosphere, which could result from a nuclear blast and which would remove much of our protection from the sun's potentially deadly rays, or it may have a cause that we cannot yet imagine.[10] The scriptures often connect fire with judgment (Deut. 28:22; 1 Cor. 3:13; 2 Pet. 3:7); this fire prefigures the scorching fire of the last judgment (Mal. 4:1). The fourth angel acts under the direction of God and by "power" that "was given unto him."

16:9 *men were scorched with great heat/blasphemed the name of God/ repented not to give him glory.* The heat of this plague is here described as "great," and the idea of "scorching" is repeated, perhaps for emphasis. But rather than acknowledge their guilt, the wicked appear to blame God for their troubles, speaking evil of him and his righteousness. Blasphemy is a recurring accusation against the wicked in Revelation (2:9; 16:11, 21). Even at this late hour in the world's history, men have an opportunity to repent—but still they refuse (9:20–21; 16:11; see the contrast in 11:13). An angel in 14:7 admonished the world to "fear God, and give glory to him," but the great body of people on earth choose their sin instead.

16:10 *the fifth angel poured out his [bowl] upon the seat of the beast/ his kingdom was full of darkness.* In the ninth plague that Moses proclaimed in Egypt, the whole kingdom was stricken with thick darkness (Ex. 10:21–23). Here, darkness fills the kingdom of the beast (Isa. 60:2; D&C 82:5; 84:49; 112:23). The darkness may be literal or spiritual—or

---

[10] For a discussion of the effects of nuclear war on the ozone layer, see Schell, *Fate of the Earth,* 20–21, 79–92.

both. Most likely, because the darkness results from an action of an angel of God, who would not be the source of spiritual darkness, it is probably a literal darkness that reflects the spiritual darkness in the beast's kingdom. The "seat of the beast" may more accurately be translated the "throne of the beast" (RSV, NEB, JB, NIV). The idea is that the Lord will attack the beast at his very headquarters, striking at his power and authority.

This plague may be a fulfillment of a curse that the Lord pronounced on the wicked in the times of Moses: "The Lord shall smite thee with madness, and blindness, and astonishment of heart: and thou shalt grope at noonday, as the blind gropeth in darkness, and thou shalt not prosper in thy ways: and thou shalt be only oppressed and spoiled evermore, and no man shall save thee" (Deut. 28:28–29).

16:10–11 *they gnawed their tongues for pain/blasphemed the God of heaven/repented not of their deeds.* The terrible pain that men suffer may be a result of the sores in 16:2, combined with the lack of clean water in 16:4 and the scorching heat of the sun in 16:9. The darkness into which they are plunged can only exacerbate their plight. Again they follow their leader, the beast, in blaspheming God (13:1, 5–6; 17:3), blaming him for their pains and sores. And still they will not repent. It seems incredible that people would not turn to God with humble spirits after suffering so much, but they follow the pattern of a scriptural type of long ago: despite all that he and his people suffered, the Egyptian pharaoh in the time of Moses only hardened his heart (JST Ex. 7–10). The plagues of this angel may also be connected with nuclear war.

16:12 *the sixth angel poured out his [bowl] upon the great river Euphrates/the water thereof was dried up.* In the days of Moses and Joshua, the Lord divided and dried up a passage through two different bodies of water to enable his people to be delivered from bondage and then to inherit their land of promise (Ex. 14:21; Josh. 3:13–17). But in John's vision, the Lord through his angel will dry up the water of a river to clear the way for destruction and war. The Euphrates formed the eastern and northeastern boundary of the land the Lord gave to Abraham and his descendants (Gen. 15:18; Deut. 1:7–8; Josh. 1:3–4) and served as a natural barrier to the enemies of Israel. When that barrier is removed, the enemies of Israel can begin their march. The Old Testament speaks often of the Lord drying up waters to accomplish his purposes (Ex. 14:21; Josh. 3:13–17; Isa. 11:15–16; 44:27; Jer. 51:36; Zech. 10:11).

that the way of the kings of the east might be prepared. It is uncertain who the kings of the east are. One commentator notes that there have been more than fifty different interpretations of this expression.[11] What most agree on is that the kings are enemies of the Lord's people and of the Lord himself and that they are prepared to go forth to war.

16:13 *I saw three unclean spirits like frogs come out of the mouth of the dragon/beast/ false prophet.* The "satanic trinity"[12] of the dragon, the beast, and the false prophet send forth evil spirits, or devils, to do their work. Their emergence from the mouths of the devil and his helpers suggests that these evil spirits are symbolic of false communications, lies, and propaganda designed to deceive the people of the world. Similarly, in 12:15, a river that may represent lies comes from the mouth of the dragon; in 13:5, blasphemies come from the mouth of the beast; and in 13:14, the false prophet, or second beast, seems to speak threats and ungodly commands.

Frogs, to which the spirits are compared, are unclean animals under the law of Moses (Lev. 11:10). One of the plagues that Moses and Aaron brought on Egypt was a plague of frogs (Ex. 8:2–6). Interestingly, Pharaoh's magicians, using Satan's power, duplicated this plague (Ex. 8:7). In nearby Persia, which was east of the Euphrates (16:12), frogs were "considered to be the instrument of Ahriman, the god of darkness."[13] Further, Ahriman had power to change his shape—and the animal form that fit him most naturally was that of a frog.[14]

The fact that three unclean spirits come forth from three different evil beings suggests that each of those beings (the dragon, the beast, and the false prophet) may send forth one of the spirits. These evil spirits are the agents and representatives of those who send them forth. As righteous men on earth can stand for God by virtue of the priesthood they hold, so can these unclean spirits stand for Satan through the evil power he bestows on them.

16:14 *For they are the spirits of devils.* Here we learn definitively who the three unclean spirits of 16:13 are—spirits of devils. Devils, of course,

---

[11] Walvoord, *Revelation of Jesus Christ,* 236.
[12] Harrington, *Revelation,* 166.
[13] Schick, *Revelation of St. John,* 2:51.
[14] *Interpreter's Bible,* 12:485.

are not body and spirit combined but are only spirits. Perhaps a better translation would be "spirits that are devils."

The Lord has told us: "Hearken, O ye elders of my church, and give ear to the voice of the living God; and attend to the words of wisdom which shall be given unto you, according as ye have asked and are agreed as touching the church, and the spirits which have gone abroad in the earth. Behold, verily I say unto you, that there are many spirits which are false spirits, which have gone forth in the earth, deceiving the world. And also Satan hath sought to deceive you, that he might overthrow you" (D&C 50:1–3).

working miracles. Jesus Christ prophesied that "there shall arise false Christs, and false prophets, and shall shew great signs and wonders; insomuch that, if it were possible, they shall deceive the very elect" (Matt. 24:24; see also commentary on 13:14). These evil spirits are part of the fulfillment of that prophecy. The miracles of Satan and the miracles of God may often be indistinguishable from one another to the outward senses. Only through the discernment given by the Spirit of God can we know the difference.

Elder Orson Pratt wrote, "The reason the Lord will suffer the devil to work miracles to deceive 'the kings of the earth and of the whole world,' is because they will previously have rejected 'the everlasting gospel;' therefore the devil will deceive them, and lead them on to destruction, as he did the Egyptians."[15]

go forth unto the kings of the earth and of the whole world. The deceiving spirits sent forth by Satan will have worldwide influence, including with the rulers of the nations of the earth. The spirits will cause the gathering of the kings and their armies together to battle.

to gather them to the battle. This battle is the great final battle at Armageddon, which will be fought by the armies of the earth (16:16). That battle, perhaps when it reaches its crisis point, will be interrupted by the coming of the Lord (Zech. 14:1–4), "the great day of God Almighty."

great day of God Almighty. See commentary on 6:17.

16:15 *Behold, I come as a thief.* See commentary on 3:3.

Blessed is he that watcheth. We have often been commanded to be alert and to watch the signs of the times as the day of Christ's return draws

---

[15] Pratt, *Divine Authenticity of the Book of Mormon,* no. 5 (1851): 66.

closer (Matt. 24:42–51; 25:1–13; D&C 45:44; 133:10–11). Watching also implies being obedient and prepared (Matt. 24:45–46, 48–51; 25:3–4, 8–9). Specifically, latter-day revelation tells us we need to be prepared by having the Holy Spirit for our guide (D&C 45:56–57).

keepeth his garments, lest he walk naked and they see his shame. To keep one's garments is to be ready for any eventuality (specifically, here, the coming of the Lord). If a soldier does not know when the battle will begin, he needs to keep the proper clothing (armor) at hand for any eventuality. If he does not, he might be caught unawares and have to go forth naked.[16]

But there is a deeper meaning, suggested by a similar statement in 3:3–5. There we read the warning that the Lord will come as a thief and the promise that those who have "not defiled their garments . . . shall walk with me in white" (3:4). To keep one's garments in this sense is to keep them pure, to avoid and resist sin. It is to keep the covenants and promises one made in the temple. As Alma said, "And may the Lord bless you, and keep your garments spotless, that ye may at last be brought to sit down with Abraham, Isaac, and Jacob, and the holy prophets who have been ever since the world began, having your garments spotless even as their garments are spotless, in the kingdom of heaven to go no more out" (Alma 7:25).

This verse is an interjection, a parenthetical warning and word of comfort to the Saints: The terrors of the last days will continue and worsen. Those who yield themselves to sin will be exposed, but those who remain prepared and pure will be blessed.

16:16 *he gathered them together/Armageddon.* Armageddon is the site of the last great battle before the coming of the Lord. The person gathering the armies together is not identified, but it is likely Satan, working through the evil spirits he sends to the earth (16:14). Armageddon is the New Testament name for Megiddo, an ancient city some sixty miles north of Jerusalem. Megiddo lay "on the north side of the Carmel ridge and command[ed] the strategic pass between the coastal plain and the valley of Esdraelon." The area "is one of history's famous battlefields, having witnessed major conflicts all the way 'from one fought by Tuthmosis III in 1468 B.C. to that of Lord Allenby of Megiddo in 1917.' 'By the waters of

---

[16] Mounce, *Book of Revelation,* 300.

Megiddo' Barak and Deborah defeated the chariots of Sisera (Judg. 4–5; cf. 5:19)."[17] In that same area, Gideon and his three hundred soldiers defeated the Midianites (Judg. 7) , and Saul and Jonathan were killed in battle (1 Sam. 31:1–6), as was King Josiah (2 Kgs. 23:29–30). "The kings of the whole world will be destroyed in final conflict outside the city of Jerusalem. . . . Armageddon is symbolic of the final overthrow of all the forces of evil by the might and power of God."[18]

The great battle of Armageddon will not be a localized conflict but the center of a worldwide war. Elder Bruce R. McConkie explained, "The center of the battle will be on the mount and in the valley of Megiddo and on the plains of Esdraelon, though, since all nations are involved, it cannot be other than a worldwide conflict."[19]

The battle of Armageddon was seen and prophesied anciently by Joel and Zechariah (see also Luke 21:20–23):

"Prepare war, . . . Beat your plowshares into swords, and your pruning-hooks into spears: let the weak say, I am strong. Assemble yourselves, and . . . come up to the valley of Jehoshaphat: for there will I sit to judge all the heathen round about. Put ye in the sickle, for the harvest is ripe: come, get you down; for the press is full, the fats overflow; for their wickedness is great. Multitudes, multitudes in the valley of decision: for the day of the Lord is near in the valley of decision" (Joel 3:9–14).

"For I will gather all nations against Jerusalem to battle; and the city shall be taken, and the houses rifled, and the women ravished; and half of the city shall go forth into captivity. . . . Then shall the Lord go forth, and fight against those nations, as when he fought in the day of battle. And his feet shall stand in that day upon the mount of Olives, which is before Jerusalem on the east, and the mount of Olives shall cleave in the midst thereof toward the east and toward the west. . . . And ye shall flee to the valley of the mountains; . . . and the Lord my God shall come, and all the saints with thee" (Zech. 14:2–5).

Ultimately, the objective of Satan and his armies is not the conquest of northern Israel nor of Jerusalem but the destruction of the Lord's temple and the Lord's work.[20]

---

[17] Mounce, *Book of Revelation,* 301.
[18] Mounce, *Book of Revelation,* 302
[19] McConkie, *Millennial Messiah,* 397.
[20] McConkie, *Millennial Messiah,* 476–94.

16:17 *the seventh angel poured out his [bowl] into the air.* Other angels poured their bowls out upon the earth, the sea, the rivers, the sun, the seat of the beast, and the Euphrates. By pouring his bowl out into the air, the angel seems to be affecting all of earth through its all-encompassing atmosphere. The sounding of the last trumpet and the pouring forth of the last bowl are quite similar in their results, both signifying the end of earth's history.

Table 5

Trumpet	Bowl
the Lord's kingdom is established (11:15)	God's purpose is accomplished (16:17)
the time of judgment is announced (11:18)	judgment falls on the earth (16:19–20)
the temple in heaven is opened (11:19)	a great voice comes from the temple in heaven (16:17)
there are lightnings, voices, thunderings, a great earthquake, and a hailstorm (11:19)	there are voices, thunders, lightnings, a great earthquake, and hail (16:18, 21)

Though there are parallels between the events following the sounding of the trumpet and the pouring forth of God's wrath from the bowl, these two events may well be different, occurring at different times. The first series seems to prefigure the second.

great voice out of the temple of heaven, from the throne, saying, It is done. Because this voice comes from the throne in the temple of heaven, it must belong to God the Father, who is seated on that throne and rules over all. By saying "It is done," he announces that all things have been accomplished and the time has come for the final destruction of Babylon and of the earth.

16:18 *there were voices, and thunders, and lightnings.* The thunders and lightnings may indicate that all nature is in an uproar as a result of the judgments poured forth from the last bowl. The voices may be God's proclamations of judgment and command as we see in the Doctrine and Covenants, where he prepares the earth to return to its paradisiacal glory: "And he shall utter his voice out of Zion, and he shall speak from Jerusalem, and his voice shall be heard among all people; and it shall be a voice as the voice of many waters, and as the voice of a great thunder, which shall break down the mountains, and the valleys shall not be found. He shall command the great deep, and it shall be driven back into the north countries, and the islands shall become one land; and the land of Jerusalem and the land of Zion shall be turned back into their own place, and the earth shall be like as it was in the days before it was divided. And the Lord, even the Savior, shall stand in the midst of his people, and shall reign over all flesh" (D&C 133:21–25). See commentary on 4:5; see also 8:5; 11:19.

there was a great earthquake. This earthquake is different from the ones mentioned in 6:12 and 11:13–14. The earthquake in 6:12 was so great that the mountains and islands are "moved out of their places" (6:14), but that earthquake occurred in the period of the sixth thousand years (D&C 77:6–7). The earthquake in 11:13–14 was the first in the seventh thousand-year period; it is of indeterminate size and intensity. The earthquake in 16:18 is described as the greatest in the history of the world. It is so great, as we read in 16:20, that it appears to be connected with the flattening of the mountains and the unifying of the continents.

"One of the plainest and most-oft-repeated statements about the ushering in of the Millennium is the promise of a great shaking of the earth, of earthquakes that are everywhere at one and the same time, and of mountains and valleys and seas and landmasses that move. 'Yet once, it is a little while,' saith the Lord, 'and I will shake the heavens, and the earth, and the sea, and the dry land; and I will shake all nations, and the desire of all nations shall come.' (Hag. 2:6–7.) Christ, the Desire of all nations, shall come amid the greatest shaking of the earth and of all things that there has ever been or ever will be in the entire history of this planet. Everything on earth—the historical events then in progress, the beasts and all forms of life, and the inanimate objects that do not act for themselves—everything on earth will be affected by the great shaking."[21] (See also Ezek. 38:19–20; Joel 3:16; D&C 133:31.)

16:19 *the great city was divided into three parts.* The great city seems to be Babylon, which at the end times is not a literal city but a figurative city, representative of all the wicked societies of the earth. The division into

[21] McConkie, *Millennial Messiah,* 620–21.

three parts suggests that the city is fully weakened and prepared for the final destructive blow.

the cities of the nations fell. The cities of the nations fall in the earthquake, but this passage also seems to refer to the destruction of governments. The events in these verses bring about the fulfillment of the latter-day prophecy made by Joseph Smith: "With the sword and by bloodshed the inhabitants of the earth shall mourn; and with famine, and plague, and earthquake, and the thunder of heaven, and the fierce and vivid lightning also, shall the inhabitants of the earth be made to feel the wrath, and indignation, and chastening hand of an Almighty God, until the consumption decreed hath made a full end of all nations" (D&C 87:6).

great Babylon came in remembrance before God. See commentary on 14:8.

the cup of the wine of the fierceness of his wrath. See commentary on 14:10.

16:20 *every island fled away/the mountains were not found.* This passage describes the great leveling of the earth as the Lord prepares it for the millennial era. This leveling will occur as a result of the tremendous earthquake in 16:18. As we read in the Doctrine and Covenants, "Continue in steadfastness, looking forth for the heavens to be shaken, and the earth to tremble and to reel to and fro as a drunken man, and for the valleys to be exalted, and for the mountains to be made low, and for the rough places to become smooth—and all this when the angel shall sound his trumpet" (D&C 49:23; 109:74; 133:21–23).

Elder Parley P. Pratt wrote of this event: "From these verses [Isaiah 40:1–5] we learn, first, that the voice of one shall be heard in the wilderness, to prepare the way of the Lord, just at the time when Jerusalem has been trodden down of the Gentiles long enough to have received, at the Lord's hands, double for all her sins, yea, when the warfare of Jerusalem is accomplished, and her iniquities pardoned. Then shall this proclamation be made as it was before by John [the Baptist], yea, a second proclamation, to prepare the way of the Lord, for his second coming; and about that time every valley shall be exalted, and every mountain and hill shall be made low, and the crooked shall be made straight, and rough places plain, and then the glory of the Lord shall be revealed, and all flesh shall see it together, for the mouth of the Lord hath spoken it. . . .

"Having restored the earth to the same glorious state in which it first existed—leveling the mountains, exalting the valleys, smoothing the rough places, making the deserts fruitful, and bringing all the continents and islands together, causing the curse to be taken off, that noxious weeds, and thorns, and thistles shall no longer be produced; the next thing is to regulate and restore the brute creation to their former state of peace and glory, causing enmity to cease from off the earth. But this will never be done until there is a general destruction poured out upon man, which will entirely cleanse the earth, and sweep all wickedness from its face."[22]

16:21 *there fell upon men a great hail out of heaven.* Deadly hailstones are one of the elements of nature God periodically uses to assist the righteous in their battles and to punish the wicked (Josh. 10:11; Mosiah 12:6), and hailstorms are often prophesied among the troubles to come (Ezek. 13:13; 38:22; Rev. 11:19; D&C 29:16). A "very grievous hail" was one of the plagues sent upon Egypt in the days of Moses (Ex. 9:18).

every stone about the weight of a talent. Each of these hailstones weighs between forty-five and ninety pounds (the exact weight of a talent is uncertain).[23] The point is that these hailstones are tremendous in size and catastrophic in their effect.

men blasphemed God because of the plague of the hail. Not only do the people of the world fail to repent but they speak evil of God for that which he does in perfect justice.

[22] Pratt, *Voice of Warning,* 159–60, 162.
[23] Douglas, ed., *New Bible Dictionary,* 1324.

REVELATION
17

BABYLON, THE MOTHER OF HARLOTS (17:1–6)

This chapter, along with chapter 18, is a teaching interlude that shows John (and us) why the judgments in chapter 16 are righteous and just. We see, in symbolic form, the depths of the evil world and we understand why God's wrath is so strong against it. We also see the source of Babylon's destruction—not God, but Babylon's own wicked lovers.

As chapter 17 begins, John is invited to see the judgment of "the whore," but first he sees her arrayed in her power. The angel bears witness that the whore has power over all the earth ("many waters") and that she has influence over the kings and people of the world. Through the power of the Spirit, John actually sees the whore, though he is seeing a symbol surrounded by other symbolic layers of meaning. He sees her excesses in her lust for wealth and pleasure, as shown by her clothing and jewelry. He sees her pride, as shown by the name on her forehead. He sees her wickedness by that name and by her murder of the righteous.

Centuries earlier, Nephi saw a similar vision. "Many generations" after the time of peace that followed the coming of Christ to the Americas, Nephi saw the "whore of all the earth." This part of his vision clearly concerns the time of the Great Apostasy and the last days. What he saw helps us understand what John saw and recorded, particularly chapters 13, 17, and 18 of John's revelation.

As 1 Nephi 13 opens, Nephi sees "the nations and kingdoms of the Gentiles" (v. 3). Among those nations, he sees "the formation of a church which is most abominable above all other churches, which slayeth the saints of God, yea, and tortureth them and bindeth them down, and yoketh them with a yoke of iron, and bringeth them down into captivity" (v. 5).

The founder of "this great and abominable church" is the devil himself (v. 6). "And I also saw gold, and silver, and silks, and scarlets, and fine-twined linen, and all manner of precious clothing; and I saw many harlots," which, the scripture explains, "are the desires of this great and abominable church" (vv. 7–8).

Next, Nephi sees Columbus discovering America (v. 12), followed by the Revolutionary War (vv. 17–19), which further helps to place the prophecies in the time of the Great Apostasy. Nephi learns that the "great and abominable church, which is most abominable above all other churches" was formed after the Bible went forth "from the Jews unto the Gentiles" (v. 26). Further, he sees that the great and abominable church takes "away from the gospel of the Lamb many parts which are plain and most precious; and also many covenants of the Lord" (v. 26). Their motive is malicious: "And all this have they done that they might pervert the right ways of the Lord, that they might blind the eyes and harden the hearts of the children of men" (v. 27). "Because of these things which are taken away out of the gospel of the Lamb, an exceedingly great many do stumble, yea, insomuch that Satan hath great power over them" (v. 29).

In the verses that follow, Nephi learns that the "abominable church . . . is the mother of harlots" (v. 34), that that church had dug a "great pit . . . for the destruction of men" (1 Ne. 14:3), and that "that great and abominable church . . . is the mother of abominations" (v. 9). Nephi learned that there are finally only two churches on the earth, "the one is the church of the Lamb of God, and the other is the church of the devil; wherefore, whoso belongeth not to the church of the Lamb of God belongeth to that great church, which is the mother of abominations; and she is the whore of all the earth" (v. 10). "The whore of all the earth . . . sat upon many waters; and she had dominion over all the earth, among all nations, kindreds, tongues, and people" (v. 11). Because of that dominion, and "because of the wickedness and abominations of the whore," the numbers of the church of the Lamb of God "were few" (v. 12).

"And it came to pass," Nephi wrote, "that I beheld that the great mother of abominations did gather together multitudes upon the face of all the earth, among all the nations of the Gentiles, to fight against the Lamb of God. . . . And it came to pass that I beheld that the wrath of God was poured out upon that great and abominable church, insomuch that there were wars and rumors of wars among all the nations and kindreds of the earth. . . .

And when the day cometh that the wrath of God is poured out upon the
mother of harlots, which is the great and abominable church of all the
earth, whose founder is the devil, then, at that day, the work of the Father
shall commence, in preparing the way for the fulfilling of his covenants,
which he hath made to his people who are of the house of Israel" (vv. 13,
15, 17).

This great and abominable church is the church of the devil. It is the
"mother of abominations." It is the "whore of all the earth." It is Babylon.

Elder Bruce R. McConkie gave a powerful description of that church:
"What is the church of the devil in our day, and where is the seat of her
power? If we accept the angelic word, if we believe as Nephi believed, and
if, the Lord willing, we see what Nephi saw, then we shall accept without
question the reality around us. The church of the devil is every evil and
worldly organization on earth. It is all of the systems, both Christian and
non-Christian, that have perverted the pure and perfect gospel; it is all of
the governments and powers that run counter to the divine will; it is the
societies and political parties and labor unions that sow strife and reap contention. It is communism; it is Islam; it is Buddhism; it is modern Christianity in all its parts. It is Germany under Hitler, Russia under Stalin, and
Italy under Mussolini. It is the man of sin speaking in churches, orating in
legislative halls, and commanding the armies of men. And its headquarters
are everywhere—in Rome and Moscow, in Paris and London, in Teheran
and Washington—everywhere that evil forces, either of church or state or
society, can be influenced. The immanent and all-pervading presence of
evil in high places is one of the signs of the times."[1]

Revelation 17:1–6

1 And there came one of the seven angels which had the seven [bowls],[2]
and talked with me, saying unto me, Come hither; I will [show] unto thee
the judgment of the great whore that sitteth upon many waters:
2 With whom the kings of the earth have committed fornication, and the
inhabitants of the earth have been made drunk with the wine of her fornication.
3 So he carried me away in the spirit into the wilderness: and I saw a
woman sit upon a scarlet coloured beast, full of names of blasphemy, having seven heads and ten horns.

[1] McConkie, *Millennial Messiah,* 54–55.
[2] The KJV *vials* may be more appropriately translated *bowls.* See, for example, RSV, GNB, NIV,
and JB.

4 And the woman was arrayed in purple and scarlet colour, and decked with gold and precious stones and pearls, having a golden cup in her hand full of abominations and filthiness of her fornication;

5 And upon her forehead was a name written, MYSTERY, BABYLON THE GREAT, THE MOTHER OF HARLOTS AND ABOMINATIONS OF THE EARTH.

6 And I saw the woman drunken with the blood of the saints, and with the blood of the martyrs of Jesus: and when I saw her, I wondered with great admiration.

NOTES AND COMMENTARY

17:1 *one of the seven angels.* One of the angels with one of the bowls of the wrath of God (15:7) approaches John and invites him to see the judgment of "the great whore."

talked with me. John is not merely observing things in his vision, for the angel is interacting with him, apparently speaking with him as one man does with another. The angel offers to show John the whore that represents the fountain of evil in the world; in 21:9 an angel (possibly the same one) takes John to see the "bride of the Lamb." In both cases, John sees the woman as a city: the first as the wicked city of Babylon, the second as the holy city of New Jerusalem.

the judgment of the great whore. The image of prostitution was commonly used in the Old Testament to depict extreme apostasy not only from religion but from all that is godly and good (Isa. 1:21; 23:16–17; Jer. 2:20–31; 13:27; Ezek. 16:15, 28–29; Hosea 2:5; Nahum 3:4).

Nephi gives us a definition of who the great whore is: "He that fighteth against Zion, both Jew and Gentile, both bond and free, both male and female, shall perish; for they are they who are the whore of all the earth; for they who are not for me are against me, saith our God" (2 Ne. 10:16). The "judgment of the great whore" means, simply, the punishment of the world of wickedness. The judgment is described in detail in Revelation 17 and 18.

Nephi also saw that great judgment: "The blood of that great and abominable church, which is the whore of all the earth, shall turn upon their own heads; for they shall war among themselves, and the sword of their own hands shall fall upon their own heads, and they shall be drunken with their own blood.

"And every nation which shall war against thee, O house of Israel, shall be turned one against another, and they shall fall into the pit which they digged to ensnare the people of the Lord. And all that fight against

Zion shall be destroyed, and that great whore, who hath perverted the right ways of the Lord, yea, that great and abominable church, shall tumble to the dust and great shall be the fall of it.

"For behold, saith the prophet, the time cometh speedily that Satan shall have no more power over the hearts of the children of men; for the day soon cometh that all the proud and they who do wickedly shall be as stubble; and the day cometh that they must be burned.

"For the time soon cometh that the fulness of the wrath of God shall be poured out upon all the children of men; for he will not suffer that the wicked shall destroy the righteous. . . .

"Behold, my brethren, I say unto you, that these things must shortly come; yea, even blood, and fire, and vapor of smoke must come; and it must needs be upon the face of this earth; and it cometh unto men according to the flesh if it so be that they will harden their hearts against the Holy One of Israel" (1 Ne. 22:13–16, 18; see also D&C 88:94).

sitteth upon many waters. The interpretation of the expression "many waters" is given in 17:15: "The waters which thou sawest, where the whore sitteth, are peoples, and multitudes, and nations, and tongues." As Nephi saw, "[the whore] had dominion over all the earth, among all nations, kindreds, tongues, and people" (1 Ne. 14:11).

17:2 *With whom the kings of the earth have committed fornication.* The rulers of the earth, who ought to lead in righteousness, instead lead the people into sin. They "commit fornication" with the whore by selling that which is good and right and true, even their very souls, for the pleasure and power the whore will give them. They commit fornication by turning from their true husband, or at least him to whom they are betrothed—God himself—to Babylon.

the inhabitants of the earth have been made drunk with the wine of her fornication. Drunkenness here is a symbol of apostasy, in which the people lose the power of good judgment because of their unwise choices. "They are drunken, but not with wine," Isaiah prophesied, "they stagger, but not with strong drink" (Isa. 29:9; see Jer. 51:6–9). The wine that makes them drunk is not the fornication of sexuality but that of unfaithfulness to God (see commentary on 14:8).

17:3 *So he carried me away in the spirit.* Nephi (son of Lehi) received the same blessing when he experienced his vision of the last days (1 Ne. 14:30; 15:1; 2 Ne. 4:25), as did Jesus in the days of his temptation (JST

Matt. 4:8). It appears that in these instances the Spirit, or the Holy Ghost, may carry a person to another location, while at the same time enabling him to transcend his physical limitations to rend the veil. In the years before the coming of Christ to the Americas, the prophet Nephi (son of Helaman) was cast into prison—but by "the power of God . . . he was taken by the Spirit and conveyed away out of the midst of them. And it came to pass that thus he did go forth in the Spirit, from multitude to multitude, declaring the word of God" (Hel. 10:16–17). Others in the scriptures who received this blessing include Adam (Moses 6:64), Lehi (1 Ne. 1:8), Ezekiel (Ezek. 37:1), and Mary, the mother of Jesus (1 Ne. 11:19).

into the wilderness. In Revelation 12 we saw the woman who represented the church of God, the bride of Christ, go into the wilderness for safety. Now we see her counterfeit, the woman who represents the church of the devil, dwelling in the wilderness. In the first instance, the wilderness symbolized a place of refuge; here it symbolizes the dryness and desolation of sin.

I saw a woman sit upon a scarlet coloured beast. This beast is most likely the same as that found in 13:1—both have seven heads and ten horns (see commentary there). The woman is the whore spoken of in 17:1. The scarlet color of the beast is the same color as the ribbon that was tied around the neck of the scapegoat on the Day of Atonement; the ribbon represented the sins of Israel.[3] In the same way, the scarlet of the beast seems to represent sin (Isa. 1:18).

full of names of blasphemy. This phrase repeats the description of the beast in 13:1. But in the earlier reference, the beast had the name of blasphemy on his seven heads; here the beast is full of those names.

having seven heads and ten horns. As we learn in 17:9–10, the seven heads represent seven mountains and seven kings. The ten horns represent ten kings that are yet to come. These numbers may well be symbolic rather than literal. See commentary on 13:1; 17:9–12.

17:4 *And the woman was arrayed in purple and scarlet colour.* Purple clothing symbolizes royalty (Judg. 8:26), and scarlet clothing symbolizes wealth and nobility (2 Sam. 1:24; Prov. 31:21; Lam. 4:5; Dan. 5:7; Matt. 27:28–29). The woman's clothing indicates her position of wealth and power in the world.

---

[3] Edersheim, *Temple,* 312.

But there is a deeper significance. In the Old Testament, purple and scarlet appear together only in Exodus (occurring twenty-six times), and in every instance the colors are used, together with blue and white linen, to describe the tabernacle of the Lord and the clothing of the high priest (see, for example, Ex. 26:1, 31, 36). Purple and scarlet were used in the curtains of the tabernacle, the hanging for the door, the hanging for the gate of the court, and the veil itself. They were used for the ephod (linen apron) of the high priest, as well as for his girdle, the hems of his robe, the breastplate, and the cloths used in the temple rituals. Thus, the woman is standing as counterfeit for the most sacred elements of the true religion—the high priest who presided over all the people, and the temple. She is trying to supplant the religion of God with a false religion, one that points the people to sin and excess and ultimately to a worship of Satan himself (13:4).

The woman who is Babylon is not only wickedness but also political power, and moreover, not only political power but religious systems that entice all men to turn their hearts to Satan. She seems to combine elements of the first and second beasts and the false prophet.

Even with all her worldly trappings, the glory of this woman pales when compared to the "woman clothed with the sun" in 12:1 and the simple beauty of the bride of the Lamb in 19:7–8.

decked with gold and precious stones and pearls. These are symbols of wealth. The word *decked* indicates that the woman wears an excessive amount of this jewelry. In fact, everything about the woman speaks of pride, worldliness, and excess.

having a golden cup in her hand full of abominations and filthiness of her fornication. A golden cup indicates wealth—and one seeing such a cup would expect to find in it something pleasurable to drink. Instead, the woman's cup is filled with "abominations and filthiness," which stem from the woman's "fornication" in turning her heart from God to Satan (Jer. 7–8; D&C 10:20–22). Abominations are offenses against God that are particularly vile and disgusting.

17:5 *And upon her forehead was a name written.* The book of Revelation mentions a mark on the forehead seven times. We read in 13:16, 14:9, and 20:4 of the mark of the beast on the forehead or in the hands of those who follow him. In 7:3, 9:4, 14:1, and 22:4 we read of the righteous receiving the name or seal of God on their foreheads. But here the woman has her own name written on her forehead. Some authorities believe it was

common in ancient Rome for prostitutes to write their names on their foreheads, probably on a headband.[4]

Mystery. The righteous know the hidden things of God, called the
"mysteries." The greatest mysteries are reserved for those who receive the
keys to such mysteries in the temple, who keep their temple covenants, and
who hunger and thirst after the things of godliness. The woman here is the
embodiment of the mysteries of Satan, the counterfeit of the mysteries of
God. These mysteries are found in false religious creeds, in "the secret
works of darkness" (2 Ne. 10:15; 9:9; 26:22; 28:9), and in secret combinations, "which . . . is most abominable and wicked above all, in the sight of
God" (Ether 8:18; Hel. 6:22–23; Moses 5:51).

Babylon the Great. "Babylon the great is the church of the devil; it is
the world with all its evil and carnality; it is every organization of every
kind, sort and form—whether religious, civic, political, fraternal, or otherwise—which espouses a philosophy or promotes a cause which leads men
away from salvation and toward the kingdoms of lesser glory in the eternal
world."[5] As the Lord says in latter-day revelation, Babylon is "the midst of
wickedness" (D&C 133:14).

mother of harlots and abominations. Babylon not only is a prostitute
herself but is the mother of other prostitutions, other harlots on the earth.
Not only does the woman embody one form of great wickedness on the
earth, but she fosters organizations, religions, governments, philosophies,
and attitudes that embrace the devil and his world. The abominations here
include those spoken of in Daniel, where the temple and other sacred
things are desecrated and corrupted (Dan. 11:31; Matt. 24:15). And they
include the evil practice of combining harlotry with idolatry (Hosea 4:12–
14). In the scriptures the Lord calls all of the following an abomination; all
are engendered by Babylon, the mother of such things:

incest (Lev. 18:6–16, 26–27)
homosexuality (Lev. 18:22)
bestiality (Lev. 18:23, 26–27)
idolatry (Deut. 7:25; 12:29–31; Mal. 2:11)
offering an impure sacrifice to God (Deut. 17:1)
offering human sacrifice (Deut. 18:10, 12)

---

[4] Mounce, *Book of Revelation,* 311.
[5] McConkie, *Doctrinal New Testament Commentary,* 3:558.

using those who practice divination, enchantments, witchcraft (Deut. 18:10, 12)

using wizards, necromancers (Deut. 18:11–12)

using those who cast spells or consult the dead (Deut. 18:11–12)

transvestism (Deut. 22:5)

taking money earned as a prostitute into the temple to pay a vow (Deut. 23:18)

being dishonest in financial dealings (Deut. 25:13–16; Prov. 11:1)

making idols (Deut. 27:15)

sodomy (1 Kgs. 14:24)

being prideful (Prov. 6:17; 16:5; Jacob 2:13, 16; Hel. 4:11–12)

lying (Prov. 6:17, 19; 12:22)

murder (Prov. 6:17)

contentiousness (Prov. 6:19)

justifying the wicked and condemning the just (Prov. 17:15)

offering sacrifice in wickedness (Prov. 21:27)

adultery (Ezek. 18:11; 22:11)

oppressing the poor and needy (Ezek. 18:12; Hel. 4:11–12)

wilfully failing to pay debts (Ezek. 18:12)

whoredoms (Jacob 2:28)

fornication (Alma 39:3–5)

secret combinations (Hel. 7:25)

cannibalism (Moro. 9:10)

rape (Moro. 9:9)

the creeds of apostate churches (JS–H 1:18–19)

17:6 *drunken with the blood of the saints/martyrs.* Babylon is the name of the spirit that comes over those who kill the prophets. That spirit has infected much of the world. (See commentary on 16:6; also see 18:24; Matt. 23:34–35; 2 Cor. 4:8–11; Heb. 9:16.) The word *drunken* suggests that through the ages the righteous have been victims of a great slaughter—a slaughter that was intoxicating to the perpetrators.

when I saw her, I wondered with great admiration. John does not "admire" this embodiment of great wickedness. A better translation of the Greek word here would be "astonishment."[6] John is amazed or astonished at the extreme level of Babylon's wickedness.

---

[6] See note *c* to 17:6 in the LDS edition of the KJV.

THE SYMBOLISM OF THE WOMAN AND THE BEAST (17:7–18)

The angel interprets some of the symbols John has seen in his vision, particularly in chapters 13 and 17: the woman, the beast, the seven heads of the beast, and the ten horns on those heads. Although the horns of the beast, which symbolize kings, make war with the Lamb, they also, in the end, turn on the woman and destroy her. In turn, the horns of the beast are "overcome" in their war with the Lamb.

Revelation 17:7–18

7 And the angel said unto me, Wherefore didst thou marvel? I will tell thee the mystery of the woman, and of the beast that carrieth her, which hath the seven heads and ten horns.

8 The beast that thou sawest was, and is not; and shall ascend out of the bottomless pit, and go into perdition; and they that dwell on the earth shall wonder, whose names were not written in the book of life from the foundation of the world, when they behold the beast that was, and is not, and yet is.

9 And here is the mind which hath wisdom. The seven heads are seven mountains, on which the woman sitteth.

10 And there are seven kings; five are fallen, and one is, and the other is not yet come; and when he cometh, he must continue a short space.

11 And the beast that was, and is not, even he is the eighth, and is of the seven, and goeth into perdition.

12 And the ten horns which thou sawest are ten kings, which have received no kingdom as yet; but receive power as kings one hour with the beast.

13 These have one mind, and shall give their power and strength unto the beast.

14 These shall make war with the Lamb, and the Lamb shall overcome them; for he is Lord of lords, and King of kings; and they that are with him are called, and chosen, and faithful.

15 And he saith unto me, The waters which thou sawest, where the whore sitteth, are peoples, and multitudes, and nations, and tongues.

16 And the ten horns which thou sawest upon the beast, these shall hate the whore, and shall make her desolate and naked, and shall eat her flesh, and burn her with fire.

17 For God hath put in their hearts to fulfil his will, and to agree, and give their kingdom unto the beast, until the words of God [are][7] fulfilled.

18 And the woman which thou sawest is that great city, which reigneth over the kings of the earth.

---

[7] JST changes the KJV *shall be.*

NOTES AND COMMENTARY

17:7 *And the angel said unto me, Wherefore didst thou marvel? I will tell thee the mystery.* The angel serves as a guide and interpreter for John (and for us) through John's vision, offering to explain the mystery of the woman, the beast on which she sits, and the seven heads and ten horns of the beast. (For other examples of angels filling this role, see Dan. 7:15–16; 8:15–26; 1 Ne. 11–14.)

17:8 *The beast that thou sawest was, and is not/shall ascend out of the bottomless pit.* The beast that John saw in Revelation 13 received what seemed to be a mortal wound; but he was healed and given life again, to the astonishment of the world. That beast *was,* meaning at one time it existed, but it *is not,* meaning that at the time of John's vision it no longer existed on the earth. So where was it? Perhaps in the bottomless pit, which is a symbol of the prison in which Satan will be kept. Yet, some time after John's vision, the beast will come forth from the bottomless pit to continue to work his evil work on the earth. For instance, after the two witnesses have completed their work on earth, the beast who ascended from the bottomless pit will "make war against them . . . and kill them" (11:7). See commentary on 9:1–2; 13:1–8.

go into perdition. Perdition is the eternal dwelling place of Satan and those who consciously choose him instead of the light. One of Satan's names is Perdition (D&C 76:26; Moses 5:24); these followers are called the sons of perdition (D&C 76:31–48). *Perdition* is used to translate the Greek *apoleia,* which means "destruction" and which likely stems from *apollumi,* which means *ruin* or *loss.*[8] In the end, the beast (meaning all those people who embrace and support that which the beast does) will be cast into perdition with Satan, his master.

they that dwell on the earth shall wonder. In 13:3 we read that "all the world wondered after the beast" when he was healed of his fatal wound. This seems to be a repetition of that same incident.

whose names were not written in the book of life. This phrase helps us to identify those who will wonder at the beast: all those who have not truly come unto Christ and been claimed as his. We have the same qualifier in 13:8, which says that all people on earth will worship the beast except

---

[8] Strong, *Exhaustive Concordance of the Bible,* "Greek Dictionary of the New Testament," nos. 622, 684.

those whose names are written in "the book of life of the Lamb." See commentary on 3:5.

from the foundation of the world. The foundation of the world is the Creation—those whose names have been written in the book of life from the Creation will not "wonder" at the beast. Perhaps this passage refers to the Lord's foreknowledge of those who will come unto exaltation (1 Pet. 1:2; Alma 13:3, 7). Or it may refer to the collective group of the righteous, whose names were written in the book of life beginning with Adam and Eve.

when they behold the beast that was, and is not, and yet is. We read at the beginning of the verse that the beast "was, and is not." Here we read that the beast "yet is." He lived, he died, and now he lives again. See commentary on 3:3.

"This is an obvious parody of the Lamb, who was put to death yet came back to life and now is alive forevermore (1:18; 2:8). The description is also an intentional antithesis to the One 'who is, and who was, and who is to come' (1:4, 8; 4:8). In the broadest sense the beast is that satanically inspired power which, although having received the stroke of death, returns to hurl himself with renewed fury against the forces of God. It is this incredible power of resuscitation that causes the inhabitants of the earth to stand in awe. He is the beast of chapter 13 who had received a death-stroke in one of his heads and yet survived (13:3, 12, 14). Down through history he repeatedly 'comes up out of the Abyss' to harass and, if it were possible, to destroy the people of God. He is the little horn of Daniel 7 (Antiochus Epiphanes) who rises out of the fourth kingdom (the 'most terrifying' fourth beast, Dan. 7:19) to make war against the saints (Dan. 7:21). He is Nero, who instigates a persecution of the Christians to avert suspicion that he is responsible for the burning of Rome. The beast *was;* at the moment he *is not.* John wrote under the shadow of an impending persecution. The beast is about to come again. This coming will be his last, for now the King of kings and Lord of lords will throw him (along with the false prophet) alive into the fiery lake of burning sulfur (19:20)."[9]

17:9 *And here is the mind which hath wisdom.* This expression is similar to that found in a comparable setting in 13:9: "If any man have an ear,

---

[9] Mounce, *Book of Revelation,* 314.

let him hear." In other words, wisdom and thoughtful searching will bring the understandings in this chapter.

The seven heads are seven mountains, on which the woman sitteth. The beast (or political/philosophical/economic/religious power) that gives the woman her headquarters or base of operations has seven heads, which the angel tells us represent seven mountains. Rome is the traditional "city on seven hills."[10] Yet John may be referring not to literal Rome but to Rome as a symbol of all that is powerful and corrupt in the world. The number seven indicates perfection or completion—in this case, complete corruption or perfectly evil power. In other words, the woman's headquarters in any age is an evil power, as Rome was in John's day.

17:10 *And there are seven kings.* The seven heads of the beast represent seven kings. Most commentators believe that these represent seven emperors of Rome, running from Augustus (27 B.C.) to Titus (A.D. 79), with Domitian (A.D. 81) as the eighth.[11] The problem with this argument is that it ignores Julius Caesar, the first Roman emperor, plus three others who put forth rival claims in A.D. 68–69, as well as two that followed Domitian. Thus, these kings of Rome do not seem to fit with either the seven kings in this verse or the ten kings in 17:12. Other scholars suggest that the seven kings are really seven *kingdoms*—one scholar, for example, lists Egypt, Nineveh, Babylon, Persia, and Greece as the kingdoms that are past, with Rome as the kingdom in the present at the time of John's vision and with the Christian empire beginning with Constantine as the kingdom yet to come.[12] Yet the Greek text clearly indicates that the seven heads are seven kings, not kingdoms.[13]

The precise identity of the kings, however, is not as important as their function in the vision. The seven kings may represent many kings of the earth, and the number seven, which indicates perfection or completeness, may tell us that all the kings of the earth, as a whole, are part of the beast and supportive of the evil woman.

five are fallen, and one is, and the other is not yet come. Of the seven kings symbolized by the beast's seven heads, five were already dead at the time of John's vision. The sixth was reigning at that time, and the seventh

[10]Virgil, *Aeneid,* 6:782; Martial, *Epigrams,* 4:64; Cicero, *Letters to Atticus,* 6:5.
[11]Dummelow, *One-Volume Bible Commentary,* 1087; and Mounce, *Book of Revelation,* 316.
[12]Alford, *Greek Testament,* 4:710–11.
[13]Mounce, *Book of Revelation,* 317.

had not yet been born or come to power. Ultimately, we can only speculate as to whom these kings might be.

when he cometh, he must continue a short space. The sixth king had already come to power when John had his vision, but he would reign for only a short time.

17:11 *And the beast that was, and is not.* This beast is the same one identified and discussed in 13:1–8 (see commentary on 17:8).

even he is the eighth, and is of the seven. The beast has seven heads that represent seven kings. But the beast himself is also a king, the eighth in the series—yet at the same time "of the seven." This is obviously a paradox, one without an easy answer. Some argue that Nero was one of the seven and that, according to a myth, he returned. Apparently, many in the first century (presumably including some of the Saints) believed in this myth. Some believed that Nero had not died at all but had gone into hiding. Others argued that the evil, bloodthirsty Domitian was a reincarnation of the evil, bloodthirsty Nero.[14] But by now both Nero and Domitian have long since perished, yet the beast continues into the latter days as part of the seventh seal, and he will be present at the destruction of Babylon at the last day. Perhaps the beast transcends all the other kings; perhaps he, as anti-Christ, is "of the seven" in the sense that his evil purpose is fulfilled in them—and, as the eighth, he may fulfill all that the others set in motion and sought to accomplish.

and goeth into perdition. This expression reiterates that the beast will be defeated and banished from the earth.

17:12 *the ten horns which thou sawest are ten kings.* These ten kings all seem to reign during the same general period; they are united in their support of the beast and his principles and goals. The number ten here seems to signify "the whole of a part"[15]—the kings symbolized here might be representative of all the kings and kingdoms of the world (except God's), particularly those when the world is ripe in wickedness (see also Dan. 7).

which have received no kingdom as yet. The kings represented by the ten horns are all in John's future, and the prophecy seems to suggest that

[14] Mounce, *Book of Revelation,* 316; Dummelow, *One-Volume Bible Commentary,* 1087.
[15] Draper, *Opening the Seven Seals,* 193.

they will hold power during the seventh seal, when they will unite against
the whore (17:16).

receive power as kings one hour with the beast. These kings will
receive their power from the beast, but they will hold it only a short time
("one hour").

17:13 *These have one mind.* The ten kings have one united purpose,
which is to support the beast. That mind and purpose are inspired by the
master of the beast, Satan himself.

"Satan has control now. No matter where you look, he is in control,
even in our own land. He is guiding the governments as far as the Lord will
permit him. That is why there is so much strife, turmoil, and confusion all
over the earth. One master mind is governing the nations. It is not the President of the United States; it is not Hitler; it is not Mussolini; it is not the
king or government of England or any other land; it is Satan himself."[16]

and shall give their power and strength unto the beast. The ten kings
will lend their support to the principles and philosophies and goals of the
evil king and evil kingdom that is called the beast.

17:14 *These shall make war with the Lamb.* The Lamb, of course, is
Jesus Christ (see commentary on 5:6). The war is part of the war that began
in heaven (12:7) and continues as the beast tries to destroy the true believ-
ers in Christ (13:7). This war will come to a bloody conclusion at Armageddon (16:13–16; 19:17–21).

the Lamb shall overcome them. Christ will be victorious over all his
enemies, "retaining all power, even to the destroying of Satan and his
works at the end of the world, and the last great day of judgment" (D&C
19:3). This event, when Christ will conquer all at his second coming, is discussed in much greater detail in 19:11–21.

for he is Lord of lords, and King of kings. One reason why the Lamb is
successful in his battle against his enemies is that he commands the hosts
(or armies) of heaven, as the "Lord of lords, and King of kings." Not only
do both the Father and the Son reign as sovereigns over all the earth and
over every earthly ruler of any kind but they also rule over heavenly lords
and kings (1:6; 5:10; 15:3; Deut. 10:17; Dan. 2:47; 1 Tim. 6:15).

they that are with him are called, and chosen, and faithful. Those who
attend the Lamb in overcoming his enemies are those who have overcome

---

[16] Smith, *Doctrines of Salvation,* 3:315.

the world. This seems to be the same group that is described in 14:4: "These are they which follow the Lamb whithersoever he goeth." And they continue with him at the Second Coming, as seen in 19:14: "And the armies which were in heaven followed him upon white horses, clothed in fine linen, white and clean." Some of the called and chosen, of course, will still be alive as mortals at the Second Coming.

In one sense, to be called and chosen is to come to priesthood blessings and powers, in which one must be faithful (D&C 121:34–46). This phrase may also refer to those who have had their calling and election made sure.[17]

17:15 *The waters which thou sawest . . . are peoples/multitudes/ nations/tongues.* Here the angel gives a clear interpretation of where the whore is located—among all peoples of the world.

17:16 *And the ten horns which thou sawest upon the beast.* See commentary on 17:12.

these shall hate the whore. Though they once sustained and assisted the whore in her evil work on the earth, as allies of the beast that supported her, in the end the ten kings will turn on her and destroy her—which will also bring their own destruction. Nephi saw the same event: "And the blood of that great and abominable church, which is the whore of all the earth, shall turn upon their own heads; for they shall war among themselves, and the sword of their own hands shall fall upon their own heads, and they shall be drunken with their own blood" (1 Ne. 22:13; Ezek. 38:18–23).

shall make her desolate and naked/eat her flesh/burn her with fire. Here is a paradox: Though the ten horns (ten kings) grow from the beast (a kingdom and ideology, as well as a specific king), and although the horns support and sustain the beast, and although the beast supports and sustains the whore (the church of the devil, the wicked world), yet the horns shall turn on the whore and help to destroy her. An old proverb says that there is no honor among thieves, meaning that though thieves may be allies for a time, in the end they will steal from each other. The Book of Mormon says that by the wicked will the wicked be punished (Morm. 4:5). Elsewhere it says that Satan will abandon his followers at the last day (Alma 30:60). In the same way, those who do the work of the devil often turn on each other.

These kings will not suddenly become righteous but will seek their own selfish ends in destroying the whore, not realizing that by their actions

---

[17] *Teachings of the Prophet Joseph Smith,* 42, 331.

they will also destroy themselves. Perhaps the crazed self-destruction of the Nephites and Jaredites illustrates the mindless killing described here (Morm. 6:7–15; Ether 15:15–32).

The fate of the whore is striking. Instead of the finery that she once wore, the kings will strip her naked. Instead of drinking from a golden cup, she herself will be consumed—by those who turn on her like wild animals. Instead of being "drunken with the blood of the . . . martyrs" (17:6), she herself will be killed. The particular method by which she is killed is important to note. Under the law of Moses, any daughter of a priest who chooses to "profane herself by playing the whore" is to be "burnt with fire" (Lev. 21:9). Revelation 18:8 gives further details about the burning of Babylon. Ultimately, of course, Babylon, or the wicked world, will be destroyed by the fire of the coming of the Lord.

The description and fate of Babylon in the last days seems to mirror an allegory told by Ezekiel:

Rev. 17:2	Babylon the whore committed fornication with the kings of the earth
Ezek. 23:17	Aholibah (representing Jerusalem, v. 4) allowed others to "[come] to her into the bed of love, and they defiled her with their whoredom"
Ezek. 23:19	"Yet she multiplied her whoredoms"
Rev. 17:16	The ten kings will come to "hate the whore"
Ezek. 23:29	"And they shall deal with thee hatefully"
Rev. 17:16	The ten kings "shall make her desolate and naked"
Ezek. 23:26, 29	"They shall also strip thee out of thy clothes, and take away thy fair jewels, . . . and shall leave thee naked and bare"
Rev. 17:16	The ten kings "shall eat her flesh"
Ezek. 23:25	"They shall take away thy nose and thine ears"
Rev. 17:16	The ten kings "shall . . . burn her with fire"
Ezek. 23:25	"Thy residue shall be devoured by the fire"
Rev. 17:18	The woman is a symbol for "that great city, which reigneth over the kings of the earth"
Ezek. 23:4	The woman is a symbol for the city Jerusalem.

17:17 *For God hath put in their hearts to fulfil his will, and to agree, and give their kingdom unto the beast.* Though the kings likely do not know it, they serve God's greater purpose in supporting the beast for a time (Isa. 7:18; 45:1). It has not been revealed why this is part of the Lord's plan.

until the words of God [are] fulfilled. God has a plan which has been prophesied through his servants. All will proceed according to the divine will until all is accomplished (D&C 1:37). In particular, in this instance God has decreed that the kingdom of the wicked must be destroyed (14:8; 16:19; 18:8).

17:18 *And the woman which thou sawest is that great city, which reigneth over the kings of the earth.* Who is the whore? She is the church of the devil, as we have seen. She is the source and instigator of great sin on the earth. She is mysterious and secretive. And she is a political entity—a city—as well as a great gathering of people. For a time she had control of the other kingdoms of the earth, but eventually they will betray her and contribute to her destruction.

In the time of John, Rome was the great city and the very essence of evil. But Rome is only one manifestation of Babylon, which can be found in one form or another until the end. The seat and embodiment of evil is found in governments, societies, churches, and other associations of humans on the earth in all ages.

REVELATION
18

THE FALL OF BABYLON (18:1–24)

The Babylonian captivity was perhaps the lowest point of Israel's history. Elder Bruce R. McConkie wrote: "Both Isaiah and Jeremiah spoke at length of the devastations of that day and of the cursings and destruction that would come upon Babylon as a result. (Isa. 13 and 21; Jer. 50 and 51.) Babylon was truly the great enemy of the Lord's people anciently, and her overthrow and the destruction of her worldliness and wickedness was one of the things of greatest interest and concern to them. What was more natural, then, than for John and all the prophets to use Babylon as the symbol of sin, and her destruction as the overthrow of wickedness on earth."[1]

The fall of Babylon was foreseen in 14:8: "And there followed another angel, saying, Babylon is fallen, is fallen, that great city, because she made all nations drink of the wine of the wrath of her fornication." In 16:17 and 19, divine action was taken to destroy the wickedness of Babylon: "And the seventh angel poured out his vial into the air; . . . and great Babylon came in remembrance before God, to give unto her the cup of the wine of the fierceness of his wrath." The angel in 17:1 promised to show John the fulfillment of that prophecy and that divine action. But we do not actually begin to see that destruction until chapter 18, which is an extended lament, or a funeral dirge, over the loss of the great city of Babylon.

Babylon was convinced that in her strength she would never fall: "I sit a queen," she said, "and shall see no sorrow." But she will fall indeed and become a "habitation of devils." Her destruction shall be complete: "She shall be utterly burned with fire," the prophecy says. Because the world has

---

[1] McConkie, *Doctrinal New Testament Commentary,* 3:559.

given herself over to Babylon's enticements, the world will lament her demise. Joining in the lament are earth's kings, merchants, and shippers. But the righteous will have cause to rejoice over her downfall.

In latter-day revelation we read, "And the great and abominable church, which is the whore of all the earth, shall be cast down by devouring fire, according as it is spoken by the mouth of Ezekiel the prophet, who spoke of these things, which have not come to pass but surely must, as I live, for abominations shall not reign" (D&C 29:21; see also Ezek. 39:6).

"For the time speedily shall come that all churches which are built up to get gain, and all those who are built up to get power over the flesh, and those who are built up to become popular in the eyes of the world, and those who seek the lusts of the flesh and the things of the world, and to do all manner of iniquity; yea, in fine, all those who belong to the kingdom of the devil are they who need fear, and tremble, and quake; they are those who must be brought low in the dust; they are those who must be consumed as stubble; and this is according to the words of the prophet" (1 Ne. 22:23).

Elder Orson Pratt adds this testimony: "John predicts another great event to take place immediately after the proclamation of the everlasting gospel, namely, the downfall of great Babylon. . . . [S]he must fall, after she has been warned with the sound of 'the everlasting gospel.' Her overthrow will be by a series of the most terrible judgments which will quickly succeed each other, and sweep over the nations where she has her dominion, and at last she will be utterly burned by fire, for thus hath the Lord spoken. Great, and fearful, and most terrible judgments are decreed upon these corrupt powers—the nations of modern Christendom; for strong is the Lord God who shall execute His fierce wrath upon them, and he will not cease until he has made a full end, and until their names be blotted out from under heaven."[2]

Revelation 18:1–24

1 And after these things I saw another angel come down from heaven, having great power; and the earth was lightened with his glory.
2 And he cried mightily with a strong voice, saying, Babylon the great is fallen, is fallen, and is become the habitation of devils, and the hold of every foul spirit, and a cage of every unclean and hateful bird.

---

[2] Pratt, *Divine Authenticity of the Book of Mormon,* no. 6 (1851): 84–85.

3 For all nations have drunk of the wine of the wrath of her fornication, and the kings of the earth have committed fornication with her, and the merchants of the earth are waxed rich through the abundance of her delicacies.

4 And I heard another voice from heaven, saying, Come out of her, my people, that ye be not partakers of her sins, and that ye receive not of her plagues.

5 For her sins have reached unto heaven, and God hath remembered her iniquities.

6 Reward her even as she rewarded you, and double unto her double according to her works: in the cup which she hath filled fill to her double.

7 How much she hath glorified herself, and lived deliciously, so much torment and sorrow give her: for she saith in her heart, I sit a queen, and am no widow, and shall see no sorrow.

8 Therefore shall her plagues come in one day, death, and mourning, and famine; and she shall be utterly burned with fire: for strong is the Lord God who judgeth her.

9 And the kings of the earth, who have committed fornication and lived deliciously with her, shall bewail her, and lament for her, when they shall see the smoke of her burning,

10 Standing afar off for the fear of her torment, saying, Alas, alas, that great city Babylon, that mighty city! for in one hour is thy judgment come.

11 And the merchants of the earth shall weep and mourn over her; for no man buyeth their merchandise any more;

12 The merchandise of gold, and silver, and precious stones, and of pearls, and fine linen, and purple, and silk, and scarlet, and all thyine wood, and all manner [of] vessels of ivory, and all manner [of][3] vessels of most precious wood, and of brass, and iron, and marble,

13 And cinnamon, and odours, and ointments, and frankincense, and wine, and oil, and fine flour, and wheat, and beasts, and sheep, and horses, and chariots, and slaves, and souls of men.

14 And the fruits that thy soul lusted after are departed from thee, and all things which were dainty and goodly are departed from thee, and thou shalt find them no more at all.

15 The merchants of these things, which were made rich by her, shall stand afar off for the fear of her torment, weeping and wailing,

16 And saying, Alas, alas, that great city, that was clothed in fine linen, and purple, and scarlet, and decked with gold, and precious stones, and pearls!

17 For in one hour so great riches is come to nought. And every shipmaster, and all the company in ships, and sailors, and as many as trade by sea, stood afar off,

18 And cried when they saw the smoke of her burning, saying, What city is like unto this great city!

19 And they cast dust on their heads, and cried, weeping and wailing, saying, Alas, alas, that great city, wherein were made rich all that had ships in the sea by reason of her costliness! for in one hour is she made desolate.

20 Rejoice over her, thou heaven, and ye holy apostles and prophets; for God hath avenged you on her.

---

[3] JST 18:12 adds *of* in two places in this verse.

21 And a mighty angel took up a stone like a great millstone, and cast it into the sea, saying, Thus with violence shall that great city Babylon be thrown down, and shall be found no more at all.
22 And the voice of harpers, and musicians, and of pipers, and trumpeters, shall be heard no more at all in thee; and no craftsman, of whatsoever craft he be, shall be found any more in thee; and the sound of a millstone shall be heard no more at all in thee;
23 And the light of a candle shall shine no more at all in thee; and the voice of the bridegroom and of the bride shall be heard no more at all in thee: for thy merchants were the great men of the earth; for by thy sorceries were all nations deceived.
24 And in her was found the blood of prophets, and of saints, and of all that were slain upon the earth.

NOTES AND COMMENTARY

18:1 *And after these things I saw another angel come down from heaven, having great power.* John now beholds a powerful angel, different from the angel that guided him through the vision of chapter 17.

the earth was lightened with his glory. This angel is so brilliant that the very earth is illuminated by his presence. In fact, this angel's glory is like that of Christ, who will yet return: "And, behold, the glory of the God of Israel came from the way of the east: and his voice was like a noise of many waters: and the earth shined with his glory" (Ezek. 43:2). "For as the light[e]ning [of the sun] cometh out of the east, and shineth even unto the west; so shall also the coming of the Son of man be" (Matt. 24:27).

18:2 *And he cried mightily with a strong voice.* The power of the angel's proclamation equals the power of his appearance—his cry is mighty, and his voice is strong.

Babylon the great is fallen, is fallen. The angel's words are almost a direct quotation from a passage in Isaiah: "Babylon is fallen, is fallen; and all the graven images of her gods he hath broken unto the ground" (Isa. 21:9; Jer. 51:8). This same expression is found in latter-day scripture: "And again, another angel shall sound his trump, which is the sixth angel, saying: She is fallen who made all nations drink of the wine of the wrath of her fornication; she is fallen, is fallen!" (D&C 88:105).

the habitation of devils/foul spirit/hateful bird. Where once Babylon boasted of being the great and powerful city that controlled kings (17:18) and was the site of opulence and wealth (17:4), it now is not fit for human habitation. Rather than being a city or kingdom with a desired place in the world, it now is the home for devils, foul spirits, and unclean birds. This symbolic description emphasizes that the mighty Babylon will be brought to the lowest possible point.

Old Testament prophets saw the fallen city of Babylon as a wasteland, good only for foul and unclean creatures: "From generation to generation it shall lie waste; none shall pass through it for ever and ever. But the cormorant and the bittern shall possess it; the owl also and the raven shall dwell in it: and he shall stretch out upon it the line of confusion, and the stones of emptiness. They shall call the nobles thereof to the kingdom, but none shall be there, and all her princes shall be nothing. And thorns shall come up in her palaces, nettles and brambles in the fortresses thereof: and it shall be an habitation of dragons, and a court for owls. The wild beasts of the desert shall also meet with the wild beasts of the island, and the satyr shall cry to his fellow; the screech owl also shall rest there, and find for herself a place of rest. There shall the great owl make her nest, and lay, and hatch, and gather under her shadow: there shall the vultures also be gathered, every one with her mate" (Isa. 34:10–16; see also Isa. 13:19–22; Jer. 50:35–36, 40; Zeph. 2:13–15).

As it was with the literal, ancient city of Babylon, so shall it be with the spiritual Babylon that spreads itself across the world in our time.

18:3 *For all nations have drunk of the wine of the wrath of her fornication.* See commentary on 14:8; 17:1–2.

the merchants of the earth are waxed rich through the abundance of her delicacies. The New English Bible gives a helpful alternative reading: "Merchants the world over have grown rich on her bloated wealth." The world's merchants have partaken of the wealth and luxury of Babylon, and they thereby have become part of her. This verse points out the worldwide power of Babylon (the wicked world, the church of the devil), as well as her involvement and influence in economic affairs.

18:4 *And I heard another voice from heaven.* This voice could be that of God, who directly addresses the Saints as "my people." More likely it is an angel speaking for God: in verses 5 and 8 the Lord is referred to in third person. The words of this angel seem to be those recorded in verses 4 through 20.

Come out of her, my people. This is the recurring cry of the prophets: Leave the world and its wickedness, and bind yourself to God. Down through the ages we hear their voices:

"Depart ye, depart ye, go ye out from thence, touch no unclean thing; go ye out of the midst of her; be ye clean, that bear the vessels of the Lord" (Isa. 52:11).

"Flee out of the midst of Babylon, and deliver every man his soul: be not cut off in her iniquity; for this is the time of the Lord's vengeance; he will render unto her a recompence" (Jer. 51:6).

"Go ye out of Babylon; gather ye out from among the nations, from the four winds, from one end of heaven to the other. . . . Go ye out from among the nations, even from Babylon, from the midst of wickedness, which is spiritual Babylon" (D&C 133:7, 14).

This counsel has particular application to the Saints in our day. There is much in our world that partakes of the pride, the lust, the materialism, and the sins of Babylon. There is much that seeks to replace God in our hearts—the endless quest for wealth, the near-worship of sports and entertainment "stars," the deep desire of most people to seek and reach their own goals rather than God's. Babylon is alive and well in our times—but, as prophesied, Babylon will fall.

that ye be not partakers of her sins. The Saints are called to leave Babylon so that they can be fortified against the temptation to partake of her sins. What are those sins? Certainly the people of Babylon are guilty of all the typical sins of mankind at their worst—murder, adultery, abortion, theft, pornography, lying, and on and on. But in addition, as Revelation records, Babylon is also guilty of persecuting and killing the Saints (17:6), leading the nations of the world into idolatry and gross wickedness (17:2–4), and fostering all manner of abominations (17:5).

that ye receive not of her plagues. This phrase is connected with the previous one. By leaving Babylon and refusing to partake of her sins, the righteous are also protected from her plagues, enumerated elsewhere in Revelation (chapters 8, 9, and 16).

18:5 *For her sins have reached unto heaven/God hath remembered her iniquities.* God is fully aware of the grossness and the extent of the sins of Babylon; not one escapes his notice. And even if he does not act immediately to judge and to punish in a given instance, he will ever remember until the time of retribution.

18:6 *Reward her even as she rewarded you.* Babylon will receive according to the law of the harvest: that which she has sown, so shall she reap. As she has given out, so shall it come back to her in punishment (Job 4:8; D&C 6:33).

"Wherefore, fear and tremble, O ye people, for what I the Lord have decreed . . . shall be fulfilled. And verily I say unto you, that they who go forth, bearing these tidings unto the inhabitants of the earth, to them is power given to seal both on earth and in heaven, the unbelieving and rebellious; yea, verily, to seal them up unto the day when the wrath of God shall be poured out upon the wicked without measure—unto the day when the Lord shall come to recompense unto every man according to his work, and measure to every man according to the measure which he has measured to his fellow man" (D&C 1:7–10; see also Jer. 50:15, 29).

double unto her double according to her works. Babylon will receive not only a full portion of punishment for her iniquities but a double portion. Under the law of Moses, a thief was to pay double for that which he had taken (Ex. 22:4, 7). A double punishment is a common consequence in the scriptures (Isa. 40:2; Jer. 16:18). The double use of *double* is a peculiarity of the King James Version (contrast, for example, RSV, NEB, JB, and NIV).

the cup which she hath filled. Babylon has filled a cup of iniquity and caused the nations of the world to drink of it (14:8). That same cup will now be filled with the wrath of God for Babylon to drink—in double portions.

18:7 *How much she hath glorified herself/lived deliciously.* Babylon, which is the wicked world, has exalted herself and lived in great pride and luxury. *Deliciously* can also be rendered *wantonly* or *riotously.*[4]

so much torment and sorrow give her. The Lord says that as Babylon has exalted herself in pride and given herself to riotous living, to that same degree Babylon will suffer torment and sorrow. This punishment will come just before the second coming of Christ.

I sit a queen, and am no widow. Babylon gives herself so thoroughly to pride and sin that she sees herself as invincible. She rules over the people of the world, a great queen over many kings. She fears nothing, not even death.

This arrogant claim repeats a prophecy found in Isaiah: "And thou saidst, I shall be a lady for ever: so that thou didst not lay these things to thy

---

[4] See note *a* to 18:7 in the LDS edition of the KJV.

heart, neither didst remember the latter end of it. Therefore hear now this, thou that art given to pleasures, that dwellest carelessly, that sayest in thine heart, I am, and none else beside me; I shall not sit as a widow, neither shall I know the loss of children" (Isa. 47:7–8).

The prophecy in Isaiah continues, foreseeing that which John also saw next: "But these two things shall come to thee in a moment in one day, the loss of children, and widowhood: they shall come upon thee in their perfection for the multitude of thy sorceries, and for the great abundance of thine enchantments. For thou hast trusted in thy wickedness: thou hast said, None seeth me. Thy wisdom and thy knowledge, it hath perverted thee; and thou hast said in thine heart, I am, and none else beside me. Therefore . . . desolation shall come upon thee suddenly, which thou shalt not know" (Isa. 47:9–11).

18:8 *Therefore shall her plagues come in one day, death, and mourning, and famine.* Some translations replace the word *death* with *disease* or *pestilence.*[5] *In one day* indicates that these things will come suddenly on the wicked.

In Deuteronomy Moses prophesied the horror of plagues and calamities to come upon the wicked: "The Lord shall send upon thee cursing, vexation, and rebuke, in all that thou settest thine hand unto for to do, until thou be destroyed, and until thou perish quickly; because of the wickedness of thy doings, whereby thou hast forsaken me. . . . Then the Lord will make thy plagues wonderful, and the plagues of thy seed, even great plagues, and of long continuance, and sore sicknesses, and of long continuance. Moreover he will bring upon thee all the diseases of Egypt, which thou wast afraid of; and they shall cleave unto thee. Also every sickness, and every plague, which is not written in the book of this law, them will the Lord bring upon thee, until thou be destroyed" (Deut. 28:20, 59–61; see also 28:16–61; 2 Ne. 6:15; 10:6).

she shall be utterly burned with fire: for strong is the Lord God who judgeth her. After the plagues comes the burning. When the Lord returns, the wicked will be destroyed by burning, and the earth itself will be cleansed by fire. "For after today cometh the burning—this is speaking after the manner of the Lord—for verily I say, tomorrow all the proud and they that do wickedly shall be as stubble; and I will burn them up, for I am

---

[5] See RSV, GNB, JB, and NEB.

the Lord of Hosts; and I will not spare any that remain in Babylon" (D&C 64:24; 3 Ne. 26:3). Certainly a god who has power to bring such a judgment is a strong and powerful god.

This scene is also depicted in latter-day scripture: "And another angel shall sound his trump, saying: That great church, the mother of abominations, that made all nations drink of the wine of the wrath of her fornication, that persecuteth the saints of God, that shed their blood—she who sitteth upon many waters, and upon the islands of the sea—behold, she is the tares of the earth; she is bound in bundles; her bands are made strong, no man can loose them; therefore, she is ready to be burned" (D&C 88:94).

18:9 *the kings of the earth, who have committed fornication and lived deliciously with her.* These kings are probably the kings of the earth in general, mentioned in 17:2. The kings represent the people of the earth, who also have joined in the "fornication" (see commentary on 14:8; 17:1–2). The kings and the people have joined together in celebrating the idolatry, immorality, and lust of the world. They have "lived deliciously" in luxury, excess, and wantonness, loving the pleasures of the world more than the treasures of God.

bewail her, and lament for her, when they shall see the smoke of her burning. When the kings of the earth see the utter destruction of Babylon, meaning the lifestyle and lust and wealth to which they had given themselves, they will weep and mourn for her loss (Jer. 51:8).

18:10 *Standing afar off for the fear of her torment.* Though they regret her loss, kings try to separate themselves from Babylon for fear that they will share in her fate.

Alas, alas, that great city Babylon, that mighty city! This cry of lament for the destruction of wicked Babylon is repeated three times in this chapter—once by the kings, once by the merchants, and once by the sea traders. "The city is Babylon; she is the similitude. The city is Rome; but she too is only a type and a figure. The city is all the cities of the world—San Francisco, Chicago, and New York City; London, Paris, and Berlin; Moscow, Tokyo, and Sao Paulo—all of which are subject to the rule and dominion of evil and carnality."[6]

for in one hour is thy judgment come. This expression suggests that the punishments and disasters that will overtake Babylon (symbolizing the

---

[6] McConkie, *Millennial Messiah,* 445.

wicked world) will come suddenly. Variations of this expression are repeated in 18:17, 19. It is worth noting that the "one hour" of persecution revealed in 17:12–14 is balanced by the "one hour" of judgment in this verse.

18:11–13 *And the merchants of the earth shall weep and mourn over her.* The merchants, symbolizing all those who seek to increase their wealth by association and dealings with a godless culture, will mourn for the loss of that culture, that society, that way of life. Their mourning will be particularly poignant because of their personal loss—they will grieve for themselves more than for Babylon.

The long list of items bought and sold in Babylon is impressive in the broad variety of that which is available there. Most of the items listed fall into the category of luxuries—in Babylon, it is not enough to wear simple clothing; one must wear "fine linen, and purple, and silk, and scarlet." It is not enough to eat bread; one must have "wine, and oil, and fine flour."

Ezekiel received a vision similar to that depicted in this chapter: "The word of the Lord came again unto me, saying, Now, thou son of man, . . . say unto Tyrus, . . . [Many merchants] traded in thy fairs . . . with horses and horsemen and mules . . . ivory and ebony . . . emeralds, purple, and broidered work, and fine linen, and coral, and agate . . . and honey, and oil, and balm . . . [and] wine . . . and white wool . . . lambs, and rams, and goats . . . [and] all spices, and with all precious stones, and gold . . . [and] blue clothes, and broidered work, and in chests of rich apparel. . . . [T]hy merchandise, thy mariners, . . . and all thy men of war, that are in thee . . . shall fall into the midst of the seas in the day of thy ruin. . . . [They] shall come down from their ships, they shall stand upon the land; and shall cause their voice to be heard against thee, and shall cry bitterly, and shall cast up dust upon their heads, they shall wallow themselves in the ashes. . . . And in their wailing they shall take up a lamentation for thee, and lament over thee, saying, What city is like Tyrus, like the destroyed in the midst of the sea? . . . The merchants among the people shall hiss at thee; thou shalt be a terror, and never shalt be any more" (Ezek. 27:1–3, 12–24, 27, 29–32, 35–36).

18:13 *slaves, and souls of men.* This passage represents the worst of the merchandising that takes place in Babylon: the merchants are trading in the souls and bodies of human beings. Throughout history, millions upon millions of men, women, and children have been kidnapped from their homes, during war or otherwise, and taken to distant places where they have been forced to labor for another.[7] In return for their labors, which were often excessive and accompanied by force and violence, the slave received only subsistence food, some clothing, shelter, and the opportunity to continue to live. Certainly such traffic in human beings is reprehensible to God.

Another form of trading and merchandising that occurs in Babylon is in what John calls the "souls of men." This expression may refer to false religions that buy and sell men's souls, as Moroni recorded: "There shall be churches built up that shall say: Come unto me, and for your money you shall be forgiven of your sins" (Morm. 8:32). Or John's vision may refer to what Hugh Nibley called the "Mahan Principle." Here is Nibley's description of how Babylon trades in the souls of men:

"The story begins . . . with Satan seeking to promote himself even in the premortal existence, and being cast out of heaven in his pride, and dedicating himself upon his fall to the destruction of this earth, 'for he knew not the mind of God' (Moses 4:6). [On earth] he . . . will control the world economy by claiming possession of the earth's resources; and by manipulation of its currency—gold and silver—he will buy up the political, military, and ecclesiastical complex and run everything his way. . . . He not only offers employment but a course of instruction in how the whole thing works, teaching the ultimate secret: 'That great secret' (Moses 5:49–50) of converting life into property. Cain got the degree of Master Mahan, tried the system out on his brother, and gloried in its brilliant success, declaring that at last he could be free, as only property makes free, and that Abel had been a loser in a free competition.

"The discipline was handed down through Lamech and finally became the pattern of the world's economy (Moses 5:55–56). . . . One may see Mahan at work all around, from the Mafia, whose adherence to the principle needs no argument, down to the drug pusher, the arms dealer, the manufacturer and seller of defective products, or those who poison the air and water as a shortcut to gain and thus shorten and sicken the lives of all their fellow creatures."[8]

18:14 *the fruits that thy soul lusted after/all things . . . dainty and goodly/thou shalt find them no more at all.* The sweet and exotic foods that

[7] "It is estimated that there were as many as 60,000,000 slaves in the Roman Empire" alone (Mounce, *Book of Revelation,* 334).
[8] Nibley, *Approaching Zion,* 165–67.

the world has enjoyed will be destroyed with Babylon itself. These foods may symbolize the excesses and extravagances of the world.

18:15 *The merchants of these things/stand afar off/weeping and wailing.* Greed and luxury are powerful motivators. Those who have become rich by trafficking in the things of the world feel great grief at the loss of their source of wealth. But even in their mourning they remove themselves from Babylon at the end, standing "afar off" for fear of partaking of her torment.

18:16 *Alas, alas, that great city.* The cry of the merchants, the sea traders, and the kings in mourning the loss of Babylon (which is the wicked world, personified by the greatest, richest, and most powerful city in the world) is one of self-interest: they feel deeply the loss of her wealth, symbolized by the linen, the royal clothing made of purple and scarlet, and the precious metals and gems.

18:17 *For in one hour so great riches is come to nought.* See commentary on 18:10.

as many as trade by sea, stood afar off. See commentary on 18:10.

18:18 *What city is like unto this great city!* When the sea traders see the destruction of Babylon, they are amazed. Babylon was so powerful and so rich—how could it be destroyed? In the same way, those who embrace the philosophies and lifestyle of a world without the true God, which world seems uniquely powerful and important, will be amazed at its destruction.

18:19 *And they cast dust on their heads.* In Middle Eastern culture, this gesture is traditionally a sign of humiliation and deep mourning (Ezek. 27:30).

Alas, alas, that great city. See commentary on 18:10, 16.

for in one hour is she made desolate. See commentary on 18:10.

18:20 *Rejoice over her, thou heaven/holy apostles and prophets.* While the wicked kings, merchants, and sea traders mourn the loss of Babylon, heaven and the righteous have cause to rejoice. Their great nemesis, the unholy antagonist of all that is good and right, has been destroyed.

God hath avenged you on her. Babylon orchestrated war against the righteous and has become "drunken with the blood of the saints" (17:6). But God will come down in vengeance and bring judgments upon her according to all her wickedness. This vengeance fulfills the promise made in 6:9–11.

18:21 *a mighty angel took up a stone like a great millstone, and cast it into the sea.* Of those who abuse or offend the Lord's "little ones," the Lord said, "It were better for him that a millstone were hanged about his neck, and that he were drowned in the depth of the sea" (Matt. 18:6). This is the very fate destined for Babylon, the wicked culture, philosophy, governments, religion, and lifestyle of the world. As an object lesson, "a mighty angel" will lift up a huge stone and throw it into the sea; and "thus with violence shall that great city Babylon be thrown down, and shall be found no more at all." This passage may also depict some otherwise undefined natural disaster.

The destruction of Babylon was foreseen by Jeremiah (Jer. 51:37), Nephi (1 Ne. 14:15–16; 22:14), and Joseph Smith (D&C 1:16), among others.

We read in Jeremiah of this impressive prophecy: "So Jeremiah wrote in a book all the evil that should come upon Babylon. . . . And Jeremiah said to Seraiah, When . . . thou hast made an end of reading this book, . . . thou shalt bind a stone to it, and cast it into the midst of Euphrates: And thou shalt say, Thus shall Babylon sink, and shall not rise from the evil that I will bring upon her" (Jer. 51:60–64).

Just as a weighty stone has no power to rise again from the depths of the sea, in the same way Babylon will have no power to rise again from the destruction a just God brings on her.

18:22 *harpers/musicians/pipers/trumpeters/heard no more at all in thee.* The sounds of people seeking worldly pleasure and entertainment will be lost when Babylon is destroyed (Isa. 24:8; Ezek. 26:13). Contrast that with the promise in 15:2, which says that those who resist the beast, gaining a personal victory over him, will have "the harps of God," making music of true joy and praise.

no craftsman . . . shall be found any more in thee. Daily labor for pay in the city will cease. The economy of Babylon will be destroyed along with the city.

the sound of a millstone shall be heard no more at all in thee. The grinding of wheat and other such daily tasks will no longer be heard in Babylon, because Babylon will be no more. This prophecy has an ominous undertone—when the millstone ceases to grind, food soon ceases to be available.

18:23 *And the light of a candle/shine no more at all in thee.* The city will be plunged into darkness. It will no longer have any light at all.

the voice of the bridegroom and of the bride shall be heard no more at all in thee. Of an earlier and parallel event the Lord said, "Then will I cause to cease from the cities of Judah, and from the streets of Jerusalem, the voice of mirth, and the voice of gladness, the voice of the bridegroom, and the voice of the bride: for the land shall be desolate" (Jer. 7:34). The loss of such sounds indicates that normal life has stopped, or that all life in that place has ceased to be.

This verse (18:23) is reminiscent of Jeremiah 25:9–12, a description of the long exile of Israel. In that passage, the Lord says he will allow Babylon to conquer his people but that Babylon would be destroyed in the end. During the exile, the Lord says, "I will take from them the voice of mirth, and the voice of gladness, the voice of the bridegroom, and the voice of the bride, the sound of the millstones, and the light of the candle" (Jer. 25:10).

thy merchants were the great men of the earth. Those who traded in and with Babylon were great, rich, and powerful, but they do not have power to save her.

by thy sorceries were all nations deceived. The Lord abhors sorcery, the use of witchcraft and evil powers to deceive others. We read in Revelation 13 of the miracles of the beast, which deceived the people of the earth and caused them to worship the beast rather than God (13:12–15). Though the sorceries of Babylon enabled her to deceive the nations and thus to rule the world, those dark, satanic powers are unable to save her in the end: "Stand now with thine enchantments, and with the multitude of thy sorceries, wherein thou hast laboured from thy youth; if so be thou shalt be able to profit, if so be thou mayest prevail. . . . Let now the astrologers, the stargazers, the monthly prognosticators, stand up, and save thee from these things that shall come upon thee. Behold, they shall be as stubble; the fire shall burn them; they shall not deliver themselves from the power of the flame: there shall not be a coal to warm at, nor fire to sit before it" (Isa. 47:12–14).

18:24 *in her was found the blood of prophets/saints/all that were slain upon the earth.* Ultimately, Babylon, or the wicked world, is responsible for the martyrdom of all the prophets and Saints who have ever been killed for their faith, as well as all who have been killed by murder and war. This persecution of the righteous is probably Babylon's greatest sin. That these things were "found" in Babylon at the end suggests that all her wickedness will be uncovered.

REVELATION
19

VICTORY SONGS IN HEAVEN (19:1–10)

This part of John's revelation reports primarily things he *hears,* rather than things he *sees.* He hears "a great voice of much people in heaven" praising God for his righteous judgments against Babylon. He hears "the voice of a great multitude" praising God and rejoicing that "the marriage of the Lamb is come." He hears an angel command him to write that those who "are called unto the marriage supper of the Lamb" are "blessed."

This section "skillfully weaves together three distinct strands from the Old Testament, all of which have been used before in the New Testament and related literature, but never together. The first is the depiction of the reign of God as a great feast (see Isa. 25:6; cf. Mark 2:19; Matt. 22:1–14; 25:1–13; Luke 14:15–24). The second is the notion of Israel as the bride of Jehovah (see Hosea 2:5; Isa. 1:21; Jer. 2:2; cf. Eph. 5:32). The final is the use of clean garments as a symbol of sanctity (see Gen. 35:2; Isa. 52:1; 61:10; Zech. 3:4; cf. Rev. 3:4; 6:11; 7:14)."[1]

Revelation 19:1–10

> 1 And after these things I heard a great voice of much people in heaven, saying, Alleluia; Salvation, and glory, and honour, and power, unto the Lord our God:
> 2 For true and righteous are his judgments: for he hath judged the great whore, which did corrupt the earth with her fornication, and hath avenged the blood of his [saints][2] at her hand.
> 3 And again they said, Alleluia. And her smoke rose up for ever and ever.
> 4 And the four and twenty elders and the four beasts fell down and worshipped God that sat on the throne, saying, Amen; Alleluia.

---

[1] Draper, *Opening the Seven Seals,* 208.
[2] JST 19:2 changes the KJV *servants.*

5 And a voice came out of the throne, saying, Praise our God, all ye his [saints],[3] and ye that fear him, both small and great.
6 And I heard as it were the voice of a great multitude, and as the voice of many waters, and as the voice of mighty thunderings, saying, Alleluia: for the Lord God omnipotent reigneth.
7 Let us be glad and rejoice, and give honour to him: for the marriage of the Lamb is come, and his wife hath made herself ready.
8 And to her was granted that she should be arrayed in fine linen, clean and white; for the fine linen is the righteousness of saints.
9 And he saith unto me, Write, Blessed are they which are called unto the marriage supper of the Lamb. And he saith unto me, These are the true sayings of God.
10 And I fell at his feet to worship him. And he said unto me, See [that][4] thou do it not: I am thy fellowservant, and of thy brethren that have the testimony of Jesus: worship God: for the testimony of Jesus is the spirit of prophecy.

NOTES AND COMMENTARY

19:1 *a great voice of much people in heaven.* The people in heaven are likely the "many angels round about the throne" mentioned in 5:11, "and the number of them was ten thousand times ten thousand, and thousands of thousands." See also commentary on 7:9–10.

saying, Alleluia. The millions of people in heaven are crying out praises to God. *Alleluia,* they cry, which is the Greek form of the Hebrew *Hallelujah,* meaning "Praise ye Jah!" or "Praise Jehovah!" The praises are specifically motivated by the judgment God has brought against the great whore, Babylon, the wicked world (19:2).

Salvation, and glory, and honour, and power, unto the Lord our God. The inhabitants of heaven cry out praises to God, acknowledging that all honor and glory for the work of salvation in the earth go to him. The King James Version *Salvation* may more properly be rendered *Victory* (Greek *Soteria*).[5] The expression *Lord our God,* indicates that the Lord is a personal God to us, one that we can claim as our own.

19:2 *For true and righteous are his judgments.* As this verse tells us, the Lord has made a judgment against the great whore, which is correct and fair and right. (See also commentary on 16:7.) All of God's judgments are true and righteous. If he were to judge otherwise, as Alma taught, he would "cease to be God" (Alma 42:13, 22).

---

[3] JST 19:5 changes the KJV *servants.*
[4] An addition found in JST 19:10.
[5] Harrington, *Revelation,* 185.

for he hath judged the great whore. The judgment of the whore is announced in 17:1; the actual judgments are detailed in chapters 6, 9, 11, and 16.

did corrupt the earth with her fornication. See commentary on 17:2.

hath avenged the blood of his [saints] at her hand. In 6:9–10, John "saw under the altar the souls of them that were slain for the word of God, and for the testimony which they held: And they cried with a loud voice, saying, How long, O Lord, holy and true, dost thou not judge and avenge our blood on them that dwell on the earth?" That question is answered in the last days when the Lord exercises his many terrible judgments against the wicked. The events that bring the downfall of Babylon are the same as those that avenge the blood of the martyrs of the Lord.

19:3 *And again they said, Alleluia.* See commentary on 19:1.

And her smoke rose up for ever and ever. The smoke of the destruction of Babylon (see 18:9, 18) will rise up to the heavens forever as a testimony of her wickedness. When Sodom and Gomorrah were destroyed, Abraham "looked . . . toward all the land of the plain, and beheld, and, lo, the smoke of the country went up as the smoke of a furnace" (Gen. 19:28). When Isaiah made his prophecy against Idumea (which represents the world; see D&C 1:36), he saw that "the land thereof shall become burning pitch. It shall not be quenched night nor day; the smoke thereof shall go up for ever: from generation to generation it shall lie waste" (Isa. 34:9–10; Rev. 14:11). As the smoke of incense rises up to God as a prayer (8:3–4), so will the smoke of the destroyed Babylon rise up as a reminder of the sin and just destruction of the wicked world.

19:4 *And the four and twenty elders.* See commentary on 4:4.

the four beasts. See commentary on 4:6.

fell down and worshipped God that sat on the throne. See commentary on 4:10.

saying, Amen; Alleluia. Those closest to the throne, the elders and the beasts, join in the chorus introduced in the previous verse, crying "Amen, Alleluia," which means "Verily, praise the Lord Jehovah!" This expression echoes the cry of the people in Psalm 106:48: "Blessed be the Lord God of Israel from everlasting to everlasting: and let all the people say, Amen. Praise ye the Lord."

19:5 *And a voice came out of the throne.* Because this voice comes from the throne of God, it may appear to be the voice of God himself. But the words spoken by the voice ("Praise our God") imply that the voice is not that of God the Father. It could be the voice of Jesus, commanding the Saints to praise the Father, though Jesus likely would have said "my God" (3:12; John 20:17). The speaker may be one of those who surround the throne.

Praise our God, all ye his [saints], and ye that fear him, both small and great. First the people in heaven cry out their praises (19:1–3), and then those who are closest to the throne (19:4). Now all Saints, "small and great," are asked to join in the praises.

19:6 *the voice of a great multitude.* See commentary on 19:1.

as the voice of many waters. The noisy sound of a huge rushing river or of the crashing breakers of the ocean is a very apt description of the sound of an immense crowd of people. See commentary on 1:15; 14:2.

as the voice of mighty thunderings. Again, this is a very apt description of the sound of many people. See commentary on 14:2.

saying, Alleluia: for the Lord God omnipotent reigneth. To paraphrase this passage: "Praise Jehovah, for the Lord who has power over all reigns as king over all the earth" (see Mosiah 3:5; Articles of Faith 1:10). This is the fourth cry of "Alleluia" recorded in Revelation 19; unlike the others, which praised him for his judgments against Babylon, this cry praises God for coming to bless and reign over his Saints. The establishment of Christ's reign is the fulfillment of the request made in the Lord's prayer: "Thy kingdom come" (Matt. 6:10).

19:7 *Let us be glad and rejoice, and give honour to him.* We do indeed have cause to be glad, to rejoice, and to give honor to the Lord. He has offered the great mediating sacrifice for us, enabling us to repent and be cleansed from our sins and to draw near to him to be joined in an eternal, holy union with him (John 17:11, 19–23). The specific reason for this present rejoicing is that union, "the marriage of the Lamb."

for the marriage of the Lamb is come. The marriage of the Lamb, who is Christ (D&C 33:17–18) to his bride, who is the Church (D&C 109:73–74) as well as the New Jerusalem (21:2, 9–10), is a metaphor for the union between the Lord and his people, made possible through the atonement of Christ. In fact, the very name of Christ's sacrifice (*at-one-ment*) suggests the purpose of that sacrifice: to make us one with both the Father and the Son (John 17:11, 19–23). To underscore the sweetness and blessing of that union, the Lord uses marriage as a symbol. There is no sweeter or more meaningful relationship on earth than that between a holy husband and a holy wife; that is the kind of relationship (in depth of feeling and completeness of union) that the Lord is inviting us to. That marriage is between Christ and the Church—but the Church is not just an organization on the earth; it is also the individual souls who belong to that organization. Though we are to prepare for the marriage all our lives (Matt. 25:1–13; D&C 45:56–57), it will be brought to its culmination (with the body of the Church) when Christ returns in glory. Of course, as individuals, we are bound to Christ as soon as we are ready. (For other references to the marriage of the Lamb, see Isa. 54:4–5; 62:5; Jer. 31:32; JST Matt. 22:1–14; Eph. 5:23, 32; D&C 58:6–11; 65:3; 88:92; 133:10, 19.)

his wife hath made herself ready. Through repentance, sanctification, and a heart that is fully turned to God, the wife of Christ, which is the Church, has prepared herself to be joined with him.

19:8 *to her was granted.* It was granted to the bride to wear fine linen, which represents the righteousness of the Saints. *To her was granted* is an interesting expression that reveals an important truth. Though we may labor hard to be righteous, in the final event even our righteousness is possible because of the grace and power and gifts of God (Deut. 30:20; John 1:12; 2 Cor. 4:7; Col. 1:10–11).

she should be arrayed in fine linen, clean and white. The great whore was arrayed in showy, expensive, worldly clothing (17:4), but the bride of Christ is wearing simple clothing, which symbolizes "the righteousness of saints" (see also 15:6). The linen is white because it was "washed . . . in the blood of the Lamb" (7:14), meaning that the Saints are sanctified through the atonement of Christ.

19:9 *And he saith unto me, Write.* An angel (identified as such in 19:10) tells John specific words to record.

Blessed are they which are called unto the marriage supper of the Lamb. This passage is another of the beatitudes of the book of Revelation (see Appendix 4). Those who are invited guests at the Lamb's celebratory marriage feast are blessed indeed. There are three persons or groups at the marriage supper: the Bridegroom, Jesus Christ, who is the Lamb; the Bride, who is the Church (as an institution but also as a collection of many individuals); and the guests, who also are likely the individual members, those who have qualified by righteousness for the grace of Christ. It seems that the individual members appear twice in this image: once in their connection with the Church (the Bridegroom) and once in representing themselves (the guests).[6]

Joseph Smith wrote of this feast and our attendance: "Those who keep the commandments of the Lord and walk in His statutes to the end, are the only individuals permitted to sit at this glorious feast. . . . [Paul wrote:] 'I have fought a good fight, I have finished my course, I have kept the faith. . . . ' . . . His labors were unceasing to spread the glorious news: and like a faithful soldier, when called to give his life in the cause which he had espoused, he laid it down. . . . Follow the labors of this Apostle from the time of his conversion to the time of his death, and you will have a fair sample of industry and patience in promulgating the Gospel of Christ. Derided, whipped, and stoned, the moment he escaped the hands of his persecutors he as zealously as ever proclaimed the doctrine of the Savior. . . . Reflect for a moment, brethren, and enquire, whether you would consider yourselves worthy a seat at the marriage feast with Paul and others like him, if you had been unfaithful? Had you not fought the good fight, and kept the faith, could you expect to receive?"[7]

This marriage supper is described in latter-day revelation, where the Lord speaks of "a feast of fat things . . . for the poor; yea, a feast of fat things, of wine on the lees well refined, that the earth may know that the mouths of the prophets shall not fail; yea, a supper of the house of the Lord, well prepared, unto which all nations shall be invited. First, the rich and the learned, the wise and the noble; and after that cometh the day of my power; then shall the poor, the lame, and the blind, and the deaf, come in unto the marriage of the Lamb, and partake of the supper of the Lord, prepared for the great day to come" (D&C 58:8–11; 65:3).

he saith unto me, These are the true sayings of God. The angel bears witness that these words, which he has instructed John to write, come from God himself.

19:10 *And I fell at his feet to worship him/See [that] thou do it not.* John has seen many angels in his vision and interacted with several of them, and he has not been inclined to worship any of them. Perhaps with praises going forth from "much people in heaven" (19:1), those who surround the throne (19:4), and a "great multitude" of the servants of God

---

[6] See Draper, *Opening the Seven Seals,* 209–10.
[7] *History of the Church,* 2:19–20.

(19:5–6), and with the angel's promise of the sublime blessing of the marriage of the Bridegroom and the Bride, John is overcome and bows before the angel. Or perhaps, with the glory of the angel and the majesty and power of his words, John mistakes the messenger of the Lord for the Lord himself. In 1:10–18 John sees the Lord himself and appropriately bows before him, and the Lord blesses him in his worship (1:17). There the Lord says, "I am Alpha and Omega, the first and the last" (1:11). In 22:12–13, a heavenly being says, "Behold, I come quickly; . . . I am Alpha and Omega, . . . the first and the last." The person speaking is an angel, speaking for the Lord. Immediately before these words (22:8–9), John has sought again to fall before the angel in worship, and again John has been warned to worship only God. With an angel having authority to stand in the place of Christ, appearing in great glory and speaking the very words of Christ, it is understandable how John could mistake the identity of his visitor.

Worship of angels is never appropriate (as John, of course, knew) because they are our fellowservants but from another sphere (Heb. 1:5–14). Instead, as the angel says here, we must "worship God" (see also Ex. 20:2–3).

I am thy fellowservant, and of thy brethren that have the testimony of Jesus. President Joseph F. Smith said, "We are told by the Prophet Joseph Smith, that 'there are no angels who minister to this earth but those who do belong or have belonged to it.' Hence, when messengers are sent to minister to the inhabitants of this earth, they are not strangers, but from the ranks of our kindred, friends, and fellow-beings and fellow-servants."[8]

worship God. God is the only being (or thing) we may appropriately worship; only worship of God brings eternal blessings. When Satan sought to entice Jesus to worship him, Jesus responded, "Get thee hence, Satan: for it is written, Thou shalt worship the Lord thy God, and him only shalt thou serve" (Matt. 4:10).

Who is the God we worship? And how do we worship him appropriately? Doctrine and Covenants 93 gives us some deep truths on the matter. There the Lord says that he has given us a revelation "that you may understand and know how to worship, and know what you worship" (v. 19).

We worship a being who is "the true light that lighteth every man that cometh into the world," who is one with the Father, and who has received

---

[8] Smith, *Gospel Doctrine,* 435.

of the fulness of the Father (vv. 2–3). He is "the light and the Redeemer of the world"; "in him was the life of men and the light of men"; and he is the creator of "all things" (v. 10). He is "full of grace and truth" (v. 11); "he received a fulness of the glory of the Father" (v. 16); "he received all power, both in heaven and on earth, and the glory of the Father was with him, for he dwelt in him" (v. 17); and "he received a fulness of truth, yea, even of all truth" (v. 26). The Father, whom we worship, is the source of the glory and power held by the Son.

How we worship is learned from the pattern shown in that same section. True worship is to follow the Son, to receive all that the Father will grant us, to obey the Lord in all things. True worship, then, is not a practice or attitude found only on the Sabbath, or in the temple, or in prayer, but in our very attitude of life.

Doctrine and Covenants 93 gives us the following clues to this divine pattern: Christ "received of [his] Father" (v. 5), and so must we, partaking of his blessings and receiving his presence through his Spirit, and likewise receiving of (and doing) his will. Christ "received not of the fulness at the first, but received grace for grace" (v. 12), and so must we, worshipping God by receiving all that he gives us, and by giving forth gifts and blessings to others. Christ received of the Holy Ghost (v. 15), and so must we. Christ was fully obedient to the Father in all things; and we must be obedient to him through the Son, keeping his commandments—which is a key to receiving "grace for grace" (v. 20). As Christ is the Firstborn of the Father, so must we be begotten through Christ, that we may be "partakers of the glory" of God (vv. 21–22). It appears that all of this is part of true worship of God.[9]

for the testimony of Jesus is the spirit of prophecy. Those who have received the spiritual witness (or testimony) that Jesus is the Christ have received a vital spiritual communication from on high. The spirit of prophecy is but another manifestation of that same Spirit. Thus, those who have a deep and true testimony of Christ have already experienced the spirit of prophecy. As President John Taylor taught, "The testimony of Jesus was the very principle, essence, and power of the spirit of prophecy whereby the ancient prophets were inspired."[10]

---

[9] See McConkie, *Doctrines of the Restoration,* ed. McConkie, 369–86.
[10] Taylor, *Gospel Kingdom,* 120.

Some of our latter-day leaders have taught that the Holy Ghost and the spirit of prophecy are virtually equivalent. President Wilford Woodruff wrote that "it is the privilege of every man and woman in this kingdom to enjoy the spirit of prophecy, which is the Spirit of God."[11] Elder Delbert L. Stapley stated that "the Holy Ghost is the spirit of prophecy."[12] Another way to put it is that those who live righteously have claim to the Holy Spirit of God, which gives them, as one of its gifts, the spirit of prophecy.

The formula for receiving the spirit of prophecy is given in Alma 17:2–3. The key requirements appear to be diligent scriptural search, much fasting, and much prayer: "Now these sons of Mosiah . . . had waxed strong in the knowledge of the truth; for they were men of a sound understanding and they had searched the scriptures diligently, that they might know the word of God. But this is not all; they had given themselves to much prayer, and fasting; therefore they had the spirit of prophecy, and the spirit of revelation."

The phrase in the Greek text adds another dimension to our understanding. In essence, it says that the testimony *about* Jesus forms the common element in all prophecy. Taken together, all prophecy comes down to a witness of Christ, his work, his atonement, and his triumph.

THE LORD ON A WHITE HORSE (19:11–16)

This section of John's revelation prophesies the actual second coming of the Lord in great power and judgment, accompanied by the armies of heaven. His appearance will be that of a mighty warrior-king, with "eyes . . . as a flame of fire," and "many crowns" on his head, and wearing a blood-red vesture (19:12, 13). He is identified as "Faithful and True," "The Word of God," "King of kings," and "Lord of lords." He will "make war" and lead "armies" and will ride a "white horse," as will his armies.

Paul spoke a similar prophecy to that found here: "The Lord Jesus shall be revealed from heaven with his mighty angels, in flaming fire taking vengeance on them that know not God, and that obey not the gospel of our Lord Jesus Christ: who shall be punished with everlasting destruction from the presence of the Lord, and from the glory of his power" (2 Thes. 1:7–9).

---

[11] Durham, *Discourses of Wilford Woodruff,* 61.
[12] Stapley, Conference Report, October 1966, 113.

Some of the earlier sections of Revelation paralleled the plagues the Lord sent on Egypt in the time of Moses (see, for example, the plagues in chapters 8 and 16). In some ways the coming of the Lord, at which time the wicked are destroyed, parallels the tenth plague in Egypt, in which the first-born of Pharaoh's people (and all others who refused the passover covenant with the Lord) were destroyed (Ex. 12:23–29). In fact, the destruction was so great that "there was a great cry in Egypt; for there was not a house where there was not one dead" (Ex. 12:30).

The description of that tenth plague recorded in the apocryphal Book of Wisdom has some interesting parallels with this section of Revelation: "While gentle silence enveloped all things, and night in its swift course was now half gone, thy all-powerful word leaped down from heaven, from the royal throne, into the midst of the land that was doomed, a stern warrior carrying the sharp sword of thy authentic command, and stood and filled all things with death, and touched heaven while standing on the earth" (Book of Wisdom 18:14–16).

Revelation 19:11–16

11 And I saw heaven opened, and behold a white horse; and he that sat upon him [is][13] called Faithful and True, and in righteousness he doth judge and make war.
12 His eyes . . . as a flame of fire, and [he had] on his head . . . many crowns; and . . . a name written, that no man knew, but . . . himself.[14]
13 And he [is][15] clothed with a vesture dipped in blood: and his name is called The Word of God.
14 And the armies which were in heaven followed him upon white horses, clothed in fine linen, white and clean.
15 And out of his mouth [proceedeth the word of God, and] with it he [will] smite the nations: and he [will] rule them with [the word of his mouth;] and he treadeth the winepress [in] the fierceness and wrath of Almighty God.[16]
16 And he hath on [a][17] vesture and on his thigh a name written, KING OF KINGS, AND LORD OF LORDS.

---

[13] JST 19:11 changes the KJV *was*.
[14] JST 19:12 makes several minor changes in this verse.
[15] JST 19:15 changes the KJV *was*.
[16] JST makes several important clarifying changes in this verse, which reads in the KJV: "And out of his mouth goeth a sharp sword, that with it she should smite the nations: and he shall rule them with a rod of iron: and he treadeth the winepress of the fierceness and wrath of Almighty God."
[17] JST 19:16 changes the KJV *his*.

NOTES AND COMMENTARY

19:11 *And I saw heaven opened.* This expression seems to be another way of saying, "I had a vision from heaven," or "I had a vision of things in heaven." For example, when Peter had his vision that taught him that the gospel should be taken to the Gentiles, he "saw heaven opened, and a certain vessel descending unto him, as it had been a great sheet knit at the four corners, and let down to the earth" (Acts 10:11). We read in latter-day revelation that "the power and authority of the higher, or Melchizedek Priesthood, is to hold the keys of all the spiritual blessings of the church—to have the privilege of receiving the mysteries of the kingdom of heaven, to have the heavens opened unto them" (D&C 107:18–19).

a white horse. To ride a horse into battle is to go forth in strength and power. The color white is often a symbol of victory.[18] See commentary on 6:2.

and he that sat upon him [is] called Faithful and True. These two titles of Christ give two of his primary characteristics. Christ is called *faithful* in 1:5 and *true* in 3:7. Here the characteristics are combined. He is faithful in that he holds steadfastly to the right and keeps all his promises. He is true in that he acts always in accordance with true and righteous principles.

in righteousness he doth judge. The Father has given the right and responsibility of judging the world (and all the individuals in the world) to his Son (John 5:22). As God, our Savior is not capable of rendering unrighteous or unfair judgment (Ps. 19:9; Isa. 11:4; 2 Ne. 9:46). This judgment will vindicate the righteous and punish the wicked.

and make war. The Lord is a God of mercy, blessing his children with his loving kindness, but he is also a God of justice, rendering judgment to all the people on the earth. He is "the Prince of Peace" (Isa. 9:6), but he is also "a man of war" (Ex. 15:3), "mighty in battle" (Ps. 24:8). His title "Lord of hosts" suggests that he is the commander of the angelic hosts of heaven as they go forth to war against the wicked (1 Chr. 17:24; Ps. 24:10; Isa. 6:5; Zech. 14:16–17).[19]

19:12 *His eyes . . . as a flame of fire.* See commentary on 1:14.

---

[18] Harrington, *Revelation,* 190; Dummelow, *One-Volume Bible Dictionary,* 1076.

[19] The Hebrew word *sebaoth,* which here is translated *hosts,* may also be translated *armies,* according to all lexicons.

[he had] on his head . . . many crowns. The many crowns on the head of Christ represent the truth proclaimed in 11:15: "The kingdoms of this world are become the kingdoms of our Lord, and of his Christ; and he shall reign for ever and ever." Contrast the *many* crowns of Christ with the seven worn by Satan, the dragon (12:3) and the ten worn by the beast (13:1). The crowns worn by the Lord are not specified in number; he has more than all other kings combined. He is the King of kings and Lord of lords (19:16), "far above all principality, and power, and might, and dominion, and every name that is named, not only in this world, but also in that which is to come" (Eph. 1:21; Col. 1:16; 2:10).

a name written, that no man knew, but . . . himself. In the book of Revelation, a name on the forehead seems to identify the person who bears it. In 17:5 the whore had a name on her forehead that identified her as "Babylon the Great, the Mother of . . . Abominations. . . ." In 14:1 the 144,000 had the Father's name written in their foreheads, suggesting that they belong to him. Here the Lord has a name written on his forehead, but it is not to identify him to others, because only he himself knows it.

"As with all glorified beings, our Lord has a new name in celestial exaltation, a name known to and comprehended by those only who know God in the sense that they have become as he is and have eternal life. See Rev. 2:12–17. Thus, Christ's 'new name' shall be written upon all those who are joint-heirs with him (Rev. 3:12), and shall signify that they have become even as he is and he is even as the Father. (3 Ne. 28:10.)"[20]

19:13 *And he [is] clothed with a vesture dipped in blood.* When Christ returns, his garments will be red, as we read in both ancient and modern revelation:

"And it shall be said: Who is this that cometh down from God in heaven with dyed garments; yea, from the regions which are not known, clothed in his glorious apparel, traveling in the greatness of his strength? And he shall say: I am he who spake in righteousness, mighty to save. And the Lord shall be red in his apparel, and his garments like him that treadeth in the wine-vat. And so great shall be the glory of his presence that the sun shall hide his face in shame, and the moon shall withhold its light, and the stars shall be hurled from their places.

---

[20] McConkie, *Doctrinal New Testament Commentary,* 3:567.

"And his voice shall be heard: I have trodden the wine-press alone, and have brought judgment upon all people; and none were with me; and I have trampled them in my fury, and I did tread upon them in mine anger, and their blood have I sprinkled upon my garments, and stained all my raiment; for this was the day of vengeance which was in my heart" (D&C 133:46–51; Isa. 63:1–3).

The blood on Christ's clothing symbolizes at least three things: the blood Christ shed in performing the Atonement (Luke 22:44; D&C 19:18); the blood, or sins, of the wicked that he took upon himself (blood and sins are equated in Jacob 1:19; see also 1 Pet. 3:18; Alma 33:22; 3 Ne. 11:11); and the blood of the unrepentant wicked he has slain in his wrath (Isa. 63:3; Lam. 1:15; D&C 133:48, 50–51).

his name is called The Word of God. In three verses we have learned of three names of Christ: Faithful and True, a name that no one knows, and The Word of God. John had earlier used this present name: "In the beginning was the Word, and the Word was with God, and the Word was God. The same was in the beginning with God." (John 1:1–2).[21]

God executes his commands through his word, as do his servants (1 Ne. 17:29–31, 46; Alma 5:5; 7:8; 3 Ne. 28:20; Morm. 8:24; 9:17; Moses 7:13). This occurs in at least two ways—when God speaks, his servants obey and carry out his will, and when God speaks, even nature obeys, bringing to pass his will through what we call miracles. Perhaps Christ is called the Word himself because he is the one who most thoroughly carries out the will of God, being the very embodiment of that will (JST 19:15).

19:14 *the armies which were in heaven followed him.* One of the Lord's titles is *Lord of hosts*—the word *hosts* is used to translate the Hebrew *tsebaah,* which generally means *armies.*[22] Christ is the Lord of the armies of heaven. Those armies include the "mighty angels" that Paul explained would return with Christ (2 Thes. 1:7) and may also include the "latter-day Church (D&C 5:14; 105:26, 30–31; 109:73) [and] the departed faithful (Dan. 4:35; Rev. 19:14; D&C 88:112)."[23] Those with the Lamb in

[21] JST 19:13 uses *Word* here to refer to the gospel. But in JST John 1:14 and 16, Christ himself is called the Word.

[22] The expression *Lord of hosts* or *Lord God of hosts* is used 341 times in the scriptures. The expression *Lord of Sabaoth,* which means the same thing, occurs 6 times. *Sabaoth* is a transliteration of the Hebrew *tsebaah* but in plural form. It occurs twice in the New Testament and four times in the Doctrine and Covenants.

[23] McConkie and Parry, *Guide to Scriptural Symbols,* 16.

war are those who are "called, and chosen, and faithful" (17:14); the 144,000 "follow the Lamb whithersoever he goeth" (14:4). Perhaps these righteous ones of the earth join the armies of heaven after death or, perhaps, after their resurrection. Those who follow Christ here will follow him in the life to come.

upon white horses. The armies of heaven, following Christ, have white horses like their master. See commentary on 19:11.

clothed in fine linen, white and clean. The armies of heaven are arrayed in fine white linen as the Bride of Christ is; or perhaps they are so arrayed because they are the Bride. See commentary on 19:8.

19:15 *out of his mouth [proceedeth the word of God, and] with it he [will] smite the nations.* Paul taught that "the sword of the Spirit . . . is the word of God" (Eph. 6:17). Elsewhere he wrote, "For the word of God is quick, and powerful, and sharper than any two-edged sword, piercing even to the dividing asunder of soul and spirit, and of the joints and marrow" (Heb. 4:12). The returning Christ will use the word of God as a powerful weapon; and with the power of those words he will smite the wicked and destroy the nations of the earth (Isa. 11:4; 49:2). See also commentary on 2:16 and 19:13.

he [will] rule them with [the word of his mouth]. The power of God is often found in his word; not only will he smite the nations with his word but he will also rule them with that word. See commentary on 12:3.

he treadeth the winepress [in] the fierceness and wrath of Almighty God. See commentary on 14:19.

19:16 *And he hath on [a] vesture, and on his thigh a name written.* The vesture is probably that which is "dipped in blood" (19:13). But the name is different from the name mentioned in 19:12, which "no man knew." The name here is "King of kings, and Lord of lords." It is uncertain why the name is written on his thigh, but the outer thigh would be prominently visible on a horseman. Some interpret this phrase to mean that the name was actually written on the garment that covered his thigh; others believe that the name was written on the sword at his side, resting on or next to his thigh.[24] Of course, the purpose of this symbolic picture is to emphasize the supremacy of the Lord.

---

[24] Mounce, *Book of Revelation,* 356; Harrington, *Revelation,* 191; note *d* to 19:16 in JB.

KING OF KINGS, AND LORD OF LORDS. This name is probably written in all capital letters to emphasize that it was presented like a sign on the thigh of the Lord. This is the fourth of the name-titles of Christ given in this chapter (19:11–13). Because Christ is the Lord over all, he has power to smite the nations and rule them "with the word of his mouth" (JST 19:15). For a discussion of what this title means, see the commentary on 17:14.

THE SUPPER OF THE GREAT GOD (19:17–21)

In the previous section, we read that Christ will "smite the nations," treading "the winepress of the fierceness and wrath of Almighty God" (19:15). His "vesture dipped in blood" (19:13) is symbolic, in part, of the righteous slaughter of the wicked.

The destruction of the wicked is a theme of much of Revelation; the judgments against the wicked in the earlier chapters are part of the process of cleansing the earth and bringing justice on those who have followed the whore and the beast. But as events draw to their bloody conclusion, "the beast, and the kings of the earth, and their armies" will gather together "to make war against" Christ and his followers. In those battles, the beast will be conquered and thrown into the lake of fire, and the armies will be slain by the Lord. These events seem to be among those that occur at the Second Coming.

The slain will be so many that the fowls of the air will be invited to come and feast on the corpses. This is called "the supper of the great God" (19:17).

Revelation 19:17–21

> 17 And I saw an angel standing in the sun; and he cried with a loud voice, saying to all the fowls that fly in the midst of heaven, Come and gather yourselves together unto the supper of the great God;
> 18 That ye may eat the flesh of kings, and the flesh of captains, and the flesh of mighty men, and the flesh of horses, and of them that sit on them, and the flesh of all [who fight against the Lamb, both bond and free],[25] both small and great.
> 19 And I saw the beast, and the kings of the earth, and their armies, gathered together to make war against him that sat on the horse, and against his army.

[25] JST 19:18 replaces the KJV *men, both free and bond* with this important clarifying phrase.

20 And the beast was taken, and with him the false prophet that wrought miracles before him, with which he deceived them that had received the mark of the beast, and them that worshipped his image. These both were cast alive into a lake of fire burning with brimstone.
21 And the remnant were slain with the [word] of him that sat upon the horse, which [word][26] proceeded out of his mouth: and all the fowls were filled with their flesh.

Notes and Commentary

19:17 *And I saw an angel standing in the sun.* This passage describes "a position of splendor appropriate to a herald of victory. From this vantage point he will be able to deliver effectively his message to the birds that circle in mid-heaven."[27]

he cried with a loud voice, saying to all the fowls that fly in the midst of heaven. The angel calls out to the carrion birds that are flying above the earth, awaiting the bloody battles between the beast and his armies and the heavenly hosts led by the Lamb.

Come and gather yourselves together unto the supper of the great God. This supper stands in great contrast to the wedding supper that occurs at the union of the Bride and the Bridegroom (19:9). Here, the bodies of the wicked are the fare at the supper. At the wedding feast, the righteous are blessed to partake of things "well refined" (D&C 58:8).

"Those with refined senses find it difficult to conceive of the desolation, destruction, and death that will prevail during the final great battles ushering in Christ's reign of peace. So great shall be the slaughter and mass murder, the carnage and gore, the butchery and violent death of warring men, that their decaying bodies 'shall stop the noses of the passengers,' and it shall be a task of mammoth proportions merely to dispose of them. Then shall Ezekiel's prophecy be fulfilled that every feathered fowl and every beast of the field shall assemble to 'eat the flesh of the mighty, and drink the blood of the princes of the earth.' (Ezek. 39.)

"That all this is an actual, literal supper, an horrible but real event yet to be, has been specifically confirmed in latter-day revelation. (D. & C. 29:18–21.)"[28]

---

[26] JST 19:21 replaces the KJV *sword* with *word* in two instances in this verse.
[27] Mounce, *Book of Revelation,* 357.
[28] McConkie, *Doctrinal New Testament Commentary,* 3:569.

19:18 *That ye may eat the flesh of kings/captains/mighty men/horses.* For a time the kings and captains and mighty men rule on the earth. But in the end, even they will fall before the power of the Lord, and they will become nothing more than flesh for the birds to feed on. Their warhorses will suffer the same fate.

Ezekiel received a revelation similar to this part of John's: "Thus saith the Lord God; Speak unto every feathered fowl, and to every beast of the field, Assemble yourselves, and come; gather yourselves on every side to my sacrifice that I do sacrifice for you, even a great sacrifice upon the mountains of Israel, that ye may eat flesh, and drink blood. Ye shall eat the flesh of the mighty, and drink the blood of the princes of the earth, of rams, of lambs, and of goats, of bullocks, all of them fatlings of Bashan. And ye shall eat fat till ye be full, and drink blood till ye be drunken, of my sacrifice which I have sacrificed for you. Thus ye shall be filled at my table with horses and chariots, with mighty men, and with all men of war, saith the Lord God. And I will set my glory among the heathen, and all the heathen shall see my judgment that I have executed, and my hand that I have laid upon them. So the house of Israel shall know that I am the Lord their God from that day and forward" (Ezek. 39:17–22).

the flesh of all [who fight against the Lamb, both bond and free], both small and great. This inclusive statement (*all, bond and free, small and great*) tells us that there will be no exceptions: everyone who fights against the Lamb will be destroyed.

19:19 *the beast/kings/armies . . . make war against him that sat on the horse.* John again sees the beast he first saw in chapter 13. The continuing battle of wicked kingdoms and philosophies against the Lamb was first begun in the war in heaven (JST 12:6), continued when the beast rose to power on the earth (13:7), and will reach its culmination at Armageddon (16:13–14, 16). Of course, the battles between Satan and Jesus Christ do not always involve armies and bloodshed (in fact, such battles may be the exception rather than the rule); often Satan engages in a war of words, of ideas, seeking to win hearts and souls. In all cases the eventual outcome is assured: "These shall make war with the Lamb, and the Lamb shall overcome them" (17:14). Old Testament prophecies of this conflict are recorded in Psalm 2:2; Zechariah 12; 14; and Joel 3.

his army. See commentary on 19:14.

19:20 *the beast was taken.* John knew in advance (as can we, by a witness from the Spirit) that the terrible beast, which had such power, will be conquered by the omnipotence of Christ, the Lord over all (17:14).

with him the false prophet that wrought miracles. See commentary on 13:14.

These both were cast alive into a lake of fire burning with brimstone. "I beheld even till the beast was slain," Daniel said, "and his body destroyed, and given to the burning flame" (Dan. 7:11). The worst of all fates awaits the beast and the false prophet, which conspired together as an anti-Christ to thwart the work of the Lord through deception and bloodshed. They will not be slain; in the sense that the beast and false prophet are individual beings, this may be because a spirit cannot be killed; in the sense that the beast and false prophet are philosophies and ideologies, this may be because such can never be destroyed but only removed from a given place and time. Rather, they will be thrown alive into the worst place imaginable—a burning lake of fire. See also commentary on 14:10.

"Although the actual word Gehenna is not used in Revelation, this is what John refers to as the fiery lake of burning sulfur. Gehenna (an abbreviation for 'valley of the son of Hinnom') was the name given to the valley lying to the south and west of Jerusalem (the modern *Wadi er Rababi).* As the site of a cultic shrine where human sacrifices were offered (2 Kgs. 16:3; 23:10; Jer. 7:31), it acquired an unholy reputation. Because of prophetic denunciation of this place of terrible wickedness (Jer. 7:32; 19:6), it came to be equated with the hell of final judgment. . . . In [New Testament] times Gehenna was a place of fire and the abode of the wicked dead (Matt. 5:22; Mark 9:43).

"In our passage the fiery lake is said to burn with sulfur, a yellow substance that burns readily in air. . . . A lake of burning sulfur would not only be intensely hot, but malodorous and fetid as well. It is an appropriate place for all that is sinful and wicked in the world. The Antichrist and the false prophet are its first inhabitants. Later the devil (20:10), Death and Hades (20:14), and all evil people (21:8) will join them in this place of ceaseless torment."[29]

Joseph Smith taught of this terrible punishment: "A man is his own tormentor and his own condemner. Hence the saying, They shall go into the

---

[29] Mounce, *Book of Revelation,* 359.

lake that burns with fire and brimstone. The torment of disappointment in the mind of man is as exquisite as a lake burning with fire and brimstone. I say, so is the torment of man."[30]

19:21 *the remnant were slain with the [word] of him that sat upon the horse.* After the beast and the false prophet are cast into the fiery lake, the Lord slays their followers by the power of his word. Interestingly, although we know the Lord brings his armies with him to face the armies of evil, we have no details of the battle. In fact, from this verse, it appears that the Lord himself simply vanquishes the enemy through his power. But it could well be that the Lord also commands his followers to engage in the battle in the strength of his power.

Latter-day Saint scholar Richard Draper observes concerning the power of the word, "The only weapon the prophets need to defeat the enemy hosts and to establish peace upon the earth is the proclamation of the gospel."[31]

all the fowls were filled with their flesh. The fowls were earlier invited to come forth and be filled with the flesh of the wicked. Here they respond and are filled indeed. See commentary on 19:17–18.

---

[30] *History of the Church*, 6:314.
[31] Draper, *Opening the Seven Seals*, 213.

REVELATION
2 0

THE LORD'S THOUSAND-YEAR REIGN (20:1–6)

Having seen the defeat and destruction of the beast, the false prophet, and the armies of the wicked, John now sees the defeat and imprisonment of their master, Satan. An angel comes from heaven, captures the devil, and throws him into a bottomless pit, where he must remain for a thousand years. The martyrs for Christ, who stood firm in the face of all the persecution and trouble brought by the beast and his followers, will be called forth in the first resurrection and given power to reign with Christ on earth. But those who joined the beast will have to wait the thousand years for the blessing of resurrection.

Revelation 20:1–6

1 And I saw an angel come down [out of][1] heaven, having the key of the bottomless pit and a great chain in his hand.
2 And he laid hold on the dragon, that old serpent, which is the Devil, and Satan, and bound him a thousand years,
3 And cast him into the bottomless pit, and shut him up, and set a seal upon him, that he should deceive the nations no more, till the thousand years should be fulfilled: and after that he must be loosed a little season.
4 And I saw thrones, and they sat upon them, and judgment was given unto them: and I saw the souls of them that were beheaded for the witness of Jesus, and for the word of God, and which had not worshipped the beast, neither his image, neither had received his mark upon their foreheads, or in their hands; and they lived and reigned with Christ a thousand years.
5 But the rest of the dead lived not again until the thousand years were finished. This is the first resurrection.

---

[1] JST 20:1 replaces the KJV *from.*

6 Blessed and holy [are they who have]² part in the first resurrection: on
such the second death hath no power, but they shall be priests of God and
of Christ, and shall reign with him a thousand years.

NOTES AND COMMENTARY

20:1 *an angel come down [out of] heaven, having the key of the bottomless pit.* In 9:1 an angel is given the key to the bottomless pit. (This follows the reading given by the Joseph Smith Translation; the King James
Version incorrectly has Satan receiving the key.) Here that angel returns to
capture the devil. We do not know the identity of this angel, but obviously it
is a being of great power. Perhaps it is Michael, who has a special commission to fight and defeat Satan (D&C 88:112–15).³ We do know that
Michael is the seventh angel, who is given the privilege of proclaiming the
victory of the Lamb (D&C 88:106–7, 112). Ultimately, of course, it is
Christ who holds the key of hell and who gives the key to whomever he
chooses to accomplish his work. See commentary on 9:1.

a great chain in his hand. Not only will the devil be cast into prison but
he will be bound there by a chain, suggesting shackles and reemphasizing
that there is no hope of his escape.

20:2 *he laid hold on the dragon, that old serpent, which is the Devil,
and Satan, and bound him.* This verse gives us in one place the four names
or titles John calls the adversary, making certain that we know the identity
of our enemy throughout the revelation: the dragon, the serpent, the devil,
and Satan. It is important to note that it is the angel who captures and binds
the devil, not the inhabitants of earth, but he remains bound because the
people refuse to hearken to him. As Nephi taught, "Because of the righteousness of his people, Satan has no power; wherefore, he cannot be
loosed for the space of many years; for he hath no power over the hearts of
the people, for they dwell in righteousness, and the Holy One of Israel
reigneth" (1 Ne. 22:26).

a thousand years. During the Millennium, which will last a thousand
years, "Satan shall not have power to tempt any man" (D&C 101:28).

Elder Eldred G. Smith said: "Many other scriptures refer to the thousand years of wonderful, glorious conditions on the earth, because Lucifer,

---

² JST 20:6 replaces the KJV *is he that hath.*
³ This was the view of George Q. Cannon, as recorded in his *Life of Joseph Smith the Prophet,*
198.

Satan, the devil, will be bound. The scriptures say he will be 'bound with a chain' and 'put into a bottomless pit.' To me, these are symbolical terms. I cannot quite conceive of steel chains or pits that could hold Satan. The only power I know of that will bind Satan, or render him powerless, is righteous living.

"The war that started in heaven has not ended yet and shall not end until everyone has proved the extent of his ability to resist Satan. Even Jesus Christ had to bind Satan when he was tempted in the wilderness. Satan had no power over him, because Jesus resisted his temptations. Then the record says, ' . . . he departed from him for a season.' (Luke 4:13.) When you have resisted a temptation until it no longer becomes a temptation, then to that extent, Satan has lost his power over you, and as long as you do not yield to him, to that degree he is bound."[4]

20:3 *cast him into the bottomless pit.* The bottomless pit is another name for outer darkness.[5] See commentary on 9:1.

set a seal upon him. Other versions of the Bible agree that it was the pit that was sealed, rather than the devil himself (see LB, RSV, GNB, NIV, JB, NEB). To ensure that the devil could not escape, the pit that is his prison will be sealed shut by the power of God.

that he should deceive the nations no more. We see in 12:9 that Satan's mission on the earth is to deceive the people and the nations of the world. But when he is captured, bound with chains, and cast into the pit, he will no longer be able to deceive the people of the earth.

till the thousand years should be fulfilled: and after that he must be loosed a little season. After the thousand-year period has expired, Satan will be loosed to turn again to his work of deception and destruction—but only for a "little season." How long will the little season last?

President Joseph Fielding Smith reasoned that it might last a full one thousand years: "Our Savior came in the meridian of time. That dispensation is called the dispensation of the meridian of time. This means that it was about half way from the beginning of 'time' to the end of 'time.' Anyone who desires can figure it for himself that our Lord came about 4,000 years from the time of the fall. The millennium is to come some time following the 2,000 years after his coming. Then there is to be the millennium

---

[4] Smith, *Improvement Era,* June 1970, 104.
[5] *Doctrine and Covenants Commentary,* 158.

for 1,000 years, and following that a 'little season,' the length of which is not revealed, but which may bring 'time' to its end about 8,000 years from the beginning."[6]

Latter-day revelation gives additional details about what will transpire during that "little season": "Satan shall be bound, that old serpent, who is called the devil, and shall not be loosed for the space of a thousand years. And then he shall be loosed for a little season, that he may gather together his armies. And Michael, the seventh angel, even the archangel, shall gather together his armies, even the hosts of heaven. And the devil shall gather together his armies; even the hosts of hell, and shall come up to battle against Michael and his armies. And then cometh the battle of the great God; and the devil and his armies shall be cast away into their own place, that they shall not have power over the saints any more at all. For Michael shall fight their battles, and shall overcome him who seeketh the throne of him who sitteth upon the throne, even the Lamb" (D&C 88:110–15).

20:4 *thrones, and they sat upon them, and judgment was given unto them.* The kings of the earth, who once occupied the world's thrones, joined with the beast to fight against the kingdom of Christ. By the power of Christ they will be defeated and slain (19:21). Then those who stood firm in righteousness will be blessed to become kings themselves, granted thrones to reign with Christ throughout the Millennium.

There apparently is a hierarchy of judgment in the time of the Millennium. First is Christ himself, who rules over all and judges all (John 5:22; Acts 10:42; Morm. 3:20). Serving under him, the Twelve Apostles from the meridian dispensation will judge the house of Israel (Matt. 19:28). The house of Israel in this context apparently means those who are true Israel, those who are true to their covenants, as Joseph Smith learned by revelation: "Mine apostles, the Twelve which were with me in my ministry at Jerusalem, shall stand at my right hand at the day of my coming in a pillar of fire, being clothed with robes of righteousness, with crowns upon their heads, in glory even as I am, to judge the whole house of Israel, even as many as have loved me and kept my commandments, and none else" (D&C 29:12). John the Revelator, of course, is one of the Twelve who will so judge.

---

[6] Smith, *Doctrines of Salvation,* 1:81.

In addition, the Nephite twelve are given the charge to judge the seed of Lehi (1 Ne. 12:9–10; 3 Ne. 27:27; Morm. 3:19). The principle would suggest that there are other divinely appointed leaders of other peoples who also will judge those they serve. Missionaries will be given the responsibility to stand in judgment on those who reject them (D&C 75:20–22). And finally, all Saints shall "judge the world" (1 Cor. 6:2).

Daniel had a similar vision of the judgment: "I beheld till the thrones were cast down, and the Ancient of days [Adam] did sit, whose garment was white as snow, and the hair of his head like the pure wool: his throne was like the fiery flame, and his wheels as burning fire. A fiery stream issued and came forth from before him: thousand thousands ministered unto him, and ten thousand times ten thousand stood before him: the judgment was set, and the books were opened. . . . I beheld, and the same horn made war with the saints, and prevailed against them; until the Ancient of days came, and judgment was given to the saints of the most High; and the time came that the saints possessed the kingdom" (Dan. 7:9–10, 21–22).

the souls of them that were beheaded for the witness of Jesus, and for the word of God. The martyrs for Christ will reign with Christ: "And whoso layeth down his life in my cause, for my name's sake, shall find it again, even life eternal" (D&C 98:13). See commentary on 6:9.

which had not worshipped the beast, neither his image. See commentary on 13:15.

neither had received his mark upon their foreheads, or in their hands. See commentary on 13:16.

they lived. As we see in 13:15, the righteous are slain for refusing to worship the beast or to receive his mark. The beast gained a temporary victory. But here they rise in the resurrection to live forevermore and to reign victorious with their King.

and reigned with Christ a thousand years. During the thousand years of the Millennium, Christ "will reign personally upon the earth" (Article of Faith 10). With him will reign the martyrs and other righteous people who resisted the great pressure to worship the beast and who were raised up in the first resurrection. "In mine own due time will I come upon the earth in judgment, and my people shall be redeemed and shall reign with me on earth. For the great Millennium, of which I have spoken by the mouth of my servants, shall come" (D&C 43:29–30).

20:5 *the rest of the dead lived not again until the thousand years were finished.* The righteous are resurrected at the coming of the Lord—they were dead but now live again, like their Master (2:8). But the wicked must wait until after the Millennium. Their resurrection, with their judgment, is described in 20:12–13.

This is the first resurrection. The first and second resurrections are described in some detail in the Doctrine and Covenants: "The curtain of heaven [shall] be unfolded, as a scroll is unfolded after it is rolled up, and the face of the Lord shall be unveiled;

"And the saints that are upon the earth, who are alive, shall be quickened and be caught up to meet him.

"And they who have slept in their graves shall come forth, for their graves shall be opened; and they also shall be caught up to meet him in the midst of the pillar of heaven—

"They are Christ's, the first fruits, they who shall descend with him first, and they who are on the earth and in their graves, who are first caught up to meet him; and all this by the voice of the sounding of the trump of the angel of God.

"And after this another angel shall sound, which is the second trump; and then cometh the redemption of those who are Christ's at his coming; who have received their part in that prison which is prepared for them, that they might receive the gospel, and be judged according to men in the flesh.

"And again, another trump shall sound, which is the third trump; and then come the spirits of men who are to be judged, and are found under condemnation;

"And these are the rest of the dead; and they live not again until the thousand years are ended, neither again, until the end of the earth.

"And another trump shall sound, which is the fourth trump, saying: There are found among those who are to remain until that great and last day, even the end, who shall remain filthy still" (D&C 88:95–102).

20:6 *Blessed and holy [are they who have] part in the first resurrection.* This passage is another of the beatitudes found in Revelation (see Appendix 5). Those who are blessed to rise first are blessed indeed, for spirits look upon "the long absence of their spirits from their bodies as a bondage" (D&C 138:50). They are further blessed because they are victors over the second death; they are made "priests of God and of Christ," and they are chosen to "reign with him a thousand years." They are holy because they are righteous and because they are made holy by the glorified bodies they are given in the resurrection (D&C 88:28–29).

on such the second death hath no power. The second death has no power over those of the first resurrection. See commentary on 2:11.

priests of God and of Christ. See commentary on 1:6; 5:10.

reign with him a thousand years. See commentary on 5:10; 20:4.

SATAN IS LOOSED (20:7–10)

Satan will be sealed up in the bottomless pit for a thousand years—but not forever. "When the thousand years are expired, Satan shall be loosed" to once again do his work of deception and destruction on the earth. He will gather followers from all nations to a battle in which the warriors are as many "as the sand of the sea." Satan's mortal hosts will surround the Saints and their "beloved city," but the Lord will act in great glory and power to devour his enemy. Then the devil will be cast away forever, to be punished for his great sins for all eternity.

The account in 4 Nephi 1 gives us a sobering preview of how the bright millennial era can be brought to a close. After the Savior's visit to the descendants of Lehi in the Americas, the people entered into a condition that was millennial in some important respects: "There was no contention in the land, because of the love of God which did dwell in the hearts of the people. And there were no envyings, nor strifes, nor tumults, nor whoredoms, nor lyings, nor murders, nor any manner of lasciviousness; and surely there could not be a happier people among all the people who had been created by the hand of God. . . . [T]hey were in one, the children of Christ, and heirs to the kingdom of God. And how blessed were they! For the Lord did bless them in all their doings" (vv. 15–18).

The breakdown in this near-perfect society had tiny beginnings: "a small part of the people . . . revolted from the church and [had] taken upon them the name of Lamanites" (vv. 20). Many years later, "in this two hundred and first year there began to be among them those who were lifted up in pride, such as the wearing of costly apparel, and all manner of fine pearls, and of the fine things of the world. And from that time forth they did have their goods and their substance no more common among them. And they began to be divided into classes; and they began to build up churches

unto themselves to get gain, and began to deny the true church of Christ"
(vv. 24–26).

From that point, the society disintegrated rapidly. Within the next
decade, "there were many churches in the land; yea, there were many
churches which professed to know the Christ, and yet they did deny the
more parts of his gospel, insomuch that they did receive all manner of
wickedness, and did administer that which was sacred unto him to whom it
had been forbidden because of unworthiness. And this church did multiply
exceedingly because of iniquity, and because of the power of Satan who
did get hold upon their hearts" (vv. 27–28).

Thus it was that in only a few years, Satan, who had essentially been
bound, was loosed again in the land. "And thus they did dwindle in unbelief
and wickedness, from year to year. . . . [And] there was a great division
among the people. . . . And the more wicked part of the people did wax
strong, and became exceedingly more numerous than were the people of
God" (vv. 34–35, 40). By the time three hundred years had passed away,
"the robbers of Gadianton did spread over all the face of the land; and there
were none that were righteous save it were the disciples of Jesus" (v. 46).

The decline and fall of this blessed society makes for troubling reading, and the lessons for our day are clear. Satan ever lies in wait to deceive
and destroy, and if he fails with one generation, he will try with redoubled
efforts to harm the next.

We cannot say whether the picture we see in 4 Nephi will be experienced toward the end of the Millennium, but it is certainly possible that the
pattern will be repeated.

Revelation 20:7–10

7 And when the thousand years are expired, Satan shall be loosed out of his
prison,
8 And shall go out to deceive the nations which are in the four quarters of
the earth, Gog and Magog, to gather them together to battle: the number of
whom is as the sand of the sea.
9 And they went up on the breadth of the earth, and compassed the camp of
the saints about, and the beloved city: and fire came down from God out of
heaven, and devoured them.
10 And the devil that deceived them was cast into the lake of fire and brimstone, where the beast and the false prophet are, and shall be tormented day
and night for ever and ever.

NOTES AND COMMENTARY

20:7 *when the thousand years are expired, Satan shall be loosed out of his prison.* Because Satan will be bound by the power of God, as well as by the choices and desires of the people, it is reasonable to suppose that both these elements will be present in his loosing. Satan will likely be loosed because the people turn to him again and because the Lord, suffering their agency, will allow it. As we read in Doctrine and Covenants 29, "When the thousand years are ended, and men again begin to deny their God, then will I spare the earth but for a little season" (v. 22).

20:8 *shall go out to deceive the nations.* In 12:9 we read that "Satan . . . deceiveth the whole world." The tragedy is that though in the Millennium the whole world will turn to righteousness and peace and Satan will not have power to tempt and deceive (1 Ne. 22:26), at the end of the Millennium he will return to that power. And those who hearken to him will be not a few. He will deceive "nations" in every part of the globe, "the four quarters of the earth."

Gog and Magog. These names are symbolic names of the hosts that will follow Satan in his war against the Saints. We find these terms in the Old Testament in Ezekiel's description of the great wars that precede the second coming of Christ (Ezek. 38–39). Here they or others who are represented by the same symbolic names fight the kingdom of Christ and his followers.

to gather them together to battle. Latter-day revelation casts additional light on the last battle between Satan and God: "And then he shall be loosed for a little season, that he may gather together his armies. And Michael, the seventh angel, even the archangel, shall gather together his armies, even the hosts of heaven. And the devil shall gather together his armies; even the hosts of hell, and shall come up to battle against Michael and his armies. And then cometh the battle of the great God; and the devil and his armies shall be cast away into their own place, that they shall not have power over the saints any more at all. For Michael shall fight their battles, and shall overcome him who seeketh the throne of him who sitteth upon the throne, even the Lamb" (D&C 88:111–15).

the number of whom is as the sand of the sea. Those mortals who follow Satan in the last battle shall be so many that they cannot be numbered. In addition, "the hosts of hell" will join in the battle (D&C 88:113).

It is instructive to compare this prophecy with the promise given to
Abraham: "I will multiply thy seed as the stars of the heaven, and as the
sand which is upon the sea shore; and thy seed shall possess the gate of his
enemies" (Gen. 22:17). Though Satan and his hosts will be innumerable, so
also will be Michael and his armies, who are all of Abraham by covenant.
And the ancient promise will then surely be fulfilled: Abraham's seed will
prevail.

20:9 *And they went up on the breadth of the earth.* This expression
suggests great hordes crossing the earth. The Good News Bible words this
passage as "they spread out over the earth"; the Jerusalem Bible renders it
as "they will come swarming over the entire country."

compassed the camp of the saints about, and the beloved city. "The
two terms, 'camp of the saints' (Palestine) and 'beloved city' ([New] Jerusalem), stand together for the people of God. 'Camp' is the word used in
Exodus for Israel's wilderness home. . . . The 'beloved city' stands in contrast to 'the great city' (11:8); it is the new Jerusalem."[7]

fire came down from God out of heaven, and devoured them. This passage reminds us of an experience of Elijah, who when faced with enemies
said, "If I be a man of God, let fire come down from heaven, and consume
thee and thy fifty. And the fire of God came down from heaven, and consumed him and his fifty" (2 Kgs. 1:12). It also brings to mind an experience
Jesus had with James and John in the New Testament, when the apostles
wanted Jesus to call down fire from heaven to destroy a people who would
not receive them (Luke 9:51–56).

It may be that the fire is symbolic of heavenly power—latter-day revelation tells us that Michael and his heavenly hosts will fight these battles at
the end (D&C 88:111–15).

20:10 *And the devil that deceived them was cast into the lake of fire
and brimstone, where the beast and the false prophet are.* We read in 19:20
that the beast and the false prophet are cast into the lake of fire and brimstone (see commentary there). Here the devil is cast into the lake of fire as
well.

shall be tormented day and night for ever and ever. Torment is the
essence of dwelling in the lake of fire and brimstone; in fact, torment and
punishment are probably the purpose of the lake. In contrast to this torment

---

[7] Harrington, *Revelation,* 198.

of the damned is the everlasting joy of those who are saved in the kingdom of God. As we read in the Doctrine and Covenants, "The graves of the saints shall be opened; and they shall come forth and stand on the right hand of the Lamb, . . . and they shall sing the song of the Lamb, day and night forever and ever" (D&C 133:56).

Nephi taught that in the resurrection "they who are righteous shall be righteous still, and they who are filthy shall be filthy still; wherefore, they who are filthy are the devil and his angels; and they shall go away into everlasting fire, prepared for them; and their torment is as a lake of fire and brimstone, whose flame ascendeth up forever and ever and has no end" (2 Ne. 9:16).

THE LAST JUDGMENT (20:11–15)

In his vision of the Last Judgment, John sees God sitting on his throne as the great Judge of all. He sees the dead resurrected and brought to stand before God, to be judged "according to their works," as those works were recorded in both earthly and heavenly books (see also D&C 128:6–8). He also sees another book, "the book of life." Those whose names are not recorded in the book of life are "cast into the lake of fire." In addition, death and hell themselves are "cast into the lake of fire."

Revelation 20:11–15

> 11 And I saw a great white throne, and him that sat on it, from whose face the earth and the heaven fled away; and there was found no place for them.
> 12 And I saw the dead, small and great, stand before God; and the books were opened; and another book was opened, which is the book of life: and the dead were judged out of those things which were written in the books, according to their works.
> 13 And the sea gave up the dead which were in it; and death and hell delivered up the dead which were in them: and they were judged every man according to their works.
> 14 And death and hell were cast into the lake of fire. This is the second death.
> 15 And whosoever was not found written in the book of life was cast into the lake of fire.

NOTES AND COMMENTARY

20:11 *a great white throne.* This throne, which we first see in 4:2, symbolizes God's kingship and power. It is called "great" to suggest that this is no ordinary throne but one fit for the king of all creation. White may symbolize victory or purity and righteousness—or a combination of these attributes of God. In addition, the word *white* (Greek *leukos*) may mean "bright" or "gleaming."[8] God dwells in "everlasting burnings,"[9] and his throne would therefore be white, bright, and gleaming. For other references to the throne, see 4:2–3, 9; 5:1, 7, 13; 6:16; 7:10, 15; 19:4; 21:5.

him that sat on it. The Being on the throne is God, the Eternal Father.

from whose face the earth and the heaven fled away. "When the thousand years are ended, and men again begin to deny their God, then will I spare the earth but for a little season; And the end shall come, and the heaven and the earth shall be consumed and pass away, and there shall be a new heaven and a new earth. For all old things shall pass away, and all things shall become new, even the heaven and the earth, and all the fulness thereof" (D&C 29:22–24). These things will come by the power of God.

there was found no place for them. The old heaven and earth must give way so that the new may come (21:1). Just as Satan and his followers were cast out of the presence of God—"neither was their place found any more in heaven" (12:8)—so will the old heaven and the old earth themselves have no place before God. The earth will be changed to a celestial order after the Millennium (see 21:1).

20:12 *the dead, small and great, stand before God.* These individuals are "the rest of the dead" who were not resurrected earlier (20:5). The righteous dead have already been raised up unto glory (20:4). All who remain—whether they were weak or strong, rich or poor, famous or insignificant in the eyes of the world—will be raised from the dead to stand before God the Judge to determine what their eternal reward or punishment will be.

the books were opened. Joseph Smith explained: "You will discover in this quotation [Rev. 20:12] that the books were opened; and another book was opened, which was the book of life; but the dead were judged out of those things which were written in the books, according to their works; consequently, the books spoken of must be the books which contained the record of their works, and refer to the records which are kept on the earth [which probably includes Church records of ordinances and Church

---

[8] Mounce, *Book of Revelation*, 375.
[9] *History of the Church*, 6:317.

histories]. And the book which was the book of life is the record which is kept in heaven; the principle agreeing precisely with the doctrine which is commanded you in the revelation contained in the letter which I wrote to you previous to my leaving my place [D&C 127]—that in all your recordings it may be recorded in heaven" (D&C 128:7; see also Dan. 7:10).

another book was opened, which is the book of life. Those whose names are recorded in the book of life are saved from being cast into the lake of fire, which is the second death. As Jesus said to the apostles, "Rejoice not, that the spirits are subject unto you; but rather rejoice, because your names are written in heaven" (Luke 10:20). See commentary on 3:5.

the dead were judged out of those things which were written in the books, according to their works. The things we do here on earth are entered into the record books of both heaven and earth, and our works form the basis of our judgment. Jacob wrote: "When all men shall have passed from this first death unto life, insomuch as they have become immortal, they must appear before the judgment-seat of the Holy One of Israel; and then cometh the judgment, and then must they be judged according to the holy judgment of God" (2 Ne. 9:15). And Paul later testified, "Every one of us shall give account of himself to God" (Rom. 14:12).

As mentioned earlier, the dead here are those who were not worthy to come forth in the first resurrection but were reserved until after the Millennium was completed. The righteous will also likely stand before the judgment bar at this time but only to have their earlier judgment—and blessing of glory—confirmed.[10] For examples of individuals and groups that received an earlier judgment, see 20:4; Mosiah 15:21–25; D&C 101:30–31; 132:37.

Joseph Smith gave a valuable and comforting lesson on the judgment: "The Great Parent of the universe looks upon the whole of the human family with a fatherly care and paternal regard; He views them as His offspring, and without any of those contracted feelings that influence the children of men. . . . [He] will judge all men, not according to the narrow, contracted notions of men, but, 'according to the deeds done in the body whether they be good or evil,' or whether these deeds were done in England, America, Spain, Turkey, or India. He will judge them, 'not

---

[10] McConkie, *Doctrinal New Testament Commentary,* 3:576–77.

according to what they have not, but according to what they have,' those who have lived without law, will be judged without law, and those who have a law, will be judged by that law. . . . He will award judgment or mercy to all nations according to their several deserts, their means of obtaining intelligence, the laws by which they are governed, the facilities afforded them of obtaining correct information, and His inscrutable designs in relation to the human family; and when the designs of God shall be made manifest, and the curtain of futurity be withdrawn, we shall all of us eventually have to confess that the Judge of all the earth has done right."[11]

President Joseph Fielding Smith added this insight: "Every man will be judged according to his works, his opportunities for receiving the truth, and the intent of his heart."[12]

20:13 *the sea gave up the dead which were in it.* The sea may represent those whose bodies are most lost of all, even more than those who were buried in the earth. The bodies were carried away, and no one knows their final resting place. Even these will be resurrected. In addition, "It was widely believed that those lost at sea had no access to Sheol (Hades); in specifically naming the sea John emphasizes that he is describing the *general* resurrection."[13]

death and hell delivered up the dead which were in them. According to Jacob, brother of Nephi, death is the state in which body and spirit are separated, and hell is the state of spiritual death. All those in both states will be brought forth in the great, universal resurrection. Jacob said: "O how great the goodness of our God, who prepareth a way for our escape from the grasp of this awful monster; yea, that monster, death and hell, which I call the death of the body, and also the death of the spirit. And because of the way of deliverance of our God, the Holy One of Israel, this death, of which I have spoken, which is the temporal, shall deliver up its dead; which death is the grave. And this death of which I have spoken, which is the spiritual death, shall deliver up its dead; which spiritual death is hell; wherefore, death and hell must deliver up their dead, and hell must deliver up its captive spirits, and the grave must deliver up its captive bodies, and the bodies and the spirits of men will be restored one to the other; and it is by the power of the resurrection of the Holy One of Israel" (2 Ne. 9:10–12).

[11] *Teachings of the Prophet Joseph Smith,* 218.
[12] Smith, *Doctrines of Salvation,* 2:21.
[13] Harrington, *Revelation,* 203.

they were judged every man according to their works. See commentary on 20:12.

20:14 *death and hell were cast into the lake of fire.* This expression seems to be a symbolic way of saying that the great consequences of sin— physical and spiritual death—will suffer the same fate as the master insti- gator of sin, Satan. "Jesus Christ . . . hath abolished death," Paul wrote (2 Tim. 1:10), and he likewise abolishes hell for all who attain to a state of glory. The lake of fire itself is a hell for those who are cast into it (Satan, his angels, and the sons of perdition), and that hell will continue through the eternities (D&C 29:38; 76:44; 2 Pet. 2:4). For a discussion of the lake of fire, see commentary on 19:20.

But for those who are "heirs of salvation" (D&C 76:88), meaning all who attain to a kingdom of glory, death and hell will forever cease to exist.

This is the second death. The torture of the second death is typified by the lake of fire. See commentary on 2:11.

20:15 *whosoever was not found written in the book of life was cast into the lake of fire.* In close proximity we have seen the following cast into the lake of fire: the beast and the false prophet (19:20), the devil (20:10), death and hell (20:14), and all those who are not found in the book of life (20:15). For discussion of the book of life, see commentary on 3:5; for discussion of the lake of fire, see commentary on 19:20.

REVELATION
21:1-27;
22:1-5

THE NEW HEAVEN AND NEW EARTH (21:1–8)

With death and hell abolished, along with Satan and his followers, the earth is ready to be transformed. All the people of the world are also ready to dwell on a new creation, having "put off the old man" and having "put on the new man, . . . after the image of him that created him," which is Jesus Christ (see Col. 3:4–10), and having come forth from the grave in celestial glory. With evil gone and the inhabitants of the earth glorified, the earth itself is changed to a habitation of great glory.

The new earth is much more than simply a globe made new. It is also a new society, a new way of living. It is a place where God may dwell. It is a state of being in which there is no death, sorrow, or pain. It is a habitation for the heirs of God.

Revelation 21:1–8

> 1 And I saw a new heaven and a new earth: for the first heaven and the first earth were passed away; and there was no more sea.
> 2 And I John saw the holy city, new Jerusalem, coming down from God out of heaven, prepared as a bride adorned for her husband.
> 3 And I heard a great voice out of heaven saying, Behold, the tabernacle of God is with men, and he will dwell with them, and they shall be his people, and God himself shall be with them, and be their God.
> 4 And God shall wipe away all tears from their eyes; and there shall be no more death, neither sorrow, nor crying, neither shall there be any more pain: for the former things are passed away.
> 5 And he that sat upon the throne said, Behold, I make all things new. And he said unto me, Write: for these words are true and faithful.

6 And he said unto me, It is done. I am Alpha and Omega, the beginning and the end. I will give unto him that is athirst of the fountain of the water of life freely.
7 He that overcometh shall inherit all things; and I will be his God, and he shall be my son.
8 But the fearful, and unbelieving, and the abominable, and murderers, and whoremongers, and sorcerers, and idolaters, and all liars, shall have their part in the lake which burneth with fire and brimstone: which is the second death.

NOTES AND COMMENTARY

21:1 *a new heaven and a new earth.* The new earth is described in the Doctrine and Covenants: "Therefore, [the earth] must needs be sanctified from all unrighteousness, that it may be prepared for the celestial glory; for after it hath filled the measure of its creation, it shall be crowned with glory, even with the presence of God the Father; that bodies who are of the celestial kingdom may possess it forever and ever; for, for this intent was it made and created, and for this intent are they sanctified. . . . And again, verily I say unto you, the earth abideth the law of a celestial kingdom, for it filleth the measure of its creation, and transgresseth not the law—wherefore, it shall be sanctified; yea, notwithstanding it shall die, it shall be quickened again, and shall abide the power by which it is quickened, and the righteous shall inherit it" (D&C 88:18–20, 25–26).

"And again, verily, verily, I say unto you that when the thousand years are ended . . . the end shall come, and the heaven and the earth shall be consumed and pass away, and there shall be a new heaven and a new earth. For all old things shall pass away, and all things shall become new, even the heaven and the earth, and all the fulness thereof, both men and beasts, the fowls of the air, and the fishes of the sea; and not one hair, neither mote, shall be lost, for it is the workmanship of mine hand" (D&C 29:22–25).

the first heaven and the first earth were passed away. Heaven and earth as we know them will cease to exist, having "passed away," as we pass away in death. In their place will be a renewed, resurrected earth,[1] and the heavens surrounding the earth will likewise be renewed.

there was no more sea. Perhaps one reason there will be no sea is that the entirety of the earth will have one surface, "like a sea of glass and fire" (D&C 130:7).

---

[1] See *Discourses of Brigham Young,* 375; Smith, *Doctrines of Salvation,* 1:74; 2:281, 322; Talmage, *Jesus the Christ,* 322.

This expression may also have a symbolic meaning, as Latter-day Saint scholar Richard Draper explains: "The abode of chaos, the home of the satanic beast, the old seat over which the whore held sway, has vanished. Under the force of the Lamb's radiance, the source of Babylon's seaborne luxuries and what helped feed and sustain her corruption has boiled into oblivion. But the sea and the abyss are one and the same. Therefore, the destruction of the sea represents the annihilation of the primeval deep, the home of malevolence and evil. Up to this point, it has dominated the world. As the stronghold of Satan's supporters, its existence mocked the hope of a complete victory and a complete sovereignty of the Lord. It has no place in the transformed world where all things spontaneously obey their Lord and their God."[2]

21:2 *the holy city, new Jerusalem, coming down from God out of heaven.* In the last days, a "remnant of the house of Joseph shall be built upon this land; . . . and they shall build up a holy city unto the Lord, like unto the Jerusalem of old. . . . And there shall be a new heaven and a new earth; and they shall be like unto the old save the old have passed away, and all things have become new. And then cometh the New Jerusalem; and blessed are they who dwell therein, for it is they whose garments are white through the blood of the Lamb" (Ether 13:8–10).

This New Jerusalem "should come down out of heaven, and the holy sanctuary of the Lord," Moroni wrote (Ether 13:3). Thus, the New Jerusalem built up on the earth by the Saints of God will be joined by the New Jerusalem from heaven, which includes the original Zion, Enoch's city, "the City of Holiness, . . . [which] was taken up into heaven" (Moses 7:19, 21).

As the Lord promised Enoch, "Righteousness and truth will I cause to sweep the earth as with a flood, to gather out mine elect from the four quarters of the earth, unto a place which I shall prepare, an Holy City, that my people may gird up their loins, and be looking forth for the time of my coming; for there shall be my tabernacle, and it shall be called Zion, a New Jerusalem. And the Lord said unto Enoch: Then shalt thou and all thy city meet them there, and we will receive them into our bosom, and they shall see us; and we will fall upon their necks, and they shall fall upon our necks, and we will kiss each other; and there shall be mine abode, and it shall be

[2] Draper, *Opening the Seven Seals,* 228.

Zion, which shall come forth out of all the creations which I have made; and for the space of a thousand years the earth shall rest" (Moses 7:62–64).

In Revelation 21, it appears that John is seeing the heavenly New Jerusalem descend *after* the final battle when Satan is cast away forever, while in Moses 7, it seems that the city will descend *before* the Millennium. Perhaps the Lord may send the holy city down at the beginning of the Millennium, remove it during the final time of wickedness on the earth (because the earth may not be worthy to have the city present in that period), and, finally, restore it to its rightful place after Satan is conquered and cast out for good.

prepared as a bride adorned for her husband. See commentary on 19:7.

21:3 *great voice out of heaven.* The revelation does not explain whose voice this is, whether of God or of an angel. Its function is to explain the meaning of what John is now seeing.

the tabernacle of God is with men, and he will dwell with them. In the time of Moses, God dwelt among men in the great tent they provided for him—his tabernacle (Lev. 26:11–12). In the celestialized earth, God will personally come down to earth and stay with his people. "After [the earth] hath filled the measure of its creation, it shall be crowned with glory, even with the presence of God the Father" (D&C 88:19).

they shall be his people, and God himself shall . . . be their God. The Lord is able to dwell with the people of the celestialized earth because they are his people. They have become one with him and are worthy of his presence. This passage fulfills a promise made repeatedly through the Lord's prophets: "I will set my tabernacle among you: and my soul shall not abhor you. And I will walk among you, and will be your God, and ye shall be my people" (Lev. 26:11–12; Jer. 7:23; 11:4; 30:22; Ezek. 36:28; 37:23, 27; Zech. 8:8; 2 Cor. 6:16).

21:4 *And God shall wipe away all tears from their eyes.* See commentary on 7:17.

there shall be no more death/sorrow/crying/pain. This promised reward is the reverse of the fate of Babylon. There, all sounds of joy have ceased forever (18:22). In the celestial Zion, the heavenly New Jerusalem, all sorrow has ceased forever. Death, sickness, and physical pain are no more. And the sources of sorrow and emotional pain—including crime, poverty, contention in the home, jealousy, marital unfaithfulness, and a host of others—likewise have totally ceased (see also Isa. 65:17–20).

for the former things are passed away. The former things are those belonging to the old heaven and earth. The old heaven and earth, with the death, sorrow, pain, and suffering that were integral parts of them, are gone forever.

21:5 *he that sat upon the throne said, Behold, I make all things new.* The One who sits on the throne in heaven is God the Father. He has power to renew or rejuvenate or regenerate. That process of renewal begins in the hearts of those who will turn to God and yield themselves to him (Hel. 3:35). It continues when the dead are raised to glory and concludes when the earth itself is transformed into a new world (see commentary on 21:1). The Lord does not make just some things new—he proclaims that all things are made new by his power.

he said unto me, Write; for these words are true and faithful. John has repeatedly been commanded to record things he hears and sees, and he is also told what to write (1:10–11; 1:19; 14:13). "Faithful and True" are given to John as two of the names of Christ (19:11), whose words are always trustworthy (the translation given in JB, NIV, NEB, and RSV) and true (2 Ne. 31:15; D&C 1:37; 71:11).

21:6 *It is done.* Because Christ is the Alpha and Omega, the beginning and the end, he is fully able to see the end from the beginning. That which he has ordained to come to pass is as though it has already happened. Thus, to God, blessings promised in the future are as certain of fulfillment as if they had already been received.

I am Alpha and Omega, the beginning and the end. See commentary on 1:8.

I will give unto him that is athirst of the fountain of the water of life freely. Water is an essential source of life; Jesus Christ is the source of eternal life. As such, he is the fountain of the water of life,[3] which water of life is the principles and ordinances of the gospel.[4]

In the remarkable exchange with the woman of Samaria, Jesus said, "If thou knewest the gift of God, and who it is that [speaketh] to thee, . . . thou wouldest have asked of him, and he would have given thee living water. . . .

---

[3] Jeremiah taught clearly that Christ was "the fountain of living waters" (Jer. 2:13; 17:13).

[4] *Discourses of Brigham Young,* 235; McConkie, *Doctrinal New Testament Commentary,* 1:151–52.

But whosoever drinketh of the water that I shall give him shall never thirst; but the water that I shall give him shall be in him a well of water springing up into everlasting life" (John 4:10, 14). As the Lord promised through John, this water is offered freely to all who will recognize their spiritual thirst and come unto Christ to be satisfied (Isa. 55:1; Alma 5:34; 42:27; D&C 10:66). See commentary on 7:17.

Living water may also represent the Holy Ghost. Jesus said, as John recorded elsewhere: "He that believeth on me, as the scripture hath said, out of his belly shall flow rivers of living water. (But this spake he of the Spirit, which they that believe on him should receive: for the Holy Ghost was not yet given; because that Jesus was not yet glorified)" (John 7:38–39).

21:7 *He that overcometh shall inherit all things.* When we overcome the temptations of the adversary and rise above the trials of life, when we endure to the end in righteousness, we receive the great blessing of becoming "heirs of God and joint-heirs with Christ" (Rom. 8:17). Then the King shall say to us, "Come, ye blessed of my Father, inherit the kingdom prepared for you from the foundation of the world" (Matt. 25:34), and "all that my Father hath shall be given unto him" (D&C 84:38). Then "they are gods, even the sons of God—wherefore, all things are theirs, whether life or death, or things present, or things to come, all are theirs and they are Christ's, and Christ is God's. And they shall overcome all things" (D&C 76:58–60). Certainly overcoming will require sacrifice and suffering, but as Paul taught, "I reckon that the sufferings of this present time are not worthy to be compared with the glory which shall be revealed in us" (Rom. 8:18).

This promise follows on other, similar promises made to those who overcome—that they will become pillars in the temple of God, to go no more out; that the very name of God, and Christ's new name, will be written upon them; that they will be privileged to sit with Christ on his throne (3:12, 21). See Appendix 5 for a list of blessings that will be granted to those who overcome.

I will be his God, and he shall be my son. This marvelous promise is given to all who enter the celestial kingdom. Earlier the Lord said, "They shall be his people, . . . and God himself shall be . . . their God" (21:3). But here the Lord makes it personal and individual—we will become his sons and his daughters, not just part of a collective group. This assurance is a fulfillment of what Paul promised: "Wherefore thou art no more a servant, but a son; and if a son, then an heir of God through Christ" (Gal. 4:7). And again, "For as many as are led by the Spirit of God, they are the sons of God" (Rom. 8:14).

In another setting, John the Revelator gave the same testimony: "Behold, what manner of love the Father hath bestowed upon us, that we should be called the sons of God: therefore the world knoweth us not, because it knew him not. Beloved, now are we the sons of God, and it doth not yet appear what we shall be: but we know that, when he shall appear, we shall be like him; for we shall see him as he is" (1 Jn. 3:1–2).

The underlying feeling conveyed by this phrase is that the Lord is assuring us of *relationship*, a close relationship between us and him. He will claim us as his own, draw us to him, hold us closely, and treat us tenderly. We will in very deed be his sons and daughters.

21:8 *But the fearful, and unbelieving, and the abominable, and murderers, and whoremongers, and sorcerers, and idolaters, and all liars.* It is interesting—and important—that the Lord begins this list of those to be condemned with "the fearful, and unbelieving." Certainly to have fear and lack belief are not as serious as the sins that follow in the list. Yet it is the fearful and unbelieving who yielded to the enticings of the beast, who failed to stand firm and true in the face of the great persecutions and temptations that come upon the faithful. Perhaps fear and unbelief lead to the other sins the Lord lists (D&C 63:17–18; 76:36–37, 103–6).

All these are in stark opposition to the character of Christ, who is faithful and true (3:14; 19:11). They have been led astray by the devil, "which deceiveth the whole world" (12:9). They follow their father, Satan; as Christ said, "Ye are of your father the devil. . . . There is no truth in him. . . . He is a liar, and the father of it" (John 8:44).

This verse might be seen both as a warning and an invitation: a warning that those who do not repent of ungodliness will not be able to enjoy the sweet existence on the new, paradisiacal earth, and an invitation to turn from such wickedness.

the lake which burneth with fire and brimstone. This expression is a metaphor for the second death. Latter-day Saint scholar Richard Draper has written: "Such sinners are Lucifer's but only for a time. While they are under his power, his full wrath will be spent upon them. For a thousand years [the Millennium] their tears, their torment, their misery will be his wine, and their scorched souls and burning consciences the butter of his bread."[5] See commentary on 19:20.

which is the second death. See commentary on 2:11.

THE CITY OF NEW JERUSALEM (21:9–27; 22:1–5)

In Revelation 19 we briefly saw Zion portrayed as a bride. Here we see a more developed image of Zion as a holy, celestial city. That city will send forth a wonderful light. It will have high walls with foundations made of precious stones, and its gates will be made of pearl and guarded by twelve angels. The city itself will be "pure gold, like unto clear glass." Within the city is a "pure river of water of life" and "the tree of life." The inhabitants of the city will dwell in the presence of God, "and they shall see his face, . . . and they shall reign for ever and ever."

In the apocryphal book of 4 Ezra, the seer experienced a similar shift in his vision. First he sees a woman mourning for her children, not realizing that the woman is Zion. Then, "while I was talking to her, her face suddenly shone exceedingly, and her countenance flashed like lightning. . . . And I looked, and behold, the woman was no longer visible to me, but there was an established city, and a place of huge foundation showed itself" (4 Ezra 10:25–27).

The images of the holy city in Revelation 21 stand in bold contrast to the wicked city in Revelation 17. The city of righteousness (a symbol for her people) is everything good and holy and true that the city of wickedness (also a symbol for her people) is not.

It is easy to be distracted by the details of measurements and precious stones in this vision and thus to miss impressions that come from other images in this passage: the celestial city (and the people) are bound to Christ in an intimate relationship; the city is holy and has come from the presence of God; she shines with precious light; one gains entry to the city through passing by angels that are set as sentries there, and by belonging to one of the twelve tribes of Israel; the "twelve apostles of the Lamb" are a key element of the city's foundation; the Father and the Son shine with the light of their being to illuminate the city; only those who are pure and clean are allowed to enter; the city provides both living water and the fruit of the

---

[5] Draper, *Opening the Seven Seals,* 232–33.

tree of life to its inhabitants; both the Father and the Son dwell there, and the servants of Christ "shall see his face."

Ezekiel had a similar vision of the holy city (Ezek. 40:1–47:12; 48:30–35).

Revelation 21:9–27; 22:1–5

9 And there came unto me one of the seven angels which had the seven . . .[6] last plagues, and talked with me, saying, Come hither, I will shew thee the bride, the Lamb's wife.

10 And he carried me away in the [S]pirit[7] to a great and high mountain, and shewed me that great city, the holy Jerusalem, descending out of heaven from God,

11 Having the glory of God: and her light was like unto a stone most precious, even like a jasper stone, clear as crystal;

12 And had a wall great and high, and had twelve gates, and at the gates twelve angels, and names written thereon, which are the names of the twelve tribes of the children of Israel:

13 On the east three gates; on the north three gates; on the south three gates; and on the west three gates.

14 And the wall of the city had twelve foundations, and in them the names of the twelve apostles of the Lamb.

15 And he that talked with me had a golden reed to measure the city, and the gates thereof, and the wall thereof.

16 And the city lieth foursquare, and the length is as large as the breadth: and he measured the city with the reed, twelve thousand furlongs. The length and the breadth and the height of it are equal.

17 And he measured the wall thereof, an hundred and forty and four cubits, according to the measure of a man, that is, of the angel.

18 And the building of the wall of it was of jasper: and the city was pure gold, like unto clear glass.

19 And the foundations of the wall of the city were garnished with all manner of precious stones. The first foundation was jasper; the second, sapphire; the third, a chalcedony; the fourth, an emerald;

20 The fifth, sardonyx; the sixth, sardius; the seventh, chrysolite; the eighth, beryl; the ninth, a topaz; the tenth, a chrysoprasus; the eleventh, a jacinth; the twelfth, an amethyst.

21 And the twelve gates were twelve pearls; every several gate was of one pearl: and the street of the city was pure gold, as it were transparent glass.

22 And I saw no temple therein: for the Lord God Almighty and the Lamb are the temple of it.

23 And the city had no need of the sun, neither of the moon, to shine in it: for the glory of God did lighten it, and the Lamb is the light thereof.

24 And the nations of them which are saved shall walk in the light of it: and the kings of the earth do bring their glory and honour into it.

---

[6] JST 21:9 omits the KJV *vials full of the seven.*
[7] JST 21:10 capitalizes *Spirit.*

25 And the gates of it shall not be shut at all by day: for there shall be no night there.

26 And they shall bring the glory and honour of the nations into it.

27 And there shall in no wise enter into it any thing that defileth, neither whatsoever worketh abomination, or maketh a lie: but they which are written in the Lamb's book of life.

22:1 And he shewed me a pure river of water of life, clear as crystal, proceeding out of the throne of God and of the Lamb.

2 In the midst of the street of it, and on either side of the river, was there the tree of life, which bare twelve manner of fruits, and yielded her fruit every month: and the leaves of the tree were for the healing of the nations.

3 And there shall be no more curse: but the throne of God and of the Lamb shall be in it; and his servants shall serve him:

4 And they shall see his face; and his name shall be in their foreheads.

5 And there shall be no night there; and they need no candle, neither light of the sun; for the Lord God giveth them light: and they shall reign for ever and ever.

NOTES AND COMMENTARY

21:9 *one of the seven angels which had the seven . . . last plagues.* This is one of the angels that poured plagues from the seven bowls, or vials (17:1).

Come hither, I will shew thee the bride, the Lamb's wife. The angel's invitation parallels a similar invitation in 17:1: "Come hither; I will shew unto thee the judgment of the great whore that sitteth upon many waters." In the former instance, as in this, John saw a city. The wicked city of the whore, however, is destined to receive eternal destruction, while the holy city of New Jerusalem will be filled forever with the glory of God. See commentary on 19:7.

21:10 *And he carried me away in the [S]pirit.* See commentary on 17:3.

to a great and high mountain. This place may have simply been a vantage point from which John could view the city (as in JST Matt. 4:8–10), but more likely this high mountain was the "holy mountain of God" (Ezek. 28:14, 16), the holy temple on earth rather than in heaven.

shewed me that great city, the holy Jerusalem, descending out of heaven from God. See commentary on 21:2.

21:11 *Having the glory of God.* The city is filled with God's glory, meaning his light, his power, his majesty, and, crowning all, his presence. "Therefore, [the earth] must needs be sanctified from all unrighteousness, that it may be prepared for the celestial glory; for after it hath filled the measure of its creation, it shall be crowned with glory, even with the presence of God the Father; that bodies who are of the celestial kingdom may possess it forever and ever; for, for this intent was it made and created, and for this intent are they sanctified" (D&C 88:18–20; Isa. 60:1–2; Ezek. 43:1–2).

her light was like unto a stone most precious, even like a jasper stone, clear as crystal. A jasper is a precious stone with great religious significance, for it was one of the stones in the high priest's breastplate (Ex. 28:20; 39:13). In 4:3, we read that the One on the throne, God the Father is "like a jasper" (see commentary there). Here, the holy city of New Jerusalem, which has "the glory of God," is also "like a jasper stone," perhaps meaning the city will have a beauty and glory like God himself.

The celestial city will shine like a precious stone in the same way that the earth itself will shine: "The angels . . . reside in the presence of God, on a globe like a sea of glass and fire, where all things for their glory are manifest, past, present, and future, and are continually before the Lord. The place where God resides is a great Urim and Thummim. This earth, in its sanctified and immortal state, will be made like unto crystal and will be a Urim and Thummim to the inhabitants who dwell thereon" (D&C 130:6–9).

The stone that is the city is like the "stone" that is Christ: "Therefore thus saith the Lord God, Behold, I lay in Zion for a foundation a stone, a tried stone, a precious corner stone, a sure foundation" (Isa. 28:16).

We also will be like precious stones, each contributing our part to Zion. Peter explained: "Ye also, as lively stones, are built up a spiritual house, an holy priesthood, to offer up spiritual sacrifices, acceptable to God by Jesus Christ. Wherefore also it is contained in the scripture, Behold, I lay in Sion a chief corner stone, elect, precious: and he that believeth on him shall not be confounded. Unto you therefore which believe he is precious: but unto them which be disobedient, the stone which the builders disallowed, the same is made the head of the corner" (1 Pet. 2:5–7).

It is reasonable that these images would be similar—a holy, celestial environment must be completely consistent with its Maker and with its holy, celestial inhabitants.

21:12 *a wall great and high.* This expression suggests that the people inside the city will enjoy absolute peace and complete security—and that no one can enter except by the gates.

twelve gates. Though the city is surrounded by an impregnable wall, those who qualify may freely enter; that there are twelve gates indicates a ready entrance for the faithful. The twelve gates may represent the twelve tribes of Israel, or the Twelve Apostles, who will judge the worthiness of the people to enter the holy city.

at the gates twelve angels. The angels may well be guardians or sentinels, assigned to prevent entrance into the city by "any thing that defileth" (21:27). It may be that these angels represent the angels Brigham Young described when he defined the temple endowment: "Your endowment is, to receive all those ordinances in the House of the Lord, which are necessary for you, after you have departed this life, to enable you to walk back to the presence of the Father, passing the angels who stand as sentinels, being enabled to give them the key words, the signs and tokens, pertaining to the Holy Priesthood, and gain your eternal exaltation in spite of earth and hell."[8]

names written thereon, which are the names of the twelve tribes of the children of Israel. On the gates were written the names of the twelve tribes, probably with a different gate assigned to each tribe. To enter the celestial city of Zion, we must enter as members of the family of Abraham, according to the Abrahamic covenant (Abr. 2:6–11). That may be the purpose of the symbolism here—that we enter Zion through the gate of, or by membership in, one of the twelve tribes of Israel.

21:13 *On the east three gates.* Ezekiel recorded, "And at the east side . . . three gates; and one gate of Joseph, one gate of Benjamin, one gate of Dan" (Ezek. 48:32).

on the north three gates. Ezekiel wrote, "And the gates of the city shall be after the names of the tribes of Israel: three gates northward; one gate of Reuben, one gate of Judah, one gate of Levi" (Ezek. 48:31).

on the south three gates. Again from Ezekiel: "And at the south side . . . three gates; one gate of Simeon, one gate of Issachar, one gate of Zebulun" (Ezek. 48:33).

on the west three gates. Again from Ezekiel: "At the west side . . . three gates; one gate of Gad, one gate of Asher, one gate of Naphtali" (Ezek. 48:34).

---

[8] Brigham Young, *Journal of Discourses,* 2:31.

21:14 *the wall of the city had twelve foundations, and in them the names of the twelve apostles of the Lamb.* Other translations indicate that the city wall was made of twelve foundation *stones* (LB, GNB, JB, NEB), each one representing one of the twelve apostles. The symbolism in this vision seems to say that the earthly organization of the Church is so important that it truly forms a foundation for the celestial city in which we hope eventually to dwell.

This passage from Paul's writings thus appears to have a significance beyond mortality: "Now therefore ye are no more strangers and foreigners, but fellowcitizens with the saints, and of the household of God; and are built upon the foundation of the apostles and prophets, Jesus Christ himself being the chief corner stone; in whom all the building fitly framed together groweth unto an holy temple in the Lord" (Eph. 2:19–21).

21:15 *he that talked with me had a golden reed.* This golden reed is a measuring rod (see commentary on 11:1). Perhaps only a measuring rod made of gold is appropriate to be used with the holy city of gold.

to measure the city, and the gates thereof, and the wall thereof. The angel has apparently been commissioned to measure the heavenly city and convey the information to John and thus to us.

21:16 *the city lieth foursquare/twelve thousand furlongs/The length and the breadth and the height of it are equal.* After the angel measures the city, John learns that it is shaped like an enormous cube—like the holy of holies in Solomon's temple (1 Kgs. 6:20). The holy of holies was the holiest place on earth, the innermost chamber of the temple, the earthly place where God would visit. The city in John's vision was likewise the holiest place on the new earth and likewise was the dwelling place of God. Both were formed in the shape of a cube, "a symbol of perfection."[9]

A furlong is about 607 English feet.[10] Altogether, then, the city was about 1,400 miles on each side. It was also 1,400 miles high. "The heavenly Jerusalem stretches from earth to heaven and unites them into one."[11] The number 1,400 comes close to being a multiple of 12 times 120 (1,440), perhaps a repetition of the emphasis on the twelve apostles and the twelve tribes of Israel.

---

9 Harrington, *Revelation,* 213–14.
10 See note *b* to 21:16 in the LDS edition of the KJV.
11 Davidson, ed., *New Bible Commentary,* 1197.

21:17 *And he measured the wall thereof, an hundred and forty and four cubits, according to the measure . . . of the angel.* "The repetition of the number twelve in the stones and gates stands as a constant reminder of the priestly power that guards and envelops all aspects and operations of the holy city. This is seen especially in the measurement of the walls. John notes they are 144 cubits, after the measure of an angel. The size of an angelic cubit is unknown. What is important is the number—twelve squared—signifying the fullness of priesthood authority. This is what surrounds and stands as a great bulwark to the city."[12]

21:18 *the building of the wall of it was of jasper.* We see in 21:11 that the city is like jasper, as God himself is like jasper (4:3). Here the wall of the city is jasper. The symbolism seems to be that the very walls of the city give glorious testimony to the presence of God.

the city was pure gold, like unto clear glass. In 4:6, John sees that God's throne is "a sea of glass like unto crystal." In 21:11, the city is likened to clear crystal. In the Doctrine and Covenants the earth itself is "like unto crystal" and the globe where God and his angels dwell is "like a sea of glass and fire" (D&C 130:9, 7). In 21:21, the streets are "pure gold, as it were transparent glass." These images of pure gold, transparent glass, and perfect crystal suggest perfection and clarity. They suggest great worth, value, and preciousness. They suggest materials that reflect and magnify the brilliance of light. Perhaps these things will all work together with the Urim and Thummim that is the earth itself (D&C 130:9) to create an environment in which great truths are more readily made manifest to the inhabitants of the earth.

21:19–20 *the foundations of the wall of the city were garnished with all manner of precious stones.* "Here is a city, in size and dimensions, in splendor and glory, which is so far beyond human experience or comprehension that there is no way to convey to the finite mind what the eternal reality is. Hence, expressions relative to precious stones, to streets of gold, and to pearly gates."[13]

Isaiah used a similar description of the heavenly city to indicate the love and attentiveness of God: "O thou afflicted, tossed with tempest, and not comforted, behold, I will lay thy stones with fair colours, and lay thy

---

[12] Draper, *Opening the Seven Seals,* 236.
[13] McConkie, *Doctrinal New Testament Commentary,* 3:588.

foundations with sapphires. And I will make thy windows of agates, and thy gates of carbuncles, and all thy borders of pleasant stones. And all thy children shall be taught of the Lord; and great shall be the peace of thy children. In righteousness shalt thou be established: thou shalt be far from oppression; for thou shalt not fear: and from terror; for it shall not come near thee" (Isa. 54:11–14).

The stones listed in these verses may be compared with those on the breastplate of the high priest anciently, each of which bore the name of one of the twelve tribes (Ex. 28:17–21; 39:10–14; Ezek. 28:13). In the New Jerusalem, however, these stones are linked to the Twelve Apostles rather than to the twelve tribes of Israel (21:14).

These stones may also be contrasted with the precious stones worn by the harlot, who is a symbol of another city. See commentary on 14:8; 17:1, 4.

21:21 *the twelve gates were twelve pearls.* Pearls were viewed as very precious in New Testament times (Matt. 13:45–46; 1 Tim. 2:9). Pearls are not mentioned in the Old Testament, but the Lord revealed through Isaiah concerning this same city, "I will make . . . thy gates of carbuncles" (Isa. 54:12). Like pearls, carbuncles were valued as precious stones.[14] The truth common to both passages is that the gates were made of priceless materials, indicating the great value the people, and the Lord, placed on the holy city itself.

every several gate was of one pearl. The pearls used in constructing the gates were so remarkable that one marvelous pearl was all that was needed to make each gate. This detail seems to emphasize again the magnificence of the different elements of the city.

the street of the city was pure gold, as it were transparent glass. See commentary on 21:18.

21:22 *no temple therein.* There are at least two possible reasons why no temple is needed in the celestial city. First, the entire city is "the house of the Lord"—the Lord is ever-present there. Second, all the inhabitants have made the necessary covenants. All the ordinance work for the living and the dead has been completed. All are fully qualified for a celestial life; nothing more remains to be done.

---

[14] Carbuncles may have been clear crystals or "a precious stone of bright red color." LDS Bible Dictionary, 631, s.v. "carbuncle"; see also Parry, Parry, and Peterson, *Understanding Isaiah,* 486.

Of course, in another sense, there is a temple in heaven, as John saw repeatedly in his vision (3:12; 7:15; 11:19; 14:17; 15:5; 16:17). But a deeper truth is that all of heaven is the temple, as we can deduce from the description of the heavenly city in this chapter of Revelation. And a truth deeper still is that God himself is the temple. What John may mean, then, is that there may be no single structure called a temple in heaven; everything about the heavenly experience partakes of the spirit and beauty and light of the temple.

the Lord God Almighty and the Lamb are the temple of it. We go to the temple in mortality to receive ordinances, make covenants, and draw closer to the Lord. In the celestial world we will actually live in God's presence. Perhaps, rather than go to a sacred edifice to draw near to the Lord, we will seek to go to him directly; rather than go to a sacred edifice to make covenants and agreements with God, we will most likely go to him directly. In the celestial kingdom, the temple ceases to be a means to come unto God—we will go to him directly.

21:23 *the city had no need of the sun, neither of the moon, to shine in it: for the glory of God did lighten it, and the Lamb is the light thereof.* When God, with his brightness, is present, we do not need the secondary light sources of the sun and moon (Isa. 60:19–20). After all, the sun and moon have power to shine in the first place because of the light of Christ (D&C 88:7–13).

21:24 *the nations of them which are saved shall walk in the light of it: and the kings of the earth do bring their glory and honour into it.* The Father and the Son give their light to the heavenly city, and that city gives its light to the nations of the saved on the earth. In turn, "the kings of the earth will bring it their treasures" (JB), or "the kings of the earth shall bring into it all their splendour" (NEB).

But what are these nations on the celestial world, and who are the kings? The kings of the earth were destroyed in 19:19, 21 and 20:9. John testified at the beginning of the book that Christ "hath made us kings and priests unto God" (1:6). Here he shows us that the Lord, in triumph, will indeed bring us forth in glory as kings.

These kings—who will be us and our fellows, as exalted, glorified souls—will bring the riches of their inheritance, as well as the glory of their own beings, into the city.

21:25 *the gates of it shall not be shut at all by day.* This expression indicates the degree of security and peace in the land (see also Isa. 60:11).

for there shall be no night there. Because God is the light of the city, and because he is ever-present, his light shines constantly. There will be neither day nor night there, but one constant, never-ceasing period of light.

21:26 *they shall bring the glory and honour of the nations into it.* See commentary on 21:24.

21:27 *there shall in no wise enter into it any thing that defileth, neither whatsoever worketh abomination, or maketh a lie.* This passage may seem to go without saying, because the city is now in the celestial kingdom. All things that defile, that work abomination, or that make a lie have been cast into the lake of fire (21:8), but the Lord apparently wants to underscore this truth: "No unclean thing can enter into his kingdom" (3 Ne. 27:19; 1 Ne. 10:21; Alma 11:37; Moses 6:57).

but they which are written in the Lamb's book of life. Those whose names are not written in the Lamb's book of life—specifically, all those who worship the beast (13:8)—have been prohibited from entering the holy city of New Jerusalem. See commentary on 3:5.

22:1 *he shewed me a pure river of water of life.* In the heavenly city of New Jerusalem is a river of water of life, which flows from the throne of God; beside the river are two trees of life (see commentary on 7:17; 21:6).

These features are reminiscent of the Garden of Eden; as we read in Genesis: "And out of the ground made the Lord God to grow every tree that is pleasant to the sight, and good for food; the tree of life also in the midst of the garden, and the tree of knowledge of good and evil. And a river went out of Eden to water the garden" (Gen. 2:9–10).

"There is a river," the psalmist wrote, "the streams whereof shall make glad the city of God, the holy place of the tabernacles of the most High" (Ps. 46:4).

In Lehi's great vision, he also saw the tree of life and "near the tree" was "a river of water" (1 Ne. 8:13). When Nephi learned the interpretation, he discovered that the tree represents "the love of God, which sheddeth itself abroad in the hearts of the children of men; wherefore, it is the most desirable above all things" (1 Ne. 11:22). He also learned that "the rod of iron, which my father had seen, was the word of God, which led to the fountain of living waters, or to the tree of life; which waters are a representation of the love of God; and I also beheld that the tree of life was a representation of the love of God" (1 Ne. 11:25).

Thus, the tree of life and the "pure river of water of life" both represent the same thing: the love of God. Could it be that the pure love of God (given as a gift from him to us and then returned with full hearts back to him and to others) is what brings us to eternal life and then sustains and empowers us there?

clear as crystal. See commentary on 21:18.

proceeding out of the throne of God and of the Lamb. Ezekiel saw waters flowing from beneath the temple, or house of God. Here they flow from the throne, which might represent the holy of holies in the heavenly temple. The waters of life, then, or the waters of love, come forth from God's throne, from the heart of God's holy city. The symbolism suggests that these waters come directly from God himself. The love of God is a motivating power unto eternal life, as John declared elsewhere: "For God so loved the world, that he gave his only begotten Son, that whosoever believeth in him should not perish, but have everlasting life" (John 3:16). For further discussion of the throne of God, see commentary on 1:4.

Earlier in John's vision he sees the throne of God in heaven (4:1–2), but now it has come down to earth in the New Jerusalem, for God will dwell with his people. It is noteworthy that God the Father and Jesus the Son seem here to share one throne, which may be representative of the perfection of their union. That union was expressed in Jesus' great intercessory prayer (John 17:11, 21–23).

22:2 *In the midst of the street of it, and on either side of the river.* This sentence is made clearer by other translations. In its context we read, "Then the angel showed me the river of the water of life, . . . flowing . . . down the middle of the great street of the city. On each side of the river stood the tree of life, bearing twelve crops of fruit, yielding its fruit every month" (NIV).

the tree of life. The tree of life here lies "in the midst of the street." Perhaps that street represents the straight and narrow path that Lehi saw (1 Ne. 8:20), which leads through the trials and temptations of mortality upward to the tree and, ultimately, to the celestial city of God. See also commentary on 2:7; 22:1.

We know that in the Garden of Eden was a real tree called the tree of life (Gen. 2:9; 3:24). In that setting, as well as elsewhere in the scriptures, the tree of life also functions as a symbol for eternal life.

The tree of life in the celestial city has no cherubim guarding it, as did the tree in the Garden of Eden (Gen. 3:24; Alma 12:21), for all in the city have a right to freely partake. And there is no mention of the tree of knowledge of good and evil; the inhabitants of the city, having successfully passed through mortality, have experienced both good and evil, and they have rejected all evil and turned wholly to the good. They are now entitled to eternal life, which the fruit of the tree symbolizes.

There is also possibly a deeper level of meaning here. Trees often symbolically stand for people, and the tree of life symbolizes that perfect Man who brings us life.[15] But the Greek in this verse may well be plural (*trees*).[16] It may be that the trees of life in the celestial city include the exalted souls who have come unto Christ and become like him, souls who have gained eternal life.

which bare twelve manner of fruits, and yielded her fruit every month. This passage suggests that each tree bears a different fruit every month, for a total of twelve varieties each year. Further, unlike most fruit trees, which bear their fruit seasonally, the fruit of the tree of life is ever available. The tree of life is always living and growing, never subject to death, not even subject to the normal sequence of a winter's "death," a spring's sprouting, a summer's growth, an autumn's harvest, and another winter's death.

Lehi described the fruit of the tree of life as "desirable to make one happy" and "desirable above all other fruit" (1 Ne. 8:10, 12). He said "it filled my soul with exceedingly great joy" (1 Ne. 8:12). Alma described this fruit as "most precious, which is sweet above all that is sweet, . . . and ye shall feast upon this fruit even until ye are filled, that ye hunger not, neither shall ye thirst" (Alma 32:42).

If the trees of life are the exalted souls in the celestial glory, the fruit of the tree may be their goodness and their good works that bless others forever.

the leaves of the tree were for the healing of the nations. Ezekiel saw the same tree and received the same understanding: "[An angel] brought me again unto the door of the house [the temple]; and, behold, waters issued out from under the threshold of the house eastward: . . . and the waters came down from under from . . . the south side of the altar. . . . Then

---

[15] McConkie and Parry, *Guide to Scriptural Symbols,* 103–4.
[16] Metzger, *Breaking the Code,* 102; JB 22:2.

said he unto me, . . . by the river upon the bank thereof, on this side and on that side, shall grow all trees for meat, whose leaf shall not fade, neither shall the fruit thereof be consumed: it shall bring forth new fruit according to his months, because their waters they issued out of the sanctuary: and the fruit thereof shall be for meat, and the leaf thereof for medicine" (Ezek. 47:1, 8, 12).

Because the tree symbolizes the love of God, it is only consistent to understand that the leaves of the tree would help to bring peace, union, and spiritual strength—in a word, healing—to the nations of the world. This use is probably symbolic, though there may actually be plants in the worlds of glory that bring blessing to those who gain the right to use them.

The nations mentioned here may be those in 21:24–26, which have been saved by the power of Christ. As he said to us all, by way of invitation, "Will ye not now return unto me, and repent of your sins, and be converted, that I may heal you?" (3 Ne. 9:13). Or, as Elder Parley P. Pratt wrote, "When John sees it [the tree of life], the nations have no need of healing, for there is no death, neither pain, nor sorrow, for the former things have passed away, and all things are become new; consequently, he speaks in the past tense, and says they were for the healing of the nations; of course, referring to the times when they existed temporally, according to Ezekiel, before their final change."[17]

22:3 *there shall be no more curse.* This passage seems to refer to the curses that were pronounced on Adam and Eve at the time of the Fall—that they would "surely die" by partaking of the forbidden fruit, that the woman would bear children in sorrow, and that the man would eat his bread "in the sweat of thy face." The ground itself, in fact, was "cursed . . . for thy sake; in sorrow shalt thou eat of it all the days of thy life" (Gen. 2:17; 3:16, 17, 19). Those in the celestial world would be subject to these curses no more. It is interesting to note that the Bible begins with a record of humankind being cursed and ends with a vision of those curses being removed.

but the throne of God and of the Lamb shall be in it. The *but* that joins this phrase with the preceding phrase suggests that the presence of God and the Lamb is an essential reason why a curse could not exist in the New Jerusalem—the presence of God blesses all that receive it. In particular, the

---

[17] Pratt, *Voice of Warning,* 138.

curse of spiritual death is removed by the presence of God. See commentary on 22:1.

his servants shall serve him. See commentary on 7:15.

22:4 *they shall see his face.* One great purpose of the temple is to bring us into the presence of God. Much of the symbolism of the temple ordinances demonstrates how we can find our way back to him. When we dwell in the heavenly temple, or in the heavenly city, we will see God's face always, for we will always be in his presence. Jesus pointed to this blessing when he said, "Blessed are the pure in heart: for they shall see God" (Matt. 5:8).

When we live in the holy city, we will regularly have the privilege that Moses had on the rarest of occasions: "And the Lord spake unto Moses face to face, as a man speaketh unto his friend" (Ex. 33:11; Moses 1:11, 31). Moses "sought diligently to sanctify his people that they might behold the face of God" as well, but they refused to qualify themselves and lost the blessing (D&C 84:23–24).

But the promise of the Lord continues among us: "Sanctify yourselves that your minds become single to God, and the days will come that you shall see him; for he will unveil his face unto you, and it shall be in his own time, and in his own way, and according to his own will" (D&C 88:68). "Verily, thus saith the Lord: It shall come to pass that every soul who forsaketh his sins and cometh unto me, and calleth on my name, and obeyeth my voice, and keepeth my commandments, shall see my face and know that I am" (D&C 93:1).

Perhaps not many will receive this blessing in mortality, but all who enter the holy, celestial city of the New Jerusalem surely will.

his name shall be in their foreheads. In the symbolism of the book of Revelation, an individual bears the name or mark of the person with whom he or she is allied (3:12; 13:16). Further, to bear another's name seems to indicate that one has become like that other person. Therefore, with the Father's name in our foreheads, we can know that "when he shall appear, we shall be like him; for we shall see him as he is" (1 Jn. 3:2). See commentary on 3:12.

22:5 *there shall be no night there/need no candle/neither light of the sun.* A light emanates from the person of God, as Joseph Smith saw in the Sacred Grove: "I saw a pillar of light exactly over my head, above the brightness of the sun. . . . I saw two Personages, whose brightness and glory defy all description" (JS–H 1:16–17). God, with the great light of his being, will dwell in the celestial city, and thus there will never be night, nor need for artificial light of candle, nor need for the sun (Zech. 14:6–7). See commentary on 21:23.

they shall reign for ever and ever. When we ascend to our glory, as "heirs of God, and joint-heirs with Christ," we will reign with them forever (Rom. 8:17). As "sons of God . . . we shall be like him" (1 Jn. 3:2). We ourselves "shall . . . be gods" (D&C 132:20). We will truly be like our Father and our Lord: "Every man who reigns in celestial glory is a God to his dominions."[18] The righteous are the rulers of heaven.

---

[18] *Teachings of the Prophet Joseph Smith,* 374.

REVELATION
22:6–21

"SURELY I COME QUICKLY" (22:6–21)

As his vision concludes, John hears a repeated testimony of its truth-fulness: "These sayings are faithful and true," the angel says. Speaking in Jesus' name, the angel says, "I Jesus have sent mine angel to testify unto you these things"; "he which testifieth these things saith, Surely I come quickly." And John adds his own testimony: "I John saw these things, and heard them."

The angel pronounces two blessings and a curse. "Blessed is he that keepeth the sayings of the prophecy of this book," he proclaims. "Blessed are they that do his commandments," for they will "have right to the tree of life" and will be able to "enter in through the gates into the city." Cursed is any man who will "add unto" these things or "take away" from them.

These concluding verses also give us insight to some of the names and titles of Christ: "Alpha and Omega, the beginning and the end, the first and the last"; "the root and the offspring of David"; and "the bright and morning star."

Finally, speaking for the Lord, the angel repeats three times, "I come quickly" and adds, "the time is at hand." Though we may not see the imme-diate signs of Christ's coming, yet we must always be ready to receive him in righteousness. Then we can join with John in his deep-felt desires in say-ing, "Even so, come, Lord Jesus."

Revelation 22:6–21

> 6 And he said unto me, These sayings are faithful and true; and the Lord God of the holy prophets sent his angel to shew unto his servants the things which must shortly be done.

7 Behold, I come quickly: blessed is he that keepeth the sayings of the prophecy of this book.

8 And I John saw these things, and heard them. And when I had heard and seen, I fell down to worship before the feet of the angel which shewed me these things.

9 Then saith he unto me, See [that]¹ thou do it not: for I am thy fellow-servant, and of thy brethren the prophets, and of them which keep the sayings of this book: worship God.

10 And he saith unto me, Seal not the sayings of the prophecy of this book: for the time is at hand.

11 He that is unjust, let him be unjust still: and he which is filthy, let him be filthy still: and he that is righteous, let him be righteous still: and he that is holy, let him be holy still.

12 And, behold, I come quickly; and my reward is with me, to give every man according as his work shall be.

13 I am Alpha and Omega, the beginning and the end, the first and the last.

14 Blessed are they that do his commandments, that they may have right to the tree of life, and may enter in through the gates into the city.

15 For without are dogs, and sorcerers, and whoremongers, and murderers, and idolaters, and whosoever loveth and maketh a lie.

16 I Jesus have sent mine angel to testify unto you these things in the churches. I am the root and the offspring of David, and the bright and morning star.

17 And the Spirit and the bride say, Come. And let him that heareth say, Come. And let him that is athirst come. And whosoever will, let him take the water of life freely.

18 For I testify unto every man that heareth the words of the prophecy of this book, If any man shall add unto these things, God shall add unto him the plagues that are written in this book:

19 And if any man shall take away from the words of the book of this prophecy, God shall take away his part out of the [tree]² of life, and out of the holy city, and from the things which are written in this book.

20 He which testifieth these things saith, Surely I come quickly. Amen. Even so, come, Lord Jesus.

21 The grace of our Lord Jesus Christ be with you all. Amen.

NOTES AND COMMENTARY

22:6 *And he said unto me.* The speaker here might be the last angel guide given to John (21:9, 15; 22:1). Or the angel who here concludes the vision may be the same angel who began it (1:1).

These sayings are faithful and true. See commentary on 21:5.

the Lord God of the holy prophets. Jesus is the God of the Old Testament. He is Jehovah, who spoke plainly to Adam, Enoch, Noah, Abraham,

---

¹ This is an addition from JST 22:9.
² This change from the KJV *book of life* is found in virtually all other translations, including NIV, NEB, JB, RSV, and others.

Moses, Isaiah, and all the other prophets of the Old Testament, as well as the God of the prophets in the Book of Mormon and in other sacred scripture yet to come forth. The angel bears testimony that this Lord of truth and power has sent the angel to communicate the great truths of the vision to John.

sent his angel to shew unto his servants the things which must shortly be done. See commentary on 1:1.

22:7 *Behold, I come quickly.* See commentary on 2:5.

blessed is he that keepeth the sayings of the prophecy of this book. See commentary on 1:3.

22:8 *And I John saw these things, and heard them.* John repeats his testimony that he himself saw and heard the things of the vision (1:1, 9). The vision truly was from God; it is not a figment of John's imagination, nor is it a work of fiction.

I fell down to worship. See commentary on 19:10.

22:9 *See [that] thou do it not/I am thy fellowservant.* See commentary on 19:10.

of thy brethren the prophets, and of them which keep the sayings of this book. John himself is a prophet, and the other prophets of all ages are his peers. The angel tells John that he (the angel) is one of the fellowship of the prophets and that he does not consider himself better than the prophets or the other Saints who keep the Lord's commandments.

worship God. See commentary on 19:10.

22:10 *Seal not the sayings of the prophecy of this book.* Daniel was given a vision and told to seal it up "to the time of the end" (Dan. 8:26; 12:4, 9)—it was not the Lord's purpose for the world to know the things Daniel received. Earlier in John's vision, he is told to "seal up those things which the seven thunders uttered, and write them not" (10:4). Perhaps the time has not yet come for these specific things to be revealed. But the rest of the prophecy was intended for the world and the Saints, and John was commanded not to seal it up but to let it go forth for others to read and to seek to understand.

for the time is at hand. See commentary on 1:3.

22:11 *He that is unjust, let him be unjust still/he that is holy, let him be holy still.* What is true of a person's spirit as it moves from this life to the next is also true of the person as he or she faces the time of the second coming of Christ. If we procrastinate the day of our repentance until the Lord's coming, we will continue in our filthiness after he arrives—and, likewise, the righteous and holy will continue in their holiness. Jacob taught the same principle, using some of the same words, in reference to our state at the final judgment: "They who are righteous shall be righteous still, and they who are filthy shall be filthy still" (2 Ne. 9:16; Alma 7:21; 41:10–15; D&C 88:35).

22:12 *behold, I come quickly.* See commentary on 2:5.

my reward is with me. When the Lord returns in glory, he will bring with him a judgment on every person on earth—a reward for the righteous, and a punishment for the wicked. "Behold, the Lord God will come with strong hand, and his arm shall rule for him: behold, his reward is with him, and his work before him" (Isa. 40:10; Rev. 11:18).

to give every man according as his work shall be. We will be judged according to the works we have performed on the earth. See commentary on 20:12; 2:23.

22:13 *I am Alpha and Omega, the beginning and the end, the first and the last.* These are the words of the angel, speaking in behalf of Christ (1:1–6, 12–20; 22:6–16). See commentary on 1:8.[3]

22:14 *Blessed are they that do his commandments.* This passage is another of the beatitudes found in Revelation. Those who do as the Lord commands them to do are blessed indeed. As the verse explains, they are privileged to partake of the fruit of the tree of life and to enter into the heavenly city. In other words, those who obey the Lord's commands are blessed with a celestial glory.

have right to the tree of life. See commentary on 2:7.

may enter in through the gates into the city. See commentary on 21:12.

22:15 *For without are dogs.* "'Dogs' is a traditional Jewish designation of heathen Gentiles."[4] The dogs, or the unbelievers, must stay outside ("without") the city—they are not blessed with celestial glory.

sorcerers, and whoremongers, and murderers, and idolaters, and whosoever loveth and maketh a lie. In 21:8, we learn that the sinners in this list will be cast into the lake of fire and brimstone and will suffer the second death. Here we see that such sinners will also be barred from entering into

---

[3] For a discussion of divine investiture of authority, the principle whereby Christ can speak for the Father and an angel can speak for Christ, see the First Presidency epistle of 30 June 1916, in Talmage, *Articles of Faith,* appendix 2, 470–71.

[4] Harrington, *Revelation,* 223.

the celestial city of New Jerusalem. This list echoes that of the earlier one—but "whosoever loveth and maketh a lie" is much more emphatic and descriptive than "all liars." These people will be not only outside ("without") the city but outside the entire kingdom, having been assigned to a lesser kingdom, called telestial (D&C 76:98, 103).

22:16 *I Jesus have sent mine angel to testify unto you these things in the churches.* See commentary on 1:1, 4.

I am the root . . . of David. See commentary on 5:5.

offspring of David. Jesus Christ was a direct and literal descendant of king David (Matt. 1:1–17). In addition, the Messiah was seen as the fulfillment of Israel's expectation to be saved by a king like their beloved and powerful David. In his second coming, Christ, the offspring of David, will indeed deliver his people, as did the first David (Isa. 16:5; Jer. 23:5; 30:9; Ezek. 34:23–24; 37:24–28), and will be their King.

the bright and morning star. In scriptural symbolism, stars typically refer to individuals (Gen. 37:9; Num. 24:17; Job 38:7; Jude 1:13). Jesus is "the bright and morning star," the one that shines first and longer than all his brothers and sisters, even into the daytime, greater, brighter, more constant than all the others (2 Pet. 1:19). See commentary on 1:16; 2:28; 12:1.

22:17 *the Spirit and the bride.* The Spirit is the Holy Ghost, which speaks to prophets and righteous members alike. The bride is the New Jerusalem, or, in a broader sense, the righteous members of the Church. For more on the identity of the bride, see commentary on 19:7.

Come. This word seems to be an invitation to Christ to return in triumph and glory to the earth (22:20). Those making the invitation include the Holy Spirit, the bride of Christ (the Church), and all those who hear the words of John's vision.

him that heareth. Here John speaks to all those who hear (or read) the words of his book, but he speaks particularly to those who truly hear with their hearts and not with their ears alone (D&C 136:32). John invites them to join the Spirit and the bride in seeking the coming of Christ.

let him that is athirst come. As John invites those who hear his words to seek the second coming of Christ, he also invites those who are spiritually thirsty to come as well, to partake freely of the water of life that they may be ready to welcome their Savior and rejoice with all those who have received admittance into the celestial city. The living water of which we partake, of course, is Christ himself, who gives us spiritual life with his love, his truth, and his atoning power.

"And Jesus said unto them, I am the bread of life: he that cometh to me shall never hunger; and he that believeth on me shall never thirst" (John 6:35).

"If any man thirst," he said, "let him come unto me, and drink. He that believeth on me, as the scripture hath said, out of his belly shall flow rivers of living water" (John 7:37–38).

whosoever will, let him take the water of life freely. See commentary on 21:6.

22:18 *For I testify unto every man that heareth the words of the prophecy of this book.* John here is not bearing testimony to the words of the book but is pronouncing a curse under the direction of the Spirit. The curse is that if any man adds to or takes away from what John has recorded, seeking to alter the scripture itself, that man will receive great punishment from God.

If any man shall add unto these things. "Of course a careful reading of this text shows very clearly that John the Revelator was speaking only of the book of Revelation and not of any collection of other sacred writings. Moses used a similar expression in speaking to ancient Israel when he said: 'Ye shall not add unto the word which I command you, neither shall ye diminish ought from it, . . . ' This is found in the fourth chapter of the book of Deuteronomy (verse 2). In the 12th chapter of the same book Moses said this: 'What thing soever I command you, observe to do it: thou shalt not add thereto, nor diminish from it.' (Verse 32.)

"Can anyone suppose that in these words Moses laid down a prohibition against all subsequent revelations and against all books which might be called scripture in years to come? Did he have the power to silence all future prophets and forbid them to speak or write as God intended that they should? Of course not, or we would be without most of the Old Testament and would have none of the New Testament at all.

"It was the same with John the Revelator. In warning against additions to the book of Revelation he spoke of that book only, insisting that no one attempt to change or corrupt what he had said. The Bible was not compiled when John wrote the book of Revelation, so he could not possibly have referred to it. Furthermore, scholars tell us that the Gospel of John was written after the book of Revelation, and if this be true it becomes another indication that John had no thought of precluding other writings but only of protecting this particular book of Revelation from change or corruption."[5]

God shall add unto him the plagues that are written in this book. John's curse, spoken by the Spirit, is that if anyone tries to add to this book of scripture, the book of Revelation, that person will suffer from the plagues recorded in the book.

22:19 *if any man shall take away from the words of the book of this prophecy.* "God alone can add to or diminish from holy writ. What he has spoken, he has spoken, and none but he can alter. When a prophet speaks by the power of the Holy Ghost, it is the voice of God; and none can change it without suffering the penalty prescribed for perverting the pronouncements of Deity."[6]

God shall take away his part out of the [tree] of life/out of the holy city/from the things which are written in this book. This passage describes dire punishments. If a person seeks, with malice, to change the words of God as God has given them to his children, that person will lose the blessings the scripture speaks of and will lose his opportunity to join the righteous in the celestial kingdom of God.

22:20 *He which testifieth these things.* "He" is Jesus Christ, as seen by the first-person reference in the next phrase; however, it very well could be John's angelic visitor speaking in the name of Christ (1:1–6, 12–20; 22:6–16).

Surely I come quickly. See commentary on 2:5.

Amen. See commentary on 1:6.

Even so, come, Lord Jesus. John joins his voice to those of the Spirit, the bride, and those who read and believe John's revelation, asking the Lord to come quickly, as he has promised. See commentary on 22:17.

22:21 *The grace of our Lord Jesus Christ be with you all. Amen.* This is a benedictory statement from John to his readers, a blessing offered on their heads. It matches, like a bookend, the introduction John made at the very beginning of the book (1:4). This benediction was common in New Testament writings; every one of Paul's epistles ends with this kind of statement (all but two, Romans and 1 Corinthians, have it in the last verse) and sometimes the language is identical. The statement underscores an

---

[5] Petersen, Conference Report, October 1964, 121.
[6] McConkie, *Doctrinal New Testament Commentary,* 3:594.

important truth that John and Paul both desired to teach: that it is the grace, or gift, of Christ (when coupled with our faith, repentance, and obedience) that enables us to live and do and reach and grow and, in the end, to be exalted.[7]

The grace of Christ is indeed offered to all. Therefore, "let him that is athirst come. And whosoever will, let him take the water of life freely" (22:17).

---

[7] See LDS Bible Dictionary, 697, s.v. "grace."

—⤳⤳⤳—

REVELATION,
A BOOK OF CONTRASTS

Things pertaining to Deity	Things pertaining to Satan and wickedness
Saints of God	followers of Satan
seal of God (7:2–3)	mark of the beast (13:16)
"Faithful and True Witness" (3:14)	deceitful serpent (12:9)
virgin	harlot
armies of heaven—100 million (5:11)	armies of earth—200 million (9:16)
four angels of heaven (7:1)	four angels of the abyss (9:14)
marriage supper of the Lamb (19:9)	supper of the great God (19:17)
hymns of praise to God	cries of anguish of the wicked
fruit of the tree of life (2:7)	cup (wine) of wrath of God (14:10)
celestial temple of heaven	telestial earth
New Jerusalem	Babylon
sea of glass (4:6)	lake of fire (21:8)
heavenly living creatures (4:6)	beasts of the earth
temple in heaven	great abyss
seven	three and one-half/666
Michael and his angels (12:7)	Satan and his angels (12:7)

Things pertaining to Deity	Things pertaining to Satan and wickedness
Church of God	Church of the Devil
Lamb of God (5:6, 12)	beast with two horns like a lamb (13:11–13)
Christ was, is and will be (1:4, 8)	"beast that was, and is not, and yet is" (17:8)
mark in forehead (7:3; 9:4; 14:1, 3–5; 19:12; 20:4; 22:4)	name on forehead (13:16–17; 14:9; 17:5)
woman (12:1), bride, Lamb's wife (21:9)	mother of harlots (17:5)
righteous kings and priests (1:6)	kings of the earth (18:9)
heavenly harpers (14:2)	worldly harpers and musicians (18:22)
fine linen, clean and white (19:8)	fine linen, purple, silk, scarlet, and riches (18:12)
angels worship God day and night (7:15)	Satan accuses the saints "day and night" (12:10)
slain Lamb (5:6, 12)	wounded beast (13:3)
"many crowns" of Jesus (19:12)	ten crowns of the beast (13:1)
God gives power to two prophets (11:2)	dragon gives power to the beast (13:2)
144,000 virgins (14:3–4)	those who consort with the mother of harlots and commit fornication (17:2, 5)
incense smoke represents prayers of righteous (5:8)	smoke of the burning of Babylon and wicked (14:11)
colors associated with high priest	colors associated with mother of harlots (see commentary on 17:4)
God's cup of indignation (14:10; 16:19)	golden cup of whore (17:4)

Things pertaining to Deity	Things pertaining to Satan and wickedness
white and pure linen of Lamb's wife (19:8)	the linen of Babylon (18:12, 16)
God's glory lightens the celestial city (21:23)	No candle will light in Babylon after her destruction (18:23)

—

NAMES AND TITLES OF DEITY FOUND IN REVELATION

Almighty (1:8)
Almighty God (19:15)
Alpha and Omega (1:8) (4 times)
Amen (3:14)
beginning of the creation of God (3:14)
beginning and the ending (1:8) (3 times)
bright and morning star (22:16)
Christ (11:15) (4 times)
Faithful and True (19:11)
faithful and true witness (3:14)
faithful witness (1:5)
Father (1:6) (4 times)
first and the last (1:11) (4 times)
first begotten of the dead (1:5)
hidden manna (2:17)
him that liveth for ever and ever (4:10)
him which is, and which was, and which is to come (1:4) (4 times)
holy (3:7)
holy and true (6:10)
God (1:1) (83 times)
God Almighty (16:14)

God of heaven (11:13)
God of the earth (11:4)
Jesus (14:12) (5 times)
Jesus Christ (1:1) (6 times)
King of kings (17:14) (2 times)
King of saints (15:3)
Lamb (5:6) (28 times)
Lion of the Tribe of Juda (5:5)
living God (7:2)
Lord (1:8) (9 times)
Lord God (18:8) (3 times)
Lord God Almighty (4:8) (5 times)
Lord God omnipotent (19:6)
Lord Jesus (22:20)
Lord Jesus Christ (22:21)
Lord of lords (17:14) (2 times)
Lord our God (19:1)
morning star (2:28)
prince of the kings of the earth (1:5)
root and offspring of David (22:16)
Root of David (5:5)
Son of God (2:18)
Son of man (1:13) (2 times)
true (3:7)
Word of God (19:13)

—⁓—

SYMBOLS OF REVELATION
AND THEIR INTERPRETATION

This list of symbols is far from complete. It includes only those symbols discussed within this book.

Symbol	Interpretation
seven stars	seven servants of the Church (JST 1:20)
seven lampstands	seven churches of Asia (1:20)
seven lamps of fire	seven servants of God (JST 4:5)
golden bowls of incense	prayers of the Saints (5:8)
great multitude of heaven	exalted Saints (7:9, 13–14)
dragon	Satan (12:9)
serpent	Satan (12:9)
the waters	peoples, and multitudes, and nations, and tongues (17:15)
the woman	great city, which reigneth over kings (17:18)
seven heads of the beast	seven mountains (17:9)
ten horns of the beast	ten kings (17:12)
morning star (2:28)	Christ (22:16)

Symbol	Interpretation
woman clothed with the sun (12:1)	Church of God (JST 12:7)
twenty-four elders (4:4)	faithful members of the seven churches (D&C 77:5)
rod of iron (2:27; 19:15)	word of God (1 Ne. 15:23–24)
white stone (2:17)	Urim and Thummim (D&C 130:10)
seven seals (5:1)	seven one-thousand-year time periods (D&C 77:7)
book with seven seals (5:1)	contains will, mysteries, and works of God (D&C 77:6)
two witnesses (11:3)	two prophets (D&C 77:15)
little book (10:2)	mission and ordinance (D&C 77:14)
sea of glass (4:6)	earth in its sanctified state (D&C 77:1)
four beasts (4:6)	"figurative expressions" (see D&C 77:2–3)
eyes of the beasts (4:8)	light and knowledge (D&C 77:4)
wings of the beasts (4:8)	power to move and to act (D&C 77:4)
twelve horns/twelve eyes of Lamb (JST 5:6)	twelve servants of God (JST 5:6)

Symbols introduced with *like* or *as* are *similes:*

A great voice, *as* of a trumpet (1:10)
His head and his hairs were white *like* wool (1:14)
His feet *like* unto fine brass, *as* if they burned in a furnace (1:15)
His voice *as* the sound of many waters (1:15)
His countenance was *as* the sun shineth in his strength (1:16)
I fell at his feet *as* dead (1:17)
His eyes *like* unto a flame of fire (2:18)
They shall be in his hands *as* the vessels of clay in the hands of a potter (JST 2:27)
I will come on thee *as* a thief (3:3)
The first voice which I heard was *as* it were of a trumpet talking with me (4:1)

He that sat was to look upon *like* a jasper and a sardine stone (4:3)

There was a rainbow round about the throne, in sight *like* unto an emerald (4:3)

A sea of glass *like* unto crystal (4:6)

The first beast was *like* a lion (4:7)

The second beast *like* a calf (4:7)

The third beast had a face *as* a man (4:7)

The fourth beast was *like* a flying eagle (4:7)

I heard, *as* it were the noise of thunder, one of the four beasts, saying (6:1)

Moon became *as* blood (6:12)

Sun became black *as* sackcloth of hair (6:12)

Stars of heaven fell unto the earth, even *as* a fig tree casteth her untimely figs (6:13)

The heaven departed *as* a scroll when it is rolled together (6:14)

As it were a great mountain burning with fire was cast into the sea (8:8)

There fell a great star from heaven, burning *as* it were a lamp (8:10)

There arose a smoke out of the pit, *as* the smoke of a great furnace (9:2)

There came out of the smoke locusts upon the earth: and unto them was given power, *as* the scorpions of the earth have power (9:3)

And their torment was *as* the torment of a scorpion, when he striketh a man (9:5)

The shapes of the locusts were *like* unto horses prepared unto battle (9:7)

On their heads were *as* it were crowns *like* gold (9:7)

Their faces were *as* the faces of men (9:7)

They had hair *as* the hair of women (9:8)

Their teeth were *as* the teeth of lions (9:8)

They had breastplates, *as* it were breastplates of iron (9:9)

The sound of their wings was *as* the sound of chariots of many horses running to battle (9:9)

They had tails *like* unto scorpions (9:10)

The heads of the horses were *as* the heads of lions (9:17)

Their tails were *like* unto serpents (9:19)

His face was *as* it were the sun (10:1)

His feet *as* pillars of fire (10:1)

Cried with a loud voice, *as* when a lion roareth (10:3)

It shall be in thy mouth sweet *as* honey (10:9)

It was in my mouth sweet *as* honey (10:10)

There was given me a reed *like* unto a rod (11:1)

The serpent cast out of his mouth water *as* a flood after the woman (12:15)

The beast which I saw was *like* unto a leopard (13:2)

His mouth *as* the mouth of a lion (13:2)

I saw one of his heads *as* it were wounded to death (13:3)

He had two horns *like* a lamb (13:11)

He spake *as* a dragon (13:11)

I heard a voice from heaven, *as* the voice of many waters, and *as* the voice of a great thunder (14:2)

Second angel poured out his vial upon the sea; and it became *as* the blood of a dead man (16:3)

I saw three unclean spirits *like* frogs come out of the mouth of the dragon (16:13)

I come *as* a thief (16:15)

A mighty angel took up a stone *like* a great millstone (18:21)

I heard *as* it were the voice of a great multitude, and *as* the voice of many waters, and *as* the voice of mighty thunderings (19:6)

His eyes were *as* a flame of fire (19:12)

The number of whom is *as* the sand of the sea (20:8)

New Jerusalem . . . prepared *as* a bride adorned for her husband (21:2)

Her light was *like* unto a stone most precious, even *like* a jasper stone, clear *as* crystal (21:11)

The city was pure gold, *like* unto clear glass (21:18)

The street of the city was pure gold, *as* it were transparent glass (21:21)

Pure river of water of life, clear *as* crystal (22:1)

APPENDIX 4

———◈———

THE SEVEN CHURCHES

The letters to the seven churches, recorded in Revelation 2 and 3, have a distinct pattern that is orderly, interesting, and instructive.

Each of the seven letters begins with an introduction, or commission, in which John is instructed to "write" to the servants of the seven churches.

The commission is followed by a description of Jesus Christ. Each of the seven descriptive statements ("he that hath the seven stars in his right hand," "the first and the last," "he which hath the sharp sword with two edges," and so on) recalls similar statements in Revelation 1, in which John describes the resurrected Lord. For example, the description of the "seven stars" in Christ's right hand in 2:1 harks back to the same phrase in 1:16.

The next part of the pattern speaks of Christ's knowledge of the churches' works. Seven times Christ states, "I know thy works," once to each of the seven churches. Christ then admonishes each of the seven churches, telling them to "remember," "be faithful," "repent," and so on.

The call to hear, the next aspect of the pattern, informs the reader that "he that hath an ear, let him hear what the Spirit saith unto the churches" and is repeated to each of the seven churches.

The final part of the pattern is promises and blessings, which are extended to the righteous, specifically those who overcome the world. The promises and blessings are most wonderful. For example, to the Saints of Sardis, the Lord promises that "he that overcometh, the same shall be clothed in white raiment; and I will not blot out his name out of the book of life, but I will confess his name before my father, and before his angels" (3:6).

Certainly this inspired pattern, given to John the Revelator, pertains to us as well as to the early Saints. Its admonitions, call to hear, and promises and blessings give us guidance, peace, hope, and comfort as we prepare to hear the additional truths revealed in the remaining chapters of Revelation, truths that pertain to the last days and the second coming of the Savior.

Names of churches	Ephesus (2:1–7)	Smyrna (2:8–11)	Pergamos (2:12–17)
Commission	Unto the angel of the church of Ephesus write; (v. 1)	And unto the angel of the church in Smyrna write; (v. 8)	And to the angel of the church in Pergamos write; (v. 12)
Description of Jesus Christ	These things saith he that holdeth the seven stars in his right hand, who walketh in the midst of the seven golden candlesticks; (v. 1)	These things saith the first and the last, which was dead, and is alive; (v. 8)	These things saith he which hath the sharp sword with two edges; (v. 12)
Christ and the churches	I know thy works . . . (v. 2)	I know thy works . . . (v. 9)	I know thy works . . . (v. 13)
Christ admonishes the churches	Remember therefore from whence thou art fallen, and repent, and do the first works . . . (v. 5)	be thou faithful unto death . . . (v. 10)	Repent . . . (v. 16)
Call to hear	He that hath an ear, let him hear what the Spirit saith unto the churches; (v. 7)	He that hath an ear, let him hear what the Spirit saith unto the churches; (v. 11)	He that hath an ear, let him hear what the Spirit saith unto the churches; (v. 17)
Promise and blessing	To him that overcometh will I give to eat of the tree of life, which is in the midst of the paradise of God. (v. 7)	He that overcometh shall not be hurt of the second death. (v. 11)	To him that overcometh will I give to eat of the hidden manna, and will give him a white stone, and in the stone a new name written, which no man knoweth saving he that receiveth it. (v. 17)

Thyatira (2:18–29)	Sardis (3:1–6)	Philadelphia (3:7–13)	Laodicea (3:14–22)
And unto the angel of the church in Thyatira write; (v. 18)	And unto the angel of the church in Sardis write; (v. 1)	And to the angel of the church in Philadelphia write; (v. 7)	And unto the angel of the church of the Laodiceans write; (v. 14)
These things saith the Son of God, who hath his eyes like unto a flame of fire, and his feet are like fine brass; (v. 18)	These things saith he that hath the seven Spirits of God, and the seven stars; (v. 1)	These things saith he that is holy, he that is true, he that hath the key of David, he that openeth, and no man shutteth; and shutteth, and no man openeth; (v. 7)	These things saith the Amen, the faithful and true witness, the beginning of the creation of God; (v. 14)
I know thy works . . . (v. 19)	I know thy works . . . (v. 1)	I know thy works . . . (v. 8)	I know thy works . . . (v. 15)
But that which ye have already hold fast till I come. (v. 25)	Remember therefore how thou hast received and heard, and hold fast, and repent. (v. 3)	hold that fast which thou hast, that no man take thy crown. (v. 11)	be zealous therefore, and repent. (v. 19)
He that hath an ear, let him hear what the Spirit saith unto the churches. (v. 29)	He that hath an ear, let him hear what the Spirit saith unto the churches. (v. 6)	He that hath an ear, let him hear what the Spirit saith unto the churches. (v. 13)	He that hath an ear, let him hear what the Spirit saith unto the churches. (v. 22)
And he that overcometh, and keepeth my works unto the end, to him will I give power over [many kingdoms]: And he shall rule them . . . : even as I received of my Father. And I will give him the morning star. (vv. 26–28)	He that overcometh, the same shall be clothed in white raiment; and I will not blot out his name out of the book of life, but I will confess his name before my Father, and before his angels. (v. 5)	Him that overcometh will I make a pillar in the temple of my God, and he shall go no more out: and I will write upon him the name of my God, and the name of the city of my God, which is new Jerusalem . . . : and I will write upon him my new name. (v. 12)	To him that overcometh will I grant to sit with me in my throne, even as I also overcame, and am set down with my Father in his throne. (v. 21)

THE BEATITUDES OF
THE BOOK OF REVELATION

The Beatitudes spoken by the Lord on the Sermon on the Mount are well-known: "Blessed are the poor in spirit: for theirs is the kingdom of heaven. Blessed are they that mourn: for they shall be comforted" (Matt. 5:3–4). All together, Matthew records nine of these Beatitudes (see Matt. 5:3–12).

Less well-known, but conveying deep and important truths, are the Beatitudes recorded in the book of Revelation. Through inspiration of the Spirit, John has given us seven such truths. We note one important difference between the Beatitudes recorded in Matthew and those found in Revelation: the earlier set, those spoken by the mortal Jesus, follow a formula wherein he states that certain people are "blessed"; then he gives the form the blessing will take. In the Beatitudes listed below, specific groups of people are pronounced "blessed," but the specific form of their blessing is often not given:

1. "Blessed is he that readeth, and they that hear the words of this prophecy, and keep those things which are written therein: for the time is at hand" (1:3).

2. "Blessed are the dead which die in the Lord from henceforth: Yea, saith the Spirit, that they may rest from their labours; and their works do follow them" (14:13).

3. "Behold, I come as a thief. Blessed is he that watcheth, and keepeth his garments, lest he walk naked, and they see his shame" (16:15).

4. "Blessed are they which are called unto the marriage supper of the Lamb" (19:9).

5. "Blessed and holy [are they who have] part in the first resurrection: on such the second death hath no power, but they shall be priests of God and of Christ, and shall reign with him a thousand years" (20:6).

6. "Behold, I come quickly: blessed is he that keepeth the sayings of the prophecy of this book" (22:7).

7. "Blessed are they that do his commandments, that they may have right to the tree of life, and may enter in through the gates into the city" (22:14).

BLESSINGS TO THOSE
WHO OVERCOME

The book of Revelation records a number of very important blessings that are granted to "him that overcometh" the world and the temptations and trials of the adversary, enduring to the end. All of these statements make symbolic promises of the blessings of eternal life for those who overcome (see the commentary in this volume on the respective verses).

1. "To him that overcometh will I give to eat of the tree of life, which is in the midst of the paradise of God" (2:7).

2. "He that overcometh shall not be hurt of the second death" (2:11).

3. "To him that overcometh will I give to eat of the hidden manna, and will give him a white stone, and in the stone a new name written, which no man knoweth saving he that receiveth it" (2:17).

4. "[To him who] overcometh, and keepeth my [commandments] unto the end, . . . will I give power over [many kingdoms]" (2:26).

5. "He that overcometh, the same shall be clothed in white raiment; and I will not blot out his name out of the book of life, but I will confess his name before my Father, and before his angels" (3:5).

6. "Him that overcometh will I make a pillar in the temple of my God, and he shall go no more out: and I will write upon him the name of my God, and the name of the city of my God, which is new Jerusalem, which cometh down out of heaven from my God: and I will write upon him my new name" (3:12).

7. "To him that overcometh will I grant to sit with me in my throne, even as I also overcame, and am set down with my Father in his throne" (3:21).

8. "He that overcometh shall inherit all things; and I will be his God, and he shall be my son" (21:7).

SOURCES CONSULTED

Alford, Henry. *The Greek Testament.* 4 vols. Chicago: Moody Press, 1958.

Anchor Bible Dictionary. Ed. David Noel Freedman. 6 vols. New York: Double-day, 1992.

Andersen, H. Verlan. *The Great and Abominable Church of the Devil.* Provo: H. Verlan Andersen, 1972.

Beckwith, I. T. *The Apocalypse of John.* New York: Macmillan, 1922.

"Book of Revelation Overview." *Ensign,* October 1983, 50–53.

Bratcher, Robert G., and Howard A. Hatton. *A Handbook on the Revelation of John.* New York: United Bible Societies, 1993.

Bullinger, E. W. *Commentary on Revelation.* Grand Rapids, Mich.: Kregel, 1984.

———. *Number in Scripture.* Grand Rapids, Mich.: Kregel, 1967.

Cannon, George Q. *Life of Joseph Smith the Prophet.* Salt Lake City: Deseret Book, 1986.

Charles, R. H. *A Critical and Exegetical Commentary on the Revelation of St. John.* 2 vols. Edinburgh: T&T Clark, 1985.

Cicero. *Cicero's Letters to Atticus.* Trans. D. R. Shackleton Bailey. New York: Penguin Books, 1978.

Dahl, Larry E., and Donald Q. Cannon. *The Teachings of Joseph Smith.* Salt Lake City: Bookcraft, 1997.

D'aragon, Jean-Louis. "The Apocalypse." In *Jerome Biblical Commentary,* ed. R. E. Brown, 477. Englewood Cliffs, N. J.: Prentice-Hall, 1968.

Davidson, Francis, ed. *The New Bible Commentary.* 2d ed. Grand Rapids, Mich.: Eerdmans, 1954.

Davis, R. Dean. *The Heavenly Court Judgment of Revelation 4–5.* Lanham, Md.: University Press of America, 1992.

Deissmann, Gustav Adolf. *Light from the Ancient East.* Trans. Lionel R. M. Strachan. Grand Rapids, Mich.: Baker Book House, 1978.

Douglas, J. D., ed. *The New Bible Dictionary.* Grand Rapids, Mich.: Wm. B. Eerdmans, 1962.

Draper, Richard D. *Opening the Seven Seals: The Visions of John the Revelator.* Salt Lake City: Deseret Book, 1991.

Dummelow, J. R. *A Commentary on the Holy Bible.* New York: Macmillan, 1908, 1909.

———. *One Volume Bible Dictionary.* New York: Macmillan, 1984.

Durham, Reed C. "Revelation: The Plainest Book Ever Written." *New Era,* May 1973, 21–27.

Edersheim, Alfred. *The Temple: Its Ministry and Services As They Were at the Time of Jesus Christ.* 1908. Reprint. Grand Rapids, Mich.: Eerdmans, 1975.

Ehat, Andrew F., and Lyndon W. Cook. *The Words of Joseph Smith.* Provo: Brigham Young University Religious Studies Center, 1980.

"The Father and the Son: A Doctrinal Exposition by the First Presidency and the Twelve." In James E. Talmage, *Articles of Faith,* 470–71. Salt Lake City: Deseret Book, 1977.

Ford, J. Massyngberde. *Revelation: Introduction, Translation and Commentary.* Vol. 38 of *Anchor Bible Commentary.* New York: Doubleday, 1975.

Friedrich, Gerhard, and Gerhard Kittel, eds. *Theological Dictionary of the New Testament.* 10 vols. Grand Rapids, Mich.: Wm. B. Eerdmans, 1964–76.

Glasson, T. F. *Revelation of John.* Cambridge: Cambridge University Press, 1965.

Good News Bible: The Bible in Today's English Version. New York: American Bible Society, 1976.

Haran, Menahem. *Temples and Temple Service in Ancient Israel.* Winona Lake, Ind.: Eisenbrauns, 1985.

Harrington, Wilfrid J. *Revelation.* Vol. 16 of Sacra Pagina Series, ed. Daniel J. Harrington. Collegeville, Minn.: Liturgical Press, 1993.

Hersey, John. *Hiroshima.* New York: Bantam Books, 1946, 1975.

Holy Bible. Authorized King James Version. Salt Lake City: The Church of Jesus Christ of Latter-day Saints, 1979.

Holy Bible. Revised Standard Version. New York: Nelson, 1946, 1952.

Hymns of The Church of Jesus Christ of Latter-day Saints. Salt Lake City: The Church of Jesus Christ of Latter-day Saints, 1985.

The Interpreter's Bible. 12 vols. New York: Abingdon, 1952–57.

Jerusalem Bible. Reader's Edition. Garden City, N. Y.: Doubleday, 1968.

Joseph Smith's "New Translation" of the Bible. Independence, Mo.: Herald, 1970.

Kimball, Spencer W. "Temples—Now and in the Future." Address to Genealogical Seminar, 4–5 August 1977. Provo: Brigham Young University Media Services, 1977. Audiocassette.

Krodel, Gerhard A. *Revelation.* Minneapolis, Minn.: Augsburg, 1989.

Living Bible. Wheaton, Ill.: Tyndale, 1976.

Lund, Gerald N. "Seeing the Book of Revelation as a Book of Revelation." *Ensign,* December 1987, 46–52.

Martial. *The Epigrams of Martial.* Sel. and trans. James Michie. New York: Vintage Books, 1973.

Matthews, Robert J. *"A Plainer Translation": Joseph Smith's Translation of the Bible.* Provo: Brigham Young University Press, 1975.

McConkie, Bruce R. *Doctrinal New Testament Commentary.* 3 vols. Salt Lake City: Bookcraft, 1965–73.

———. *Doctrines of the Restoration: Sermons and Writings of Bruce R. McConkie.* Ed. Mark L. McConkie. Salt Lake City: Bookcraft, 1989.

———. *The Millennial Messiah.* Salt Lake City: Deseret Book, 1982.

———. *A New Witness for the Articles of Faith.* Salt Lake City: Deseret Book, 1985.

———. *The Mortal Messiah.* 4 vols. Salt Lake City: Deseret Book, 1979–81.

———. "Understanding the Book of Revelation." *Ensign,* September 1975, 85–89.

McConkie, Joseph Fielding, and Donald W. Parry. *A Guide to Scriptural Symbols.* Salt Lake City: Bookcraft, 1990.

Metzger, Bruce M. *Breaking the Code: Understanding the Book of Revelation.* Nashville: Abingdon Press, 1993.

Mounce, Robert. *The Book of Revelation.* Grand Rapids, Mich.: Eerdmans, 1977.

New English Bible. Oxford: Oxford University Press, 1961.

New International Version of the Holy Bible. Grand Rapids, Mich.: Zondervan, 1986.

Nibley, Hugh W. *Approaching Zion.* Salt Lake City: Deseret Book and FARMS, 1989.

Parry, Donald W. "Sinai as Sanctuary and Mountain of God." In *By Study and Also by Faith: Essays in Honor of Hugh W. Nibley,* 1:482–500. 2 vols. Ed. John M. Lundquist and Stephen D. Ricks. Salt Lake City: Deseret Book, 1990.

Parry, Donald W., Jay A. Parry, and Tina M. Peterson. *Understanding Isaiah.* Salt Lake City: Deseret Book, 1998.

Parry, Jay A., and Donald W. Parry. "The Temple in Heaven: Its Description and Significance." In *Temples of the Ancient World: Ritual and Symbolism,* ed. Donald W. Parry, 515–32. Salt Lake City: Deseret Book and FARMS, 1994.

Petersen, Mark E. Conference Report, October 1964, 121.

Pratt, Orson. In *Journal of Discourses,* 14:242–43. 26 vols. London: Latter-day Saints' Book Depot, 1854–86.

Pratt, Parley P. *Divine Authenticity of the Book of Mormon,* nos. 5 and 6 of 6. Liverpool: R. James, 1851. In *LDS Collectors Library* [CD-ROM]. Salt Lake City: Infobases International, 1995.

———. *Key to the Science of Theology.* Salt Lake City: Deseret Book, 1973.

———. *A Voice of Warning.* Salt Lake City: Deseret News Press, n.d.

Robinson, Stephen E. "Early Christianity and 1 Nephi 13–14." In *The Book of Mormon: First Nephi, The Doctrinal Foundation,* ed. Monte S. Nyman and Charles D. Tate Jr., 177–91. Provo: Brigham Young University Religious Studies Center, 1988.

Russell, David S. *The Method and Message of Jewish Apocalyptic.* Philadelphia: Westminster, 1964.

Schell, Jonathan. *The Fate of the Earth.* New York: Alfred A. Knopf, 1982.

Schick, Eduard. *Revelation of St. John.* Trans. Werner Kruppa. 2 vols. New Testament for Spiritual Healing Series. New York: Herder and Herder, 1971.

Scott, Walter. *Exposition of the Revelation of Jesus Christ.* 4th ed. Grand Rapids, Mich.: Kregel, 1979.

Smith, Eldred G. "Choose Ye This Day." *Improvement Era,* June 1970, 104.

Smith, Hyrum M., and Janne M. Sjodahl. Introduction to and commentary on *The Doctrine and Covenants.* Rev. ed. Salt Lake City: Deseret Book, 1951.

Smith, Joseph. *History of The Church of Jesus Christ of Latter-day Saints.* Ed. B. H. Roberts. 2d ed. rev. 7 vols. Salt Lake City: The Church of Jesus Christ of Latter-day Saints, 1932–51.

———. *Lectures on Faith.* Comp. N. B. Lundwall. Salt Lake City: N. B. Lundwall, n.d.

———. *Teachings of the Prophet Joseph Smith.* Sel. Joseph Fielding Smith. Salt Lake City: Deseret Book, 1938.

Smith, Joseph F. *Gospel Doctrine.* 5th ed. Salt Lake City: Deseret Book, 1939.

Smith, Joseph Fielding. *Church History and Modern Revelation.* 4 vols. Salt Lake City: Council of the Twelve Apostles of The Church of Jesus Christ of Latter-day Saints, 1946–49.

———. *Doctrines of Salvation.* 3 vols. Comp. Bruce R. McConkie. Salt Lake City: Bookcraft, 1954–56.

The Restoration of All Things. Salt Lake City: Deseret Book, 1945.

———. *Man, His Origin and Destiny.* Salt Lake City: Deseret Book, 1954.

Sperry, Sidney B. *Doctrine and Covenants Compendium.* Salt Lake City: Bookcraft, 1960.

Stapley, Delbert L. Conference Report, October 1966, 113.

Strand, Kenneth A. "An Overlooked Old Testament Background to Revelation 11:1." *Andrews University Seminary Studies* 22 (1981): 317–25.

Strong, James. *The Exhaustive Concordance of the Bible.* Nashville: Abingdon, 1890.

Talmage, James E. *The Articles of Faith.* 12th ed. Salt Lake City: The Church of Jesus Christ of Latter-day Saints, 1924.

———. *Jesus the Christ.* 3d ed. Salt Lake City: The Church of Jesus Christ of Latter-day Saints, 1916.

Taylor, John. *The Gospel Kingdom.* Sel. G. Homer Durham. Salt Lake City: Bookcraft, 1943.

———. *The Mediation and Atonement.* Salt Lake City: Deseret News, 1882.

Virgil. *The Aeneid of Virgil.* Trans. Kevin Guinagh. New York: Holt, Rinehart and Winston, 1970.

Vincent, Marvin. *Word Studies in the New Testament.* Grand Rapids, Mich.: Eerdmans, 1976.

Walvoord, John F. *Revelation of Jesus Christ.* Chicago: Moody, 1966.

Whitney, Orson F. *Saturday Night Thoughts.* Salt Lake City: Deseret News, 1927.

Woodruff, Wilford. *The Discourses of Wilford Woodruff.* Sel. G. Homer Durham. Salt Lake City: Bookcraft, 1990.

———. In *Journal of Discourses,* 13:163. 26 vols. London: Latter-day Saints' Book Depot, 1854–86.

———. "The Temple Worker's Excursion." *Young Women's Journal,* August 1894, 505–16.

Young, Brigham. *Discourses of Brigham Young.* Sel. John A. Widtsoe. Salt Lake City: Deseret Book, 1941.

SCRIPTURE INDEX

SUBJECT INDEX

Calf, image of, 62
Calling and election made sure, 91, 94–96, 175, 231
Camp, 276
Candlesticks, symbolism of, 18–19, 21, 26, 139
Carbuncles, 296
Celestial kingdom, 14, 19, 287–88, 298. *See also* New Jerusalem, Temple in heaven
Child, as kingdom of God, 148–52
Church, Christ's: in the meridian, 148–54, 156–61, 174; to join with Christ, 251–53. *See also* Restoration
Church of the devil, 216–18. *See also* Babylon
Clouds, symbolism of, 16, 191
Colossae, 14
Court, of temple, 136
Creation, 227
Creator, 63–64
Creatures, 61, 73. *See also* Beasts
Crowns, 151, 153, 259
Crystal. *See* Sea of glass
Cube, symbolism of, 294
Curses, removed, 301–2. *See also* Plagues

Daniel, visions of: Christ, 19–20; beasts, 145, 166–67; last days, 155–56; Second Coming, 191; judgment, 271
Darkness, as plague, 206–7
David, key of, 47–48
Death: as name of horseman, 75, 82; to one-fourth humanity, 77, 82; to one-third humanity, 122; of two prophets, 141–42; at Second Coming, 263; cast into fiery lake, 281; ceases to exist, 285–86
Death, spiritual: 34, 280, 288–89
Destruction: at opening of seals, 82, 86–88; at first four trumpets, 105–13; at fifth trumpet, 114–20; at sixth trumpet, 120–23; at death of two prophets, 143; of Babylon, 241. *See also* Plagues
Diana, temple of, 28
Dogs, symbolism of, 307
Domitian, 229
Double, consequences, 240
Dragon, 148–49, 153–54
Drunkenness, 220

Eagle, 62, 160

Earth: represents worldliness, 4; as sanctified, 60, 72, 282–83; temporal existence of, 67, 78; at time of Noah, 80; four corners of, 92–93; significance of, 127; obeys God, 160–61; leveling of, 214–15
Earthquakes, 86–89, 143, 213–14
Economy, world, 175
Edom, 187
Egypt, plagues of, 107–11, 116–17, 140–42, 204–8, 257
Elders, twenty-four, 55–56, 58–59, 63, 65, 70–71, 145
Elias, 93–94, 130
Emerald, 58
Enoch, 79
Ephesus, 14, 27–32, 322
Euphrates, plague on, 207
Eyes, 51–52, 62–63, 70
Ezekiel, 18, 130–31

Famine, 80–81, 111, 140
Fire: plague of, 110; as weapon, 122, as torment, 188; God can dwell within, 197; connected to judgments, 206; destroys Babylon, 241, 250; symbolic of heavenly power, 276
Forehead, marks or names on: followers of Satan use, 95, 175; righteous use by Deity, 94–95, 175, 178–80, 302; whore uses, 222–23; Christ uses new name as, 259
Fornication, symbolism of, 186–87, 220
Forty-two, significance of, 137–38, 162, 168–69
Four, meaning of, 76
Fowls, 262–63, 266
Frogs, 208
Fruit, of tree of life, 300–301

Gabriel, 104–5
Garden of Eden, 298–300
Garments, spotless, 210
Gathering of righteous, 192
Gehenna, 265
Gematria, 176
Gentiles, 136
God: as our Heavenly Father, 15–16; on throne in heaven, 55–56, 286; attributes of, 99; oaths of, 128; alone in temple,

200; how to worship, 254–55; judgment of, 278–80; shall dwell with men, 285, 302; is the temple, 297; list of things pertaining to, 312–14; names of, 315

Gog and Magog, 275

Gold, pure, 295

Gospel, restoration of, 183–84. *See also* Restoration

Government, church, 151–52

Green, significance of, 58

Gutenberg, Johannes, 155

Hail, 110, 215

Harps, 59, 70–71, 180, 197

Harvest, 191–92

Heaven, 4. *See also* Celestial kingdom, Temple of heaven

Heavens, sanctified, 282–83

Hell, 82, 265–66, 281

Hierapolis, 14

High priests, 57–58, 91, 95–96

Holy Ghost, 221, 255–56, 287, 308

Holy of holies, 19, 147, 294–95

Horns, symbolism of, 70, 153, 229–30

Horsemen, 75–82

Horses, 75–82, 258

Hypocrites, 201

Idolatry, 34–36, 38, 40, 122–23, 186–87

Incense, symbolism of, 59, 71, 104–6, 188

Iron rod, 41, 152–53, 298

Izmir. *See* Smyrna

Jasper, 58, 292, 295

Jerusalem, 132–33, 136–37, 141–42. *See also* New Jerusalem, Zion

Jesus Christ: sends vision to John, 2; is focus of Revelation, 3, 6, 9, 13–14; is identified by different names, 12–15, 17, 260–62, 304, 315; appears to others, 19–24; comforts John, 24–25; calls Ephesians to repentance, 29–31; message of, to Smyrna, 32–34; message of, to Pergamos, 34–38; message of, to Thyatira, 38–42; message of, to Sardis, 43–46; message of, to Philadelphia, 46–49; message of, to Laodicea, 50–54; can open seals, 65, 68–72; opens first four seals, 78–82; opens fifth seal, 83–85; opens sixth seal,

85–86; to come from east, 94; as fountain of living waters, 100–101, 286–87; opens seventh seal, 103; wrath of, 146–47; stands on temple mount, 178–79; gathers righteous, 191; suffers for all, 194; will be victorious, 230; sets example of worshiping God, 255; Second Coming of, 255–62; establishes relationship with righteous, 287–88, is cornerstone of New Jerusalem, 292. *See also* Atonement, God, Temple in heaven

Jezebel, 38, 40

Joel, vision of, 190

John the Revelator: identity of, 1–2; bears testimony of Christ, 13–14, 310–11; as angel from the east, 93–94; told not to write, 128; as an Elias, 130–31; told to write, 189; not to seal revelations, 306; curses those who add to his writings, 309–10

Judgments: against the wicked, 4, 82; through signs of the times, 85–90; angels mete out, 92–94; follow silence in heaven, 103–4; symbolized by coals, 106; begin with seven trumpets, 107–13; call wicked to repentance, 185; seven, in bowls, 199–200; against Babylon, 241–42, 249–50; during Millennium, 270–71; Final, based on book of life, 278–80, 307

King, Martin Luther, 155

Kingdom(s): of the world, 144–45, 149, 165; of God, 148–49, 152–53

Kings and priests, 72, 297–98

Kings of the earth, 228–32, 242

Lake, fiery, 265, 276–77, 288

Lamb, 15, 65, 69–70, 179

Lampstands, 18–19, 57, 60

Laodicea, 14, 50–54, 323

Last days, 3, 6–7, 9–11, 85–90, 169

Leaves of tree of life, 300–301

Lehi, 18, 41, 130

Light, from God, 297–98, 302–3

Lightnings, 59–60, 86–87

Lion, 62, 65–69

Locusts, 116–19

Love of God, 298–99

Sores, plague of, 204
Spirit, being in the, 18
Spirits, evil, 208–9
Stars: symbolism of, 23, 26, 151, 308; to fall
    from the sky, 88, darkened, 112
Stone(s), 37, 292, 295–96
Suffering, 285–86
Sun, 87, 112, 116, 151, 297
Supper: marriage, 252–53; of the great God,
    262–63
Sword, two-edged, 23
Symbols: understanding, 5–6; list of, 316–
    17

Tabernacle of testimony (witness), 199
Telestial world, 127
Temple in heaven: vision takes place in, 4–5,
    19, 181; God's throne in, 14; silence in,
    102–4; receives resurrected Saints, 147;
    meaning of, 297
Temples, 100, 134–35, 296–97
Ten, significance of, 33, 153, 229
Ten thousands, meaning of, 16
Ten thousand times ten thousand, 61, 72
Thief, analogy of, 45, 210
Thigh, name on, 261–62
Third, significance of, 107
Three and one-half, 137–38, 141–42
Throne of God, 55–57, 277–78
Thunderings, 59–60, 86–87
Thunders, seven, 127–28
Thyatira, 14, 38–42, 323
Time, 129
Torment, 118, 276
Tralles, 14
Tree of life, 32, 41, 298–301
Tribes of Israel, 92, 96, 293
Tribulation(s), 99–101. See also Destruction,
    Martyrs, Plagues
Troas, 14
Trumpet(s): voice of Christ as, 21, 57; given
    to seven angels, 102–5; of first four
    angels, 106–13; of fifth angel, 114; of
    sixth angel, 120–21; of seventh angel,
    144–47
Twelve, symbolism of, 70, 151, 153, 293–95
Twenty-four elders, 55–56, 58–59, 63, 65,
    70–71, 145

Uriel, 104
Urim and Thummin, 37, 60, 292, 295

Vegetation, 111
Vespasian, 162
Virgins, meaning of, 181
Vision, being in the spirit, 18
Volcano, 111

War: at time of second seal, 79; from
    "locusts," 117–20; destroys one-third of
    humanity, 120–22; of Satan against
    Church, 148–49; in heaven, 154, 156–57;
    effects of nuclear, 204
Water(s), lukewarm, 51; plague on, 204–5
White: symbolic of purity, 22, 278; symbolic
    of victory, 59, 79, 258; robes of, 83–94,
    98; symbolic of sanctification, 252
Whitney, Newel K., 31
Whore, 216–24. See also Babylon
Wicked: shall mourn, 17; will die spiritual
    death, 34, 288–89; are blotted from book
    of life, 46; at time of Noah, 80; warned
    and judged by signs, 85–90; at time of
    trumpets, 113; do not repent, 120–23; at
    death of two prophets, 141–43; at open-
    ing of seventh seal, 147; worship beast,
    168–70; are called to repentance, 185;
    drink of God's wrath, 187–89; are gath-
    ered to be burned, 192–93; suffer seven
    plagues, 202–8; mourn fall of Babylon,
    242–45; resurrection of, 272; at end of
    Millennium, 273–75; cannot enter New
    Jerusalem, 298, 307–8
Wilderness, 154, 160, 221
Winds, 93
Winepress, 190, 194–95
Wings, of beasts, 62
Witnesses, two, 133, 138
Woes, 113–14, 120–21
Woman, as Christ's Church, 148–52
Word of God, 261, 298
Wormwood, 112
Worshippers, measured, 134–36

Zeezrom, 188
Zion, 85, 116–17, 284, 289. See also New
    Jerusalem